AREAS OF SOCIAL WORK PRACTICE

AREAS OF SOCIAL WORK PRACTICE

An Essential Text for Students of Social Work

Editors

Archana Kaushik

R R Patil

Bishnu Mohan Dash

Sunil Prasad

BLOOMSBURY

NEW DELHI • LONDON • OXFORD • NEW YORK • SYDNEY

BLOOMSBURY INDIA
Bloomsbury Publishing India Pvt. Ltd
(A wholly owned subsidiary of Bloomsbury UK)
Second Floor, LSC Building No. 4, DDA Complex,
Pocket C – 5 & 7, Vasant Kunj,
New Delhi 110070

BLOOMSBURY, BLOOMSBURY PRIME and the Diana logo are
trademarks of Bloomsbury Publishing Plc

First published in India 2024
This edition published 2024

ISBN: 978-93-61312-42-7
2 4 6 8 10 9 7 5 3 1

Printed and bound in India by Replika Press Pvt. Ltd

To find out more about our authors and books, visit
www.bloomsbury.com and sign up for our newsletters

Contents

Foreword vii
Preface xiii
List of Contributors xvii

1. Social Work with Older Persons: Current Practices and Scope 1
Archana Kaushik
2. Social Work Practice with Refugees and Asylum Seekers 23
Ravindra Ramesh Patil, Saniya Zehra and Mehak Jafri
3. Social Work in Correctional Settings 50
Gauri Sharma
4. Social Work in School Settings: Understanding the Need and Scope 65
Anna Taney Varghese
5. Social Work Practice in HIV/AIDS 84
Sheeba Joseph and Bishnu Mohan Dash
6. Industrial Social Work: Scope, Applications and Trends 103
Rutwik Gandhe and Richi Simon
7. Social Work Intervention in Health Care System 130
Kasturi Sinha Ghosh
8. Social Work Practice with Youth in India for Strong Nation-Building 148
Vishal Mishra and Rambabu Botcha
9. Social Work with Families during COVID-19 177
Ragini Tyagi
10. Social Work with Women: Practices, Policies and Scope 193
Gayatri Menon
11. Social Work Practice with LGBTQIA+ 218
Sayantika Sen and Vani Narula
12. Social Work in Urban Setting 239
Chandrakala Diyali
13. Social Work with Families in Conflict Zones 260
Seilienmang Haokip

14. Social Group Work Practice in Tribal Communities 271
Veena Suresh and Vivek S.

15. Social Work Practice in Child Welfare Setting 283
Kumar Satyam

16. Development-Induced Displacement and Resettlement (DIDR): Social Work Perspectives 293
Aneesh T.V.

17. Rural Development and Social Work 316
Arul Actovin C and Sunil Prasad

Author Index 331
Editors' Profiles 333

Foreword

Man is by nature a social animal; an individual who is unsocial naturally and not accidentally is either beneath our notice or more than human. Society is something that precedes the individual.

– Aristotle[1]

Society is a natural extension of an individual, not just a congregation of individuals. It is human psychology to interact with others. It's not naturally possible to be alone. That's why solitary confinement is the toughest punishment administered in prisons, only on hardened criminals in case of unruly behaviour. Human beings establish relationships naturally. Expansion of mind comes naturally to humans. That's how they are referred to as social animals. These natural interactions and relationships form societies. The eternal wisdom of Bharat views society as a gradual manifestation of individual identity, rooted in the divine and infinite origin of humans. Ego or esteem called 'asmitā', literally meaning 'sense of being', in *Yoga Shastra*, gives finite identification to the person.

Personality is self-defined by the finite boundaries drawn to limit otherwise infinite capacities. Physical, mental, emotional or intellectual limitations give an individual a definite identity. But the root being One and Infinite, the urge to connect with the divine infinity becomes the primary motive of humans. Thus, the individual expands into family not just biologically but also psychologically and then into various spheres of social existence again through deeper emotional expansion and not just mundane interactions. Society is also not mere contractual, existential or interactive artificial entity, but a sublime psychological, cultural and even spiritual larger existence of all the individuals involved. In this view, the society is a dynamic flow of relationships rather than a simple system of interactions. Hence, every community is unique in its texture and expression everywhere. The individual, *vyaṣṭi*, is constantly blossoming into a collective identity called society, *samaṣṭi*. This samaṣṭi has gradually unfolding natural layers starting from family, community, organisation and most profound *rāṣṭra*. Nation as understood politically is not a synonym to this concept of *rāṣṭra*. It is more a cultural expression of a collective consciousness rather than just a legally constituted state. All these layers in Bharatiya perspective are part of society or more specifically, samaṣṭi.

The social order undergoes numerous changes and transformations in the perennial flow of time. Social ebb of human collective faces various problems, challenges and inadequacies. The ultimate goal of humanity being harmony and oneness, there are continuous efforts to address all of these. Problems need solutions but challenges demand more delicate resolutions. Inadequacies are always to be provided for. There have been various mechanisms to deal with these social needs. The diversity is due to the basic philosophy or beliefs and customs & traditions evolved through ages. In the harmonious outlook of society based on oneness of existence, there are in-built mechanisms to create an interdependent, interrelated and complementary social order resulting in social harmony. When disrupted, a more targeted intervention is needed. There are several ways of social correction, fulfilment and resolution. Beginning with Charity, philanthropy, social service to organised social work there are various forms of remedies. Charity is for fulfilling physical needs like food, clothing, shelter. Philanthropy though etymologically means loving people in Greek language, in English usage it connotes more of economic support or sponsorship necessary for charity or social service.

Social service is a voluntary work done out of empathy. Satisfaction is the only return expected. The highest motivation for social service is spiritual, where the worker looks at the service activity as an opportunity for spiritual practice, *sādhanā*. The person engaged in social service activity with this intention is a seeker, *sādhaka*. Some are motivated by the needs of the society. This social urge propels them to work for solving the problems of the society by providing for the lacunae. The underprivileged or deprived sections, groups or individuals need special attention in basic sectors such as education, health or employment. Social service activities provide for these primary needs. In social service, the doer is at the center as the activity is voluntary. The ideation, planning and execution all are according to the understanding of the volunteer or group of volunteers or in some cases the organisation of volunteers. There is no personal or collective reciprocation. No remuneration or wages are given or even expected as it is an act of renunciation and giving only. The time, energy and resources are in the form of donations. The beneficiary of social service is receiver. Such service projects are more personal, but when these philanthropic activities grow in scale though initiated as social service need to be managed professionally. Here comes the role of social worker. Social work on the other hand is structured activity done by properly educated professionals.

In the great text Shrimad Bhagavatam, author Maharshi Vyasa explains three stages of dāna, literally meaning donations, but in deeper sense referring to the acts of social service. The first or primary stage is the stage of anna dāna or food donation. In this stage, service done to fulfill physical needs like food, clothing, shelter, etc., is included. The higher stage is vidyā dāna, donating education. It is said that donating food is great, but greater is the donation of knowledge as it can provide lifelong.

annadānaṃ paraṃ dānaṃ vidyādānamataḥ param।
annena kṣaṇikā tṛptiryāvajjīvaṃ ca vidyayā॥[2]

The offering of food is great; the offering of education is even greater. While food satisfies only momentarily, education gives satisfaction during the entire course of life.

Swami Vivekananda gives example of a Japanese proverb meaning – if you feed fish, hunger for one time is satiated but if you teach them how to catch fish, they will be fed for life. Thus, education empowers the beneficiary to stand on own feet. Hence its more effective than mere charity or temporary donation. According to the *sanātana* texts and vision of life, next stage of social service is greater than imparting education. It is called *ātmajñāna dāna*, or donating the knowledge of realisation of the goal of life. If the needy is awakened to the deeper meaning and purpose of life, he/ she will not only be able to lead a well provided life, but would strive for a purposeful life. Social service thus has to be provided at one or many or all of these stages depending on the context, need and situation of the target community. But Swami Vivekananda goes a step beyond the texts and adds that the highest service is in creating a self-reliant society where no one will need any service or charity.[3] Based on this way of life, hundreds of thousands of service projects are functioning today. Almost all the religious, cultural and political organisations run a large number of service projects. There are broadly three types: educational services, health services and finally projects for self-reliant community. Most of these are run by service minded voluntary organisations or missions.

With growing awareness all over the world about human rights and the entitlement to an adequate life for all with equity and harmony, many professional 'community service organisations' (CSOs) are also working. Their worldview is legal and moral instead of cultural, religious or spiritual with activities focused on the rights and requirements of the needy and respective government schemes. Many of these CSOs are government funded expected to act as a bridge between the welfare state and the society. With statutory mandate of Corporate Social Responsibility (CSR) for all the companies to spend a part of their profit for the benefit of the society or affected community, the CSOs are getting corporate funding also. Some corporations have formed their own foundations for social service activities. All these projects and activities need well educated social work professionals. Social work education must address this growing need and produce efficient, competent and committed social workers. Social work education is relatively a young field of knowledge. Educators in this area are preparing and evolving to meet the challenges of diversity and contextualisation. A lot more needs to be done.

In all kinds of professional education, practical aspect has always been very important. Engineering, Medical, legal education etc. has always given equal, if not more, value to practical learning along with theoretical knowledge. Social work to be fully professional needs to incorporate more practical aspects in its education. Just informing about various theories of social interactions and functioning will not prepare the social workers appropriately to face the challenges in the society they have to work. Proper delivery and impact depend on application of this knowledge in practice. This demands attitudinal preparation as well as actual practical exposure. Experience of the real-life situation followed by study of theories will facilitate professionalisation of social work education. Not just the quantitative emphasis but qualitative priority of practical approach is needed. The chronology should be experience first, followed by information and analysis to form a pragmatic and dynamically fluid theory of social work.

All education is aimed at three levels: Heart, Head and Hand. Emotional, intellectual and behavioural aspects are all developed in man-making education. Lopsided intellectual content and pedagogy has been the bane of education all over the world for almost half a millennium. Paradigm shift is in the offing everywhere. Project based learning, hands on pedagogy, skill development etc. are adding practical component to the logic dominated educational process. Emotional factor is yet to be explored. According to Swami Vivekananda, education of heart that is emotional culturing is most important part of man making process. First, the heart needs to be addressed and sensitised to feel, then the head plans by using the intellect and finally expressed in action through hands. The chronology of educational process is Heart-Head-Hand. This triple 'H' approach is mandatory in the professional education in general and more specifically in the socially sensitive fields like social work. If one does not understand the social fabric of the target area, any strengthening, empowering or problem solving will just be superficial and theoretical. Capacity to empathise is most basic quality of an ideal social work professional.

This is an era in which multiple intelligence theories are trying to define and quantify various intelligences such as emotional and spiritual intelligence beyond IQ. There is a sea change in the concept of social intelligence also. When it was first defined in 1920 by Edward Thorndike it only related to the common-sense ability to relate with others. More leaning towards skills of socialisation. Recent researches by Daniel Goleman[3] drawn on social neuroscience claims that social intelligence is made up of social awareness (including empathy, attunement, empathic accuracy, and social cognition) and social facility (including synchrony, self-presentation, influence, and concern). This indicates that social relationships have a direct effect on physical health, and it is directly proportional to the depth of relationship. Deeper relationships have deeper impact. Based on these findings, the social work education has to be transformed into a more dynamic field of knowledge. Emotional dynamics of relationships need to be understood both by the professionals as well as their educators. Even the spiritual quotient is fast becoming a parameter of human evaluation. This is prime motivator in many traditional communities. Hence proper understanding of spiritual intelligence irrespective of personal beliefs is very essential for impactful social work. Both these factors contribute to the individual and collective social intelligence. Correlation between these three, though yet a subject of deeper research for final theorisation, is sufficiently established for practical usage of social workers. The business community is already using this for aggressive marketing in the digital era of artificial intelligence. Robust big data mined through social media and other internet usage is being used by machines to define social profiles of consumers for customised and targeted aggressive advertising. This should inspire more benevolent fields like social work where human intelligence is more important than the artificial one.

Human intelligence is developed by direct experience instead of artificial data collection. Hence field work becomes most important. Present book provides a practical guide for the same. It elaborates not just the principles involved in the field work but gives practical guidelines for both student social workers as well as their educators. Various chapters deal with diverse situations in the modern society in which the field work can be undertaken. The chapters are written by experienced professors of the subject. The book will serve as a much-needed tool in the field of evolving social work education. Let this contribute to preparation of social work professionals for meeting the challenges of fast-moving societies and communities all over the globe.

Mukul Kanitkar
Eminent Educationist & Author
https://uttarapath.wordpress.com/

REFERENCES

1. 'Politics' by Aristotle
2. Subhashit Trishati
3. Says Vyasa: Giving alone is the one work in this Kali Yuga; and of all the gifts, giving spiritual life is the highest gift possible; the next gift is secular knowledge; the next, saving the life of man; and the last, giving food to the needy. Of food we have given enough; no nation is more charitable than we. So long as there is a piece of bread in the home of the beggar, he will give half of it. Such a phenomenon can be observed only in India. We have enough of that, let us go for the other two, the gifts of spiritual and secular knowledge. And if we were all brave and had stout hearts, and with absolute sincerity put our shoulders to the wheel, in twenty-five years the whole problem would be solved, and there would be nothing left here to fight about…

   https://advaitaashrama.org/cw/volume_3/lectures_from_colombo_to_almora/reply_to_the_address_of_welcome_at_shivaganga_and_manamadura.htm
4. Social intelligence by Daniel Goleman https://archive.org/details/socialintelligen00gole

Preface

This new textbook, *Areas of Social Work Practice*, offers a comprehensive exploration of various areas within the field of social work, especially meant for undergraduate and graduate students in India. This book intends to equip aspiring professional social workers and educators with the knowledge and skills necessary to address a wide range of social issues in India. The chapters of the book span a diverse array of topics covering varied issues and critical role of social work. Each chapter provides detailed information about specific areas of social work along with, relevant concepts, theories, models, application and solution. The book largely delves into contemporary challenges such as elderly, refugee, migration, school social work, HIV/AIDS, industrial social work, health care systems, youth development, issues of women, issues of LGBTQIA+ community, tribals, and the impact of COVID-19 on families and society. With a focus on both urban and rural settings, and highlighting the importance of cultural competency and inclusivity, this textbook is an essential resource for understanding and practicing social work in the Indian context.

In the first chapter, 'Social Work with Older Persons,' Kaushik delves into the socio-psychological and physiological changes associated with aging and necessary interventions. This chapter also addresses the position of the elderly in the modern world and the skills required to work with them. In the second chapter, 'Social Work with Refugees,' Patil, Zehra, and Jafri explore various aspects of refugee vulnerability that call for social work interventions. The chapter provides information on the main causes and problems of refugees, international policies, programs and organizations for refugees, and the prospective role of social work with refugees in India. The third chapter, 'Social Work Practice in Correctional Settings,' emphasizes the importance of reformation and rehabilitation in correctional settings. It discusses the need to clearly define the social worker's role in bridging gaps between prisoners, prison officials, families, the community, and the government, both during and after imprisonment. This chapter also highlights the need for systemic changes, rehabilitation, and the use of humanizing language in the criminal justice system. Chapter four, 'School Social Work,' serves as a resource for understanding effective school social work models. It discusses the tasks, responsibilities, and skills required for social workers in a school context. In chapter five, 'Social Work Interventions with HIV/AIDS,' Joseph and Dash discuss the gravity of HIV/AIDS globally and in India, along with interventions by various government and non-governmental organizations. The chapter covers symptoms, modes of transmission, co-infections, legislation, and social work interventions related to HIV/AIDS. Chapter six examines 'Industrial Social Work,' discussing the concept, scope, and evolution of industrial social work in India and the West. It highlights traditional and contemporary roles and challenges faced by industrial social workers. Chapter seven, 'Social Work Practice in Health Care Systems,' discusses the role of social workers in promoting health and developing community awareness about health rights, as well as the role of government in enhancing the healthcare system. Chapter eight, 'Social Work with Youth,' explores approaches and models for working with youth towards nation-building. Chapter nine, 'Social Work with Families During COVID-19,' examines the impact of the pandemic on the family system and the role of family social workers during the crisis. Chapter ten, 'Social Work with Women,' defines key concepts in the context of women's issues and examines the forms of vulnerabilities women face. It also covers the skills and strategies needed to empower women. Chapter eleven, 'Social Work Practice with LGBTQIA+,' by Sen and Narula, explores the differences between gender and sexual orientation and the role of social work in supporting the needs of the LGBTQIA+ community. It discusses social challenges and solutions for inclusivity and cultural competency. Chapter twelve, 'Social Work in Urban Settings,' discusses urbanization, industrialization, modernization, and the associated problems and challenges. It presents solutions and highlights the roles of social workers in urban settings. Chapter thirteen, 'Social Work Practice with Families in Conflict Zones,' provides an understanding of violence and the challenges it imposes, focusing on the importance of family resilience. Chapter fourteen, 'Social Group Work Practice in Tribal Communities,' highlights the application of social group work principles in engaging with tribal communities. Chapter fifteen, 'Social Work Practice in Child Welfare Settings,' describes issues related to children within families and communities and discusses the roles of social workers in child welfare. Chapter sixteen analyzes the impact of development-induced displacement on the socio-economic and cultural lives of displaced persons in Kerala, with a focus on Cochin International Airport Limited (CIAL). It argues for the decolonization of the development process and the inclusion of indigenous paradigms in social work curricula. The final chapter discusses approaches and principles of rural development, providing comprehensive guidelines for social workers in rural settings.

In conclusion, this textbook serves as an indispensable resource for students, educators and practitioners of social work in India. It provides a detailed information and practical application about various areas of the fields of social work. The chapters in this book jointly emphasized the significance of understanding and addressing the diverse needs of different groups namely the elderly, refugee, migrants, school children, HIV/AIDS patients'/family members, industrial workers, health care systems workers, youths, women, LGBTQIA+ community, development induced displacement, tribals, etc. The uniqueness of this book is it's handling of multifaceted nature of areas of social work, integrating theoretical knowledge with practical applications and emphasis on compassion, inclusivity, cultural competency, advocacy while understanding and addressing different areas of social work practice in socio-culturally diverse India. Therefore, this textbook is must read for students and educators of social work as its not only enhances their academic learning but also contributes to their professional development as a social worker to make meaningful contributions to the society.

In closing this preface, we extend our heartfelt thanks to all who have directly or indirectly contributed to this endeavor. We express our deepest gratitude to Mr. Mukul Kanitkar, eminent educationist, political ideologue, and author, for graciously writing the Foreword for this book. We are truly grateful to our contributors, who diligently met deadlines and patiently accommodated last-minute editing requests. We have gained valuable insights from the works of numerous scholars who have written on various areas of social work practice. Our association with colleagues, friends, students, and family members has also provided us with significant perspectives. We also appreciate Mr. Paul Vinay Kumar and Mr. Satyabrat Mishra of Bloomsbury for his ongoing support and guidance throughout this project. Special thanks go to Mr. Rajbilochan Prasad for tirelessly multiple drafts of the manuscript and making countless revisions.

Ultimately, if this humble effort sparks interest among young social work students and professionals, motivating and inspiring them to improve their practice, we will feel our mission has been accomplished. The intellectual effort invested over the years in creating this book will be more than rewarded.

Prof. Archana Kaushik
Prof. R.R. Patil
Prof. Bishnu Mohan Dash
Dr. Sunil Prasad

List of Contributors

- **Aneesh T.V.**, Assistant Professor, Department of Social Work, Aditi Mahavidyalaya, University of Delhi.
- **Anna Taney Varghese,** Consultant – Learning and Innovation in Room to Read.
- **Archana Kaushik,** Professor, Department of Social Work, University of Delhi.
- **Arul Actovin C,** Assistant Professor, Department of Social Work, Sri Ramakrishna Mission Vidyalaya College of Arts and Science, (Autonomous) Coimbatore, India.
- **Bishnu Mohan Dash,** Professor, Department of Social Work, Dr Bhim Rao Ambedkar College (University of Delhi), Delhi.
- **Chandrakala Diyali,** Assistant professor, Department of Social Work, Amity University, Noida.
- **Gauri Sharma,** Freelance Development Consultant.
- **Gayatri Menon,** Social worker, PhD Scholar and ICSSR Doctoral Fellow, Department of Social Work, University of Delhi.
- **Kasturi Sinha Ghosh,** Assistant Professor, Department of Social Work, Netaji Subhas Open University, West Bengal.
- **Kumar Satyam,** Assistant Professor, Department of Social Work, Department of Social Work, Dr Bhim Rao Ambedkar College, University of Delhi.
- **Mehak Jafri,** Jamia Alumna-2023, Department of Social Work, Jamia Millia Islamia, New Delhi.
- **Ragini Tyagi,** Research Scholar, Department of Social Work, University of Delhi, Delhi.
- **Rambabu Botcha,** Assistant Professor, Department of Social Work, Rajiv Gandhi National Institute of Youth Development (RGNIYD), Ministry of Youth Affairs and Sports, Government of India, Sriperumbudur, Tamil Nadu, India.
- **Ravindra Ramesh Patil,** Professor, Department of Social Work, Jamia Millia Islamia, New Delhi.
- **Richi Simon,** Assistant Professor, Department of Social Work, The Bhopal School of Social Sciences.
- **Rutwik Gandhe,** Assistant Professor, Department of Social Work, The Bhopal School of Social Sciences.
- **Saniya Zehra,** Deputy Manager, Centum Learning Ltd, New Delhi.

- **Sayantika Sen,** PhD Scholar, Department of Social Work, Jamia Millia Islamia.
- **Seilienmang Haokip,** Assistant Professor, School of Social Work, Martin Luther Christian University, Shillong, Meghalaya.
- **Sheeba Joseph,** Professor, Department of Social Work, Bhopal School of Social Sciences.
- **Sunil Prasad,** Assistant Professor, Department of Social Work, North Eastern Regional Institute of Management (NERIM), Guwahati, Assam.
- **Vani Narula,** Professor, Department of Social Work, Jamia Millia Islamia.
- **Veena Suresh,** Assistant Professor, Department of Social Work, Amrita Vishwa Vidyapeetham, Amritapuri Campus, Kerala.
- **Vishal Mishra,** Assistant Professor, Department of Social Work, Rajiv Gandhi National Institute of Youth Development (RGNIYD), Ministry of Youth Affairs and Sports, Government of India, Sriperumbudur, Tamil Nadu, India.
- **Vivek S,** Assistant Professor, Department of Social Work, Amrita Vishwa Vidyapeetham, Amritapuri Campus, Kerala, India.

CHAPTER–1

Social Work with Older Persons: Current Practices and Scope

ARCHANA KAUSHIK

Professor, Department of Social Work, University of Delhi

Grow old along with me! The best is yet to be, the last of life, for which the first was made.

– Robert Browning

ABSTRACT: *It is generally accepted that ageing is a normal and inevitable process that occurs in all living things, including humans. Recent increases in the number and proportion of the elderly have given rise to the concept of population ageing. Currently, certain developments are altering the social relationship with the elderly. Changes in family structure and societal values have made the elderly more vulnerable.*

This chapter examines the various changes associated with ageing, including social changes, psychological changes, and physiological changes. Because of these changes, the elderly population requires specialised intervention, so this chapter also discusses gerentology, a subfield of social work intervention with the elderly.

Therefore, this chapter discusses the position of the elderly in the modern world and the skills required to work with them.

Keywords: *Older Persons, Gerontology, Geriatric Care, Health Vulnerability, Elder-Abuse, Social Security*

Learning Objectives

After reading this chapter, you will be able to:

- Develop an understanding of the differential needs and vulnerabilities of the elderly population
- Understand reasons for demographic transition named population ageing and its implications on the family and society
- Understand the age-related changes in the bio-psycho-social domains
- Know Social work professionals' current and potential roles in the care, support, and well-being of the elderly

INTRODUCTION

Old age has been a universal phenomenon. It is considered the last stage of the human life cycle. Age-related biological changes have been there since the beginning of humankind. However, social contexts have changed drastically, that have added to the vulnerability of aged people. In India, elderly people have enjoyed utmost care and respect since ancient times. However, at present, certain factors like urbanization, industrialization, modernization and now globalization have influenced most social systems and institutions, including social relations that have made the elderly stand at crossroads. They are facing several challenges and are being considered a vulnerable social group. Medical advancement and improvement in the public health system have resulted in a demographic transition called 'population ageing'. Other factors, such as a change in the family system's structural and functional aspects, have also made the elderly vulnerable. These situations have led to changes in the roles and status of the elderly, impacting their psychological well-being.

In this chapter, details are provided on these aspects. Let us first gain a better conceptual understanding of old age and its characteristic features.

OLD AGE: CONCEPTS AND FEATURES

Old age is considered a natural and universal phenomenon of all living beings, including humans. It is illustrated as deteriorating body strength and vigour, reduced body functioning, and changes in roles and relationships. More often than not, ageing is equated with vulnerability, weakness and disease. For a layperson, 'ageing' and 'old age' are interchangeably used terms.

Ageing is taken as a biological process that is characterized by a range of changes such as greying of hair, wrinkling of the skin, fading of sensory capabilities like eyesight and hearing, and curtailment of independence in the functioning of daily living and retirement from work-life. It is degenerative, continuous, universal, irreversible and intrinsic to living organisms. Birren and others (1963) have said that "ageing is a process of change involving all aspects of the organism. Its consequences range from altered structures and functions of the component tissues of the body to an altered relationship of the organism to its physical and social environment.

Ageing is a progression of adult changes, characteristic of the species, and should occur in all individuals if they live long enough" (p. 3).

Following this, ageing has three aspects, which are overlapping:

- **Biological age:** Also called physiological age, it measures how well or poorly one's body functions relative to one's actual calendar age. It estimates an individual's present position concerning his/ her potential lifespan. Genetic factors, lifestyle, nutrition and other factors influence biological age. It is closely related to chronological age, but the two are not the same.

- **Psychological age:** It refers to the adaptive capacities of an individual in comparison to the average. It means how old one feels and behaves and is not necessarily equal to chronological age. It also includes subjective reactions of the individual to changes brought about due to biological and social aspects of ageing.
- **Social age** refers to societal expectations of how people should behave at a particular chronological age. Cultural aspects have an essential bearing on social age. In India, a man is considered old when he retires from his job, while a female is perceived as old when her son brings home her bahu (daughter-in-law) when she becomes mother-in-law.

Thus, people have different rates of ageing that do not necessarily correspond to their chronological ageing.

It should be remembered that elderly individuals are not a homogenous group but differ on account of several variables like heredity, age, gender, occupation, nutrition, marital status, lifestyle, dealing with stress, tensions and crisis in life, accidents, disability, family support, achievements and failures in life and such others.

POPULATION AGEING: WORLD AND INDIA

While ageing is universal, the increasing proportion of the elderly in the general population is relatively a recent phenomenon. Worldwide, the number and proportion of the elderly are increasing, giving rise to a phenomenon called 'population ageing'. Due to advancements in medical facilities and the betterment of the public health system and control over infectious diseases, there has been a sharp decline in the death rate or mortality rate, resulting in a rise in life expectancy. This has led to an unprecedented change in the population structure, also known as the 'greying of nations', which varies from country to country.

As a result, the traditional pyramid shape of the population in any society (where the base shows children, the middle part shows working population or youth, and the apex depicts the aged population) is gradually changing to a rectangle, implying that the elderly population is becoming equal to child-population in the society.

Every year, about nine million older persons are added to the world's older population. Today, more developed countries are faced with an elderly boom as they have undergone a change to become aged societies (United Nations, 2009).

The ageing phenomenon and its related issues are not essentially confined to developed countries alone. Demographic trends show that developing countries are ageing faster than developed countries. About 60% of the world's elderly live in developing nations, and by the year 2030, East and Southeast Asia are the fastest ageing regions (UN DESA, 2023). While developed nations like France or Belgium took 80–100 years to double their elderly population from 9 per cent to 18 per cent, countries with emerging economies, especially in East Asia and Latin America, are doubling their elderly population to the same level in 20–30 years (World Economic Forum, 2023).

This has resulted in a new phase of life post-retirement known as 'third age'. Thus, till a century back, we were living in a 'world of children', and now it is rapidly becoming a world of old people. It is estimated that in the next 50 years, there may be more grandparents than grandchildren, particularly in developed countries (UN DESA, 2023). The table below (Table 1) shows the proportion of elderly in the world's major regions. It clearly depicts that Europe is the *oldest* region and Africa the youngest. The

Table 1: Age wise proportional representation of elderly persons in different regions of the world

Region	*Year*	*65 & Above (%)*	*75 & Above (%)*	*80 & Above (%)*
Europe	2000 2015 2030	15.5 18.7 24.3	6.6 8.8 11.8	3.3 5.2 7.1
North America	2000 2015 2030	12.6 14.9 20.3	6.0 6.4 9.4	3.3 3.9 5.4
Oceania	2000 2015 2030	10.2 12.4 16.3	4.4 5.2 7.5	2.3 3.1 4.4
Asia	2000 2015 2030	6.0 7.8 12.0	1.9 2.8 4.6	0.8 1.4 2.2
Latin America	2000 2015 2030	5.5 7.5 11.6	1.9 2.8 4.6	0.9 1.5 2.4
North Africa	2000 2015 2030	4.3 5.3 8.1	1.4 1.9 2.8	0.6 0.9 1.3
Sub Saharan Africa	2000 2015 2030	2.9 3.2 3.7	0.8 1.0 1.3	0.3 0.4 0.6

Source: UNDESA, World Population Ageing, 2019

world's population is slowly and steadily aging in which Eastern and South Eastern Asia would likely remain with a largest share of 37 per cent till 2050. Next would be Europe and Northern American region which would shrink to around 19 per cent. Central and South Asian region would see a tremendous increase in the elderly population. The sub – Saharan African and Northern African countries would raise their elderly population to 7 and 6 per cent respectively (UN DESA, 2019).

Indian Situation

The global phenomenon of the ageing population impacts India also. Though, at present, the population of the elderly in the country is nearly eight per cent, it is expected to gain momentum in the coming decades. In the span of 100 years from 1961, the total population will be five times, while the elderly population would be 13 times, with an absolute number of 340 million. It implies that the World's elderly would be concentrated in developing countries, and in absolute numbers, India may have the highest number of elderly in the World. Added to this, the majority (three-fourths) of the elderly people are in rural areas (Census, 2011). State-wise data show that small states/ UTs like Dadra & Nagar Haveli, Nagaland, Arunachal Pradesh, and Meghalaya have around 4 per cent of the elderly population, whereas Kerala has more than 10.5 per cent elderly.

Certain characteristic features of the aged population in India may be looked into.

Life-expectancy

National data trends show a modest but significant gain in longevity by the elderly over the decades. At the time of Independence, in India, the expectancy of life at birth was just 32 years, and female longevity was even less. Within a span of a few decades, life expectancy has markedly changed. During 2002–06, life expectancy at birth was 64.2 years for females and 62.6 years for females. At 60 years, the average remaining length of life is about 18 years (16.7 for males and 18.9 for females). At 70 years, life expectancy is 12 years (10.9 for males and 12.4 for females). It also shows the trend of feminization of ageing as there is a greater increase in the number of older women than of older men.

Sex Ratio

The skewed sex ratio in the country tells the story of existing prejudices and discriminations against females. Quite interestingly, after 60 years, women outnumber their male counterparts. The figure below depicts the ratio of elderly women per thousand males as per Census 2011. Feminization of ageing is clearly visible.

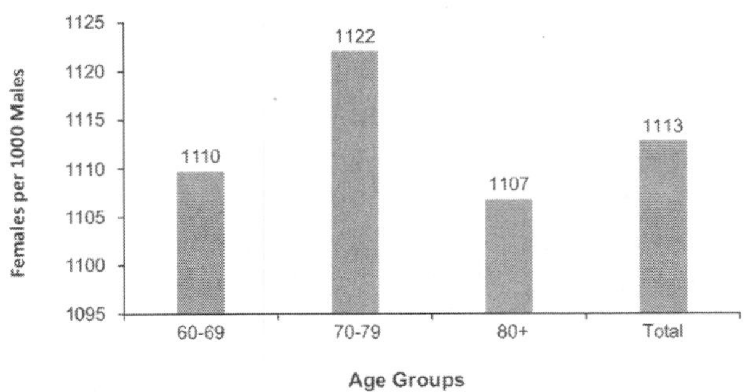

Figure 1: Sex Ratio (Females per 100 Males) – Census 2011

Marital Status

Census 2011 brings out that about 60 per cent of the elderly were currently married, and 38 per cent were widowed. The incidence of widowhood is much higher among aged females than among elderly men, as 13.7 per cent are widowers in contrast to 58.5 per cent widows. At the age of 70 years and above, about 80 per cent of women and 27 per cent of men experience widowhood. Higher life expectancy for females at 60 plus and women marrying older men has resulted in a large number of elderly widows.

Work Participation

Labour participation of the elderly depicts their economic compulsion driven by poverty. Census 2011 shows that the work participation rate among the elderly is 24.2 per cent, constituting 39 per cent of males and 11 per cent of females. In rural areas, it may be because of the involvement in

Did You Know?

Ministry of Statistics and Programme Implementation (2011) provides the following relevant data:

- The old-age dependency ratio has risen from 10.9 per cent in 1961 to 13.1 per cent in 2001. For females and males, the value of the ratio was 13.8 per cent and 12.5 per cent respectively.
- Nearly 65 per cent aged had to depend on others for their day-to-day maintenance and more than 80 per cent elderly women were economically dependent.
- The proportion of physically mobile elderly men and women decline from about 94 per cent in the age-group of 60-64 years to about 72 per cent for men and 63 to 65 per cent for women of age 80 or more.
- Prevalence of heart diseases among older people was much higher in urban areas than in rural parts.
- About 64 per thousand rural older people and 55 per thousand urban elderly suffer from one or more disabilities. Most common disability was loco-motor disability as 3 per cent of them suffer from it.

agriculture or other traditional occupations, 42 per cent of males and 11.6 per cent of females are working. Corresponding figures in urban areas are 29.7 per cent male and 9 per cent female. There are 13.2 per cent males and 2.7 per cent females above the age of 80 years in the workforce.

Review Questions

(a) What do you understand by ageing?
(b) Explain what you understand by the term 'greying of the nation'. Explain how the idea of feminizing ageing is received in the Indian culture.

BIOLOGICAL CHANGES IN AGEING

Ageing is taken as progressive, cumulative and degenerative changes that occur in an organism over a period of time. It means that a decline in specific functional abilities characterizes the natural process of ageing. In old age, even though the body becomes susceptible to a number of ailments, this does not imply that ageing is synonymous with illness or diseases. It suggests that the criteria or parameters of 'being healthy' differs in different stages of the human life cycle, including old age.

An ageing human experiences a gradual waning of almost all body functions, mainly in the agility, strength, muscle strength, endurance, digestion of food, renal and respiratory functions, cardiac performance, sensory faculties, etc., resulting in increased dependence on others for daily functioning (Elizabeth, 2006).

Considering the biochemistry of the body, there is a reduction in anabolic or 'building-up' reactions and an increase in catabolic or 'breaking down' reactions. So, billions of cells in different tissues and organs die in a programmed manner, and, unlike in youth-hood, they are not replaced anymore by fresh cells. Tissue growth (at in younger age) is replaced by tissue atrophy. Body organs, including the brain, become smaller in size, corresponding to reduced functioning. Hard and tough tissues like bones and cartilage also undergo changes. Bones become porous and are prone to break easily, and cartilage tissues get eroded and lose their flexibility, leading to disabilities.

These and several other anatomical and physiological changes bring out certainly visible manifestations, which can be easily identified. The common ones are greying of hair or loss of hair, stooping posture, slow pace while walking, and requirement of some support like a walking stick.

Eye disorders that are common in old age include senile cataract (clouding of the lens of the eye), Glaucoma (increased fluid pressure in the eye), Macular degeneration disease of the macula (responsible for central vision) causing loss of vision, Astigmatism (images look blurry or shadowed caused due to asymmetric steepening of the cornea or natural lens, resulting in uneven focusing of light), Retinopathy disease in the retina generally caused by diabetes or high blood pressure, Myopia (or nearsightedness or problem in seeing far away objects clearly), Hyperopia (or farsightedness or trouble in seeing nearby objects clearly), and Presbyopia (which is caused by loss of elasticity of the lens of the eye resulting in difficulty in reading) are other common disorders of vision. Further, age-related hearing loss is called presbycusis. The ability of the elderly to detect sounds decreases, and they may face problems in maintaining balance in sitting, standing and walking. In old age, due to the shrinking of taste buds and less saliva production in the mouth. The sense of taste gets affected. Likewise, the sense of smell also diminishes in old age due to loss of nerve endings and less mucus production in the nose (Elizabeth, 2006).

Social Changes in Ageing: 'Social Ageing'

The term 'social ageing' refers to the process through which a person's role and relationship shift as they get older, both in their personal life and in the larger social contexts of their community, employment, and religious institution. Individual differences in social ageing are not negated by the cultural norms regarding the elderly. An individual's social ageing will be brighter and more joyful in a society that has a good outlook on getting older than one that does not. However, as we may see, in many western countries people have predominantly negative view of ageing, which has serious implications for the elderly. Indian culture, on the other hand, has a favourable view of the ageing population, which has helped the country earn a respectable standing as a counterpoint to the West (Kaushik, 2011).

Though old age is taken as the closing period of life characterized by a decline in strength, active state, role engagements and other aspects, some development theorists have considered old age a developmental phase just like adolescence and babyhood. Adjusting well to the age-related changes is the developmental task of humans as they reach old age. Havighurst has given the following developmental tasks for the people above 60 years, which, if fulfilled, would lead to satisfaction and well-being.

1. **Adjusting to decreasing physical strength and health:** Elderly people have to come to terms with declining energy and strength. They need to accept certain limitations in their movement or increased dependency on others for accomplishing activities of daily living. Failure to do so would lead to disappointment and frustration, anxiety and depression.

2. **Adjusting to retirement and reduced income:** Retirement often brings along role loss, increased free time, and reduced income and activity levels. If not accepted, retirement may cause extreme stress in males because they invariably derive their identity from their profession/ occupation. Loss of job thus leads to loss of self-esteem, increased propensity to fall sick, loneliness, etc. Those who adjust to their retired life may take up new roles, develop and revive personal and social associations and may indulge in creative pursuits and hobbies.
3. **Adjusting to the death of a spouse/significant other:** Aged people have to come to terms with the fact that death is an inevitable reality of life and have to adjust to the death of their peers, spouse, friends, etc., and then to their own death. There are personal variations in the level of death fear. Widowhood may force the elderly to loneliness, worry and tension, and sleeplessness, and maybe change in relationships with significant others and neighbourhood.
4. **Establishing an explicit affiliation with one's age group:** If the elderly fail to have affiliations with peers and friends, they may be pushed into loneliness, depression, and alienation, while those who establish strong social networks of family and friends enjoy satisfaction, security, happiness and well-being.
5. **Meeting social and civic obligations:** Older people who are able to contribute in any way to the family, community and society develop a sense of satisfaction and meaningfulness. They feel integrated. Contrarily, the aged who fail to accomplish this developmental task remain aloof, lonely, depressed and disengaged.
6. **Establishing satisfactory physical living arrangements:** Fulfillment of this developmental task would ensure a sense of security, and connectivity with family and friends, while aged who fail to do so suffer physical discomfort, ill-health, frustration and depression.

Did You Know?
The Silver Economy is Booming!

By 2050, older adults will constitute over 20% of the global population, driving the Silver Economy—economic activities catering to their needs. Valued at over $17 trillion globally, industries such as healthcare, tourism, and technology are increasingly focusing on older consumers, emphasizing their active role in economic growth.

Source: European Commission, 2021

Elder Abuse

Elder abuse is one of the consequences of societal change. Abuse of elderly people is on the rise, which is taken as a gross violation of human rights and human dignity. The elderly who have once enjoyed utmost power and respect are becoming increasingly vulnerable, marginalized and prone to abuse and exploitation.

87-yr-old say: Son starved, humiliated her

An 87-year-old woman, the wife of a former undersecretary in the defense ministry, after six days of hospitalization, realized that her son had dumped her, with whom she was staying. She said that he took away her pension passbook, jewellery and cash, and she has suffered physical and mental abuse after her husband passed away...[*The Times of India*, January 16, 2019].

Elder abuse is defined as a single or repeated act or lack of appropriate action occurring within any relationship where there is an expectation of trust which causes harm or distress to an older person. American Psychological Association (2005) categorizes elder abuse into seven types, as follows:

- **Physical abuse** (beating, hitting, pushing, kicking, shoving, burning or biting, inflicting bodily pain, injury, or impairment);
- **Emotional or psychological abuse** (avoiding, shouting, name-calling, yelling, making insulting or disrespectful comments, isolating, threatening, inflicting mental anguish or emotional distress);
- **Financial exploitation** (misappropriation and illegal use of an elder's assets, funds, property, misusing his/her funds to embezzlement; forgery, forced property transfers, fraud, taking money under false pretences, etc.);
- **Sexual abuse** (non-consensual sexual contact of any kind, forceful showing of pornography, rape, sodomy or coerced nudity). Sexual abuse is perhaps the most egregious but least reported type of elder abuse;
- **Neglect** (failure to provide basic needs like food, water, clothing, medications and assistance with activities of daily living);
- **Abandonment** (desertion of an elderly person by an individual who has physical custody of the elder or by a person who has assumed responsibility for providing care to the elder);
- **Self-neglect** (behaviours of an elderly that threaten his/her own health or safety, such as not eating, not going to the doctor, etc.).

Help-age India, in its annual research, has found that almost one-third (33 per cent) of the elderly in India are facing abuse. To make the matter worse, cases of elder abuse often remain unreported and unaddressed.

Who are the victims of elder abuse?

Several research studies have found that:

- The elderly who are bedridden, suffering from a terminal illness, and/ or require the help of others in activities of daily living like eating, getting up and sitting, walking, etc., are more prone to be abused.
- The elderly suffering from mental illnesses such as schizophrenia, depression, and dementia, have higher chances of being abused.
- Gender is an interesting variable. A large majority of women suffer from domestic violence in their youth-hood, and that continues in old age too. For most of them, abuse continues as they become old. However, for men, abuse increases as after retirement from work-life, they become 'useless' for the family as women still are 'useful' as they participate in domestic chores and help in child care.
- Chances of elder abuse increase if the caregivers, who often are their children or daughters-in-law, are quite stressed out with the caregiving burden and do not have effective coping skills to deal with their stress. Caregivers vent out their stress in the form of elder abuse.
- Caregivers who abuse alcohol or drugs often have low tolerance power. They tend to abuse their elderly relatives more often. In addition, caregivers with mental disorders too have a higher tendency to mistreat their elderly.
- Children who have seen their parents abusing their aged relatives or each other may learn to inflict violence on their elderly/ spouse.
- Elderly living in poverty, those who migrated to different cultural or ethnic settings often face abuse by their caregivers, and they have no clue whom to report for rescue.

Quite interestingly, socio-demographic factors such as educational level, socio-economic status, and rural-urban location do not influence elder abuse. It means that educated and illiterate elderly, rich or poor aged, rural or urban elderly are abused at almost the same rate.

Psychological Changes with Ageing

The ageing process, just like in physiological and social domains, leads to changes in the psychological functioning of an individual. Before we look at these changes, it may be kept in mind that humans are bio-psycho-social units, and there are strong interconnections between these sub-units. So, any change in the physiological domain would have implications on social relationships and psychological well-being and vice-versa. Only for better understanding these sub-units have been dealt with separately. The psychological changes are seen in the following significant aspects:

- **Senescence:** Along with physical changes and mental decline, though slow and gradual, is inevitable. The rate of this decline or senescence differs from individual to individual. In old age, people tend to become eccentric, forgetful, absentminded, socially withdrawn, and poorly adjusted, which is usually described as senility. Reasons for these deteriorative changes are partly structural (changes in body cells/ tissues) and partly functional (decline in the efficiency of body organs, say, specific parts of the brain). An unfavourable attitude towards oneself, significant others, work, and life, in general, can lead to senility (Kaushik, 2011).
- **Negative self image:** Due to physical changes like wrinkling skin, and greying hair, elderly people consider themselves ugly as they do not fit into the social norms of beauty that favour young people. Moreover, the media often propagates negative stereotypes against old people by highlighting anti-ageing creams and other products, showcasing vulnerabilities and crimes against the elderly. People fear old age as it brings along many degenerative body changes. And this fear, at times, gives rise to a subtle level of hatred towards aged people too. Negative self-image has deleterious effects on the well-being of older persons.
- **Rolelessness:** Role-less state is a major challenge faced by the elderly in contemporary society. After the loss of roles due to retirement and settlement of children in their respective careers and families, the elderly find themselves in a void due to this 'role-less' state. It significantly contributes to loneliness, depression, alienation and similar other negative feelings.
- **Dealing with losses:** Old age brings along many losses: role, income and status loss due to retirement; loss of loved ones (friends, spouse) to death; and loss of independence in activities of daily living due to ill-health. An individual derives his/ her image from the occupation/ profession he/she is involved in. After retirement, that image no longer holds, and the individual starts having negative self-images such as being spent-force, unproductive, and useless. Reduction in income (in the form of pension) or loss of income deepens the sense of economic dependence on children and insecurity, making the person anxious and miserable. Social interactions decrease significantly. Further, loss of spouse and friends lead to loss of companionship, making the person bereaved and grief-stricken. There are few people to communicate with. It severely hampers the well-being of an elderly person (Khan & Kaushik, 2008).
- **Death fear:** Death, for most of us, is confined to old age. Many elderly people find it difficult to come to terms with the death of their significant

others—spouse and friends—and their own death. Widowhood often leads to mental health problems like loneliness, alienation, worry, tension, heightened fear of death, hallucinations, hypochondrias, depression, along with increased morbidity rates.

Review Questions

(a) Describe the various alterations that ageing brings?
(b) Explain the development task of elderly person, given by Havighurst?
(c) Justify the causes of elder abuse in your own words?

SOCIAL WORK AND AGEING

Ageing is a big challenge for the entire world in the present scenario. The population of elderly is increased day by day and it generates new challenges for the care giver of elderly thereby creating requirement of professionals who experts in the field gerontology.

The scope of social work with older persons has expanded to address the evolving needs of this population. Societal changes, such as advancements in healthcare and technology, have shifted care from hospital-based to outpatient and community settings. As improved health services extend life expectancy, the elderly population has become more diverse, presenting new challenges in caregiving. Social workers play a critical role in assisting families with decision-making and providing expertise in gerontology. However, they often face obstacles, including the need for skills in clinical tasks, case management, and care coordination. The demand for specialized services for older adults is growing, yet ageist attitudes among both healthcare professionals and social workers, along with a lack of motivation to work with the elderly, pose significant barriers. These biases result in a shortage of qualified professionals and services, limiting the effectiveness of social work in supporting this vulnerable group. However, prejudices and biases about older people make it difficult to implement such programmes efficiently. In addition to negative public opinions about older people, ageist bias adopted by the social workers

Did You Know?
Age Doesn't Limit Success!

Colonel Sanders founded KFC at 65. Anna Mary Robertson Moses, aka Grandma Moses, began painting at 78. In India, Falguni Nayar, founder of Nykaa, became a billionaire at 59, showing how entrepreneurship and success can flourish in later years. These examples challenge the notion that aging means decline—proving that creativity, innovation, and success have no age limit!

Source: Forbes, 2020; *Economic Times*, 2021

and healthcare professionals such as nurses and doctors constitutes a big challenge for implementation of these programmes. Low motivation and less desire to work with older groups is creating a lack of qualified staff and services for this disadvantaged group (Kaushik, 2020).

Gerontological Social Work

Gerontological social work a specialized branch along with multi-disciplinary sub-field of social work in which a social worker is studying or working with older adults, and is responsible for educating, researching and advancing the broader causes of older people. Gerontology as a term is emerging in society as a result of larger population of elderly in the world. In this subject, people study about process of ageing and psychosocial factors which are associated with the elderly along with problems of caregivers of the elderly. Gerontological professionals assess the multidimensional processes of ageing, which are associated with biological, psychological and social domains. Gerontological social workers play a crucial role in promoting healthy and productive aging, addressing the various challenges that arise in later life. Their unique skills, values, and roles make them well-suited to provide supportive and educational services to both elderly individuals and their caregivers. Gerontological social work focuses on the complex physical, psychological, familial, organizational, and societal factors that affect the well-being of older adults, often creating barriers to their physical and emotional health.

Interventions in gerontological social work aim to enhance dignity, self-determination, personal fulfillment, and optimal functioning for older individuals, while promoting a decent standard of living in the least restrictive environments possible. Social workers' commitment to the uniqueness of each individual within a systems perspective equips them to design and implement equitable and effective programs for the increasingly diverse older population.

This field highlights the indispensable contributions of social workers within elder care systems and underscores the importance of social work research in understanding and responding to the needs of aging populations. Social work is recognized for its critical and strategic role in ensuring that care systems are responsive to the diverse needs of older adults (Kaushik, 2020).

Gerontological social work plays a crucial role in addressing the multifaceted needs of older adults. It aims to:

- Enhance the capacity of schools and departments to train students in the field of aging.
- Provide students with exposure to a wide range of programs and services available to older persons within the country.

- Familiarize students with current and emerging policy issues affecting service systems for older adults.
- Offer opportunities for students to develop essential skills and knowledge for working with older persons.

The field addresses a wide array of issues, such as financial well-being, family caregiving, mental health, the health consequences of aging, kinship care, care management, life roles and relationships, end-of-life care, living arrangements, autonomy, prevention, aging in diverse communities, resource utilization, and welfare management.

Understanding the Role of Gerontological Social Work

Despite its critical importance, the role of social work in aging is often misunderstood. Many organizations and individuals believe that anyone with good intentions can provide services for the elderly. However, social workers must recognize that delivering quality care for older adults requires specialized knowledge. Social work's holistic approach focuses on the person-in-environment, considering bio-psycho-social factors that affect the elderly. This approach means that both the client and their family are seen as the unit of care, and providing concrete resources is just as important as offering mental health counseling (Elizabeth, 2006).

Social workers are skilled in a variety of areas relevant to aging, including age discrimination, client rights, domestic violence, loss, end-of-life concerns, substance use disorders, depression, and living with physical challenges. These professionals must be adept at assessing bio-psycho-social factors that contribute to older adults' well-being and must have a deep understanding of the social, familial, and economic aspects of aging.

Specialized Training for Gerontological Social Workers

Given the increasing needs of the aging population, social workers should pursue additional specialized education and advanced training related to older persons. Major advancements have been made in infusing aging-related content into social work courses in academic programmes. This has created a snowball effect, with more future social workers preparing to work in gerontology. These efforts are essential to addressing the growing demand for well-trained professionals who understand the unique needs of older adults and their families.

Scope of Gerontological Social Work

Gerontological social work professionals play a key role in educating family members about the behaviors and challenges elderly individuals face. They help families manage the psycho-social aspects of aging, inform them about symptoms related to old age, and facilitate access to healthcare services for the elderly. These professionals act as catalysts, bridging the gap between older adults and the healthcare system, ensuring that the aging population has access to the resources they need.

As society ages, there is a growing demand for social workers skilled in working with older adults and their families. However, a gap remains in knowledge and expertise, particularly in the areas of mental health and aging disciplines. Social work practice with older adults encompasses a broad range of functions, whether working in micro or macro settings. The primary goal is to address the specific challenges of the aging process, promoting independence, autonomy, and dignity in later life.

Social workers interact with older adults in various settings, including hospitals, adult day care centers, independent and assisted living communities, public agencies, and, increasingly, in homes. They must be knowledgeable about the aging process, the issues faced by older adults, and the needs of their caregivers. Additionally, social workers must be skilled at accessing resources for their clients and advocating for the rights of older adults.

Key Areas of Knowledge and Expertise

Gerontological social workers require expertise in several areas, including:

- Assessment of older adults' needs and functional capacity.
- Knowledge of physical and mental health issues affecting older adults.
- Case and care management, which involves coordinating services and support for elderly clients.
- Understanding long-term care options, such as nursing homes, assisted living facilities, and home care services.
- Addressing elder abuse, including identifying and responding to signs of physical, emotional, and financial abuse.
- Promoting quality of life and advance care planning, which involves helping older adults make informed decisions about their healthcare and living arrangements.
- By developing these skills, social workers can better advocate for older adults and ensure they receive the support they need to maintain their independence and quality of life.

Skills Required to Work with Older Persons

Working with the elderly presents unique challenges that require both personal and professional skills. Social workers who choose to work with older adults must cultivate compassion and patience. Older individuals may sometimes feel demeaned or resistant to younger professionals, believing they are "too young" to understand their situation. While many older adults are a joy to work with, some may have experienced abuse or neglect, which can amplify feelings of negativity and mistrust.

In addition to compassion, social workers must be prepared to handle severe mental illnesses such as dementia and Alzheimer's disease. These conditions often cause confusion, fear, and behavioral changes, making it difficult for the elderly to communicate effectively. Social workers must be able to distinguish between reality and the misconceptions that individuals with cognitive impairments may experience, while also addressing their emotional and psychological needs.

Professionally, social workers must possess a range of social work skills tailored to the needs of older adults. This includes strong communication skills, the ability to navigate complex healthcare systems, and knowledge of legal and ethical issues related to elder care. Social workers must also be skilled at coordinating services across multiple sectors, such as healthcare, housing, and social services, to provide comprehensive support for older adults.

Gerontological social work is an essential and expanding field that requires specialized training, skills, and knowledge to meet the growing demands of an aging population. Social workers play a critical role in advocating for older adults, ensuring they have access to the resources and support necessary to live independently and with dignity. The unique challenges of aging require a holistic approach that addresses not only physical health but also the emotional, social, and psychological well-being of older adults.

By developing a deep understanding of the aging process and the factors that influence the well-being of older individuals, social workers can better serve this vulnerable population. The need for well-trained gerontological social workers is greater than ever, as society continues to age and the challenges of elder care become more complex.

Review Questions

(a) Explain the concept of gerontology social work.
(b) Enlist some skills required to work with older persons.

In the near future, India will become one of the largest countries of the world which have more number of elderly. Earlier with joint family system people could give proper time to the elderly but in present times every person is busy in his own life so anyone is unable to give proper time to elderly. The term 'Elderly Care' in India seeks adequate attention to provide positive interventions for strengthening social support systems for the elderly. Being a multifaceted profession, social work has a greater role to play in the area of gerontology. Gerontological social work aims at developing the ability of the students in the schools and departments of social work to train students in the field of aging, exposing them to a range of programs and services for elderly within the country, making them aware of the current and emerging policy issues which affect the social service system in the context of elderly. Gerontological social work is particularly concerned with those issues which are related with elderly vis-à-vis physical, psychological, familial, institutional and societal. These issues create barriers to their physical and emotional well-being in later life.

SUMMARY

In this chapter, we learnt about the notion of ageing, old age and elderly people and understood about chronological ageing, biological ageing, social ageing, and psychological ageing. This helped in understanding the multi-dimensional aspects of ageing process. Elderly people are a heterogeneous group as many are healthy, active and productive while others are frail, lonely and dependent. All these age categories have differential needs and behaviour patterns. We studied the socio-demographic profile of the elderly in India while briefly looking at the increasing number and proportion of older people in the world. Factors leading to population ageing and implications of this phenomenon on the healthcare system, social and economic resources are delineated. Challenges that families, communities and nations are encountering due to increased number of elderly people have been discussed. Lastly, need and scope of geriatric care is outlined.

GLOSSARY

- **Chronological age** refers to the actual time a human has been alive and in India a person is considered an elderly or aged when he/she achieves sixty years or above while in most developed countries the cut off for old age is 65 years.
- **Young-old** (that is, 60 to 69 years) are the most healthy, productive and energetic sub-group among the elderly population. Generally, their biological functioning is almost comparable to a middle-aged person.
- **Middle-old** (that is, 70 to 79 years) become dependent in certain activities of daily living and have somewhat diminished energy and body strength.
- **Old-old** (that is, 80 to 89 years) during this period their biological functions have declined significantly and they suffer from many physiological and mental limitations.
- **Oldest-old** (90 years and above) individuals most often require the help of care-givers for their daily living.

- **Independent:** The elderly in this group are fully functional, do not require any support in carrying out their activities of daily living.
- **Assisted:** These older people require some help in their activities of daily living due to certain limitations in the body functioning because of some ailments.
- **Dependent:** They are invariably bed-ridden and require constant and long-term care and support.
- **Septuagenarian:** A person in his/her seventies (70s).
- **Octogenarian:** A person who is between 80 to 89 years. More females than males are octogenarians.
- **Centenarian:** A person who lives to the age of hundred years. In 2012, the United Nations estimated that there were 316,600 living centenarians worldwide.
- **Gerontology:** It is a scientific discipline that deals with the phenomenon of aging and all issues related to this process; it usually entails the psycho-social aspects of ageing.
- **Geriatrics or Geriatric Medicine:** It is a branch of medicine that deals with biological aspects of old age.
- **Gero-psychology:** It is a branch of psychology devoted to the study of aging.

TOP TEN TAKEAWAY POINTS

1. Socio-cultural changes affecting the function and status of the elderly have been identified.
2. In the contemporary world, they are confronted with role-less state and are becoming increasingly vulnerable and marginalized due to changing family structure, values of consumerism, etc.
3. Akin to biological changes, people experience changes in their psyche and behaviour in old age. Age related changes in personality, intelligence, memory, learning, problem solving, perception, attention, motivation, have been discussed.
4. Common mental health ailments in old age such as anxiety, phobia, depression, dementia with their common symptoms are provided in the chapter.
5. There is a relationship between all types of change (biological, social, psychological).
6. The maltreatment of the elderly is associated to the constant evolution of society.
7. Gerontology is a new field in social work education that requires more training to meet the needs of an ageing population.

8. There is a special place for elders in Indian culture, but the country's rapid industrialization and urbanisation have led to a shift in cultural norms that makes it difficult for elders to take advantage of it.
9. The needs of the elderly are unique and call for a specialised approach to development.
10. Practitioners of Gerontology, a subfield of social work, need specialised training to effectively assess and work with the elderly.

MULTIPLE CHOICE QUESTIONS

1. Subjective feeling of one's age, irrespective of chronological age is known as his/her
   (a) Physiological Age (b) Psychological Age
   (c) Social Age (d) Middle Age
2. __________ is the branch of psychology to study ageing issues
   (a) Gero-Psychology (b) Gerontology
   (c) Social work with ageing (d) Geriatrics
3. Factors like genetic endowment, life style, nutrition, etc., one's
   (a) Mental Age (b) Biological Age
   (c) Psychological Age (d) Functional Age
4. In Old age people have ample free time but experience
   (a) Happiness (b) Sadness
   (c) Role-less (d) Energetic
5. What is chronological age?
   (a) Psychological age (b) Social age
   (c) Actual time a human has been alive
   (d) Old age
6. As per the ministry of Statistic and Programme Implementation the old age dependency ratio has risen in 2001?
   (a) 10.9 per cent (b) 13.1 per cent
   (c) 65 per cent (d) 60 per cent
7. Unfavourable attitude toward oneself, others, work and life in general may lead to
   (a) Negativity (b) Denial
   (c) Senility (d) Self-Neglect
8. Age related hearing loss?
   (a) Presbycusis (b) Presbyopia
   (c) Senile Cataract (d) Catabolic reaction
9. What do you understand by the Alzheimer's disease
   (a) Flashback of traumatic event
   (b) Paralyzing fear of something that usually poses no threat
   (c) Ongoing sadness, lack of interest in activities previously enjoyed

(d) progressive mental deterioration that can occur in middle or old age

10. As per the 2011 census, which state has highest old population in India? (in Percetnage)
    (a) Andhra Pradesh (b) Kerala
    (c) Gujrat (d) Uttar Pradesh

Answers

1. (b), 2. (a), 3. (b), 4. (c), 5. (c), 6. (b), 7. (c), 8. (a), 9. (d), 10. (b).

REFERENCES

1. American Psychological Association (2005). *Introduction: Elder Abuse*. Accessed at http://www.apa.org/pi/prevent-violence/resources/elder-abuse.aspx
2. Birren, J. E., Butler, R. N., Greenhouse, S. W., Sokoloff, L., & Yarrow, M. R. (1963). Introduction to the Study of Human Aging. In J. E. Birren, R. N. Butler, S. W. Greenhouse, L. Sokoloff, & M. R. Yarrow (Eds.), *Human aging: A biological and behavioral study* (pp. 1–4). US Dept of Health, Education, & Welfare. HYPERLINK "https://psycnet.apa.org/doi/10.1037/10776-001" https://doi.org/10.1037/10776-001
3. Census (2011) Government of India. Accessed at http://censusindia.gov.in
4. Elizabeth J. Clark, Ph.D., ACSW, MPH (2006). Preparing for the Aging Boom, Accessed at http://www.socialworkers.org/pubs/news/2006/03/clark.asp.
5. Helpage India. 2012. *Elderly Abuse in India*. New Delhi: Helpage India.
6. Kaushik, A. (2011). *Media Representation of Elderly in India*. New Delhi: The Readers' Paradise Publications.
7. Khan, M.Z. & Kaushik, A. (2008). Ageing: Policies and Programmes in India. *BOLD, Quarterly Journal of the International Institute on Ageing* (United Nations – Malta), August, 18(4).
8. Kaushik, A. (2020). Addressing Marginalization Among the Elderly: A Social Work Perspective. In Malakapur Shankardas (Ed.) *Ageing Issues and Responses in India*. Springer Nature.
9. UNDESA (2003) World Public Sector Report 2003: E-Government at Cross Road—Global E-Government Survey. Department of Economic and Social Affairs, United Nations, New York.
10. UNDESA (2019) World Population Ageing 2019. Accessed at https://www.un.org/en/development/desa/population/publications/pdf/ageing/WorldPopulationAgeing2019-Report.pdf
11. United Nations, Department of Economic and Social Affairs, Population Division (2020). World Population Ageing 2019 (ST/ESA/SER.A/444).
12. United Nations (2009). World Population Prospects. New York: United Nations.

13. World Economic Forum (2023). Elderly Care: How can Countries cope with ageing. HYPERLINK accessed at https://www.weforum.org/agenda/2023/08/elderly-social-care-dementia-villages/

RECOMMENDED READINGS

1. Paltasingh, T. & Tyagi, R. (Eds.) (2015). "Caring for the elderly: Social Gerontology in Indian Context", New Delhi: Sage.
2. Ian Stuarat-Hamilton (2006). "The Psychology of Ageing: An Introduction", London & Philadelphia: Jessica Kingsley Publishers.
3. Binstock, R.H., & George, L.K. (2001). "Handbook of Aging and Social Science". New York: Academic Press.
4. Jackson, S.L. & Hafemeister, T.L. (2013). "Understanding elder abuse: New Directions for developing theories of elder abuse occurring in a domestic setting," United States: Department of Justice, National Institute of Justice.
5. World Health Organization (2002). "Active Ageing: A Policy Framework", Geneva: WHO.
6. Ramamurthi, P.V., Jamuna, D. (eds.) (2004). "Handbook of Indian Gerontology". New Delhi: Serial Publication.
7. Rajan, S.I., Mishra, U.S., Sarma, P.S. (eds.) (1999). "India's Elderly: Burden or Challenge", New Delhi: Sage Publications.
8. Crawford, K., & Walker, J. (2004). "Social Work with Older People": Learning Matters.

CHAPTER–2

Social Work Practice with Refugees and Asylum Seekers

RAVINDRA RAMESH PATIL[1], SANIYA ZEHRA[2] AND MEHAK JAFRI[3]

[1]*Professor, Department of Social Work, Jamia Millia Islamia, New Delhi*
[2]*Project Manager, Centum Foundation, New Delhi*
[3]*MSW, Jamia Alumna-2023, Department of Social Work, Jamia Millia Islamia, New Delhi*

People escaping violence or persecution must be able to cross borders safely. They must not face discrimination at borders or be unfairly denied refugee status or asylum due to their race, religion, gender, or country of origin.

– UN Secretary-General António Guterres

ABSTRACT: *The world has been witnessing the highest levels of displacement and refugee crisis. As per estimate, the global forced displacement has reached to 103 million and there are around 32.5 million people are refugees in the year 2022 representing highest number of refugee children below 18 years of age living in vulnerable and unprotected condition. Majority 72 per cent of refugees in the world come from the countries namely Syria, Venezuela, Ukraine, Afghanistan and South Sudan due to socio-political and ethnic issues forcing people into severe crisis(Refugee Data Finder, UNHCR, 2022). In India, as per statistics available, there are around 2,12,413 refugees belongs to Afghanistan, Bhutan, Tibet, Myanmmar, Nepal, Pakistan and Bangladesh sought asylum in different parts of the country.*

In this chapter, detailed information has been provided about various aspects of refugee and their vulnerability for social work intervention. The chapter covers information about refugee: definition, meaning & concepts, refugee population: world and India, refugee: main causes and problems, international policy related to refugees, programmes and organizations for refugees and prospective role of social work with refugees in India.

Keywords: *Refugee, Asylum, Policies, Programme, Social Work Practice*

Learning Objectives

After reading this chapter, you will be able to:

- Understand about definition, concept and types of refugee
- Know about magnitude of refugees in India and the world

- Develop understanding about different causes and problems of the refugee population
- Know about the existing international policies on refugees
- Know about different organizations and programmes for refugees
- Understand about role of social work practice with refugees

INTRODUCTION

It is estimated that there are more than 100 million people are forcibly displaced in the world at the end of 2022. This massive number has been swollen due to the war between Russia and Ukraine and other conflicts around the world. Conflict, violence and persecution are the major reasons behind millions of refugees in the world, who are forcibly displaced each year and living in deplorable condition in the refugee camps and asylum of recipient countries.

These millions of refugee population worldwide are forced to flee their homes and living in vulnerable condition in different countries is the major international human crisis of the contemporary times. All the humanitarian organizations and international community must come together to give refugees more help, support and opportunities to rebuild their life. Similarly, the different nation-state should accept them at the time of crisis and develop country specific refugee friendly policies for the protection and well-being of refugees. The role of humanitarian professions like social work is pertinent in the well-being of the refugee population. Social work professionals should understand the issues and crisis of refugee population to develop social work interventions for psycho-social care and human development of refugees in the host countries. While working with refugees, social workers should adopt social inclusion approach for long-term solutions for refugees and forcibly displaced people allowing them to adjust and survive in a host country and preparing them to repatriate safely to their home countries. In this chapter, the main concern is to highlight challenges faced by the refugee populations worldwide and the prospective role of social work practice to minimize refugees' distress.

REFUGEE: DEFINITIONS, CONCEPTS & TYPES

Definitions

There are different definitions given by various organizations to describe the refugees . Majority of these definitions are based on the understanding given by the United Nations and other international conventions and organizations. In order to simplify the term refugee, the different definitions of term refugee are described below.

The World War-I (1914-1918) and World War-II (1939-1945) and, the Holocaust in real sense responsible for the issues of refugees, forced displacement and genocide of millions of people. In this context, the UN 1951 Refugee Convention defined 'refugee' (in Article 1.A.2) as any person who:

> *owing to well-founded fear of being persecuted for reasons of race, religion, nationality, membership of a particular social group or political opinion, is outside the country of his nationality and is unable or, owing to such fear, is unwilling to avail himself of the protection of that country; or who, not having a nationality and being outside the country of his former habitual residence as a result of such events, is unable or, owing to such fear, is unwilling to return to it* (UNHCR, 1951, p. 6)

In 1967 UN Protocol relating to the Status of Refugees has had expanded the scope of definition given by UN Refugee Convention in 1951 as it was largely pertaining to World War II and European refugees. The 1967 UN Protocol has incorporated the problems of displacement spread around the world and the problems of refugees in Africa in its definition, which was adopted by Organization of African Unity in 1969, which is as follows:

> '*The term refugee shall also apply to every person who, owing to external aggression, occupation, foreign domination or events seriously disturbing public order in either part or the whole of his country of origin or nationality, is compelled to leave his place of habitual residence in order to seek refuge in another place outside his country of origin or nationality*' (UNHCR, 2013: 5).

Similarly, the Cartagena Declaration on Refugees (Cartagena Declaration, 1984), which has developed protection mechanism for refugees in Latin American context defines refugees as follows:

> '*Persons who have fled their country because their lives, safety or freedom have been threatened by generalized violence, foreign aggression, internal conflicts, massive violation of human rights or other circumstances which have seriously disturbed public order*' (UNHCR, 2013:4).

In addition to definition given in the UN Refugee Convention, 1951, UNHCR further made addition to its existing definition on 2011, which recognizes persons as refugees:

> '*who are outside their country of nationality or habitual residence and unable to return there owing to serious and indiscriminate threats to life, physical integrity or freedom resulting from generalized violence or events seriously disturbing public order*' (UNHCR, 2011:19).

To summarize, above definitions describe refugees as that person, who resides outside his/ her country of origin due to conflict, war, displacement or fear of persecution and is unable or unwilling to avail for himself/herself of that country's protection (UNHCR, 1999).

Concept

The concept of refugees is one that has been shaped by years of conflict, persecution, and forced displacement across the world. The Refugees face threats to their life, safety and security due to violence, conflict, war and persecution. They are forced to flee their home and take shelter in other countries, where they hope to find safety and protection from the dangers that they faced in their own countries. The concept of refugees has been a part of human history for centuries, and it continues to be a pressing issue in the modern world. As reported by the United Nations High Commissioner for Refugees (UNHCR), at present there are over 31.6 million refugees worldwide and the millions more internally displaced within their own countries (www.unhcr.org.in).

One of the primary causes of refugee crises is conflict. War and violence can force individuals and families to flee their homes for safety and security. The ongoing civil war in Syria, for example, has led to the displacement of millions of people, with many fleeing to neighbouring countries such as Lebanon, Turkey, and Jordan. Similarly, the conflict in Yemen has forced thousands to flee to nearby countries, such as Djibouti and Somalia.

Persecution is another reason why individuals may become refugees. Political persecution, religious discrimination, and other forms of targeted violence can make it unsafe for individuals to remain in their home countries. The Rohingya crisis in Myanmar, for example, has led to the displacement of thousands of Rohingya's, who had fled Myanmar due to persecution based on their ethnic and religious identity. Environmental factors, such as natural disasters and climate change, can also contribute to refugee crises. Rising sea levels, drought, and other environmental challenges can make it difficult for people to remain in their homes, forcing them to seek refuge elsewhere. This is particularly true in regions such as the Pacific Islands, where rising sea levels are putting entire communities at risk of displacement.

Once individuals become refugees, they face a variety of challenges. These may include difficulty accessing basic needs such as food, water, and shelter, as well as navigating unfamiliar legal systems and cultures. Many refugees also face discrimination and hostility from the communities where they seek refuge, making it difficult to integrate and rebuild their lives.

In this situations, it is a responsibility of international community to provide support and assistance to refugees by providing access to basic needs such as food, water, and shelter, as well as legal and financial assistance to help refugees navigate the complex process of seeking asylum. In addition, the international community can work to address the root causes of refugee crises, such as conflict and persecution, through diplomatic efforts and other means (United Nations High Commissioner for Refugees 1951).

Types of Refugees

According to the United Nations High Commissioner for Refugee (UNHCR), by the end of 2021, there were approximately 82.4 million forcibly displaced people worldwide, comprising refugees, asylum seekers, and internally displaced persons (IDPs). It is the highest number ever recorded and represents an increase of 4 per cent from the previous year.

It is also estimated that out of above mentioned 82.4 million forcibly displaced people, 26.4 million were refugees, comprising both conventional refugees and asylum seekers from Syria, Venezuela, Afghanistan, South Sudan, and Myanmar.

In addition to refugees, there were approximately 48 million internally displaced persons (IDPs) who had been forced to flee their homes due to conflict, persecution, and natural disasters, but remained within their own country's borders. The largest numbers of IDPs were in Syria, Colombia, and the Democratic Republic of Congo.

Finally, there are approximately 4.1 million stateless people worldwide who are not considered citizens of any country and therefore lack legal protection and access to basic rights and services.

The global refugee crisis remains a significant challenge, with millions of refugee population are in need of humanitarian assistance and protection. The international community continues to work to provide support to refugees and to address the root causes of displacement.

There are several types of refugees, each with their own unique circumstances and reasons for seeking refuge:

1. **Convention Refugees:** Convention refugees are people who are not able to return to their own country due to a well-founded fear of persecution on the base of race, religion, nationality, political opinion, or membership in a particular social group.
2. **Asylum Seekers:** Asylum seekers are anyone who have fled their own country and have applied for asylum in another country. They may or may not meet the criteria to be recognized as a convention refugee.
3. **Stateless Persons:** Stateless persons are individuals or group of people, who are not considered citizens of any country and therefore do not have a nationality or legal status in any country. They may have been forced to flee their own country due to discrimination or persecution.

4. **Internally Displaced Persons (IDPs):** IDPs are individuals or group of people, who have been forced to flee their own homes due to conflict, persecution, or natural disaster, but they have not crossed an international border of their country. They remain within their own country and are often in need of humanitarian assistance.
5. **Environmental Refugees:** Environmental refugees are individuals or group of people who are forced to leave their homes due to environmental disasters such as floods, droughts, or hurricanes. These individuals do not necessarily meet the criteria for refugee status under the 1951 Refugee Convention.
6. **Repatriates:** Repatriates are individuals who have returned to their home country after being displaced, often due to conflict or persecution, and are in need of assistance to reintegrate into their communities.
7. **Returnees:** Returnees are individuals or group of people, who have returned back to their own country voluntarily or involuntarily after being displaced, often due to conflict or persecution. They may also require assistance to reintegrate into their communities.

Review Questions

(a) What do you understand by the term 'refugee'?
(b) Explain the concept of refugees and asylum seekers.
(c) Explain different types of refugees?

REFUGEE POPULATION: WORLD AND INDIA

The issue of refugees has been a persistent problem in the world for a very long time. India has been a host to refugees for decades—from neighbouring countries such as Afghanistan, Bangladesh, Bhutan, Myanmar, and Sri Lanka. With estimates ranging from 200,000 to over 400,000 refugees, India also among the largest refugee populations in the world. The majority of the refugees in India are from Tibet, Sri Lanka, and Afghanistan. The refugee situation in India has been largely overshadowed by the country's internal problems. The country's large population, poverty, and social issues have made it difficult for refugees to integrate into Indian society. However, the Indian government has made various efforts to address the issue, and the country has been relatively open to refugees (UNHCR, 2020).

The situation in the world is much worse, with millions of refugees fleeing their homes due to conflicts, wars, and persecution. According to the United Nations, the number of refugees worldwide reached a record high of 26 million in 2020. Syria, Afghanistan, and South Sudan are the largest sources of refugees, with millions of people fleeing from these countries due to conflict and war.

The refugee crisis has put immense pressure on countries that host refugees, with issues such as overcrowding, lack of resources, and social tensions arising. The international community has been working to address the issue, with organizations such as UNHCR working to provide assistance to refugees and their host countries. However, the situation remains challenging; with many countries don't have pro-refugee policies (UNHCR, 2021).

Magnitude of Refugees in India

India has a significant number of refugee population. However, there are still many refugees are undocumented and living in informal settlements in India. According to the UNHCR, as of 2021, there were around 205,252 refugees and asylum seekers were registered in India.

The majority of refugees in India come from neighboring countries such as Afghanistan, Myanmar, Pakistan and Sri Lanka. Afghanistan has the largest refugee population in India, with over 116,000 refugees and asylum-seekers registered with the UNHCR. Most of these refugees are ethnic Pashtuns who have fled violence and conflict in their home country Afghanistan.

In addition to these registered refugees, there are also a significant number of undocumented refugees and asylum seekers in India. For example, there are believed to be tens of thousands of Rohingya refugees from Myanmar living in informal settlements in India. These refugees face significant challenges accessing basic services and are at risk of exploitation and abuse.

Apart from that, India is host to a significant number of refugees, with most coming from neighboring countries. Here are some examples of refugees in India:

- **Afghan refugees:** India has been hosting Afghan refugees since the Soviet invasion in 1979. As of 2021, there were over 15,000 Afghan refugees and asylum seekers in India, primarily in New Delhi and the earstwhile northern state of Jammu and Kashmir.
- **Tibetan refugees:** India has been hosting Tibetan refugees since 1959, when the Dalai Lama fled Tibet. There are currently over 100,000 Tibetan refugees living in India, primarily in settlements in the northern state of Himachal Pradesh.
- **Rohingya refugees:** India has been host to Rohingya refugees who have fled persecution in Myanmar. These Rohingya refugees are found in the northern states and other parts of India.
- **Sri Lankan refugees:** India has hosted Sri Lankan Tamil refugees since the 1980s, with most living in camps in the southern state of

Tamil Nadu. As of 2021, there were over 100,000 Sri Lankan refugees in India.

- **Bhutanese refugees:** India has hosted Bhutanese refugees since the early 1990s, when they were forced to flee Bhutan due to political persecution. As of 2021, there were around 8,000 Bhutanese refugees living in camps in the eastern state of Assam.
- **Pakistani refugees:** There are hundreds of Hindu Pakistani refugees seeking asylum in India. They come to India out of fear of persecution back in their home country. In Pakistan, they are facing religious apartheid and nobody raising questions against the disgrace and differential treatment meted against the Hindus living in Pakistan. The Hindus are considered as unequal citizens in Pakistan and the Constitution of Pakistan is only favourable to the followers of Islam.

Review Questions

(a) What is the magnitude of refugees in India and the world?
(b) Which are those countries that have a major refugee crisis in the world?
(c) Why is there a major inflow of refugees in India from other South Asian countries?

REFUGEE: MAIN CAUSES AND PROBLEMS

Causes of Seeking Refuge

Religious/National/Social/Racial/Political Persecution

Persecution, which can be religious, national, social, racial, or political, is the most frequent cause of refugees worldwide. Christians and Muslims are split about equally among religious refugees in the United States of America. Pew Research Centre reports that in 2016, total 46 per cent of refugees who entered the US were Muslims and 44 per cent were Christians; the remaining 10 per cent were other, including Hindus, Buddhists, and Jews.

Religious refugees can be found all over the world, including Christians in the Central African Republic, Hindus in Pakistan, and Muslims who are being persecuted in Burma.

Many well-known people have fled their country for political reasons at some point. This includes Alexander Ginsburg, who escaped the Soviet Union during the Cold War, Gloria Estefan, who fled the Castro regime in Cuba, and the Dalai Lama, who is the exiled leader of Tibet.

War

As stated earlier, War is one of the cause of refugee crisis worldwide. The vast majority of history's evacuees have been the immediate or backhanded result of war. Right now, the biggest gathering of exiles on the planet are escaping the common struggle in Syria, which has been seething starting around 2011 and has killed 400,000 Syrians and uprooted 6.3 million insides in the country. Another 5 million have left the nation totally.

Be that as it may, before Syria, evacuees escaped battles in Iraq and Afghanistan in large numbers in the mid-1980s, 1990s and 2000s. Afghanistan, quite, had the biggest number of refugees of any country on the planet for over twenty years somewhere in the range of 1981 and 2013, preceding being surpassed by Syria that year.

Orientation/ Sexual Direction

The sexual orientation other than male and female also one of the main cause of discrimination in many societies. The LGBTQ+ population due to their different sexual orientation faces various kinds of discriminations and harassments, which further forcing them to leave their place of origin and become refugees in other countries. In June of 2023, France turned into the main country to acknowledge a gay Chechen evacuee—a stupendous choice that had worldwide resonations.

Due to issues of LGBTQ+ refugees, the UNHCR also refreshed its rules to incorporate refugees because of reasons of orientation or sexual orientation in 2012.

"It is widely documented that LGBTI individuals are the targets of killings, sexual and gender-based violence, physical attacks, torture, arbitrary detention, accusations of immoral or deviant behaviour, denial of the rights to assembly, expression and information, and discrimination in employment, health and education in all regions around the world.4 Many countries maintain severe criminal laws for consensual same-sex relations, a number of which stipulate imprisonment, corporal punishment and/or the death penalty" (UNHCR, 2012:2).

Hunger

Hunger is another major cause of refugee crisis worldwide. Mostly in Africa and sub-Saharan Africa, large majority of people suffer due to acute food shortages, which forcing them to leave their own country and take refuge in neighbouring countries. It's assessed that 20 million individuals in four nations namely Somalia, South Sudan, Nigeria, and Yemen are confronting an outrageous dry season, and a significant number of these people are becoming outcasts, constrained from their countries looking for stable food sources.

There are around 17 million uprooted people across the African landmass, and just a little extent of them is arriving at the shores of the European mainland. Many end up in rambling, casual exile camps like the town of Monguno in north-eastern Nigeria. Displaced people escaping appetite can, obviously, additionally be getting away from different variables simultaneously, including the ascent of radical gatherings like Boko Haram in Nigeria and the effects of environmental change.

Environmental Change

The climate change and disaster are another cause of refugee crisis in the contemporary time. Large majority of people are getting displaced due to flood, drought, tsunami, etc. It's assessed that in the following 83 years, a dazzling 13 million seaside occupants could be uprooted by environmental change, joining the overflowing crowds of refugees and dislodged individuals.

Formally, environmental change isn't yet a legitimate justification behind a refuge guarantee. In 2013, the principal environmental change displaced person refuge case was shot down somewhere near the New Zealand High Court when a Kiribati man endeavoured to guarantee that status by regulation.

Be that as it may, as man-made environmental change deteriorates, and seas rise, the 1951 and 1967 shows might have to extend their extension.

Similarly, India is home to a large number of refugees who have fled their home countries due to a variety of reasons. The causes and factors that lead to refugees in India are complex and multifaceted, but can generally be grouped into a few broad categories.

One major cause of refugees in India is *armed conflict and political instability* in neighboring countries. This has been particularly true for refugees from Afghanistan and Myanmar, where long-standing political turmoil and violent conflict have driven people from their homes in search of safety. The ongoing civil war in Syria has also led to an influx of refugees in India in recent years. The refugees from these countries often face significant challenges in India, including limited access to basic services like education and healthcare, as well as discrimination and hostility from some members of the local population.

Another significant factor that contributes to the refugee population in India is *environmental degradation and climate change*. The displacement of people due to environmental factors like drought, flooding, and sea level rise is a growing global concern, and India is no exception. Climate change is having a particularly acute impact on the lives of people in the Sundarbans, a delta region shared by India and Bangladesh, where rising sea levels and increasingly severe cyclones have made life increasingly difficult for those who call the region home (*Oxfam India*, 2020).

The *persecution of ethnic and religious minorities* is also a major cause of refugees in India. For example, the Rohingya people, a Muslim minority from Myanmar, have faced brutal violence and persecution at the hands of the Myanmar government, leading many to flee across the border to India. Similarly, the Tamil minority in Sri Lanka faced decades of discrimination and violence at the hands of the Sri Lankan government, leading to a large population of Tamil refugees in India (*The Diplomat*, 2019).

Finally, *economic factors* also play a role in driving people to flee their home countries and seek refuge in India. Many refugees are drawn to India by the promise of economic opportunity, or because they see India as a more stable and secure place to live than their home countries. For example, many Afghan refugees in India are professionals or business people who were forced to flee their country due to the ongoing conflict, but who have been able to rebuild their lives in India (*The Hindu*, 2019).

Challenges Faced by Refugees

There are number of challenges faced by the refugees at the countries of their refuge. Some of the challenges faced by the refugees are as follows:

- **Fear and Insecurity:** Refugee status is full of vulnerabilities and insecurities. Generally, refugees are not accepted at the countries of their refuge and not treated well by the local residents. They also face often physical violence and torture from the local residents and always remains under fear and insecurity.
- **Deprived of Basic Amenities:** Refugees are always deprived of basic amenities and minimum human needs such as food, shelter and employment. Refugee camp sites are always in poor condition mostly at the outskirts, where refugees hardly get any basic amenities. Similarly, refugees mostly work in unorganized sectors, where they forced to work at low wages with no high status or privileges.
- **Lack of Well-Defined Framework for their Protection:** Many countries are not receptive to refugees' despite of agreement to different international treaties. Majority of them do not have policy or having ad hoc policy related to refugees has created an atmosphere of confusion regarding human rights of refugees. Thus, lack of well-defined framework for refugees' protection is one of cause of deprivation and insecurity of refugee worldwide.

- **Time Consuming Process of Identification:** In order to establishing identity of refugees United Nations High Commissioner for Refugees (UNHRC) issues a refugee card through the refugee status determination process. This process takes a long time up to 20 months to complete the procedure. In this 20 months period if any refugee caught by the police, he/she will be arrested, detained and deported back to their respective country without consulting the UNHCR.
- **Misidentified as Immigrants:** In order to get employment and better economic opportunities, many refugees have illegally immigrated to other countries. For example, 98 per cent of Mexican illegally immigrated to USA and resides there without citizenship. This illegal identity and stay in the host countries always put them under fear of arrest and detention in the USA.

Refugee Problems in India

India has long been a destination for refugees from neighboring countries, such as Afghanistan, Bangladesh, Bhutan, Myanmar, Nepal, Pakistan, and Sri Lanka. While the Indian government has offered refuge to those who have been displaced, refugees in India face numerous challenges, including legal issues, economic difficulties, and social exclusion.

One of the major problems faced by refugees in India is their *lack of legal status*. It is fact that India is a signatory to the United Nations Convention Relating to the Status of Refugees but it does not have any specific law for the protection of refugees. This means that refugees in India are often unable to access basic rights and services, such as education, healthcare, and employment. Additionally, without proper documentation, refugees are vulnerable to harassment and abuse by law enforcement authorities (Nayar, 2018).

Another significant problem faced by refugees in India is *economic hardship*. Mostly refugees in India are unable to find any source of livelihood due to their lack of legal status and discrimination based on their nationality or ethnicity. This can lead to extreme poverty and a lack of basic necessities, such as food and shelter. Many refugees also face difficulty accessing healthcare, which can exacerbate their economic hardship.

Social exclusion is also a major issue faced by refugees in India. Refugees are often viewed with suspicion by the local population and are subjected to discrimination and harassment. They may also face difficulty integrating into Indian society due to cultural differences and language barriers. This can lead to a sense of isolation and a lack of community support (Nayar, 2018).

Additionally, refugees in India are often subject to *exploitation and abuse*. Many refugees are vulnerable to human trafficking and forced labor, and women and children are particularly at risk of sexual exploitation and trafficking. These issues are compounded by the lack of legal protection and documentation for refugees in India.

Review Questions

(a) Explain the major causes of refugee problem.
(b) Explain the major problems/ challenges faced by refugees.
(c) What are the different problems faced by refugees in India?

INTERNATIONAL POLICY RELATED TO REFUGEES

The international policy of refugees refers to the set of guidelines, principles, and laws that govern the treatment of refugees worldwide. Refugees are individuals who have fled their own country due to fear of persecution, war, or violence, and are unable to return to their country of origin due to well-founded fear of persecution. The international community has recognized that refugees deserve protection and assistance and has established legal frameworks to ensure their safety and well-being under different international conventions and treaties.One of the most important international policies related to refugees is the Convention relating to the Status of Refugees, 1951. This convention defines who a refugee is and outlines the legal obligations of states to protect refugees. The convention stipulates that refugees should not be returned to their home country if they would face persecution or threat to their life, and that they should be granted access to basic rights such as education, healthcare, and employment. Over 150 countries are party to the convention, making it one of the most widely recognized and respected international agreements related to refugees. Another important international policy related to refugees is the United Nations High Commissioner for Refugees (UNHCR), 1950. The UNHCR is responsible for coordinating international efforts to protect refugees and ensuring that they are treated with dignity and respect. The UNHCR works closely with governments, NGOs, and other stakeholders to provide refugees with basic needs such as shelter, food, and water, as well as access to education, healthcare, and legal assistance.

The UNHCR also plays a crucial role in advocating for the rights of refugees and raising awareness about their situation. The agency works to educate the public about the challenges facing refugees and to dispel myths and stereotypes about them. By raising awareness about the issue, the UNHCR hopes to mobilize support and resources to help refugees rebuild their lives. In addition to the 1951 Convention and the UNHCR, there are a number of other international policies related to refugees. These include the Guiding Principles on Internal Displacement 1998, the Protocol relating to the Status of Refugees 1966, and the Convention on the Rights of the Child 1989. Each of these policies seeks to protect the rights and dignity of refugees and ensure that they are treated fairly and with compassion.

Despite these international policies, however, the situation facing refugees around the world remains challenging. Millions of people continue to be displaced from their homes due to conflict, violence, and persecution, and many face discrimination and abuse in their countries of refuge. In many cases, refugees are forced to live in overcrowded and unsafe conditions, with limited access to basic necessities such as food, water, and healthcare. To address these challenges, it is crucial that countries around the world continue to uphold their legal obligations to protect refugees and provide them with access to basic rights and services. This includes providing refugees with access to education and employment, as well as ensuring that they are able to live in safety and security. It also requires that governments work together to address the root causes of displacement, such as conflict and poverty, and to find sustainable solutions that allow refugees to return to their homes and rebuild their lives (UNHCR, 2021).

Review Questions

(a) What is the international policy for refugees?
(b) Explain briefly about different international policies on refugees.
(c) What are the problems faced by refugees despite international policies on refugees?

INTERNATIONAL CONVENTION/PROGRAMMES ON REFUGEES

There are different international conventions/ programmes on refugees, which are as follows:

- **1951 Convention relating to the Status of Refugees:** This convention defines who is a refugee and describes the rights and obligations of refugees and the responsibilities of countries that provide refuge to them. It also establishes the principle of non-refoulement, which means that a refugee cannot be returned to a country where they may face persecution.
- **1967 Protocol relating to the Status of Refugees:** This protocol expands the scope of the 1951 Convention to cover refugees who were displaced before 1951.
- **United Nations High Commissioner for Refugees (UNHCR):** The UNHCR is a UN agency that is responsible for protecting refugees,

asylum-seekers, and stateless persons worldwide. It provides assistance, protection, and solutions to those who have been forced to flee their homes due to conflict, persecution, or other reasons.

- **Global Compact on Refugees:** This is a framework for cooperation and responsibility-sharing among countries to address the global refugee crisis. It aims to improve the lives of refugees, enhance their self-reliance, and increase their access to education, healthcare, and employment.
- **Comprehensive Refugee Response Framework:** This is a program launched by the UNHCR and its partners to enhance the effectiveness of the international response to large-scale refugee issues worldwide. It seeks to improve the protection of refugees, expand their access to assistance, and support their inclusion in host communities.
- **Regional initiatives:** There are also several regional initiatives aimed at addressing refugee situations, such as the African Union Convention for the Protection and Assistance of Internally Displaced Persons in Africa and the Cartagena Declaration on Refugees in Latin America.

Indian Government's Programmes and Schemes for Refugees

India has various programmes and schemes for refugees, particularly for those who have come from neighbouring countries due to persecution or conflict. Some of the major ones include:

- **Long Term Visa:** The Indian government provides long term visas to refugees from neighbouring countries, who are unable to return to their home countries due to fear of persecution or conflict. The visa is valid for up to five years and can be renewed.
- **Swavalamban:** Swavalamban is a livelihood support programme for refugees and asylum seekers in India. The programme provides vocational training, job placement assistance, and support for self-employment to help refugees become self-sufficient.
- **Education:** Refugees in India have access to primary and secondary education under the Right to Education Act, regardless of their legal status. The government has also established special schools for refugee children in some areas.
- **Healthcare:** Refugees in India are entitled to free healthcare services provided by government hospitals and dispensaries. The government has also established special clinics for refugees in some areas.
- **Repatriation:** The Indian government has a repatriation policy for refugees who wish to return to their home countries voluntarily. The government provides financial assistance to cover transportation costs and some resettlement expenses.

Similarly, the ancient Indian philosophy of *Vasudhaiva Kutumbakam*, means 'The World is one family' strongly believes in assimilating with different culture and people has helped highly to the refugee population. India has had an outstanding record on the protection of refugee in its territory. The Constitution of India also respects the life, liberty, and dignity of human beings. The Article 21 of the Constitution encompasses the right of non-refoulement. Non-refoulement is the principle under international law which states that a person fleeing persecution from his own country should not be forced to return to his own country.

Further, the Supreme Court in the National Human Rights Commission vs. State of Arunachal Pradesh (1996) held that 'while all rights are available to citizens, persons including foreign citizens are entitled to the right to equality and the right to life, among others.'

Review Questions

(a) What do you understand by the right to non-refoulement?
(b) Explain briefly about different International conventions and programmes on refugees.
(c) What are different programmes and schemes for refugees in India?

ORGANISATIONS WORKING FOR REFUGEES IN THE WORLD

The details about the different organizations working for the protection and well-being of refugees working in the world are as follows:

- **United Nations High Commissioner for Refugees (UNHCR):** The UNHCR is a UN agency that is responsible for protecting refugees, asylum-seekers, and stateless persons worldwide. It provides assistance, protection, and solutions to those who have been forced to flee their homes due to conflict, persecution, or other reasons.
- **International Rescue Committee (IRC):** The IRC is a humanitarian organization that responds to the world's worst humanitarian crises and helps people whose lives and livelihoods are shattered by conflict and disaster to survive, recover, and gain control of their future.
- **Doctors Without Borders (MSF):** MSF is a medical humanitarian organization that provides medical assistance to people affected by conflict, epidemics, and disasters, regardless of their race, religion, or political affiliation.
- **International Committee of the Red Cross (ICRC):** The ICRC is an independent, neutral organization that provides humanitarian assistance and protection to victims of armed conflict and other situations of violence.

- **Save the Children:** Save the Children is a global organization that works to improve the lives of children in over 120 countries. They provide humanitarian aid and protection to children affected by conflict, disasters, and displacement.
- **Oxfam International:** Oxfam is a global organization that works to alleviate poverty, suffering, and injustice. They provide humanitarian assistance and long-term support to refugees and displaced persons.
- **World Vision:** World Vision is a Christian humanitarian organization that works to improve the lives of children and families in need. They provide humanitarian assistance, education, and support to refugees and displaced persons around the world.

Organisations Working for Refugees in India

Details of organizations working for refugees in India are as follows:

- One of the most important organizations working for refugees in India is the Indian Council for Social Welfare (ICSW) 1947. The ICSW is a non-governmental organization that works for the welfare and development of vulnerable sections of society, including refugees. The organization provides various services such as health care, education, and vocational training to refugees to help them become self-reliant and integrated into society.
- The Refugee Council of India (RCI) 1993 is another organization that works for refugees in India. The RCI is a non-profit organization that is dedicated to providing necessary assistance and support to refugees and asylum seekers in India. This organization works in partnership with the government and other non-governmental organizations to provide essential services such as legal aid, shelter, and education to refugees (Refugee Council of India 1993).
- The Jesuit Refugee Service (JRS) 1980 is another important organization working for refugees in India. The JRS is a non-governmental organization that provides assistance and support to refugees and asylum seekers around the world. In India, the organization works with refugees and asylum seekers from various countries, providing essential services such as legal aid, shelter, and education to help them rebuild their lives.
- The Indian government also has various programmes in place to provide assistance to refugees. The government provides refugees with legal protection, access to education, health care, and other essential services. The government also offers financial assistance to refugees through the 'Central Sector Scheme of Assistance to Stateless Persons' (Ministry of Home Affairs, 2019). This scheme aims to provide financial

assistance to stateless individuals who are not covered under any other scheme. The financial assistance covers the cost of living, education, and medical treatment. The government also provides assistance in the form of food, shelter, and financial aid to refugees in need (Ministry of Home Affairs, 2019).

Review Questions

(a) Explain briefly about the different organizations working for refugees in the world.
(b) Explain briefly about the different organizations working for refugees in India.
(c) What is 'Central Sector Scheme of Assistance to Stateless Persons' of Government of India?

ROLE OF SOCIAL WORK WITH REFUGEES

Social work with the refugees and asylum seekers is relatively broad complex activities that are targeted to find lasting solution to the situation of every individual refugee, their families and to the refugees' community as a whole. Particularly, social work interventions with refugees is envisioned as their adaptability and inclusion into a new society and provide all necessary help, support and solutions to the refugees within international protection procedure and country specific laws and provisions. Some of the focused social work role and interventions with the refugees are as follows:

Social Work Intervention with Refugee Individual and Families

Social work profession has much to offer in protection and well-being of refugee population. Social worker can respond to the complex needs of individual refugee and their families at the refugee sites and camp. Starting from helping and enabling refugees to cope up with situation and strengthen psycho-social support through social case work and social group work method. More individualistic and family centered approach shall enhance intra-personal and inter-personal coping mechanism among refugee population helped them to negotiate with the social welfare system and survive in the difficult situation. Similarly, this social work approach shall help refugees to understand the importance of family relationships and social institution to fulfill their complex needs at the country of their refuge.

While intervening with refugees at the individual and family level, the social workers must do a thorough need identification pertaining to different aspects of refugee life and then plan structure of services for the refugee individual and families such as recreational activities, play groups, support group, psycho-socio care services, counseling to contribute to the healing and well-being of refugees.

Did You Know?

- As per UNHCR estimate, the global forced displacement has reached to 103 million and there are around 32.5 million people are refugees in the year 2022 representing highest number of refugee children below 18 years of age living in vulnerable and unprotected condition.
- Majority 72 per cent of refugees in the world come from the countries namely Syria, Venezuela, Ukraine, Afghanistan and South Sudan due to socio-political and ethnic issues forcing people into severe crisis(Refugee Data Finder, UNHCR, 2022).
- There are approximately 4.1 million stateless people worldwide who are not considered citizens of any country and therefore lack legal protection and access to basic rights and services.
- The World War-I (1914-1918) and World War-II (1939-1945) and, the Holocaust in real sense responsible for the issues of refugees, forced displacement and genocide of millions of people.
- Environmental factors, such as natural disasters and climate change, also contributing to refugee crises. Rising sea levels, drought, and other environmental challenges can make it difficult for people to remain in their homes, forcing them to seek refuge elsewhere.
- India is not a signatory to the 1951 Refugee Convention or its 1967 Protocol. Yet, India has been a host to refugees for decades—from neighbouring countries such as Afghanistan, Bangladesh, Bhutan, Myanmar, Sri Lanka and Pakistan. Total Refugee population estimates between 200,000 to over 400,000 in India.
- Afghanistan has the largest refugee population in India, with over 116,000 refugees and asylum-seekers registered with the UNHCR.
- In India such refugee colonies and camps are located at different geographical locations such as Assam, Arunachal Pradesh, Kolkata, Delhi, Bengaluru, Mumbai, Chennai, etc.
- United Nations High Commissioner for Refugees (UNHCR) is responsible for coordinating international efforts to protect refugees and ensuring that they are treated with dignity and respect.
- The Article 21 of the Indian Constitution encompasses the right of non-refoulement. Non-refoulement is the principle under international law which states that a person fleeing persecution from his own country should not be forced to return to his own country.
- The Indian government provides **long term visas** to refugees from neighbouring countries, who are unable to return to their home countries due to fear of persecution or conflict. The visa is valid for up to five years and can be renewed.
- **Swavalamban** is a livelihood support programme for refugees and asylum seekers in India.
- The Indian Government also offers financial assistance to refugees through the 'Central Sector Scheme of Assistance to Stateless Persons' (Ministry of Home Affairs, 2019).

Social Work Intervention with Refugee in the Institutional Settings

The studies reveal that refugees are also found in different institutions such as old age home, hospitals, mental health institutions, prison, juvenile delinquent home, child care institutions and schools. They are facing varied problems related to maladjustment, maltreatment and discrimination in these institutional settings. The role of social worker here is towards supporting the adjustment and integration of refugee inmates in the institutions. Especially at the school settings, the refugee children have major issues related to social integration into schooling system, scholastic performance and coping with the language barriers. Social worker here should perform the role of school social worker and design school based programme to support refugee integration. While designing school based integration programme cultural and linguistic background of refugee children should be taken care for effective school social work practice with refugee children.

Social Work Intervention with Refugees in the Community

The studies have revealed that the influx of refugees also created a refugee colonies and camps in the different countries. In India such refugee colonies and camps are located at different geographical locations such as Assam, Arunachal Pradesh, Kolkata, Delhi, Bengaluru, Mumbai etc. The issues and problems of refugees in such colonies and camps are varied such as lack of basic life necessities, lack of basic amenities, lack housing, lack of medical and health facilities, lack of livelihood and employment, culture and language difference, insecurity and fear, prejudice and discrimination, social exclusion etc. The role of social worker with refugees in the community settings is multi-dimensional and demands different community based interventions to foster well-being and social inclusion among refugees in the community settings. By adopting community based approach, social worker should identify the needs of the refugees and plan community based interventions to address their issues of basic amenities, livelihood, service delivery health, safety, security, vulnerability, discrimination, social integration and social inclusion. While working with refugees in the community settings social worker should develop the skills of cultural competence, collaboration, participation, social-politico networking, advocacy, community involvement, peer support, need assessment, programme planning, capacity building to effectively promote well-being and human rights of refugee population.

Review Questions

(a) Explain the social work intervention with the refugee individual and families.

(b) Explain the social work intervention with the refugees in the institutional settings.

(c) Explain the social work intervention with the refugees in the community settings.

SUMMARY

In this chapter, we learnt about the emergence of refugee as a phenomenon in the contemporary period. The chapter discussed in detailed various aspects of refugee and their vulnerability for social work intervention. The chapter covered information about definition, meaning and concepts of refugee, magnitude of refugee population in the world and India, main causes and problems of refugee, international policies related to refugees, programmes and organizations for refugees and prospective social work intervention with refugees at the individual, family, institutional and community settings. Each section in this chapter provided with review questions for the exercise and revision purpose.

GLOSSARY

- **Convention Refugees:** Convention refugees are people who are not able to return to their own country due to a well-founded fear of persecution on the base of race, religion, nationality, political opinion, or membership in a particular social group.
- **Asylum Seekers:** Asylum seekers are anyone who have fled their own country and have applied for asylum in another country. They may or may not meet the criteria to be recognized as a convention refugee.
- **Stateless Persons:** Stateless persons are individuals or group of people, who are not considered citizens of any country and therefore do not have a nationality or legal status in any country. They may have been forced to flee their own country due to discrimination or persecution.
- **Internally Displaced Persons (IDPs):** IDPs are individuals or group of people, who have been forced to flee their own homes due to conflict, persecution, or natural disaster, but they have not crossed an international border of their country. They remain within their own country and are often in need of humanitarian assistance.
- **Environmental Refugees:** Environmental refugees are individuals or group of people who are forced to leave their homes due to environmental disasters such as floods, droughts, or hurricanes. These

individuals do not necessarily meet the criteria for refugee status under the 1951 Refugee Convention.

- **Migrant:** A person who moves from one place to another, especially to find work or better living conditions. Unlike refugees, migrants are not fleeing persecution or violence.
- **Repatriates:** Repatriates are individuals who have returned to their home country after being displaced, often due to conflict or persecution, and are in need of assistance to reintegrate into their communities.
- **Returnees:** Returnees are individuals or group of people, who have returned back to their own country voluntarily or involuntarily after being displaced, often due to conflict or persecution. They may also require assistance to reintegrate into their communities.
- **Temporary Shelter:** Short-term accommodation provided to displaced persons in the immediate aftermath of displacement.
- **Resettlement:** The transfer of refugees from an asylum country to another state that has agreed to admit them and ultimately grant them permanent residence.
- **Non-Refoulement:** A principle of international law which forbids a country from returning asylum seekers to a country in which they would be in likely danger of persecution based on nationality, race, religion, social group, etc.
- **Refugee Convention:** It is a United Nations multilateral treaty that defines who is refugee, their rights, legal obligations of states to protect refugees.

TOP TEN TAKEAWAY POINTS

1. Refugee crisis and the concept of refugees is one that has been shaped by years of conflict, persecution, and displacement across the world.
2. Refugees are individuals who are forced to flee their homes due to threats to their safety and security, often as a result of war, persecution, or violence. These individuals seek refuge in other countries, where they hope to find safety and protection from the dangers that they faced in their home countries.
3. One of the primary causes of refugee crises is conflict. War and violence can force individuals and families to flee their homes in search of safety. The ongoing war between Russia-Ukraine; Israeli-Palestinian and Civil war/violence in Syria, Sudan and Myanmar for example, have led to the displacement of millions of people, with many fleeing to neighbouring countries for refuge.
4. Persecution is another reason why individuals may become refugees. Political persecution, religious discrimination, and other forms of

targeted violence can make it unsafe for individuals to remain in their home countries. The Rohingya crisis in Myanmar, for example, has led to the displacement of hundreds of thousands of people who were forced to flee due to persecution based on their ethnic and religious identity.

5. Environmental factors, such as natural disasters and climate change, can also contribute to refugee crises.
6. Refugee face a variety of challenges such as difficulty in accessing basic needs like food, water, and shelter, as well as navigating unfamiliar legal systems and adjusting with different cultures.
7. According to the United Nations Refugee Agency (UNHCR), as of the end of 2021, there were approximately 82.4 million forcibly displaced people worldwide, including refugees, asylum seekers, and internally displaced persons (IDPs).
8. Many refugees also face discrimination and hostility from the communities where they seek refuge, making it difficult to integrate and rebuild their lives.
9. The international community and UN organizations have a responsibility to provide support and assistance to refugees. This includes providing access to basic needs such as food, water, and shelter, as well as legal and financial assistance to help refugees navigate the complex process of seeking asylum.
10. Refugee crisis is a new field of social work education, which requires urgent social work intervention to protect the rights of refugee and meet the human development needs of the refugees.

MULTIPLE CHOICE QUESTIONS

1. _______ are individuals who are not considered citizens of any country and therefore do not have a nationality or legal status in any country.
   (a) Refugee (b) Asylum Seekers
   (c) Stateless Persons (d) Internally Displaced Persons
2. The majority of the refugees in India are from________________
   (a) Tibet, Sri Lanka, and Afghanistan
   (b) Pakistan, Bangladesh, Myanmar
   (c) Nepal, Bhutan, Maldives (d) Sudan, Syria, Congo
3. According to the UNHCR, 2021, there were approximately__________ refugees and asylum seekers registered with the agency in India.
   (a) 205,252 (b) 305,000
   (c) 405,000 (d) 505,000
4. _______________ working to provide assistance to refugees and their host countries.

(a) United Nations Development Program
(b) United Nations High Commissioner for Refugees
(c) International Organization for Migration
(d) International Rescue Committee

5. ________________ is the principle under international law which states that a person fleeing persecution from his own country should not be forced to return to his own country.
(a) Rehabilitation (b) Resettlement
(c) Repatriation (d) Non-refoulement

6. ____________ is a livelihood support programme for refugees and asylum seekers in India.
(a) PM POSHAN Abhiyan (b) Swavalamban
(c) Deendayal Antyodaya Yojana
(d) PM Garib Kalyan Yojana

7. The Indian government provides long term visas ________________ to refugees from neighbouring countries, who are unable to return to their home countries due to fear of persecution or conflict.
(a) valid upto two year and can be renewed
(b) valid upto three year and can be renewed
(c) valid upto four year and can be renewed
(d) valid upto five year and can be renewed

8. How many countries are party to the convention relating to the Status of Refugees, 1951?
(a) Over 150 (b) Over 170
(c) Over 180 (d) Over 190

9. According to the United Nations High Commissioner for Refugees (UNHCR), there are currently over ___________ refugees worldwide.
(a) 20 million (b) 25 million
(c) 31.6 million (d) 35 million

10. While working with refugees in the community settings social worker should develop the skills of ________________.
(a) Coping mechanism (b) Psycho-social care
(c) Counselling (d) Cultural Competence

Answers

1. (c), 2. (a), 3. (a), 4. (b), 5. (d), 6. (b), 7. (d), 8. (a), 9. (c), 10. (d).

REFERENCES

1. Bhadwal, S. (2017). *Refugees and the state: Practices of asylum and care in India, 1947-2000*. Oxford University Press, Oxford.

2. Chakraborty, R. (2022). The Rohingya Refugee Crisis: A Challenge for India. *Asian Journal of Social Science Studies*, 6(1), 1–11
3. *Economic Times* (2022). India among top three host countries of international migrants, refugees and asylum seekers in South-East Asia region in 2020. Retrieved March 30, 2023, from https://m.economictimes.com/news/india/india-among-top-three-host-countries-of-international-migrants-refugees-and-asylum-seekers-in-south-east-asia-region-in-2020/articleshow/93011530.cms
4. Fitzpatrick, J. (1996) 'Revitalising the 1951 Refugee Convention', *Harvard Human Rights Journal*, vol. 9 pp.229-53.
5. Hathway, J. (1956), *The Law of Refugee Status*. Butterworths, Toronto, 1991.
6. *Hindustan Times* (2022, March 14). Delhi has highest share of inter-state migrants. *Hindustan Times*. https://www.hindustantimes.com/delhi-news/delhi-has-highest-share-of-inter-state-migrants-story-QCYXSWlnSYAJbNb25ljcPL.html
7. Holborn, L.W. (1946–52). The International Refugee Organization: A Specialized Agency of the United Nations: Its History and Work 1946-1952.
8. James C., (2005). *The Rights of Refugees Under International Law*. Cambridge University Press, UK.
9. Jean Yves Carlier, Dirk Vanheules Klaus Hullmann and Carlos Pena Galiano (eds) (1997). Who is a Refugee: A Comparative Case Law Study. Kluwer Law International, The Hague. 1997.
10. Kapoor, R. (2022). *Making Refugees in India*, Oxford University Press, Oxford.
11. Knox, A.W. (2020). 'Integration of Social Work Practices with Refugees: An Action Research Study', Walden Dissertations and Doctoral Studies Collections, Walden University, Minnesota, USA.
12. MHA (2019). 'Asylum to Citizen of other countries', December 4, Rajya Sabha, Unstarred Question No. 1796, Government of India.
13. Ministry of Home Affairs. (2019). Central Sector Scheme of Assistance to Stateless Persons. Retrieved from https://www.mha.gov.in/sites/default/files/Assistance_to_Stateless_Persons_0.pdf
14. Nair, A. (2007) 'National refugee law for India: Benefits and roadblocks'. in *IPCS Research Papers*, 11.
15. Nair, R. (2021). 'Refugee Protection in India in the Absence of Specific Legislation: An Overview', Social and Political Research Foundation, New Delhi.
16. Natarajan, A., M. Moslimani & M. H. Lopez (2022). 'Key facts about recent trends in global migration', December 16, Pew Research Center, Washington, DC.
17. Nawaz, S. (2019). Pakistani Hindu Refugees: Causes, Consequences and Challenges. *South Asian Studies*, 34(1), 83-97.

18. Nayar, P. K. (2018). India and refugees: The Rohingya crisis. *Strategic Analysis*, 42(2), 125-136. doi: 10.1080/09700161.2018.1434207
19. Raj, P. (2020). 'Understanding Citizenship and Refugees' Status in India', Vol. 55, Issue No.23, 06 June, *Economic and Political Weekly*, Sameeksha Publication, Mumbai.
20. Raj, S. (2020). 'Safe but Betrayed: Pakistani Hindu Refugees in India', January 22, *The Diplomat*, Retrived from https://thediplomat.com/2019/01/safe-but-betrayed-pakistani-hindu-refugees-in-india/dated 28.01.2024.
21. Raj, T.K. (2019). 'Wrong on the Rohingya', *The Hindu*, February 5, https://www.thehindu.com/opinion/op-ed/wrong-on-the-rohingya/article26176985.ece/dated 28.01.2024.
22. Social Impact Guide. (n.d.). Organizations that support refugee rights. Retrieved March 30, 2023, from https://socialimpactguide.com/journal/organizations-support-refugee-rights/
23. Stevenson, L. (2022), *A Global Overview on Refugee Status Determination.* State Academic Press, USA.
24. Tharoor, S. (2022). 'India needs a refugee and asylum law' *The Hindu*, February 19, https://www.thehindu.com/opinion/lead/india-needs-a-refugee-and-asylum-law/article65063388.ece/dated 28.01.2024.
25. UNHCR, (1950). 'Statute of the office of the United Nations High Commissioner for Refugees' December 14, https://www.unhcr.org/sites/default/files/legacy-pdf/3b66c39e1.pdf/dated 28.01.2024
26. UNHCR (1951). The Refugee Convention, 1951, Retrieved from https://www.unhcr.org/sites/default/files/legacy-pdf/4ca34be29.pdf/ dated 28.01.2024
27. UNHCR (1951). Text of the 1951 Convention Relating to the Status of Refugees. Retrieved from https://www.unhcr.org/1951-refugee-convention.html
28. UNHCR (1984). Cartagena Declaration on Refugees, Cartagena De Indias, Columbia
29. UNHCR (1999). Protecting Refugees: A Field Guide for NGOs, United Nations Publication, Geneva
30. UNHCR (2011). A Year of Crisis, UNHCR Global Trends, Retrieved from https://www.unhcr.org/statistics/country/4fd6f87f9/unhcr-global-trends-2011.html/dated 28.01.2024
31. UNHCR (2012). 'UNHCR Guidelines on International Protection No. 9: Claims to Refugee Status based on Sexual Orientation and/or Gender Identity' Retrieved from https://www.unhcr.org/media/unhcr-guidelines-international-protection-no-9-claims-refugee-status-based-sexual-orientation dated 27.07.2024
32. UNHCR (2013). 'The 1969 OAU Refugee Convention and the Protection of People fleeing Armed Conflict and Other Situations of Violence in the Context of Individual Refugee Status Determination', by Marina Sharpe, Legal and Protection Policy Research Series, Division of International Protection, Geneva, Switzerland: UNHCR.

33. UNHCR (2013). 'The Cartagena Declaration on Refugees and the Protection of People Fleeing Armed Conflict and Other Situations of Violence in Latin America', by Michael Reed-Hurtado, Legal and Protection Policy Research Series, Division of International Protection, Geneva, Switzerland: UNHCR.
34. UNHCR (2018). Refugee protection: A guide to international refugee law (Handbook for parliamentarians). Retrieved from https://www.unhcr.org/publications/legal/3d4aba564/refugee-protection-guide-international-refugee-law-handbook-parliamentarians.html
35. UNHCR (2020). Global Report, UNHCR, Geneva, Switzerland: UNHCR.
36. UNHCR (2021). 'India Fact Sheet', April 30, 2021. Geneva, Switzerland: UNHCR.
37. UNHCR (2021). Global Report, 2021, Geneva, Switzerland: UNHCR.
38. UNHCR (2022). Global Report, 2022, Geneva, Switzerland: UNHCR.
39. UNHCR (2022). Statelessness Statistics, Refugee Data Finder. Retrieved from https://www.unhcr.org/refugee-statistics/methodology/dated 28.01.2024
40. UNHCR (2023). Global Trends Forced Displacement in 2022, Retrieved from https://www.unhcr.org/refugee-statistics/dated 28.01.2024
41. Valtonen, K. (2008). *Social Work and Migration: Immigrant and Refugee Settlement and Integration (Contemporary Social Work Studies)* (1st ed.). Routledge., Ashgate, England.
42. Wonderopolis (n.d.). What causes people to become refugees? Retrieved March 30, 2023, from https://wonderopolis.org/wonder/What-Causes-People-to-Become-Refugees

RECOMMENDED REFERENCES

1. Samaddar, R. (2003). Refugees and the law. Kolkata: Stree.
2. Basu, S. P. (2013). Refugees in India: Socio-economic and legal dimensions. Kolkata: Levant Books.
3. Goodwin-Gill, G. S., & McAdam, J. (2011). The refugee in international law (3rd ed.). Oxford: Oxford University Press.
4. United Nations High Commissioner for Refugees,(2022). Global trends: Forced displacement Geneva: UNHCR.
5. Behrman, S., & Kent, A. (Eds.). (2018). Climate refugees: Global, local and critical approaches. Cambridge: Cambridge University Press.
6. Sezgin, Z., & Dijkzeul, D. (Eds.). (2015). The new humanitarians in international practice: Emerging actors and contested principles. London: Routledge.

CHAPTER–3

Social Work in Correctional Settings

GAURI SHARMA

Freelance Development Consultant

It is said that no one truly knows a nation until one has been inside its jails. A nation should not be judged by how it treats its highest citizens, but its lowest ones.

– Nelson Mandela

ABSTRACT: *Correctional institutions, also known as prisons, jails, detention centers, or halfway houses, have evolved to focus on both imprisonment and rehabilitation. The concepts of crime, punishment, and intervention have changed significantly over time. Reformation began in the West during the 19th century and spread to India with the establishment of the Indian Jail Committee in 1919-20. Although India has policies prioritizing rehabilitation and aftercare, these efforts are still in their early stages. This chapter examines prisons as correctional settings and highlights the importance of reformation and rehabilitation.*

Social workers play a crucial role in bridging gaps between prisoners, officials, families, and the community, both during imprisonment and after release. The field of corrections involves multiple services and philosophies, but a key challenge is integrating specialized skills for prisoners' care. Social work emphasizes advocating for systemic changes, promoting rehabilitation, and using humanizing language in the criminal justice system.

Keywords: *Correctional Institutions, Prison Reforms, Social Work, Rehabilitation, Reformation, Incarceration, Prisoners' Rights*

Learning Objectives

After reading this chapter, you will be able to:

1. To develop an understanding of the prison system.
2. To develop a better understanding of the different realms of correctional social work.
3. To understand the importance of reformation and rehabilitation in a correctional setting.
4. To emphasize the role of the social worker in the correctional work setting.
5. To provide suggestions for social work interventions to enhance the effectiveness of prisoners' rehabilitation.

INTRODUCTION

Crime and punishment have been part of human social life since time immemorial. However, the notion of punishment has seen a significant change over the years. From 1000 to 1200 AD crime was viewed from a more religious and superstitious context, and so were the nature of punishments. With time the notion of crime became more scientific in the 18th and 19th centuries leading to a better understanding of punishment such as punishment should fit the crime. Thus, with time the society's perception of crime and punishment has also changed, which in turn changes the intervention strategies. Thus, in the era when religion and superstition influenced crime people did not believe in treating the offenders and they were mostly kept locked inside the prisons. But with the superstition being taken over by scientific knowledge there has been a change in the belief, and lately, few people are beginning to accept crime in shades of grey', that is, they are opening to the idea of accepting that offenders can reform themselves. Prisons are no longer viewed as dungeons or detention centres for prisoners, but rather as correctional institutions. Thus, the term 'correctional' indicates a positive attitude toward a prisoner, as it provides opportunities and chances for them to reform and reintegrate into society.

Correctional institutions in this chapter are referred to as prisons/ jails, detention centres, or halfway houses for convicted prisoners seeking imprisonment and rehabilitation. The correctional setting works under police, judiciary, prosecution and prison (correctional institutions).

Prison: Correctional Institution

This section will provide a basic overview of the correctional institution, and the prison system. The evolution of the prison system can be divided into three phases: the first one lasting until the middle of the 16th century was dungeons where prisoners were kept; in the second phase, imprisonment was for punishment for certain offenders; and in the third phase, imprisonment was the substitute for capital punishment (Nagda, 2017).

Bureau of Police Research and Development (2003) and Government of India (n.d.) in its Prison Act 1894, defines prison as any jail or place used permanently or temporarily under the general or special orders of a state government for the detention of prisoners, and includes all lands and buildings appurtenant thereto; but does not include:

(a) Any place for the confinement of prisoners who are exclusively in the custody of the police;
(b) Any place specially appointed by the state government under section 541 of the Code of Criminal Procedure, 1882; or

(c) Any place which has been declared by the state government, by general or special order, to be a subsidiary jail.

Structure of Prisons

1. **Central prison:** Inmates who have been imprisoned for a longer duration (more than two years are sent to central prisons. These prisons have a higher capacity to retain inmates and also have more rehabilitation opportunities.
2. **District prison:** These prisons have a lesser capacity as compared to central prisons. Theoretically, which in practice may not hold, district prisons are mostly for undertrials.
3. **Sub jails:** These are smaller institutions in the states.
4. **Women jails:** These are for women prisoners and the prison staff are primarily women officials.
5. **Open jails:** These are jails without any walls with minimum security and the inmates are allowed to work outside the prison premises.

According to the Bureau of Police Research and Development [BPR&D] (2016), the following terms have been defined:

1. **Prisoner:** Any person confined in prison under the order of a competent authority.
2. **Convict:** Any prisoner under sentence of a court exercising criminal jurisdiction or court-martial and includes a person detained in prison under the provisions of Chapter VIII of the Code of Criminal Procedure of 1973 (Central Act 2 of 1974) and the Prisoners Act of 1900 (Central Act 3 of 1900).
3. **Undertrial prisoners:** A person who has been committed to judicial custody pending investigation or trial by a competent authority.
4. **Open prison, semi-open prison and open colonies:** Any place declared as such for the detention of prisoners under any Act or rules for the time being in force.

At present, as per Prison Statistics India (2019), India's overall prison population is 4,78,600, compared to a capacity of 4,03,739 and both the number of prisons has increased by 0.82 per cent and the occupancy rate has increased from 117.6 per cent to 118.5 per cent in 2019. Hence one can see that the issue of overcrowding is very much prevalent inside the prison but that there is one welfare officer for every 2,033 prisoners and one psychologist for every 21,650 prisoners, whereas the Model Prison Manual of 2016 recommends one correctional officer for every 200 prisoners and one psychologist for every 500 prisoners. The data reflects that there is a staffing shortage, which adds to the mental and physical stress on the personnel. As a result, all of these system-based issues should be addressed in addition to working with the prisoners. Thus social workers are placed inside prisons, they will not only support the day-to-day operations of the prison systems but will also enrich to improve the prison culture and environment.

Alternatives to Punishment

Community service occurs when an offender, or a person accused of a crime, completes work that benefits his or her local community as a method of repaying a debt to society. Community service is often used as an alternative to imprisonment and is designed to connect offenders to the victim or society so that they understand how their actions affect others (Smith, n.d.).

Parole and Furlough

Parole and furlough have been accepted as the most appropriate correctional method in modern penology for reformation, rehabilitation and reintegration. They provide a platform for offenders to reconnect with their community.

Paranjape (2015) has quoted Dr Sutherland who has defined parole as the act of releasing or the status of being released from a penal or reformatory institution in which one has served part of his maximum custody and under the guidance of the institution or some other agency approved by the State until a final discharge is granted.

Furlough is one of the rehabilitation measures to help prisoner maintain their family relationships. Unlike parole, for furlough, an inmate does not need to have a specific reason.

Probation

Walker (1985) has stated that probation as an alternative to incarceration of offenders if properly used shall eliminate three deleterious consequences that flow from preconisation, namely, loss of a job, separation from family and contamination due to association with professional offenders (Walker, 1985: 101).

Open Prisons and Semi-Open Prisons

Open prisons are commonly known as prisons without walls or prisons with minimal security Anand (2017, para 1-2). Semi-open jails are in many ways similar to open jails but the difference in this setting is that the prisoners cannot move out of the prison campus to work, and nor can their families come and stay with them.

Review Questions

(a) How has the idea of crime and punishment changed from the past to now?

(b) How does the word 'correctional' show the role of modern prisons and the change in how prisoners are managed?

(c) What are some alternatives to imprisonment?

Did You Know?

As of 2022, there were 1,330 prisons in India, reflecting a 0.8% increase from 1,319 prisons in 2021. The total prison capacity in 2022 was 436,266, with 573,220 prisoners, leading to an occupancy rate of 131.4%, up from 130.2% in 2021 (PSI, 2022).

The Necessity of Reformative Activities and Rehabilitation in a Correctional Setting

A prison is an anthropogenic system that aims at correction, reformation and rehabilitation. It is also expected to function as a curative and correctional centre. The primary function of a prison is a custodial one and the objective can be delineated as retribution, retaliation, penitence, neutralization, vindication, deterrence, general deterrence, special deterrence, removal from society and rehabilitation. The two components of the Indian prison system, rehabilitation and reintegration, are still given less priority than prison security, which is ironic given that prisons are now known as correctional institutions. It is believed that in the 19th century, the concept of reformation had started in the western countries, and India, the notion of reformation and rehabilitation came forth after the Indian Jail Committee 1919–20 was set up.

Further, rehabilitation and after-care have been examined from the perspectives of theorists like Robert M. Murton believed that prison is a dark chamber and nothing works in the context of rehabilitation of the inmates as a longer duration inside prison leads to prisonization and isolates the offenders from the realities of society. In juxtaposition, theorists such as Garafalo, Bentham asserted that rehabilitation can help inmates to reintegrate into society if they are provided with learning opportunities.

The Indian prison system has various guidelines and policies which highlight the issue of rehabilitation and aftercare and so do the international treaties yet the movement of rehabilitation of prisoners still seems to be at a nascent stage. It still lacks the attention of policymakers and social planners for the welfare, well-being and rehabilitation of prisoners and this has been visible in many forums the most recent being the Sustainable Development Goals (SDGs) 2030 which came into force on 1 January 2016 and comprise 17 goals and 169 targets and indicators to monitor and review progress towards the goals. Goal 16 of SDG is directly related to the criminal justice system as it entails justice for all, and safeguarding not just the prisoners but their children who reside with them inside the prison and their families. The goal mentions 'Promote peaceful and inclusive societies for sustainable development, provide access to justice for all and build, effective, accountable and inclusive institutions at all levels. Hence, this goal is very closely linked with the criminal justice system'.

The theoretical understanding of rehabilitation has been examined from the perspectives of theorists like Robert. M, Murton believed that nothing works in the context of rehabilitation of the inmates and juxtaposition, theorists such as Garafalo, Bentham asserted that rehabilitation can help an inmate to reintegrate into society if they are provided with learning opportunities. Since not a single theory fits the concept of rehabilitation, an 'eclectic approach' was applied to develop a conceptual-theoretical understanding.

Sharma (2020) mentions the seeds of rehabilitation are sown inside the prison in the form of activities conducted there that facilitate inmates to adjust and adapt to the prison environment and behave as law-abiding citizens of the country by not getting into fights, doing their tasks well, following the rules and regulations of the prison, and creating a healthy prison environment. One of the principal objectives of the United Nations in the area of prison reform is to contribute to the successful reintegration of prisoners into society following their release.

It is important to understand that one needs to develop an understanding of the prison culture and environment and how it impacts the mental, physical, social, emotional, and cognitive well-being of the prisoners and the officials. Another important concept while designing reformative activities is the concept of prisonization as an alternate mode of adaptation is something that makes it worse for the prisoners as its impact continues even after their release and thus, this hinders the successful rehabilitation and reintegration into society. It was mentioned that the prisoners at times adopt behaviour that they would normally dislike and thus, either they become partially or completely prisonized (Srivastava, 1977). Hence, Sharma (2020) mentions it can be said that while planning the reformative activities and the rehabilitation plan the duration of the imprisonment is an important element to understand when working with the prisoners. Further, Sharma adds in such a volatile environment it is essential that the importance of in-prison rehabilitation activities such as dancing, tailoring, baking, educational activities and gardening must be given importance as these activities not only keep an inmate busy but also help them develop a better perspective towards life which will help them re-adjust in the society upon release, and may also help in reducing recidivism of prisoners.

Hence, the above gives a snapshot of the framework of social work, the significance of reformative activities and rehabilitation in a prison institution.

Social Work Intervention in Correctional Setting

Beckett and Maynard (2005) state that social work is a value-based profession and can never be neutral. Social workers' role is very challenging and may have far-reaching consequences in the lives of people, whom they work with. The role of the social worker should be well defined in the correctional settings as it will help bridge the gap between the prisoners and the prison officials, families, society and government after their release. Further, the field of correction includes not only a variety of services but also a variety of philosophies that determine those services. In meeting the many needs of any correctional institution, one major administrative problem (limitation) is to mobilize and integrate the specialized skills required for the custody and treatment of the inmate population (Konopka, 1963 &1972).

The social worker will be using casework and group work principles in a prison setting, but the most important classroom learning that the social worker needs to instill is ethical considerations when working in a correctional setting. Mentioning a few are as follows:

- Maintain confidentiality
- To share the purpose and objectives of the project or programme
- To not be biased or judgemental
- To stay objective and not give false promises
- Emphasize the importance of consent and practise it by asking the inmates
- Not to make the prisoners feel uncomfortable at any given time
- Maintain professional relationships and create a safe space
- To ensure the safety of oneself and the prisoners

Did You Know?

Open prisons are commonly referred to as prisons without walls or prisons with minimal security, designed to promote the rehabilitation and reintegration of inmates into society.

Role of Social Worker in a Prison Setting

The role of a social worker is very important as they make prisoners aware of their rights at the entry point that is at the police station by informing them of free legal aid, provisions for their children, contacting family members and providing a lawyer are the basic rights of all the prisoners. The social worker would ensure that inside the prison the prisoners are aware of the schemes that can be availed by them and their families and also act as a bridge between them and their families and the society by keeping in mind the rules and security mechanism in place.

For children who live with their mothers inside the prison, a social worker can ensure that child-friendly ways of communicating are being used, as well as ensuring the environment and all of the children's rights are protected. The social worker can work in collaboration with the prison officials and conduct home visits, of those children who are released or placed in the hostels and could help bridge the gap between the mother and the child.

The social worker can work in collaboration with the prison officials and conduct home visits before and after the release of the prisoners from any of the settings to provide them support and care (after-care) and connect them with schemes and other organizations. They can also act as counsellors not just for the prisoner but also for the family.

The role of the social worker in general and in the above issue is to play in liaising between the system and civil society to prevent the neglect of vulnerable groups and work towards pro-social change that is the social worker needs to play a bridge between the community, victims, government and networking with other organizations thus needs to strengthen peoples' organizations. Sensitization workshops are held with various stakeholders, to make people aware of the existence of this group and regarding the semi-open and open jails.

A policy needs to be framed for prisoners, on national and international platforms. One of the reasons for neglect and ignorance towards this group, the researcher feels is the lack of political will and adding to this whenever one thinks of development; prisoners' are placed right at the end or not thought of, as one thinks they are not productive enough to contribute to the economy. Secondly, there is no independent machinery to verify if the guidelines are being implemented. This point has been stressed time and again that concrete and stern action needs to be taken by the Government. Hence, the social workers with other alliances can lobby for their rights and make the Government understand that prison is not a place where people can be discarded but are correctional home.

The social worker can help increase community participation in society by raising advocacy issues, awareness and sensitization, and networking with other organizations and institutions which work in the area of prisons and prisoners' rights. Community participation is essential as it will enable society to give a second chance to prisoners who have reformed themselves and wish to lead a crime-free life. Thus, in short, a correctional social worker provides support and comfort to the prisoners, humanization, and human rights, planning various skill-based activities such as education, training, and working on the intervention, to keep check any behavioural change a prisoner going through, conducting training to the prison officials, and facilitating rehabilitation.

Rehabilitation is one of many areas which gets neglected whereas, in reality, the major focus of the criminal justice system should be on rehabilitation. The proper social system needs to be built if we speak of the reformation of prisoners, vocational training, guidance and reintegrating them into society. The importance and awareness of semi-open and open jails need to be highlighted.

Thus, a social worker needs to be extremely innovative while working in this area and needs to assess which alternative will best suit the individual's needs.

The vital role of social workers in all correctional settings is reiterated. Social work professionals can help in chalking out customized rehabilitation plans for each inmate, helping in availing schemes that would help in their well-being, empowerment and reintegration into society. Social workers can provide services to inmates living inside prisons, their families and also to released inmates. Proper information and the process of availing them can be chalked out by social workers.

The social worker and other stakeholders can work towards ensuring that state governments aid in helping inmates in need to avail of such schemes. Here, the prison officials and courts can play a crucial role by highlighting the need and importance of rehabilitation schemes for the prisoners both living inside and outside the prison to help them become active and responsible citizens as everyone deserves a second chance. The prisoner is going through, conducting training for the prison officials, and facilitating rehabilitation.

Rehabilitation is one of many areas which gets neglected whereas, in reality, the major focus of the criminal justice system should be on rehabilitation. A proper social system needs to be built if we speak of the reformation of prisoners, vocational training, guidance and reintegrating them into society. The importance and awareness of semi-open and open jails need to be highlighted.

Inside the prison, technology plays an important part in prison management. The social worker can assist in educating the prisoners and officials about appropriate technology usage. the social worker through their stakeholder management skills, can bring in resources and connect with other partners to help prisons become more technologically advanced while ensuring security. Lalli (2016) states that the Internet is another powerful tool to spread and share information and the state prison departments' websites must contain the good practices initiated in the prisons. Inside the prisons, technology is being used for security, closed-circuit television (CCTV) cameras, documentation work and maybe with time and so on. It also plays a crucial role in connecting the prisoners' families (Sharma, 2020). In the pandemic situation when the visitation from the families or mulakats were paused, video calling was one of the biggest emotional and psychological reliefs the prisoners experienced. Also, with the courts being closed during the pandemic the trials and hearings were held through video conferencing.

Thus, a social worker needs to be extremely innovative while working in this area and needs to assess which alternative will best suit the individual's needs. At the same time work more towards bringing about systemic changes and not just focus on reforming the prisoners. It is critical to recognise that reforming convicts alone will neither reduce recidivism nor address the issue of overcrowding; instead, structural concerns must be addressed to bring about significant changes in the prison system.

The vital role of social workers in all correctional settings is reiterated. Social work professionals can help in chalking out customized rehabilitation plans for each inmate, helping in availing schemes that would help in their well-being, empowerment and reintegration into society. Social workers can provide services to inmates living inside prisons, their families and also to released inmates. Proper information and the process of availing them can be chalked out by social workers.

The social worker and other stakeholders can work towards ensuring that state governments aid in helping inmates in need to avail of such schemes. Here, the prison officials and courts can play a crucial role by highlighting the need and importance of rehabilitation schemes for the prisoners both living inside and outside the prison to help them become active and responsible citizens as everyone deserves a second chance.

Review Questions

(a) What is the main purpose of a prison when it comes to correction, reformation, and rehabilitation?
(b) How does Robert M. Murton believe long-term imprisonment affects rehabilitation?
(c) How do social workers bridge the gap between prisoners, officials, families, and society?

SUMMARY

This chapter explores the evolution of correctional institutions, highlighting the shift from religious to scientific perspectives on crime and punishment. It examines the phases of prison development, with a focus on Indian prisons, addressing challenges such as overcrowding, staffing shortages, and the early stages of prisoner rehabilitation efforts. Alternatives to imprisonment, such as parole and community service, are also discussed. The chapter emphasizes the crucial role of social workers in correctional settings, where they act as mediators between inmates, officials, families, and the community. Social workers advocate for prisoner reform, provide emotional and practical support, facilitate rehabilitation programs, and address systemic issues to reduce recidivism. Their work ensures a dual focus on individual rehabilitation, broader systemic change and highlights the importance of using humanizing language. The chapter underscores the significance of social work in promoting humanizing language, vocational training, and rehabilitation activities. It concludes by calling for systemic improvements and increased professional involvement to support the successful rehabilitation and reintegration of prisoners into society.

GLOSSARY

- **Correctional Institutions:** These are prisons, jails, detention centers, or halfway houses that focus on both confinement and rehabilitation, helping prisoners reintegrate into society.
- **Rehabilitation:** The process of helping offenders change their behavior and return to society as law-abiding citizens through planned interventions, such as education and skills training.
- **Reformation:** The act of improving prisoners' attitudes and behaviors through activities that prepare them for life after prison, focusing on transformation rather than punishment.
- **Parole:** The conditional release of a prisoner before completing their full sentence, allowing them to reintegrate with family and community while following certain conditions.
- **Prisonization:** The process by which inmates adapt to prison life, adopting its norms and behaviors, which can make it harder for them to adjust to life outside prison.
- **Social Worker:** A professional who helps bridge the gap between prisoners, authorities, families, and society, advocating for prisoners' rights and assisting with their rehabilitation and reintegration.
- **Community Service:** An alternative to jail where offenders perform unpaid work that benefits the community, helping them understand the consequences of their actions.

- **Aftercare:** Support provided to prisoners after their release, helping them adjust to life outside prison and avoid returning to crime.

TOP TEN TAKEAWAY POINTS

- **Evolution of prisons and the types of prisons:** Correctional institutions prioritize rehabilitation over punishment, and prisons, including central, district, and sub-jails, grapple with issues of overcrowding.
- **Changing perspectives of crime:** it highlights the shift from religious and superstitious crime views to scientific and reformative approaches.
- **Social workers' pivotal role:** Social workers play a critical role in bridging gaps among prisoners, officials, and families, prioritizing ethical considerations.
- **Prison challenges:** Overcrowding, staff shortages, and systemic issues pose challenges to effective reformation and rehabilitation of prisoners.
- **Rehabilitation challenges:** Overemphasis on security, prisonization, and insufficient policymaker attention hinder prisoner rehabilitation.
- **Rehabilitation in a nascent stage:** Despite existing standards and policies, prisoner rehabilitation is in a nascent stage. Overcrowding, staffing shortages, and a lack of attention from policymakers are notable challenges in the prison system.
- **Alternatives to punishment:** The alternatives to punishment such as community service, parole, furlough, probation, and open, and semi-open prisons offer alternatives to traditional imprisonment.
- **Effective social work strategies:** Advocacy, rehabilitation planning, systemic improvements, use of humanizing language and ethical considerations are crucial components for impactful social work interventions in correctional settings.
- **Significance of in-prison activities:** Educational, vocational, life-skills, recreational, and mental health activities are crucial for prisoner rehabilitation and reintegration, equipping inmates with essential personal and occupational skills for life after imprisonment.
- **Role of technology in prison management:** Technology enhances prison management by improving security, enabling communication with families, and providing access to speedy and timely legal services.

MULTIPLE CHOICE QUESTIONS

1. What is the primary focus of the criminal justice system, according to the chapter?
   (a) Retribution
   (b) Rehabilitation
   (c) Deterrence
   (d) Vindication

2. Which goal of the Sustainable Development Goals (SDGs) is directly related to the criminal justice system?
   (a) Goal 5 (b) Goal 10
   (c) Goal 16 (d) Goal 17
3. What historical shift influenced the perception of crime and punishment in the 18th and 19th centuries?
   (a) Economic perspectives
   (b) Religious and superstitious contexts
   (c) Political ideologies (d) Technological advancements
4. What term refers to the adaptation of individuals to the norms and culture within a prison environment?
   (a) Prisonization (b) Parole
   (c) Probation (d) Furlough
5. In what period did the concept of reformation and rehabilitation emerge in Western countries, according to the chapter?
   (a) 18th century (b) 19th century
   (c) 20th century (d) 21st century
6. What term is used to describe an inmate's release from a penal or reformatory institution under certain conditions?
   (a) Furlough (b) Parole
   (c) Probation (d) Community service
7. According to the Model Prison Manual (2016), what is the recommended staff ratio for correctional officers to prisoners, emphasizing the need for effective rehabilitation?
   (a) 1:500 (b) 1:1000
   (c) 1:200 (d) 1:100
8. What is the primary role of a social worker in a correctional setting, as emphasized in the chapter?
   (a) Strict law enforcement (b) Advocacy for longer sentences
   (c) Bridging gaps between prisoners, officials, families, and communities
   (d) Isolation of prisoners
9. How does the chapter emphasize the role of technology in prison settings?
   (a) Minimal relevance in correctional institutions
   (b) Solely focused on security measures
   (c) Critical for security, communication, and reforms
   (d) Encourages reliance on traditional prison practices
10. According to Walker (1985), what does probation eliminate if properly used as an alternative to incarceration?
   (a) Loss of a job (b) Separation from family

(c) Contamination due to association with professional offenders
(d) All of the above

11. What are Open Prisons commonly known as?
    (a) High-security prisons (b) Jails without walls
    (c) District prisons (d) Women jail
12. What is highlighted as a key aspect of social work in correctional institutions in the chapter?
    (a) Advocacy, rehabilitation planning, systemic improvements, and adherence to ethical considerations
    (b) Exclusive focus on custodial responsibilities
    (c) Strict adherence to punitive measures
    (d) Minimal interaction with prisoners and their families

Answers

1. (b), 2. (c), 3. (b), 4. (a), 5. (b), 6. (b), 7. (c), 8. (c), 9. (c), 10. (d), 11. (b), 12. (a)

REFERENCES

1. Anand. U. (2017). *SC Asks States to Establish 'Open Prisons' as Part of Jail Reforms.* Retrieved March 15, 2017 from http://www.news18.com/news/india/sc-asks-states-to-establish-open-prisons-as-part-of-jail-reforms-1519241.html
2. Bureau of Police Research and Development (2003). *Model Prison Manual for the Superintendence and Management of Prisons in India.* Retrieved February 20, 2015 from http://bprd.nic.in.http://bprd.nic.in/writereaddata/linkimages/1445424768-Content%20%20Chapters.pdf
3. Bureau of Police Research and Development (2016). *5th National Conference of Heads of Prisons of States & UTs on Prison Reforms. Compendium.* New Delhi
4. Bureau of Police Research and Development.(2016). *Model Prison Manual for the Superintendence and Management of Prisons in India.* Retrieved November 10, 2017 from bprd.nic.in/content/423_1_Model.aspx
5. Government of India. (n.d.). *The Prison Act, 1984 (Act IX of 1984)* (as modified up to the 1st January, 1957). Retrieved on June 10, 2016 from http://mha.nic.in. http://mha.nic.in/pdfs/ Prisons_act1894.pdf.
6. Konopka, Gisela. (1972, 1963). *Social Group Work: A Helping Process (2nd ed.).* Englewood Cliffs, N.J: Prentice-Hall, Inc.
7. Lalli (2016). Identification of Best Practises (2009). In Bureau Of Police Research And Development (2016). *5th National Conference of Heads Of Prisons of States & UTs on Prison Reforms. Compendium.* New Delhi
8. Nagda, P. (2017). A socio-legal study of prison system and is reforms in India. *International Journal of Law*, 3(4), pp. 49–56.

9. Paranjape, N.V. (2015). *Criminology and Penology with Victimology.* Allahabad: Central Law Publications.
10. Prison Statistics India (2019). *National Crime Records Bureau Ministry of Home Affairs.* New Delhi. Retrieved November 15, 2021 from https://ncrb.gov.in/sites/default/files/PSI-2019-27-08-2020.pdf
11. Prison Statistics India (2022). *National Crime Records Bureau Ministry of Home Affairs.* New Delhi. Retrieved September 2024, https://www.ncrb.gov.in/uploads/nationalcrimerecordsbureau/custom/psiyearwise2022/1701613297PSI2022ason01122023.pdf
12. Sharma, Gauri (2020). *Rehabilitation of Prisoners: A Case Study of Selected Prisons in India* (PhD Disseration). University of Delhi, New Delhi.
13. Srivastava, S.P. (1977). *Indian Prison Community.* Lucknow: Pushtak Kendra.
14. Walker, N. (1985). *Sentencing: Theory and Practice.* London: Butterworths.

RECOMMENDED READINGS

1. Chakraburtty (n.d.). The open prisons of Rajasthan. Rajasthan State Legal Services Authority. Jaipur: Rajasthan High Court.
2. Chattoraj, B. N. (1988). Aftercare services for the rehabilitation of offenders in India. *The Indian Journal of Criminology and Criminalistics*, VIII (January-June).
3. Jones, H., Cornes, C., & Stockford, T. (1977). Open prisons. Great Britain: Lavenham Press Ltd.
4. Reckless, W. C. (1952). Report on jail administration in India. New Delhi: Government of India.
5. Reddy, K. V. (n.d.). All India Committee on Jail Reforms (1980-83). Retrieved October 25, 2015, from http://www.scribd.com: http://www.scribd.com/doc/21248287/Mulla-Committee-on-Prisons.
6. Re-inhuman conditions in 1382 vs State of Assam (2018, September 25). Indian Kanoon. WRIT PETITION (CIVIL) NO. 406 OF 2013. Retrieved November 20, 2019, from https://indiankanoon.org/doc/531661/.
7. Srivastava, S. P. (1977). Indian prison community. Lucknow: Pushtak Kendra.

CHAPTER – 4

Social Work in School Settings: Understanding the Need and Scope

Anna Taney Varghese

Consultant – Learning and Innovation in Room to Read

That's how I try to think of education – a school is a miniature society where children learn to function in a real world.

– Marva Collins

Abstract: *School social workers play a crucial role in providing both direct and indirect services to students, families, and school personnel, aimed at enhancing students' academic performance and social well-being. These professionals, equipped with a Bachelor of Social Work (BSW) or a Master of Social Work (MSW) degree, are trained in mental health and act as essential intermediaries between the home, school, and broader community for students, parents, and staff. Their interventions help students navigate and manage stressful situations before these challenges negatively impact their well-being. This chapter is designed for social workers and students interested in working with children, particularly within educational settings. It offers an overview of the historical developments in school social work, both in India and globally, providing a concise yet insightful exploration of the field's evolution. Additionally, the chapter serves as a valuable resource for those seeking to understand established school social work models. It also includes a comprehensive list of tasks, responsibilities, and competencies that social workers should possess to effectively operate in a school environment.*

Keywords: *School Social Work, School Social worker, Visiting teachers, Interdisciplinary team, Ecological perspective*

Learning Objectives

After reading this chapter, you will be able to:

- Understand school as a field for practicing social work
- Comprehend the advancements made in the field through knowing history of school social work
- Get acquainted to various models of school social work
- Note various roles and responsibilities of a school social worker
- Know various skills important for a school social worker

INTRODUCTION

The education system plays a vital role in shaping the personality and life of a child. However, at times, children face challenges and struggles at several points of their progress. They encounter stress and find tough to respond to the demands. Most of the children in a school system adjust and adapt to the stress, but few might not due to various internal or external factors. These are the children who can benefit from school social work services. In order to assist pupil, achieve academic attainments, school social workers serve as a vital link between school, family, and community. They provide leadership in the formation of school disciplinary policies, mental health intervention, crisis management, and support services, and they interact directly with school administrations, students, and families.

When students are having difficulty adjusting to school, social workers assist parents in assisting their children. They might, for example, offer programmes to help new students adjust to school or to support children who have been absent for a lengthy period of time due to illness or family pressures such as divorce or death. They may also be able to assist parents of children with special needs in finding programmes tailored to their requirements. Social workers can help all students, as well as their parents and families, deal with stressful events before they affect children. Low socioeconomic status, may produce significant pressures for families affecting their capacity to maintain healthy relationships, raise their children, and adapt to changing circumstances. In these instances, social workers engage with parents to connect them with school and community resources that can help them reduce stress and enhance their family's outcomes. Social workers may not be able to change structural challenges like low socioeconomic position or racial injustice, but they can help families deal with issues that are related to these variables (Finigan-Carr & Shaia, 2018).

School social workers help more than only children and their families. They can also provide crucial information to school officials to help them better understand aspects that may influence student performance and conduct. In conclusion, social workers can contribute significantly to professional development. They can, for example, assist teachers and administrators in identifying evidence-based practices for maintaining a safe and effective learning environment without relying too heavily on suspensions, expulsions, and other coercive disciplinary measures, thus disrupting the school-to-prison pipeline (Finigan-Carr & Shaia, 2018).

HISTORY OF SCHOOL SOCIAL WORK

United States of America

A lot of conditions in the educational system, legislations and concerns in the society, influenced the growth of school social workers. Common schools, compulsory attendance, child labor legislation, migrations all were antecedents to social service in school settings.

The history of school social workers in US can be dated back to 1906–07, under the title 'Visiting teacher'. The 'visiting teachers service was first established in New York, Chicago, Boston, and Hartford, Connecticut. They were to liaison between home and school to help pupil better. In New York they were strongly supported by Public Education Association (PEA), who lobbied for adoption of visiting teachers into education board, and setting high standards for practice and suggested to employ 'social work methods' that focused individual child. Almost at the same time a full time social worker was placed by Chicago University and Chicago women's Club in a school. In Boston, they called it as 'home school visitor', who helped a child perform better by offering services and creating link between home and the school. In Hartford they were known as 'special teachers', who were primarily employed to take case histories, on behalf of Hartford Psychological Clinic (Shaffer & Fisher, 2017).

A remarkable advancement was when in 1913, in Rochester, New York City in a public school system became the first to fund a visiting teacher service, without any prior demonstration (Costin 1969). After 1913, private organizations offering and financing visiting teacher services came down significantly, as by the they had started to become the integral part of public-school systems. In 1916, the first conference of The National Conference of Visiting Teachers and Home and School Visitors was organized, deliberating on how to prevent delinquency and retardation. From 1919–29, it was known as the National Association of Visiting Teachers, which had its own journal and sooner was known as American Association of Visiting Teachers from 1929–45. Subsequently came to be known as American Association of School Social Workers (1942–45). From 1945 it came to be known as National Association of School Social Workers (NASSW), which was one of the seven organizations to form National Association of Social Workers (NASW) (Shaffer & Fisher, 2017).

One of the milestone in the advancements in the profession was when in 1923, the Commonwealth Fund of New York gave immense attention to school social work, and recognized the importance of school social workers. They funded a program to prevent juvenile delinquency and hired around 30 school social workers to work in identified rural and urban settings across United States. Gradually, in 1945, it led to US office of Education determining the minimum qualification of a school social worker, that is a master's degree in social work (Dupper, 2003)

NASW kept meeting ever since its first ever meeting in 1973 and by 1976 issued first set of standard guidelines for school social work, 'prevention' as its theme. The guidelines were then revised in the year 1992 (Dupper, 2003). In early 1990s the school social work community found leadership of NASW weekend. Majorly because of two factors, firstly due to change of certain staff at the national level, where the new staffer had diminished focused on school social work, almost making it vanished. Other associations developed in response and frustration but soon disbanded due to lack of revenue. In 1994, a meeting of 60 representatives, from 19 states, which held for three days, at Southern Illinois University in Edwardsville, Illinois, and it gave birth to another independent association, School Social Work Association of America (SSWAA). It made sure there is representation of all school social worker across United States. It grew in all aspects, developed its own constitution, bylaws and membership plans. It continues to influence education policy and legislations. It continues to organize programs for state and regional leaders. Since its formation it has integrated well with other associations to serve pupil of the state better. It's important to note that NASW after a break came back again and continues to offer guidelines and standards for school social worker (Shaffer & Fisher, 2017). Both NASW and SSWAA are internationally recognized and continue to have their publications and conferences.

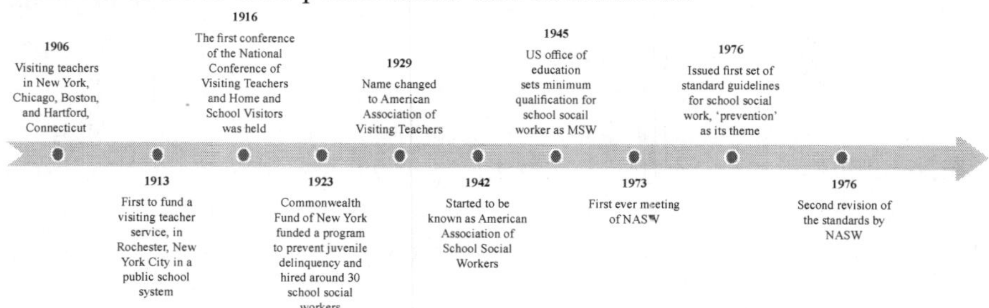

Time line of milestone in the history of school social work

India

School Social Work is yet to be recognized as a profession and necessity in India. Even if social work practitioners choose to serve in school settings, often they are diluted under the title of a counselor. The education board at any level has not accepted School Social worker as an integral part of an education system. There are no legislations yet demanding for a position of a school social worker mandate in school systems. The little growth of the profession in schools though slow, but is due to various efforts made in the past by the social work colleges, social work associations, guidance clinics and few progressive educationalists.

Gandhi (1990) explain through her work the progress of school social work in India. It' s in late 1950s and early 1960s that social work was first introduced in school settings, especially in public schools. The only model then known and practiced was social case work. It was introduced by placing social work students as part of their field work. The students through their work, sensitized the administration to the importance of a social worker in the system, thus influencing schools in some cases to appoint a social worker. It was difficult for the social work colleges to place their students in real life scenarios to practice the methods like social case work and group work. Pioneer institutes like Nirmala Niketan, Tata Institute of Social Sciences (TISS), Delhi School of Social Work (DSSW), had their own agencies, also offering placement to their students. Other educational institutions on the other hand found it difficult to establish their own agencies and thus, sought association with various other agencies thus accommodating many students. Hence, they even associated with schools and found it to be appropriate enough to practice the methods of social work in a school setting. The social case work and group work seemed applicable among children suffering with emotional, behavioral and academic issues. The important breakthrough was when in the year 1958, Kashi Vidyapeth, Varanasi (later known as Faculty of Social Work), placed two girls for their field exposure, under the supervision of a faculty member in Besant Theosophical School, a progressive private school (Goyal, 1980). Still it did not give a breakthrough for social workers as an employment opportunity in schools.

By 1959 Nirmala Niketan and TISS also started placing their students in school, with a motto of exploring new fields. They also persuaded and oriented the schools to employ social workers in school (D'Souza, 1965). A great influence was made by the placements and this marked the first ever appointment of a social worker in a private school. The placement by Nirmala Niketan paved way for a school social worker into D'Souza high school, Bombay (Maan, 2017). Another noticeable appointment of school social worker was in 1965. As a part of observing the 'World Mental Health year' in 1960, the child guidance clinic of TISS, placed students in schools, to prevent mental health illness. They under the guidance of the psychiatric social worker of the clinic and the faculty supervisor of the college did successful demonstrations (Banerjee, 1965). This created an influence and the school employed social worker in 1965, under the supervision and guidance of the clinic (C.G.C Annual Report 1960–65). Similar persuasion in Pune by Karve Institute of Social Sciences was recorded. The college convinced Pune Palak Shikshak Sang (PPSS), the Pune branch of Maharashtra parent teacher association, to accept students for field exposure in their various schools. The schools were really influenced and this led to employment of social workers in the schools in 1964 where their students were placed for field work. The word even spread to Varanasi. The advancements were so noticeable that few schools even without a demo, realized importance of social workers and appointed social workers in their schools.

These advancements led to the recognition at the national level. Deliberations were made and work was shared by school social workers in the Indian conference of social work at its XIII session held at Varanasi in December 1964. Certain recommendations by the panelists were as follows (which never got materialized):

(a) The Indian Conference of Social Work and the Indian Association of Trained Social Workers should take up the matter with the Education Commission at the centre and the All India Teachers' Association to establishing school social work sections in the board of education.'
(b) Social work profession should be introduced in the teachers' training colleges, thus orienting teachers with the profession.
(c) The salary of a social worker should be determined on the basis of qualification and experience.
(d) Fourth five year plan should include programs for social work both in rural and urban setting.

Another effort was made by Indian Association of Trained Social Workers (IATSW) in collaboration with Delhi School of Social Work (DSSW) now Department of Social Work, University of Delhi, in the private schools in Delhi. They rather placing students, oriented schools on the profession through qualified social workers. It was first introduced in Delhi to St.Thomas School, they agreed for the same and a salary of Rs.500 per month, was first offered, partially taken care by IATSW, DSSW and the parent teachers association. An 'implementation committee' was formed to check on the execution and its impact. Within two year in 1971 was convinced and as had agreed before, if satisfied, bore the full responsibility of the project. The approach was predominantly case work and clinical approach, with a gradual shift also seen towards organizing camps, workshops etc.

In all the cases it was easy to introduce and persuade private schools than public schools, as that required lot of procedure. The first attempt in public schools was made by Nirmala Niketan. Their main focus was urban slums. Poverty, broken families, hygiene issues and drop out were some major issues prevalent in the slum. They found a break through Municipal corporation, and placed their students there. This resulted in appointment of trained social workers in the corporation in the year 1971 and 1973. The partnership between Municipal corporation of Greater Bombay and college evolved and the program got another boost in the year 1979, the International year of child. Resulting in expansion to 15 more corporations. Similarly The New Delhi Municipal Corporation (NDMC) was considering for such an initiation. The education officer of the time was aware of social work profession, and opened 15 posts of school social workers in NDMC, for its schools to tackle issues of drop put and achieve universalization of education. Sadly, it could not grow in its full shape as the school social workers were supervised by educationalists who lacked knowledge of the profession.

School Social work in India still has to get its due recognition, it's still latent. Even if recognized they often lose their individuality under the banner of other various titles, like counselors, life skill trainers, etc.

Review Questions

(a) Critically evaluate the need of a social worker in a school setting?
(b) Summaries in your words the history of school social work and create a timeline of the milestone in its history in India?

Did You Know?

There are 10 fundamental rights of a child in India – the right to survival, education, protection, participation, development, health and well-being, identity, expression, non-discrimination, and a safe environment.

DEFINITION

School Social Workers are trained mental health professionals with a degree in social work who provide services related to a person's social, emotional and life adjustment to school and/or society. School Social Workers are the link between the home, school and community in providing direct as well as indirect services to students, families and school personnel to promote and support students' academic and social success (School Social Work Association of America, SSWA)

NASW standards (2002), defines, School Social work as 'Social work services provided in the setting of an educational agency by credentialed school social workers. This specialty in social work is oriented toward helping students make satisfactory adjustments and coordinating and influencing the efforts of the school, the family, and the community to achieve this goal.'

MODELS OF SCHOOL SOCIAL WORK

Ever since the inception of school social work, or visiting teacher or home school visitors, there had been several approaches practiced and emerging. All of these models focus on certain purposes, notions skills, strategies, activities and tactics. A certain pattern is designed and building on which a social worker performs or serves. Alderson (1972) has tried grouping similar patterns and identified four major models as follows: (a) the Traditional-clinical model, (b) the School-change model, (c) the Community-school model, (d) the Social interaction model. Along with these the chapter introduces to a new model of school social work developed in a three year training demonstration at the Jane Addams School of Social Work, University of Illinois, Urbana by Costin in 1975, famously known as the School-community-pupil relations model. Let's try understanding each of the models in brief.

The Traditional-Clinical Model

This model is the best known and often used model. The model focuses on individuals social and emotional difficulties that interferes their scholastic performance. The whole aim of the model is to help child function better in school, by working on the social and emotional difficulties. The understanding of the social and emotional problems are derived from psychoanalytical theory, ego psychology, case work theory and methodology. They identify the problems stemming majorly from parent child relationship. The social worker primarily chooses case work methodology with pupil and family, enabling supportive collaboration. The major criticism the model has gathered is that the school system is viewed to be benign and the pupil is supposed to adapt into the school environment. The school is barely involved as part of intervention except for the fact of gathering information about the child's behavior.

The School-Change Model

This model is in contrast to the previous model. As the name suggests the model considers school as the environment that the child is placed in and that needs alteration. It focuses on school norms, any policy or condition that is primarily the reason for the poor performance of a student. The goal is to alter the school conditions to help pupil perform better. It works directly with student/students, especially group work. Also, the major discussion and consultation is with the teachers, administrators individually or in group. The social worker often plays a role of an advocate, an intercessor or a consultant. The theoretical support it gathers from social science theories especially the theories of deviance. The model has allowed to raise above the psychopathological view of pupil's dysfunction. The model is often considered to be risky for the social worker, who according to the model targets the school system and steps in to the role of advocacy or negotiation. The exclusive focus on the school, builds a wall between pupil and the school, thus overshadowing other factors like family and community that impinges on the pupil.

The Community School Model

The community-school concept is primarily aimed at underprivileged or marginalized areas that have historically been 'out of sync' with the school's aims and norms, holding less knowledge and trust of school. The main objectives of the community school model are to increase community awareness and support of the school, for these communities, as well as to design school programmes to help students who are poor, and to lessen deprivation that affects a child's academic and social functioning abilities. Within this concept, the community is given at least equal priority to the school as a target for intervention. School workers may lack a thorough awareness of cultural differences and the effects of poverty, necessitating specialized knowledge and skills in order to deal with students and parents most effectively. The social worker is a member of an interdisciplinary crisis team, which acts as a mediator, enabler, advocate, organizer, and developer on behalf of students, teachers, and school officials. The model's biggest flaw is that some schools may not be ready for the social worker to interact so closely with the community. It's possible that questions regarding the worker's identity and loyalty develop. Active advocacy on behalf of the community and raising their concerns about the school may put the school social worker at risk positing, at the employing agency.

The Social Interaction Model

This model refers to the reciprocal influence rising out of the interaction between actions of people and groups, frequently in communication with each other. This model draws from systems and social science theories. The three main features of the model are (a) considering the field to be interactional, (b) no prominence given to any specific methodology, (c) paying attention to all the participants in the social process, their problems, actions and behaviour. The school social worker must be familiar with the numerous client systems with which he will interface. He requires the abilities to effectively engage in relationships with individuals, families, small groups, and neighbourhood groups, as well as within large and small organizations and institutions. When the worker sees multiple functional systems as clients, he or she makes a concerted effort to improve their performance by looking for commonalities, assisting in the removal of impediments, and opening up and facilitating mutually beneficial communications and transactions. The focus on the mediation though is regarded as the strength of the model, but may be difficult in its real operationality. Especially when in the interactive system power structures are resistive to change in respect to individuals who are powerless, the worker may be prone to endless mediating and may be hesitant to pursue advocacy steps.

The School-Community-Pupil Relations Model

This model also emphasizes on school, community and pupil interaction but aims majorly at expanding learning opportunities for the pupils of target groups by altering the school-community-pupil relationship system. Individual children and young people are not forgotten rather the goal is to assist them through target groups. It views, the needs and talents of groups of students as one component of the complex interplay of forces, influences, and personalities that constitutes in a school-community-pupil relationships. The focus is on a) the deficits in the school and community, and b) the interaction between specific system features and characteristics of groups of children at periods of stress in the pupil life cycle. As a result, the focus is on the situation rather than the individual. This model draws from social learning and systems theories. The social worker here respond to certain group patterns of truancy, underachievement, absenteeism, exclusion from school and other repeated indicators that schools fail to meet learning needs of significant number of students.

ECOLOGICAL PERSPECTIVE

David R. Dupper in his book 'School social work skills and interventions for effective practice' highlights a framework of an ecological perspective, within which a school social worker should create intervention plan. This perspective states that school social worker doesn't look at student mis-behavior or learning issues in isolation. NASW standards (2002) defines ecological perspective as 'The perspective of the interaction of the child and family and their environment. Important concepts include adaptation, transactions, goodness of fit between the students and their educational environments, reciprocity, and mutuality'. The ecological viewpoint emphasizes pupils' reciprocal relationships with environmental variables. This viewpoint allows school social workers to broaden their understanding of children' difficulties and expand intervention objectives. That is, difficulties that children and adolescents face in school are understood as a conflict between the academic and social requirements of the school environment and the intellectual or behavioural skills of children and youth

(Schinke & Gilchrist, 1984). To reduce this conflict or gap, Dupper suggests school social workers to be dually focused in their interventions. That is, they must target specific environmental stresses while also improving pupils' coping skills. With its twin emphasis, the ecological viewpoint allows school social workers to fulfil their unique purpose in schools: supporting children as well as eliminating harmful situations in schools, families, neighborhoods, and communities, particularly those that impact vulnerable students. The whole case right from assessment to intervention is viewed under an ecological lens. Using the ecological perspective as a guiding principle, a school social worker gets into various roles and activities to match needs of each school and student in need. The whole case right from assessment to intervention is viewed under an ecological lens.

Review Questions

(a) Create a comparison between the five models of school social work, also critically evaluate each model?
(b) Elaborate the need of fitting into the frame of an ecological perspective while practicing school social work, illustrate with a case study.

Did You Know?

According to a UNICEF and Gallup survey conducted in early 2021 with 20,000 participants across 21 countries, children in India appear hesitant to seek help for mental stress. Only 41% of Indian youth aged 15–24 believe that seeking support for mental health issues is beneficial, significantly lower than the 83% average across the surveyed nations.

ROLES AND FUNCTIONS

A social worker in a school is part of a bigger team that assists children with special needs or children facing short term or long term, behavioral academic issues. NASW standard 9 states 'school social workers shall work collaboratively to mobilize the resources of local education agencies and communities to meet the needs of students and families' (NASW, 2002). Teachers, counsellors, school psychologists, and diagnosticians are all possible members of the team. School social workers must know how to contribute to the work of an interdisciplinary team and how to operate effectively as a part of the team. 'The unique contribution of the school social worker to the interdisciplinary team is to bring home, school, and community perspectives to the interdisciplinary process' (NASW, 2002, Standard 9).

The primary purpose of school social work is to help pupils function and learn in the classroom setting. The primary objective of schools is to teach kids, not to offer social services, hence school social workers function in a secondary context. In many cases, the school social worker is the sole social worker in the school, and in certain cases, the whole school district. As a result, abilities at all levels of practice—micro, meso, and macro—are required for independent school social work practice (Openshaw, 2008). School social Work Association of America has laid down an extensive list of roles of social worker, categorizing them according to whom they are working with or assisting, which are as follows.

Overview of the Roles

- Participating in individual Educational Planning and assessment meetings.
- Working with difficulties in a child's home environment that impair the child's school performance. (at home, at school, and in the community)
- Creating a social or developmental history on a child differently abled.
- Group, individual, and/or family counselling
- Using resources from the family, school, and community to help the child learn as much as possible in his or her educational programme
- Developing positive behavior intervention techniques.

Assistance to Students

- Crisis intervention
- Developing strategies to assist pupil improve academic performance
- Helping with conflict resolutions and emotional conflicts
- Assisting in improving social interaction skills
- Helping the child in understanding concepts of self and others

Assistance to Parents/Families

- Assisting parents of children with adjustment issues in school, facilitating an easy transition
- Helping in reducing family stress that might be impact child's performance
- Assisting parents of children with special need in accessing programs available.
- Helping parents with information on and connecting with various resources in school and community

Assistance to School Personnel

- Providing essential information to staff in order for them to better understand the aspects that influence a student's performance and behaviour (cultural, sociological, economic, family, health, etc.).
- Assessing pupils who have mental health issues.

- Creating in-service training programmes for teachers and others in school.
- Helping teachers with behavior management of their students
- Providing direct assistance to school personnel.

School and the Community Liaison

- Obtaining and arranging community resources in order to address the requirements of students
- Assisting school districts in receiving necessary social and mental health services.
- Advocating for new and enhanced community/school services to fulfil needs of students and families
- Assisting the system in responding effectively to the requirements of each student.

Assistance to District

- Assist in the development and implementation of educational programmes for children with special needs.
- Creating alternate programmes for children who are in conflict with
- Detecting and reporting cases of child abuse and neglect.
- Providing consultation on legislations and policy related to school, education or child rights
- Case management for kids and families that require a variety of services.

Linda Openshaw (2008) has tried clubbing together these varied roles and functions into four basic tasks. Those are:

(a) Consultation: Being a part of interdisciplinary team, consulting with others in the team is very essential.
(b) Assessment: Applying assessment to varied roles, programmes, consultations and services.
(c) Direct intervention: Assisting individual children and parents, through individual or group modalities
(d) Assisting programme development

Not just limiting to traditional casework roles with individuals a school social worker has a wide range of roles and responsibilities. To implement the above mentioned roles and responsibilities a school social worker should have wide range of knowledge on school and community. He should have skills to initiate planned changes in the system, thus influencing the whole system and encouraging positive experiences not for just few students rather for everybody in school.

Review Questions

(a) Elucidate the four basic tasks of a school social worker given by Linda Openshaw and explain each in your own words.
(b) List down at least ten roles of a school social worker in general.

SUMMARY

Social workers as professionals are trained and committed promoting social justice, safeguarding rights of people and assisting individuals or groups facing various adverse life situations. The vocation encourages culturally sensitive practices, to create programs that values diversity of its clients. Thus, capable of serving wide range of population, children, senior citizens, women or any vulnerable or marginalized section. The skills and knowledge of a social worker makes them a well-suited professional who holds capacity in taking leads in reformations that school system should undergo ensuring a suitable environment for a child's social and emotional learning and development. The field of social work looks at issues from both a macro (society, communities, groups, and organisations) and a clinical (individual and family) perspective (Finigan-Carr & Shaia, 2018).

A school social worker extends assistance to children and youth to maximize their own strengths and learning opportunities. Social work focuses on individuals in context to their environment and interactions with different variables in the environment. Thus while assisting a pupil or group of pupil the client for the social worker doesn't limit to pupil rather is the client is a complex team, comprising of pupil, family, school and community. A child or youth inside an educational setting is supposed to accomplish varied ranges of tasks equating to their psycho-social and academic development. At times the interaction between pupil and their environment might interfere in accomplishing the tasks and thus interfering their academic functionality, learning advancements and utilizing various opportunities. Introducing an ecological perspective, a social worker focuses on the faulty interaction and creates an intervention plan that focuses on the pupil. A school social worker works directly with pupil or group of pupil and if required as well as with others to ensure the wellbeing of pupil/s.

GLOSSARY

- **Ecological Perspective:** A framework in social work focusing on the interaction between individuals and their environments, emphasizing the reciprocal relationships that affect behavior and development.
- **School Social Worker:** A trained mental health professional who provides services related to a person's social, emotional, and life

adjustment within a school environment, acting as a liaison between home, school, and community.

- **Traditional-Clinical Model:** A school social work approach that addresses individual students' social and emotional difficulties that interfere with their academic performance, often using casework methodologies.
- **School-Community-Pupil Relations Model:** A model of school social work aimed at altering the relationship between the school, community, and students to expand learning opportunities, especially for target groups facing systemic challenges.
- **Interdisciplinary Team:** A collaborative group consisting of various school professionals, such as teachers, counselors, and psychologists, working together to meet the needs of students.
- **Crisis Intervention:** Immediate assistance provided by school social workers to students experiencing emotional or behavioral crises, aimed at stabilizing their situation and preventing further disruption.
- **Visiting Teacher:** The original title for school social workers in the U.S., who served as a liaison between home and school to help students adjust to educational environments.
- **Child Guidance Clinic:** An institution that provides mental health services and support for children, often collaborating with schools to address behavioral or psychological issues affecting academic performance.

TOP TEN TAKEAWAY POINTS

1. The history of school social workers in US can be dated back to 1906-1907, under the title 'Visiting teacher'. The 'visiting teachers service was first established in New York, Chicago, Boston, and Hartford, Connecticut.
2. The influenced by Nirmala Niketan paved way for the first time ever appointment of a school social worker into a private school, D'Souza high school, Bombay. The first ever deliberation on school social worker in a social conference happened in the year 1964 in the Indian conference of social work at its XIII session held at Varanasi.
3. Alderson (1972) has tried grouping similar patterns and identified four major models of school social work, which are (a) the Traditional-clinical model, (b) the School-change model, (c) the Community-school model, (d) the Social interaction model. The fifth model, developed in a three year training demonstration at the Jane Addams School of Social Work, University of Illinois, Urbana by Costin in 1975, is known as the School-community-pupil relations model.

4. The Traditional-clinical model aims to help child function better in school, by working on the social and emotional difficulties.
5. The School-change model focuses on school norms, any policy or condition that is primarily the reason for the poor performance of a student. The goal is to alter the school conditions to help pupil perform better.
6. Community School model focuses on increasing community awareness and support of the school, for these communities, as well as to design school programs to help students who are poor, and to lessen deprivation that affects a child's academic and social functioning abilities.
7. Social interaction model refers to the reciprocal influence rising out of the interaction between actions of people and groups, frequently in communication with each other. The school social worker must be familiar with the numerous client systems with which he will interface.
8. School-community-pupil relations model also emphasizes on school, community and pupil interaction but aims majorly at expanding learning opportunities for the pupils of target groups by altering the school-community-pupil relationship system.
9. The ecological viewpoint emphasizes pupils' reciprocal relationships with environmental variables. This viewpoint allows school social workers to broaden their understanding of children' difficulties and expand intervention objectives.
10. The unique contribution of the school social worker to the interdisciplinary team is to bring home, school, and community perspectives to the interdisciplinary process.

Analytical Questions

(a) What skills and competencies a social worker should be acquainted with to be a school social worker, list down and explain a few keeping in mind the roles and functions of a school social worker?

(b) How different is a school social worker from a school counsellor or a school psychologist? List down what are the essential knowledge base that a social worker should have while serving in a school setting.

MULTIPLE CHOICE QUESTIONS

1. Who acts as a vital link between school, family and community?
   (a) Teacher (b) Counsellor
   (c) Administration (d) School Social Worker
2. The history of school social work can be dated back to ....
   (a) 1906–07 (b) 1806–07

(c) 1986–87 (d) 1886–87

3. In Hartford, US, school social worker were first known as ....
   (a) Visiting teacher (b) Special teachers
   (c) Counsellors (d) School psychologist
4. In which place US a public school became the first to fund a visiting teacher service?
   (a) Rochester, New York (b) Chicago
   (c) Hatford (d) Boston
5. When and where was first ever social work conference that recognized school social work and laid certain recommendations?
   (a) Indian conference of social work at its XIII session held at Varanasi in December 1964.
   (b) Indian conference of social work at its XIII session held at Pune in December 1964.
   (c) Indian conference of social work at its XIII session held at Delhi in December 1964.
   (d) Indian conference of social work at its XIII session held at Bombay in December 1964.
6. Who has developed School-community-pupil relations model of school social work?
   (a) Costin (b) Alderson
   (c) Linda Openshaw (d) Laura Berk
7. Which theory supports the traditional-clinical model of school social work?
   (a) Pyschoanalytical theory (b) Systems Theory
   (c) Operant Conditioning (d) Classical Conditioning
8. Which model focuses on school norms or school policies that are primarily the reason for the poor performance of a student?
   (a) The traditional-clinical model
   (b) The Community School model
   (c) The Social interaction model
   (d) The School-change model
9. Within which frame work a school social worker should create intervention plan?
   (a) Students perspective (b) Community perspective
   (c) Ecological perspective (d) Social interaction perspective
10. Linda Openshaw has clubbed the roles of school social worker as follows
   (a) Consultation, Assessment, Direct intervention, Counselling
   (b) Consultation, Assessment, Behavior modification, Assisting program development

(c) Consultation, Assessment, Direct intervention, Assisting program development
(d) Consultation, Assessment, Counselling, Behavior modification

Answers

1. (d), 2. (a), 3. (a), 4. (a), 5. (b), 6. (a), 7. (a), 8. (d), 9. (c), 10. (c)

REFERENCES

1. Alderson, J. J. (1972). Models of school social work practice. In R. Sarri & F. Maple (Eds.), *The school in the community* (pp. 151–160), Washington, DC: NASW.
2. Alderson, J. J. (1972) Continuing Education in Social Welfare: School Social work and the Effective Use of Manpower. U.S. department of health, education & welfare office of education.
3. Child Guidance Clinic, B.J. Wadia Hospital for Children, Annual Reports, 1960-1965 (Mimeographed).
4. Costin, L.B. (1969). A historical review of school social work, Social Case Work, DOI: 10.1177/104438946905000801, 1969 / 10 Vol. 50; Iss. 8
5. Costin, L. B. (1975). School social work practice a new model. Social Work, 20(2), 135–139. http://www.jstor.org/stable/23712257
6. Dupper,R.D., (2003). School Social Work Skills and Interventions for Effective Practice, John Wiley & Sons, Inc, Hoboken, New Jersey.
7. D'Souza. C., Syed. R, Sonaya. S. (1965), Social Work Forum, Vol. 3, No. 2.
8. Finigan-Carr, N. M., & Shaia, W. E. (2018). School social workers as partners in the school mission. The Phi Delta Kappan, 99(7), 26–30. https://www.jstor.org/stable/26552377
9. Shaffer, G.L. & Fisher, R.A., (2017). History of School Social Work. Leticia Villarreal Sosa Tory Cox & Michelle Alvarez (Eds), *School Social Work National Perspectives On Practice In Schools*. Oxford University Press.
10. Goyal, C.P. (1980). 'A Resume of the development of School social work movement in Kashi Vidyapeeth' (Unpublished Paper).
11. Mann, A. (2017). Significance of School Social Work: A Literature Review. *.Asian Journal Of Multidisciplinary Studies,* Vol. 5, Issue 3, ISSN: 2321-8819.
12. NASW Standards (2002). NASW Standards for School Social Work Services Approved by the NASW Board of Directors.
13. NASW (2012). NASW Standards for School Social Work Services Approved by the NASW Board of Directors.
14. Openshaw, L., (2008). Social Work in Schools: Principles and Practice. The Guilford Press New York London.
15. Schinke, S. P., & Gilchrist, L. D. (1984). Life skills counseling with adolescents. Baltimore: University Park Press.
16. School Social Work Association of America (nd). *Role of a school social worker.* https://www.sswaa.org/school-social-work

RECOMMENDED READINGS

1. 'Social Work in Schools: Principles and Practice' by Linda Openshaw. The Guilford Press, New York, London.
2. 'School Social Work Skills and Interventions for Effective Practice' by Dupper, R.D, John Wiley & Sons, Inc, Hoboken, New Jersey.
3. School Social Work, Eighth Edition: Practice, Policy, and Research Paperback – Import, 1 June 2015 by HYPERLINK "https://www.amazon.in/s/ref=dp_byline_sr_book_1?ie=UTF8&field-author=Robert−Constable&search-alias=stripbooks" Robert Constable, HYPERLINK "https://www.amazon.in/s/ref=dp_byline_sr_book_2?ie=UTF8&field-author=Carol+Rippey+Massat&search-alias=stripbooks" Carol Rippey Massat, HYPERLINK "https://www.amazon.in/Michael-S-Kelly/e/B001ITYCVK/ref=dp_byline_cont_book_3" Michael S. Kelly
4. 'Child Development and Education' by Teresa M. McDevitt and Jeanne Ellis Ormrod.

CHAPTER – 5

Social Work Practice in HIV/AIDS

SHEEBA JOSEPH[1] AND BISHNU MOHAN DASH[2]

[1]*Professor, Department of Social Work, Bhopal School of Social Sciences*
[2]*Professor, Department of Social Work, Bhim Rao Ambedkar College, University of Delhi*

HIV is not just a medical issue; it is a human rights issue. We must ensure that the voices of those affected are heard and that their dignity is respected.
– UNAIDS

ABSTRACT: *HIV/AIDS crosses all fields of practice, counselling, including mental health, community development, and health care. Social work practice continues to evolve, as social workers provide support to persons living with HIV/AIDS and those affected by the disease through direct counselling, treatment intervention, and social justice activities. This chapter is an effort to empasize on the gravity of HIV/AIDS in the global and Indian context and the intervention done by various government organizations and NGOs. The chapter also gives a brief idea about the symptoms, modes of transmission, co-infections. The legislation on HIV/AIDS and the basic human rights protection is also discussed in the chapter. Social Work intervention and HIV/AIDS is also deliberated in the present chapter.*

Keywords: *HIV, AIDS, ART, Social Work, Target Intervention*

Learning Objectives

After reading this chapter, the reader will be able to:

- Understand the basic concepts related to HIV/AIDS
- Comprehend the routes of transmission, symptoms, and the preventive measures of HIV/AIDS
- Discuss the role of social work in the field of HIV/AIDS
- The learner will understand the rights of persons with HIV/AIDs as per the constitutional law

INTRODUCTION

HIV (Human Immunodeficiency Virus) attacks all the cells in the body, making a person more vulnerable to other infections and disease conditions. Transmission of the virus is through the bodily fluids of a person with HIV, most commonly during unprotected sex (sex without a condom or HIV medicine to prevent or treat HIV), or through sharing injection drug equipment. If left untreated, HIV can lead to the disease AIDS (acquired immunodeficiency syndrome). The human body can't get rid of HIV and no effective HIV cure exists. So, once you have HIV, it will be lifelong. Antiretroviral therapy or ART is the treatment modality available for viral suppression. There are other effective methods to prevent the transmission of HIV through sex or drug use, including pre-exposure prophylaxis (PrEP), medicine people at risk for HIV take to prevent getting HIV from sex or injection drug use and post-exposure prophylaxis (PEP), HIV medicine taken within 72 hours after a possible exposure to prevent the virus from taking hold.

CONCEPTS

Acquired immunodeficiency syndrome (AIDS) is a chronic, potentially life-threatening condition caused by the human immunodeficiency virus (HIV). By damaging your immune system, HIV interferes with your body's ability to fight infection and disease.

AIDS or Acquired Immuno Deficiency Syndrome is the late stage of HIV infection that occurs when the body's immune system is badly damaged because of the virus. In the US, most people with HIV do not develop AIDS because taking HIV medicine as prescribed stops the progression of the disease.

A person with HIV is considered to have progressed to AIDS when:

- The number of their CD4 cells falls below 200 cells per cubic millimeter of blood (200 cells/mm3). (In someone with a healthy immune system, CD4 counts are between 500 and 1,600 cells/mm3.) OR
- They develop one or more opportunistic infections regardless of their CD4 count.

Without HIV medicine, people with AIDS typically survive about 3 years. Once someone has a dangerous opportunistic illness, life expectancy without treatment falls to about 1 year. HIV medicine can still help people at this stage of HIV infection, and it can even be lifesaving. But people who start HIV medicine soon after they get HIV experience more benefits—that's why HIV testing is so important.

SYMPTOMS

The symptoms of HIV and AIDS vary, depending on the phase of infection.

Primary Infection (Acute HIV)

Some people infected by HIV develop a flu-like illness within 2 to 4 weeks after the virus enters the body. This illness, known as primary (acute) HIV infection, may last for a few weeks.

Possible signs and symptoms include:

- Fever
- Headache
- Muscle aches and joint pain
- Rash
- Sore throat and painful mouth sores
- Swollen lymph glands, mainly on the neck
- Diarrhoea
- Weight loss
- Cough
- Night sweats

These symptoms can be so mild that you might not even notice them. However, the amount of virus in your bloodstream (viral load) is quite high at this time. As a result, the infection spreads more easily during primary infection than during the next stage.

Clinical Latent Infection (Chronic HIV)

In this stage of infection, HIV is still present in the body and in white blood cells. However, many people may not have any symptoms or infections during this time.

This stage can last for many years if you're receiving antiretroviral therapy (ART). Some people develop more severe disease much sooner.

Symptomatic HIV Infection

As the virus continues to multiply and destroy your immune cells – the cells in your body that help fight off germs – you may develop mild infections or chronic signs and symptoms such as:

- Fever
- Fatigue
- Swollen lymph nodes — often one of the first signs of HIV infection
- Diarrhoea
- Weight loss
- Oral yeast infection (thrush)
- Shingles (herpes zoster)
- Pneumonia

Progression to AIDS

Access to better antiviral treatments has dramatically decreased deaths from AIDS worldwide, even in resource-poor countries. Untreated, HIV typically turns into AIDS in about 8 to 10 years. When AIDS occurs, your immune system has been severely damaged. You'll be more likely to develop diseases that wouldn't usually cause illness in a person with a healthy immune system. These are called opportunistic infections or opportunistic cancers.

The signs and symptoms of some of these infections may include:

- Sweats
- Chills
- Recurring fever
- Chronic diarrhoea
- Swollen lymph glands
- Persistent white spots or unusual lesions on your tongue or in your mouth
- Persistent, unexplained fatigue
- Weakness
- Weight loss
- Skin rashes or bumps

Causes

HIV is caused by a virus. It can spread through sexual contact, illicit injection drug use or sharing needles, contact with infected blood, or from mother to child during pregnancy, childbirth or breastfeeding. HIV destroys CD4 T cells — white blood cells that play a large role in helping your body fight disease. The fewer CD4 T cells you have, the weaker your immune system becomes.

Modes of Transmission

To become infected with HIV, infected blood, semen or vaginal secretions must enter your body. This can happen in several ways:

- **By having sex:** You may become infected if you have vaginal, anal or oral sex with an infected partner whose blood, semen or vaginal secretions enter your body. The virus can enter your body through mouth sores or small tears that sometimes develop in the rectum or vagina during sexual activity.
- **By sharing needles:** Sharing contaminated injection drug paraphernalia (needles and syringes) puts you at high risk of HIV and other infectious diseases, such as hepatitis.
- **From blood transfusions:** In some cases, the virus may be transmitted through blood transfusions. Hospitals and blood banks screen the blood supply for HIV, so this risk is very small in the U.S. and other upper-middle-income countries. The risk may be higher in low-income countries that are not able to screen all donated blood.
- **During pregnancy or delivery or through breastfeeding:** Infected mothers can pass the virus on to their babies. Mothers who are HIV-

positive and get treatment for the infection during pregnancy can significantly lower the risk to their babies.

Some contextual factors that have an influence on HIV transmissions are individual factors, such as age, sexual identity, self-esteem, untreated sexually transmitted diseases, use of alcohol and drugs, interpersonal factors, such as partner commitment and the practice of safe-sex. Study and identification of these factors that lead to infection, transmission and progression of the disease is important.

RISK FACTORS OF HIV TRANSMISSION

Anyone of any age, race, sex or sexual orientation can be infected with HIV/AIDS. However, you're at greatest risk of HIV/AIDS if you:

- **Have unprotected sex:** Use a new latex or polyurethane condom every time you have sex. Anal sex is riskier than vaginal sex. Your risk of HIV increases if you have multiple sexual partners.
- **Have an Sexual Transmitted Infections (STI):** Many STIs produce open sores on your genitals. These sores act as doorways for HIV to enter your body.
- **Use illicit injection drugs:** People who use illicit injection drugs often share needles and syringes. This exposes them to droplets of other people's blood.

COMPLICATIONS

HIV infection weakens your immune system, making you much more likely to develop many infections and certain types of cancers.

Infections Common to HIV/AIDS

- **Pneumocystis pneumonia (PCP):** This fungal infection can cause severe illness. Although it's declined significantly with current treatments for HIV/AIDS, in the US, PCP is still the most common cause of pneumonia in people infected with HIV.
- **Candidiasis (thrush):** Candidiasis is a common HIV-related infection. It causes inflammation and a thick, white coating on your mouth, tongue, esophagus or vagina.
- **Tuberculosis (TB):** TB is a common opportunistic infection associated with HIV. Worldwide, TB is a leading cause of death among people with AIDS. It's less common in the U.S. thanks to the wide use of HIV medications.
- **Cytomegalovirus:** This common herpes virus is transmitted in body fluids such as saliva, blood, urine, semen and breast milk. A healthy immune system inactivates the virus, and it remains dormant in your

body. If your immune system weakens, the virus resurfaces — causing damage to your eyes, digestive tract, lungs or other organs.

- **Cryptococcal meningitis:** Meningitis is an inflammation of the membranes and fluid surrounding your brain and spinal cord (meninges). Cryptococcal meningitis is a common central nervous system infection associated with HIV, caused by a fungus found in soil.
- **Toxoplasmosis:** This potentially deadly infection is caused by Toxoplasma gondii, a parasite spread primarily by cats. Infected cats pass the parasites in their stools, which may then spread to other animals and humans. Toxoplasmosis can cause heart disease, and seizures occur when it spreads to the brain.

Cancers Common to HIV/AIDS

- **Lymphoma:** This cancer starts in the white blood cells. The most common early sign is painless swelling of the lymph nodes in your neck, armpit or groin.
- **Kaposi's sarcoma:** A tumour of the blood vessel walls, Kaposi's sarcoma usually appears as pink, red or purple lesions on the skin and mouth. In people with darker skin, the lesions may look dark brown or black. Kaposi's sarcoma can also affect the internal organs, including the digestive tract and lungs.
- **HPV-related cancers:** These are cancers caused by human papilloma-virus (HPV) infection. They include anal, oral and cervical cancer.

Other Complications

- **Wasting syndrome:** Untreated HIV/AIDS can cause significant weight loss, often accompanied by diarrhoea, chronic weakness and fever.
- **Neurological complications:** HIV can cause neurological symptoms such as confusion, forgetfulness, depression, anxiety and difficulty walking. HIV-associated neurocognitive disorders (HAND) can range from mild symptoms of behavioural changes and reduced mental functioning to severe dementia causing weakness and inability to function.
- **Kidney disease:** HIV-associated nephropathy (HIVAN) is an inflammation of the tiny filters in your kidneys that remove excess fluid and wastes from your blood and pass them to your urine. It most often affects Black or Hispanic people.
- **Liver disease:** Liver disease is also a major complication, especially in people who also have hepatitis B or hepatitis C.

PREVENTION

There's no vaccine to prevent HIV infection and no cure for HIV/AIDS. But you can protect yourself and others from infection.

To help prevent the spread of HIV:

- Pre-exposure prophylaxis (PrEP).
- Use treatment as prevention (TasP).
- Use post-exposure prophylaxis (PEP) if you've been exposed to HIV.
- Use a new condom every time you have sex.
- Tell your sexual partners if you have HIV.
- Use a clean needle.
- If you're pregnant, get medical care right away.
- Consider male circumcision.

GLOBAL AND NATIONAL SCENARIO

The first case of HIV in India was reported in 1986 in Chennai. India has the third-largest burden of human immunodeficiency virus (HIV) infection in the world. Human immunodeficiency virus (HIV), the third most widespread epidemic in the world, is a huge burden to the lower-middle-income country (LMIC), India. HIV prevalence among adults between the ages of 15 and 49 years was estimated to be 0.2 per cent in 2017. Although the number is lesser than other LMICs, India's population, estimated at 1.3 billion, manifests to 2.1 million people living with the disease (Avert, 2018).

Table 1: Summary of Global HIV Epidemic, 2022

	People Living with HIV	*People Acquiring HIV*	*People Dying from HIV Related Causes*
Total	39.0 million	1.3 million	6,30,000
Adult 15+ Years	37.5 million	1.2 million	5,40,000
Women 15+ Years	20.0 million	5,40,000	2,30,000
Men 15+ Years	17.4 million	6,40,000	3,10,000
Children <15 years	1.5 million	1,30,000	84,000

Source: UNAIDS/WHO Estimates, 2023

Table 2: Summary of the HIV/AIDS Epidemic in India, 2021

Indicators	*Value*
Adult (15-49 years) prevalence (%)	0.21 (0.17-0.25)
Number of people living with HIV (in lakh)	24.01 (19.92-29.07)
HIV incidence per 1000 uninfected population	0.05 (0.03-0.08)
New HIV Infections (in thousand)	62.97 (36.72-104.06)
Decline in new HIV infections since 2010 (%)	46.25
AIDS-related deaths (in thousand)	41.97 (26.50-67.45)
AIDS-related deaths per 100,000 population	3.08 (1.94-4.95)
Decline in AIDS-related deaths since 2010 (%)	76.54

The Government of India recognised the seriousness of the problem caused by HIV/AIDS quite early. The Ministry of Health and Family Welfare constituted the National AIDS Committee in 1986. National AIDS Control Programme (NACP) in 1987 aimed at establishing a comprehensive multi-sectional programme for the prevention and control of HIV/AIDS in India. The National AIDS Control Organisation (NACO) established in India in 1992. To strengthen HIV/AIDS control programme, various steps have been initiated at the state level, each state has a State AIDS Control Society (SACS).

STD control programme was started in 1946 and brought under the purview of NACO in the year 1992. STD clinical services are an important access point for persons at high risk for both HIV and STD, not only for diagnosis and treatment but also for health education, counselling, and prevention. Ministry of Health and Family Welfare has adopted a policy on control of HIV/AIDS/STD to integrate STD control into the existing health care system. Condom programme was initiated all over the country to ensure easy access to good quality, affordable and acceptable condom to promote safe sex encounters. The major areas in relation to condom programme are quality control of the condoms and social marketing of condoms. Blood safety programme is an integral part of the National AIDS Control Programme. The objectives of the blood safety programme is to ensure easily accessible, adequate supply of safe and quality blood and blood components for all. To minimise the risk of transmission of HIV infection through blood and blood products, government has taken a series of measures. Thrust areas are establishment of HIV testing facilities; support for testing for other blood transmittable diseases; modernisation of blood banks; appropriate clinical use of blood; and training and personnel development.

Information, education, communication (IEC), and social mobilization can be used to motivate people to adopt and maintain healthy practices and lifestyles. The IEC strategy in NACO is operationalized at the national level, political, and media advocacy, creation of a supportive environment that reduces social stigma and discrimination, and provides for better access to services. The IEC strategic plan has the following components: appropriate use of mass media,; advocacy at various levels, inter-sectoral collaboration, training, involving NGOs, and research.

The basic purpose of Targeted Intervention (TI) programme is to reduce the rate of transmission among the most vulnerable and marginalised population such as sex workers, intravenous drug users, men having sex with men (MSM), truckers, migrant labour, and street children. Targeted Intervention is one of the most important components of NACP-II. The author has discussed on various initiatives taken by the United Nations for the prevention and control of HIV/AIDS. Joined United Nations' programme on HIV/AIDS (UNAIDS) is the leading advocate for world-wide action against HIV/AIDS. Seven co-sponsoring organisations of UNAIDS offer countries a broad range of experience, effort, and resources of relevance to fight against the epidemic namely UNICEF, UNDP, UNFPA, UNDCP, UNESCO, WHO, and World Bank. The author explored and discussed some of the major collaborations with bilateral donor agencies for the prevention and control of HIV/AIDS namely US Agency for International Development (USAID), Norwegian Agency for Development (NORAD), Department of International Development (DFID), and European Union (EU).

TARGETED INTERVENTION INITIATIVES BY NACO

Targeted Interventions are preventive interventions working with high-risk groups in a defined geographic area. Targeted Intervention projects, implemented by NGOs/ Community Based Organisations (CBOs), work with both core HRGs (FSW, MSM, TG and IDU) as well as bridge populations (Migrant & Trucker) and provide preventive interventions through a peer-led approach. Targeted interventions provide HRGs with the information, means and skills needed to prevent HIV transmission and improve their access to care, support and treatment services. These programmes also focus on improving sexual and reproductive health and general health of high-risk population.

Key Risk Groups Covered Under 'Targeted Interventions'

Core High Risk Groups

- Female Sex Workers
- Men who have Sex with Men
- Transgenders
- Injecting Drug Users

Bridge Populations

- Long Distance Truckers
- High-risk Migrants

Services Offered Under the Targeted Intervention Programme

TI projects provide a package of prevention, support and linkage services to HRGs through an outreach-based service delivery model. The services offered through the Targeted Interventions projects include:

- Detection and treatment for Sexually Transmitted Infections

- Condom distribution (except in TIs for bridge population)
- Condom promotion through social marketing (for HRG and bridge population)
- Behaviour Change Communication
- Creating an enabling environment with community involvement and participation
- Linkages to Integrated Counselling and Testing Centres
- Linkages with care and support services for HIV positive HRGs
- Community organisation and ownership building

FUNDAMENTAL CONSTITUTIONAL RIGHTS OF A PERSON WITH HIV

It is also important to understand the fundamental constitutional rights of a person with HIV which ensure the respect of worth and dignity of the individual. The three of the most important rights in the HIV scenario include:

Right to Informed Consent

It is the right of every individual to lead a dignified life in spite of any condition. Testing for HIV requires specific and informed consent of the client being tested and same applies to do any research on data of HIV positive people.

Right to Confidentiality

It is one of the cardinal principles of social work profession. The matter disclosed by a client should be kept under lock and key. A person has the right to keep information on HIV status confidential. People with HIV are often afraid to go to court to vindicate their rights for fear of their HIV status open to all. However, they can take the help of Suppression of Identity under an assumed name. This ensures that PLHA can seek justice without fear of social isolation or discrimination.

Right against Discrimination

The right to be treated equally is a fundamental right whether it's something as simple as using a public well or something more serious like denial of housing. They also have the right to access any facilities enjoyed by others.

HIV and AIDS (Prevention and Control) Act, 2017

The Human Immunodeficiency Virus and Acquired Immune Deficiency Syndrome (Prevention and Control) Act, 2017 is a landmark legislation to provide a conducive environment to people infected with and affected by HIV and AIDS. The Act aims to address stigma and discrimination so that people infected with and affected by HIV and AIDS are not discriminated in household settings, establishment settings and healthcare settings. Their right to insurance, movement, holding public and private office, residence etc. should be maintained as per the prevailing laws and policies. The Act also reinstates constitutional, statutory, and human rights of people infected with and affected by HIV and AIDS. It also provides for a robust grievance redressal mechanism in form of Complaints Officer at establishments and Ombudsman at state level.

Non-discrimination is a fundamental principle of all international and human rights laws. There should be no discrimination on the basis of perceived or real HIV status. This protection is provided not only to an HIV positive person, but also extends to immediate family members and progeny who reside or have resided in the same house of HIV infected person too.

1. **Absence of discrimination at employment and occupation:** A person should not be discriminated in the institute on the basis of HIV status. Discrimination here includes the denial of, or termination from, employment or occupation and also unfair treatment in the institute.
2. **Availing healthcare facility:** A person should not be discriminated in this institution the basis of HIV status for availing healthcare facilities.
3. **Public utilities and resources:** Irrespective of HIV status, a person can hold public offices and cannot be discriminated.
4. **Right to movement:** Right to movement is a fundamental right entrusted under article 19 of Fundamental Rights of Part- III of the Constitution. No person should be denied or subjected to discontinuation or unfair treatment with regard to the right to movement.
5. **Segregation:** A person should not be segregated on the basis of HIV status. Thus, she or he or others cannot be isolated and ostracized on the basis of HIV status.
6. **HIV testing** as a pre-requisite for obtaining employment or accessing healthcare services or for the continuation of the same is completely prohibited.
7. **Confidentiality related to HIV status:** HIV positive person cannot be forced to disclose her or his or their status or any other HIV-related information. HIV-related information means any information relating to the HIV status of a person and includes: (a) information relating to the undertaking given for performing the HIV test or result of an HIV test; (b) information relating to the care, support or treatment of that person; (c) information which may identify that person; and (d) any other information concerning that person, which is collected, received, accessed or recorded in connection with an HIV test, HIV treatment or HIV-related research or the HIV status of that person.

8. **Disclosure of status to partner of HIV positive person:** In case of disclosure of status to partner of HIV positive person, no healthcare provider, except a physician or a counsellor, shall disclose the HIV positive status of a person to their partner. This kind of disclosure can be made if: (a) The healthcare provider believes that the partner is at the significant risk of transmission of HIV from such a person. (b) The HIV-positive person has been counselled to inform the partner. (c) The healthcare provider is satisfied that the HIV positive person will not inform the partner. (d) The healthcare provider has informed the HIV positive person of the intention to disclose the HIV-positive status to the partner.
9. **Confidentiality of data related to HIV:** HIV-related information is sensitive in nature and every establishment within this institute keeping the records of HIV-related information should adopt data protection measures to ensure prevention of unintended or unwanted disclosure and breach of confidentiality of the data.

SOCIAL WORK AND HIV/AIDS INTERVENTION

HIV/AIDS interventions are of two types. The first are those that are targeted at the general population. In these, the programmes are designed to improve awareness, knowledge, and attitudes to change social norms, and to create a supportive environment. In the other types of intervention targeted at special groups, such as sex workers, truck drivers and migrant workers, street children and STD patients, the efforts at prevention cover some more aspects to reduce heterosexual transmission of HIV/AIDS. These include early detection and management of sexually transmitted infections, improved behaviour in seeking treatment, sexual abstinence or delayed onset of sex, especially in adolescents, fewer sexual partners, safe-sex practices, supportive social environment to sustain behaviour change, and reduced stigma and discrimination towards those infected.

Professional Social Workers have a major task to accomplish where HIV/AIDS is concerned. Global efforts at HIV/AIDS prevention have, by and large, focused IEC campaigns. There has been extensive use of the print and electronic media. These have had an impact upon awareness generation, but have they been successful in sensitizing individuals? Have they made individuals think 'Am I at risk'? The efforts at sensitizing individuals, thereby raising their absolute and comparative risk-perception, have been conspicuously missing in this prevention programme. Social workers can do much to bridge this gap. A range of pro-HIV activities need to be focalized by a communication programme. Social workers working at the grass-roots are the best sources of information on norms and traditions, cultural practices and behavioural patterns of their community groups. With their knowledge base, they can use a variety of media to reach out to people with the message of reducing risk. Dance, drama, folk theatre, and sports events as well as television, radio, and print media can all be used to spread AIDS awareness. Earlier, it was believed that AIDS afflicted those who are given to deviant forms of behaviour. They were categorized as 'high risk groups'. Today the thinking is somewhat different. Men, women and children are all 'at risk'.

- Social workers can work in different ways to help reduce stigma and discrimination.
- Raise HIV/AIDS awareness among communities.
- Promote counselling to help people develop the right attitude towards the afflicted.
- Efforts are needed to counter prejudice and misunderstanding to protect the human rights of commercial sex workers, men who have sex with men, and other groups.
- Ensure that individuals can access comprehensive and confidential testing services. Enable the afflicted to share their positive status with their loved ones, if they so desire.

The primary aim of providing care and support is to prevent the spread of HIV including risk behaviour change for HIV positive persons. Provision of support, i.e. emotional, social, and economic consequences of infection and to provide practical assistance and advocacy including palliative care and hospice care are required.

Counselling as a medium of providing care and support. Counselling is a professional area of work and only a trained and skilled person can give counselling. All social workers are trained in the area of counselling and are qualified to give counselling even to PLHA. The Global Fund to fight AIDS, Tuberculosis, and Malaria (GFATM) is an international financing institution; invest the world's money to save lives. Hospice and palliative care as one of the important interventions by social workers all over for taking care of the infected.

Mass media is an important communication strategy to generate awareness and disseminate information on HIV/AIDS. Many social workers have published their own websites discussing the problems related to HIV/AIDS. Radio is an effective medium to reach general population, All India Radio (AIR) also airs programme related to HIV/AIDS every week. Some television programmes also contribute to bring about a change in people's attitude towards PLHA. Through formal education setting can reach children and young people and educate them about HIV/AIDS. Social workers campaign tirelessly going from school to school and colleges to colleges talking about and breaking the myths related to HIV/AIDS. In IGNOU, School of Social Work started the certificate, diploma courses in HIV/AIDS and family education. Several schools of social work-initiated awareness programme and counselling services on HIV/AIDS.

The author is in the opinion that advocacy and policy planning is necessary to protect the rights of PLHA so that they can live a life of dignity. Advocacy for HIV/AIDS prevention is the combined effort of a group of individuals or organizations to persuade individuals, groups, and organizations through various activities to adopt an effective approach. The advocacy activities undertaken by the social workers should aim to protect the rights of PLHA and it should be able to bring a balance between the long-term and short term goals of interventions for HIV/AIDS.

Behaviour Change Communication (BCC) is an interactive process with communities. BCC is an essential part of a comprehensive programme that includes both services and commodities. BCC can lead to appropriate attitude changes about perceived personal risk of HIV infection. BCC programmes can focus on teaching or reinforcing new skills and behaviours.

Review Questions

(a) Discuss the role of social workers in HIV/AIDS intervention.
(b) Explain the salient features of HIV/AIDS (Prevention and Control) Act 2017 concerning the rights of individuals infected with HIV.
(c) List the Targeted Interventions initiatives by NACO.
(d) Explain the modes of transmission of HIV.
(e) What are the symptoms of HIV?

Did You Know?

- The first recognized case of AIDS was reported in the United States in 1981, marking the beginning of a global health crisis.
- The first reported case of HIV in India was identified in 1986, setting off national and international efforts to address the emerging epidemic.
- More than 36 million people have died globally from AIDS-related illnesses, underscoring the urgent need for continued prevention and treatment efforts.
- Approximately 38 million people globally are living with HIV as of 2021, with millions benefitting from antiretroviral therapy that allows them to lead healthy lives.
- According to UNAIDS (2021), approximately one person dies from an AIDS-related illness every minute, which translates to about 1,440 deaths per day or 60 deaths per hour globally.

SUMMARY

HIV (Human Immunodeficiency Virus) compromises the immune system, increasing vulnerability to infections and diseases. It is primarily transmitted through unprotected sex and sharing injection equipment. If untreated, HIV can progress to AIDS (acquired immunodeficiency syndrome), which significantly weakens the immune system. Once infected, individuals will have HIV for life, but antiretroviral therapy (ART) can suppress the virus and prevent progression to AIDS. The symptoms of HIV vary by infection stage. In the acute phase, individuals may experience flu-like symptoms such as fever and fatigue. The chronic stage may have no symptoms but can last for years with ART. Without treatment, HIV typically progresses to AIDS within 8 to 10 years, marked by severely reduced CD4 cell counts and increased risk of opportunistic infections. Transmission occurs through sexual contact, sharing needles, blood transfusions, and from mother to child during pregnancy or breastfeeding. Contextual factors such as age, sexual behaviour, and the presence of other sexually transmitted infections (STIs) influence risk. High-risk behaviours include unprotected sex, having multiple partners, and using illicit drugs. Awareness and prevention strategies are essential for reducing HIV transmission. Professional social workers play a crucial role in HIV/AIDS prevention and awareness efforts. While global initiatives have focused on information campaigns, a notable lack of personal risk sensitization exists. Social workers, with their community insights, can utilize various media—such as drama, sports, and mass communication—to raise awareness and reduce the stigma surrounding HIV/AIDS. They are equipped to provide counselling, support, and advocacy for those affected, including marginalized groups. Effective communication and behaviour change strategies are essential for fostering understanding and acceptance, while policy advocacy is necessary to uphold the rights and dignity of people living with HIV/AIDS. A comprehensive approach involving education, support, and community engagement is vital for effective prevention and care.

GLOSSARY

- HIV (Human Immunodeficiency Virus) attacks all the cells making a person more vulnerable to other infections and disease conditions.
- Antiretroviral therapy or ART is the treatment modality available for viral suppression.
- National AIDS Control Programme (NACP) in 1987 aimed at establishing a comprehensive multi-sectional programme for the prevention and control of HIV/AIDS in India.
- Targeted Intervention (TI) programme to reduce the rate of transmission among the most vulnerable and marginalised population such as sex workers, intravenous drug users, men having sex with men (MSM), truckers, migrant labour, and street children.

- Behaviour Change Communication (BCC) is an interactive process with communities. BCC is an essential part of a comprehensive programme that includes both services and commodities.
- Acquired immunodeficiency syndrome (AIDS) is a chronic, potentially life-threatening condition caused by the human immunodeficiency virus (HIV). By damaging your immune system, HIV interferes with your body's ability to fight infection and disease.
- Pneumocystis pneumonia (PCP) is a fungal infection that can cause severe illness among people infected with HIV.
- Candidiasis (thrush) causes inflammation and a thick, white coating on your mouth, tongue, esophagus or vagina.
- Tuberculosis (TB) is a common opportunistic infection associated with HIV.
- Cytomegalovirus is a common herpes virus that is transmitted in body fluids such as saliva, blood, urine, semen, and breast milk.
- Cryptococcal meningitis is an inflammation of the membranes and fluid surrounding the brain and spinal cord (meninges).
- Toxoplasmosis is a potentially deadly infection is caused by Toxoplasma gondii, a parasite spread primarily by cats.
- Lymphoma starts in the white blood cells. The most common early sign is painless swelling of the lymph nodes in your neck, armpit or groin.
- Kaposi's sarcoma is a tumor of the blood vessel walls, Kaposi's sarcoma usually appears as pink, red or purple lesions on the skin and mouth.
- HPV-related cancers are cancers caused by human papillomavirus (HPV) infection. They include anal, oral and cervical cancer.
- Wasting syndrome referes to untreated HIV/AIDS can cause significant weight loss, often accompanied by diarrhea, chronic weakness and fever.
- HIV can cause neurological symptoms such as confusion, forgetfulness, depression, anxiety and difficulty walking. HIV-associated neurocognitive disorders (HAND) can range from mild symptoms of behavioral changes and reduced mental functioning to severe dementia causing weakness and inability to function.
- HIV-associated nephropathy (HIVAN) is an inflammation of the tiny filters in your kidneys that remove excess fluid and wastes from your blood and pass them to your urine.
- Liver disease is also a major complication, especially in people who also have hepatitis B or hepatitis C.

TOP TEN TAKEAWAY POINTS

1. HIV is a lifelong infection that attacks the immune system, increasing vulnerability to other illnesses and diseases. If untreated, HIV can progress to AIDS.
2. HIV is primarily transmitted through unprotected sex and sharing injection equipment. Effective prevention methods include antiretroviral therapy (ART), Pre-Exposure Prophylaxis (PrEP), and Post-Exposure Prophylaxis (PEP).
3. A person with HIV is diagnosed with AIDS when their CD4 cell count drops below 200 cells/mm^3 or when they develop opportunistic infections. Most individuals with HIV in the U.S. do not progress to AIDS due to timely treatment.
4. Acute HIV infection may present flu-like symptoms such as fever, headache, and swollen lymph nodes within 2 to 4 weeks of infection. These symptoms can be mild, but the viral load is high, making transmission more likely during this phase.
5. The Government of India recognized the HIV/AIDS epidemic early on, establishing the National AIDS Control Programme (NACP) in 1987 and the National AIDS Control Organisation (NACO) in 1992 to coordinate efforts at both national and state levels.
6. Targeted Intervention (TI) programs focus on vulnerable populations such as female sex workers, men who have sex with men, and injecting drug users. These programs aim to reduce transmission rates through peer-led education, access to healthcare, and support services.
7. Individuals with HIV have fundamental rights, including the right to informed consent, confidentiality, and protection against discrimination in employment, healthcare, and public services, reinforced by the HIV and AIDS (Prevention and Control) Act of 2017.
8. Information, Education, and Communication (IEC) strategies are vital in raising awareness and combating stigma. Social workers play a crucial role in using various media and community engagement to promote understanding of HIV/AIDS.
9. Counselling is essential for providing emotional and practical support to people living with HIV/AIDS. Trained social workers offer services to help individuals navigate their diagnosis, reduce risk behaviours, and improve their overall well-being.
10. Advocacy efforts by social workers aim to protect the rights of people living with HIV/AIDS, ensuring they can live with dignity. This includes promoting behaviour change communication (BCC) to enhance awareness and understanding within communities about HIV transmission and prevention.

MULTIPLE CHOICE QUESTIONS

1. Which one of the following is not a mode of transmission of HIV?
   (a) Unprotected sex
   (b) Shaking hands with infected persons
   (c) Transmission of contaminated blood
   (d) Sharing the injection/drug equipment
2. HIV that causes AIDS first starts destroying:
   (a) B-Lymphocytes (b) Lencocytes
   (c) Thrombocytes (d) T Lymphocytes
3. Which one of the following is not included in the three stages of HIV Infection?
   (a) Acute HIV infection (b) Chronic HIV infection
   (c) Medium HIV infection
   (d) Acquired immune deficiency syndrome
4. HIV occurs through ___ stages?
   (a) 5 (b) 3
   (c) 4 (d) 6
5. HIV is a __________.
   (a) Retrovirus (b) Papillomavirus
   (c) Gallivirus (d) Capripoxvirus
6. HIV is believed to be originated from which species?
   (a) Snakes (b) Mosquitos
   (c) Birds (d) Chimpanzees
7. AIDS is characterised by which of the following?
   (a) Decreased RBC Count (b) Reduction in T4-Lymphocytes
   (c) Reduction in Platelets (d) Low blood pressure
8. Which among the following organisation in India is engaged in spreading awareness and sensitise people about HIV/AIDS?
   (a) IARI (b) NCERT
   (c) NACO (d) KVIC
9. In which city the first case of HIV in India was reported in 1986?
   (a) Delhi (b) Kolkata
   (c) Mumbai (d) Chennai
10. Who is/are among the following high risk groups covered under targeted intervention?
    (a) Female sex workers (b) Men who have sex with men
    (c) Infecting drug users (d) All of the above

Answers

1. (b), 2. (d), 3. (c), 4. (b), 5. (a), 6. (d), 7. (b), 8. (c), 9. (d), 10. (d)

REFERENCES

1. Dash, B.M. (Ed.) (2016). *Fighting HIV/AIDS the gracious way*. Uppal Publishing House.
2. Avert (2018). *HIV and AIDS in India*. Mumbai, India. (Accessed 1 November 2021). https://www.avert.org/professionals/hiv-around-world/asia-pacific/india.
3. World Health Organization (2024).HIV data statistics, global HIV programme. Retrieved February 28, 2024, from https://www.who.int/hiv/data/statistics
4. World Health Organization (2022). Global health observatory data repository: HIV/AIDS. Retrieved on September 21,2024 from https://www.who.int/data/gho/data/themes/topics/topic-details/GHO/hiv-aids
5. Centre for Disease Control and Prevention. (2021). A timeline of HIV and AIDS. Retrieved on September 21, 2024 from https://www.cdc.gov/hiv/basics/whatishiv.html#timeline
6. National AIDS Control Organization (2019). Annual report 2018-19. Retrieved on September 21, 2024 from https://naco.gov.in/sites/default/files/NACO%20Annual%20Report%202018-19.pdf
7. UNAIDS (2021). Global AIDS update 2021: In dangerous waters. Retrieved on September19,2024 from https://www.unaids.org/en/resources/documents/2021/global-aids-update
8. World Health Organization (2021). HIV/AIDS. Retrieved on August 21, 2024 from https://www.who.int/news-room/fact-sheets/detail/hiv-aids
9. UNAIDS (2021). Global AIDS update 2021: In dangerous waters. Retrieved on September 21,2024 from https://www.unaids.org/en/resources/documents/2021/global-aids-update
10. National AIDS Control Organization & ICMR-National Institute of Medical Statistics (2022). *India: HIV/AIDS estimates – 2021 fact sheet*. Retrieved February 28, 2024, from https://naco.gov.in/sites/default/files/HIV%20Estimations%20Fact%20Sheet%202021.pdf

RECOMMENDED READINGS

1. Kumar, S. (2018). HIV/AIDS: Social work perspectives. New Delhi: Sage Publications.
2. NACO (2020). National AIDS control programme: A comprehensive approach. New Delhi: National AIDS Control Organization, Ministry of Health and Family Welfare.
2. Singh, A. (2019). Social work interventions in HIV/AIDS care. New Delhi: Rawat Publications.
3. Cohen, M.S., & McCauley, M. (2017). HIV prevention: A comprehensive approach. New York: Springer.
4. Parker, R., & Easton, W. (2019). HIV/AIDS and the stigma of infection: A social justice perspective. New York: Routledge.
5. Dworkin, E.R., & Menon, N. (2018). Social work and HIV/AIDS: A social justice approach. New York: Routledge.

CHAPTER – 6

Industrial Social Work: Scope, Applications and Trends

Rutwik Gandhe and Richi Simon

Assistant Professor, Department of Social Work, The Bhopal School of Social Sciences

Life's most urgent question is: What are you doing for others?

– Martin Luther King. Jr.

Abstract: *This chapter begins with a discussion on introducing the very concept of Industrial Social Work (ISW) with its changing dimensions which are making it more like Occupational Social Work (OCW). While elaborating the present-day scope of Industrial Social Work, a brief historical account of its practices and the way it emerged has been presented. Different views of Industrial social work practice have been discussed with the contrasting the present-day contemporary view leading to a discussion on issues that are merging around the Industrial and Occupational Social Work. Opportunities and changing scenario of Industrial Social Work practice has been outlined in context of changes in the labour code in India and the advent of wage code, social security code, OSHWC code and industrial relations code in India in recent times. To culminate the chapter, established models of Industrial Social Work across the globe have been focused where author suggests some emerging models like WAD, VIVAD and VED along with challenges of industrial social work practice in years to come.*

Keywords: *Industrial Social Work, Occupational Social Work, Labour Welfare, Employee Welfare*

Learning Objectives

After reading this chapter, you would be able to:

- Understand the concept, scope and evolution of industrial social work in Indian and Western scenario
- Describe major traditional and contemporary role of industrial social workers
- Discuss major challenges ad changing scenarios of industrial social work practice in India
- Explain various traditional and emerging models of industrial social work practice across the world

INTRODUCTION

Industrial Social Work, alternatively known as Occupational Social Work deals with problems and issues that confront human workforce at their workplace. This dimension and domain of social work is relatively newer than other domains of social work practice, however it is gaining momentum now. Initially it began with labour welfare, which further led to personnel management and now it encompasses all efforts that are possibly within the arc employee welfare to employee engagement, health and safety. One more significant development in this direction is the inclusion of all kinds of workplaces unlike early years of evolution of industrial social work where thinkers, and practitioners were concerned majorly about industrial work settings only. Regardless of work conditions and work setting, talking about all kind of employee's welfare, safety, heath, occupational hazards and work conditions, employee engagement leading to employee productivity and growth is under the scope of Industrial Social Work. A large part of industrial relationship management and conflict and negotiation management can also be considered within the purview of practicing Industrial Social Work. This chapter discusses emerging ideas and concepts of industrial social work, its scope, applications and practices and current trends.

Industrial social work therefore refers to the utilization of social work expertise in meeting the needs of workers or union members and the serving of broader organizational goals of the setting. For social workers, it offers the opportunity to intervene in a multiple of environmental systems that affects the individual. The main objectives of industrial social work are (a) to help employees to develop their inner resources and if necessary to mobilize other services within the enterprise to bring about changes in the work environment; (b) to help workers in their personal and family difficulties to act as a resource person to community services and to become liaison between the plant and the community services; (c) to take care of young persons, women and workers nearing superannuation; (d) to help workers for better adjustment to working hours, working conditions and work groups and to help management in evolving suitable working hours, working conditions and work group; (e) to orient and induct the employees and to assist the 'work community' as a whole to function in a better way; and (f) to direct the growth along desirable lines for which, utilizing the present facilities and resources in a better and fruitful way adjusting the individual to his complex changing world.

INDUSTRIAL SOCIAL WORK: CONCEPT AND SCOPE

'Industrial Social Work is that area of social work practice where the social worker is engaged in welfare, engagement, and development of the employees at the workplace using the specific knowledge and skills acquired for the said purpose'. This is how we define Industrial Social Work. However here after many such ideas and concepts will be discussed directly and indirectly about industrial social work in this section. It can be safely assumed that industrial social work is a complex mix of employee welfare initiatives, human resource management and industrial relations efforts at the workplace. Since it deals with a lot of workforce related issues, concerns and matters, people practicing this branch of social work ought to have the knowledge of, legal issues at workplace, human behaviour and ethics, means of engaging and motivating employees, which makes it essential to deal in the domain if human resources management and organizational behaviour in terms of modern management. However, Industrial Social Work is more than human resources management as it is concerned with health, welfare, sustainability development of employees at workplace and taking care of their families when problems are associated with work life of an employee affecting their family relationships. Therefore, we can see that umbrella of Industrial Social Work is all encompassing in the modern era. Social work practice in industries ranges from dealing with individuals and groups at workplace, to dealing with larger community issues at related to workplace. Desai (2002) observed Industrial Social Work as indigenous development as at that time it wasn't considered as social work practice specially in the US.

The scope of social work in an industrial organization is within the administrative purview of the personnel or labour welfare department, as the department is concerned with the welfare of the operative employees. Occasionally it may be directly under the management. There is much scope of social work functionary in industrial organization and when the problems are concentrated on the shop floor level, the main emphasis on the social case work method. Social work traditionally has worked with disadvantaged persons. Counselling and therapy with the individuals and families are the services needed in business and industry. An effort is made to help individuals, employers and often, their families to understand their problems in social relationships, face the problems, consider alternatives and move ahead with action that seems best of their solutions. Programmes connected with the family life and community life of the workers, there is a need of having skills in group work and community organization methods. So these three core methods of social work practice help the social worker to function at three levels (i) preventive (ii) developmental (iii) curative (Sinha, 2007).

Scope of Industrial Social Work as described by Desai (2002) is not confined to employee management, however it asks social workers to work in close association with human resource development for community organization, cultural interventions, organizational development, organizational enhancement, and even corporate philanthropy in modern times. Knowledge of human relations and psychology with ever growing challenges at workplaces has made this practice even more challenging than ever before. The labour officer of yesteryears evolved into the personnel officer. The growth actually began with the paternalistic welfare approach in the 1930s. Since then, its emphasis shifted to the field of industrial relations and labour management of the 1940s and 1950s.

Social work in industry started nearly eighty years ago, nonetheless it is still considered a relatively new concept. Many of the aspects of industrial social work function with the overall organisational structure of an enterprise. If we really trace the evolution, it all started with the European seminar on 'Personnel Social Work' held in Brussels in September 1960 internally. The report of the seminar emphasized the term 'personnel social work' and not the term of 'Industrial Social Work' because it envisioned the scope of social work profession beyond the industries and factories that evolved during industrial revolution. Since then, various definitions and interpretations have been given to the term industrial social work. However, the sphere is still in the process of defining and conceptualizing itself across the globe. In India, however this practice started little early than it started in the western world.

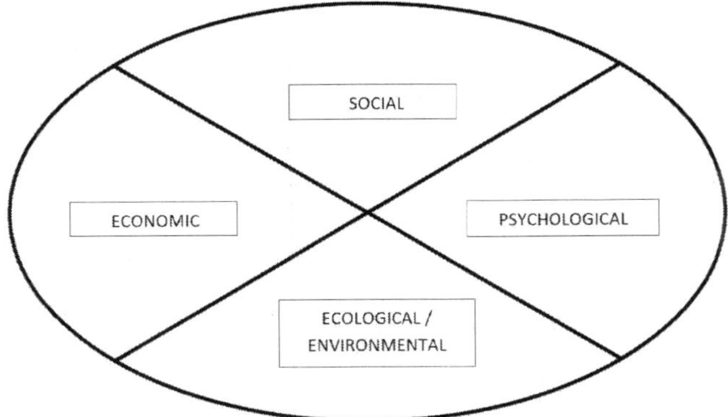

Figure 1: Dimensions of Industrial/Occupational Social Work

The expanded clinical perspective of occupational social work is based on ecological and eclectic orientation, with a conviction that social workers. to be effective in the work setting, must be receptive to acquiring new knowledge and skill (Balgopal,1989). Many social workers use the term occupational social work synonymously with industrial social work. According to Smith (1989), occupational social work offers practitioners the opportunity to rationalize and humanize contemporary society by increasing responsiveness of organizations to equal opportunity, and respect for their employees.

BRIEF HISTORICAL ACCOUNT OF INDUSTRIAL SOCIAL WORK

The second phase of the industrial era in Europe falls in the period between the World Wars (1918-1939). It was a significant period in relation to employee's welfare. The phase was marked by increasing recognition of the human factor in industry, as was evident from the fact that the worker became a subject for studies in the industry. A major breakthrough was achieved with the series of experiments conducted by the Hawthorne Works in Chicago from 1926 onwards. The experiments believed that if the employees were satisfied with their '*work situation*', they were likely to reciprocate by being more productive and efficient for the employer industry. Consequently, the facilities relating to housing, work holidays, employment of apprentices, wages, etc. became increasingly important. During the era issues pertaining to social legislation in the area of health and safety, industrial relations, works committees, social insurances, etc. assumed all the more importance. Thus, in Europe, the concept of industrial social services began to be gradually integrated into the national social policy hereafter.

In Britain, the concept of social work in industry has been virtually non-existent. It was only during the Industrial Welfare Movement between 1890–1913 that there was a brief spell of welfare activities undertaken by enlightened employers. The after-effects of the Industrial Revolution on the social conditions of industrial workers called for immediate action. Consequently, enlightened managements employed female welfare workers on their staff to look after the problems of the women and children working in the factory. The Quaker Firms of Rowntress and Cadbury's took the lead in this movement (U.N.1961).

World War II brought in its wake dislocation in industries and consequent problems of unemployment. The need for a social worker was greatly felt at this point. But with the ensuing stability in the socio-economic condition, the social workers in industry were left with no relevant functions. There were only a few practising industrial social workers after World War II, as there was a federal cut back in their services. It was not until the 1960s and 1970s that the profession and the schools of social work across the globe began to take a more serious look at industry and business as an arena of social work practice. The Industrial Social Welfare centre at Columbia University's School of Social Work was developed in the early 1960s, which gave field placement opportunities for students in Union settings. In the late 1960s, the trend was followed by the Boston College, Wayne State and Hunter College of Social Work and the University of Utah, all in USA.

Table 1: Significant Milestones in Evolution of Industrial Social Work Practice/Occupational Social Work Practice

Development/ Event	*Year*
The International Federation of Social Workers (IFSW) undertook the responsibility to explore the different directions in which social work personnel were required to be developed and groomed	1967
Technical Assistance Office of the United Nations, Geneva, and IFSW organised two International Study Groups on the functions and working methods of the personnel social workers. The study groups met in September 1967 at Zurich (Switzerland) and in March 1959 at Dortumnd (West Germany)	1957 and 1959
The report of these study groups forms the basis for the development of the concept of industrial social work; they were the outcome of European Seminar on Personnel Social Work, held under the European Social Welfare Programme	1961
The Seminar reviewed the earlier report and reiterated the need for personnel social work and highlighted its place by emphasizing that, 'the concept of personnel social work should be embodied in the personnel policy of the enterprise, regardless of whether the function is part of the organisational structure of the enterprise or is carried out by an outside agency.	UN declaration 1961
The Council on Social Work Education (CSWE) sponsored a meeting with social work practitioners, educators, representatives of organised labour and industry to discuss curriculum implications for future development in the field of social work in industry.	1976 (May)
One hundred (100) industrial social work practitioners from across the U.S. and Canada met in New York City to explore the nature of industrial social work practice and came to the conclusion that social work in industry had a very promising future and was uniquely suited to the labour and industrial setting, given the profession's commitment to a 'social functioning' perspective as opposed to a health versus illness approach common to other helping professions	1978 (June 7)
The joint project of the CSWE and NASW on social work in industrial settings has been a hallmark in the development of the domain of Industrial Social Work	March 1977-Oct.1979

The field of industrial social work is still evolving in India as well as other parts of the world. It is not yet defined and there no singular model of practice to guide the profession. Desai (1991) presents a very interesting account of development and evolution of industrial social work in India. As already mentioned, that in the initial years of its evolution this branch of social work was only limited to industrial worker's welfare, which

Table 2: Important Milestones of Evolution of Industrial Social Work in India

Milestone	*Year*
The first official administrator joined the ranks of the industrial management cadre of the Royal Commission on Labour was under the chairmanship of J.H. Whitley. This commission was appointed to inquire into and report on the conditions of labour in the industrial undertakings and plantations in British India on health, efficiency and standard of living of the workers.	1931
Provision of welfare officer in Factories Act was made.	1948
The nomenclature 'Personnel function' emerged	1950s (West) 1960s (India)
Companies Act 1956 was amended and it was made mandatory to for all for-profit public enterprises to shell out at-least 2% their profit for the welfare of the people	2013

with the passage of time became quite wide to include almost everything under the sun dealing with anything that leads to productivity and meaning engagement of the employees at all kinds of workplaces. It is noteworthy that even in the countries like United States of America and UK it is acknowledged that Industrial Social Work is relatively new domain which started growing only after 1950s and 1960s.

Desai and Dole (1979) observed that 'Social work maintained a link between the management, labour and the community resources such as community councils, boards and national fund-raising drives' Desai (1991) explicitly mentions that in India, Factories Act 1948 was instrumental in growth and development of Industrial Social Work Practice as the act then required at least one labour welfare officer wherever in industrial labour force of 500 or more is deployed in one premises. This statutory requirement created a huge demand of trained and skilled personnel who can handle the welfare issues as per the law. This particular legislation also necessitated a lot of welfare measures to be ensured and personnel administration at factory level. To meet this sudden requirement labour welfare officers in the country, Tata Institute of Social Sciences (TISS), Mumbai was asked by the government of the day to train such individuals who can play this role effectively. Eventually under the visionary leadership of Mr DM Vasudev Moorthy, the TISS started to train individuals in this domain. By that time such education was not so popular in US and UK as well. In the due course TISS gained name and fame because of industrial and personnel management training and became a world recognised institution to provide training and education in this domain and became pioneering instruction across the globe.

It has finally developed as a comprehensive function in the 1960s, a function, which has come to be integrated with the management function in an organisation. And, in the 1980s, it emerged as an Human Resource Development(HRD) function with still wider implications. This has resulted in the recognition of human resources as a great asset to the organisation. the concept of labour has itself undergone an evolution; referred to as 'labour' in the beginning and then 'employee'. The term 'personnel' came to be widely used to denote the work force of an organisation in the 1960s and 1970s. Today, they are collectively referred to as the 'human resource' of the organisation.

Another and final breakthrough appeared in this space when under Corporate Social Responsibility (CSR) umbrella all the companies were made to compulsorily allocate at least 2% of their profit to social welfare activities if their profit and turnover meets a statutory criterion. Please note that activities under CSR is not necessarily industrial social work, however engaging employees for these CSR activities which makes them feel fulling and engaged is kind of industrial social work so due to surge if CSR activities post 2013 in India, the size, volume and arena of industrial social work has expanded and evolved in perception.

Review Questions

(a) Write a note on history and evolution of Industrial Social Work in the Europe and USA.
(b) Discuss the evolution of Industrial Social Work in Indian context.
(c) Briefly discuss the concept of Industrial Social Work.
(d) Briefly describe the scope of Industrial Social Work.

MAJOR ROLES AND INTERVENTION OF INDUSTRIAL SOCIAL WORKERS: TRADITIONAL VIEW

A social worker can help the employees to overcome their problems and continue to function as productive workers. According to M.M. Desai, the professionally trained social worker can develop his/ her programmes at the levels of (a) preventive, (b) developmental, and (c) curative.

Preventive Roles

1. Informal educational programmes aimed at enlightening the workers on issues pertaining to work life like industrial safety, functional literacy, saving habits, social security, etc.
2. Promoting the use of health and medical programmes for workers and their families (health check-ups, inoculation campaigns, family planning, informative sessions on nutrition, low-cost diets, childcare, etc.

3. Personal and environmental hygiene, etc.

Developmental Roles

Industrial Social Workers have the role of developing people through various forms of activities these include refreshing, recreational, income generating activities and the likes of which employees can have enriching and fulfilling experiences in life. Such engagement at workplace gives another meaning to their professional lives. Developing recreational programmes like library services, prime sports gatherings, various skill competitions, exhibitions, film shows, etc., celebration of cultural festivals, supplementary income programmes, hobby classes, vocational guidance programmes, etc.

Curative Roles

Curative programmes are aimed at handling problem situations faced by the individual worker by helping them to make maximum use of their own potentials and the resources offered by the industry as well as the community. Counselling to the individual employees and their families can be given for problems, such as alcoholism, indebtedness, and absenteeism, etc. The counselling services can be coupled with concrete assistance. The examples of such concrete assistance could be: (1) Securing medical help within or outside the industrial facility; (2) Planning of the family budgets; (3) Providing necessary help in obtaining funds to the family members; (4) Looking for employment for worker's dependents in trying times of the workers; and (5) In case required referring the worker/his dependents to welfare agencies in the community like child guidance clinic, marriage counselling bureaus, alcoholic anonymous groups and the like, depending on the availability of such facilities

Social work skills can be actively used for preventing problems from happening, as also for enriching the life of the workers and their families. When done so, we say that effective intervention is made by the Industrial Social Workers. The intervention may be in the form of (a) proposing a new job design, (b) planning and organizing the services at all three aforementioned levels, i.e. *preventive, developmental* and *curative* levels. This requires a basic study of the organization. It is through an open and sensitive approach, rather than a predetermined blue print that the intuitive social worker can positively integrate the social work objectives with the management objectives. However, the experience of seasoned industrial welfare practitioners suggests the scope of social work in business and industry, depend upon three major factors: (1) the attitude of the management; (2) the quality of the goodness of bet between needs of business and the extent to which these needs can be addressed by social work; and (3) cost effectiveness of the services provided.

Did You Know?

India was the only country in the world to create this statutory position against the background of the social reform, social service and social movement during the 19th century.

MAJOR ROLE OF INDUSTRIAL/ OCCUPATIONAL SOCIAL WORKERS: CONTEMPOARY VIEW

According to the study group organised by the Netherlands Government, a qualified social worker is necessary in an enterprise for the following reasons: (1) their specialised training in the understanding of human problems, ability to consider the human personality as a whole; (2) their knowledge of the conditions of work; (3) their knowledge of the worker's life; (4) their knowledge of the resources of the community; (5) their professional secrecy; and (6) their capacity for co-operation. The role of Social Worker has traditionally been assigned to the Personnel/Welfare functionaries in India. In fact, the social work profession, to a great extent, owes its popularity and growth to the acceptance of social work training as a necessary preparation for personnel and welfare work in India. A comparison with other countries reveals that the importance attached to the social worker's role in the personnel field is much higher in India than elsewhere.

The role of industrial social worker is very effective when done in prevention mode for example, detection and prompt treatments may prevent some workers from becoming serious casualties at industrial facilities. Social work intervention in industrial sector can be at micro and macro level. At micro level, the social worker can provide treatment to the worker and his family, employer and union members. Social workers must extend help that may be given in relation to problems related to work, self and others around them, such as job performance, job satisfaction, absenteeism, conflict situations, etc. Further problems, such as anxiety, depression, phobia, mental disturbance, substance abuse, marital and family conflict, may also be attended to. At the macro level however, it can be organizational intervention where the social worker can provide individual and group consultation to supervisors and managers at all levels regarding understanding of human behaviour.

There are a number of trained social workers in our country who have been absorbed into industry, mainly in the personnel and labour welfare departments. In the West, Industrial Social Work has developed along different lines, where full time Social Workers are appointed in Industries to carry out the social work role and they are not burdened with other duties of Industrial relations and personnel administration, as is the case in India. India is the only country in the world where there is a statutory requirement that certain specified types of industry must employ trained social workers for labour welfare. The posts of welfare officers in industry were created by the government under the Factories Act 1947. These functionaries are paid by the individual managements, but their qualifications, method of recruitment; duties are prescribed by the government through rules framed for the purpose. Nearly all states require that the welfare officer should be a graduate of an approved University recognized by State Government for their training. Most of these institutions are schools of social work.

The field of labour welfare and personnel management has found its place on the curriculum of the schools of social work as one of the specializations and a large number of students opt for it. For their training, the students are sent to various factories where they are expected to learn about the working and functions of the labour/ personnel department. They are also expected to apply their social work knowledge and skills, while tackling the labour problems. Today many institutions have sprung up, which offer degree diploma in labour welfare and personnel management, still, we find that those having social work training are preferred over others, which indicates that the benefits of social work training are recognised by the employers. There is still not a clear-cut and well-defined role for the social worker in the industrial sector. The present scenario throws up a confused picture where the role of the social worker varies according to the size of the industry and the perception of social worker's contribution by the owners of the enterprise. In most undertakings, social workers are seen as performing tasks assigned to a personnel manager or officer, such as recruitment, selection, wage and salary administration, etc. Here the social worker has become more of a personnel man. In smaller undertakings, it is usually a one man show where he is partly a personnel man, partly a social worker, partly a timekeeper and, at other times, a public relations officer, trying to juggle with the wide-ranging responsibilities.

As of today, it is only in handful of organisations that the social workers perform a pure social work role, wherein they are appointed as industrial social workers. Their role here, irrespective of their designation, is to assist the individual and groups in their adaptation to the organisation in particular and society in general, by removing, as far as possible, the inner and outer obstacles to this adaptation. They help the employees to develop within an organisation in a healthy manner, paving way for an effective organization. However, today, a trained social worker is an asset to an organization.

EMERGING ISSUES OF INDUSTRIAL/OCCUPATIONAL SOCIAL WORK

Today's workforce is considerably different from what it was even a decade ago. The current workforce is much more diverse. Women are increasingly coming into the workforce, because of technological and economic changes. Today workers are no longer content to be just economic tools in the production of goods and services. They want to be treated as human beings who have hope, aspirations, anxieties and fears that need to be handled. They want challenge and personal growth through work. They want to be treated as equals. However, the workers' rising expectations and some perceived unresponsiveness of the industry to these expectations have resulted in increased frustration with and alienation from the workplace. Employees experience at least one major career shift before they retire. Being terminated from job for reasons other than job performance will also become much more common as global changes that affect the work place continue to occur. The changing nature of work force is leading many emerging issues in the work place some of them are discussing below.

- **More women in workforce:** For women and their families, such as patterns of child rearing and affordable child care, flexible working hours, transportation to and from work, and job training, in addition to salary, benefits, pensions, and compensation are crucial. For their employers, absenteeism and tardiness, sick leave, and employee stress become factor no matter how competent and hard working their employees are. Other some issues are decreased flexibility of the workforce as two-career families become less willing to relocate: fewer distinctions between male's and female's jobs and wage rates, increase in part time, flexible, and stay at-home jobs and decrease in total work hours per employee.
- **Aging workforce:** The two important trends in the global scenario are that the younger worker group is decreasing while older workers are the fastest growing group. The increased aging of the workforce and of society is likely to have some impacts (Sinha, 2007). A more experienced, stable, reliable workforce should increase productivity. A continuing decrease in the number of workers available to assume responsibility for those not in the workforce will have long-term implications for areas such as social security. The labour market for younger workers may actually tighten as companies initially forced to rise such as increased automation. Those aging workers who leave or lose jobs will have a difficult time seeking new jobs at their previous levels.

- **Increased Stress at workplace:** Most standard textbooks in medicine attribute anywhere from 50% to 80% of all disease to stress-related or psychosomatic origins. One of the main sources of stress is job pressures. Particularly any job has stresses. The list of stress- related illnesses includes bronchial asthma hypertension, headache, migraine, insomnia, constipation, cancer etc. Stress is also one of the causes of emotional disorders. Employers are becoming increasingly aware of the cost of stress to employees and to their businesses, absenteeism, law productivity, short- and long-term stress related illnesses, job dissatisfaction, marital difficulties and emotional disorders. Violence in work place -Work place violence is an increasing problem identified by employers and their employees. Some employees are bringing their family problems to work, or are harassed by other often family members, while at work.
- **Sexual Harassment:** It is another concern in the work place, both to employers and their employees. The costs of sexual harassment can be extremely damaging both emotionally and from a cost perspective to employers. It is difficult to obtain accurate figures about the actual incidence of sexual harassment in the workplace, because half of all people who are harassed never report it. They may fear that they will lose their jobs or experience other retribution.
- **Occupational Health Hazards:** A number of occupational health hazards affect workers. These include on-the-job accidents and work-related illnesses including job stress. Accidents and other on-the-job health hazards create additional stresses for employees and their families. Workers in chemical plants who contract cancer and miscarry or produce children born with congenial deformities, and construction workers who may be heart by heavy equipment place themselves and their families in jeopardy.
- **Work-life balance:** Researchers in one recent study found that increasing numbers of individuals are giving importance in personnel or family time than their work and salary. It is indicated that they would turn down promotion if it is seriously affected the amount of time they could spent with their families. Mental health of employees and families- Increasingly, employees, and their families lacking a support system and unable to cope with life's pressure, succumb to divorce, family violence, substance abuse, suicide, other health or emotional problems. For workers and families facing such pressures, however, options are often limited. Many individuals work because they have to in order to support their families. Women workers who work different hours than other family members, balancing work and family pressure is still difficult.

- **Issues of working parents:** Millions of children under the age of 14 are without adequate child care while their parents' work. Often, infants and toddlers are left sleeping alone at night by working parents. It is not unusual for children ages 4 and 5 to be left at home lonely for long period of time, and children as young as 8 are often left in charge of much younger children. Increases youth related delinquent acts, as well as increases teenage pregnancy, are being attributed partly to the lack of supervision provided to adolescents while their parents' work. Care of elderly parents is another problem increasingly affecting employees. Women caring for dependent adult's report health problems, emotional disorders, and problems with absenteeism and tardiness. Many middle-aged women are projected to have dual responsibilities for dependent children an elderly parents, a situation described as the 'sandwich phenomena' (Sinha, 2007).

Did You Know?

According to many scholar's Occupational social work is the specialized field most suited to address the needs of workers under stress at the work place, yet it has been in decline in the United States since the 1990s as per the employment statistics released by the government. The factors contributing to this decline are (a) availability of alternative care institutions, (b) managed care, (c) the dominance of the advanced clinical social work license, and (d) the lack of a social work presence in occupational stress effectiveness research.

OPPORTUNITIES OF INDSTRIAL SOCIAL WORK

Industrial Social Work or any other branch of social work doesn't work in isolation. It has certain intersections with many other branches of social work. That is where deep opportunities lie and we really get to know the real scope, arena and opportunities for particular kind of social work practice. For example, Gerontology address issues such as pension adequacy, advancing programmes in pre- and post-retirement counselling, increasing services to retirees and assisting with job re-entry and training and retraining for old workers, all of which relate directly to the work experience of older people (Crawley, 1992). The Gerentlogical method of enquiry, which examines the inter relationship of social, psychological and physical changes in aging can provide social workers with a realistic, dynamic perspective and a deeper understanding of the older workers.

In spite of obstacles and seeming hindrances, there are bright prospects for social work practice in business and industry. With the increasing realization on the part of the employers of their social responsibility and obligations, the value of social work and the contribution it can make is bound to grow. In the Indian context, the social work welfare/ personal officers, who are also professional social workers, are largely carrying out the social worker's role in industry. However, increasingly, the need for full time social workers is being felt and in big and progressive units, they have already found a place for themselves. Once full-time social workers come to be accepted in Indian industries, the social work role, which is being presently carried out by welfare/personnel officers with social work training, will be given its legitimate place in industry.

Further, social work is no longer only confined to industry, but is seen as extending its expertise to all occupations and work situations; hence the term occupational social work is finding favour with the experts. This is so because today, employees, irrespective of the setting, are beset with many problems, which can interfere with their personal effectiveness and overall productivity. It is a challenge to the social work profession to apply its skill and knowledge to these non-conventional fields in new and innovative ways to increase productivity and organisational effectiveness and, thereby, create a niche for itself.

Today, more and more women are joining the workforce, posing new equations at home and at workplace. In the changing scenario, both men and women have to find new ways of adapting. The stress on them and their children can be tremendous, making mental health at workplace a serious issue. Consequently, many companies will have to develop programmes of childcare, paternity/maternity leave policies, flexitime and so on. According to Berry (1990), the world of work today poses various challenges. For old workers, it means learning and accommodating to new entrants with different styles, concerns and values. For new entrants, it means growth, learning and developing the persistence needed to achieve full membership.

Today, there are emerging areas of practice for social workers, which have been recognized in the West and are gradually making a conduit to the Indian Business and Industry. To mention a few, Employee Assistance Programs (EAP), Employee Relations (ER), Organisation Development (OD), Dislocated Worker's Services, Plans and Benefits Management (DWSPBM), Employee Volunteering Programmes (EVP), Employee Welfare Programs (EWP) and Employee Voluntary Initiative Programs (EVIP) are quite in prevailing ones. A person's self-esteem, sense of well-being and prosperity is, in some way, linked to his job. Today, we are into tumultuous times of job upheavals, economic restructuring, competition downsizing, which have weakened the 'social safety nets' around us. Workers in all settings are faced with multitude of problems, which come in the way of their effective performance and overall productivity.

The skills, techniques and knowledge of social work, which has so far been offered to the poor and destitute, can be put to great use in enhancing the ability of human resources to improve the world of work. Counselling, group work, research, policy analysis, program development and planning, need assessment and other such social work techniques can be used by business and industry to increase productivity and overall organisational effectiveness. Social work integrates into it, knowledge and practice insights from sociology, education, clinical psychology, labour relations, organisational behaviour, etc., which can provide answers to the problems of workplace. The future of social work in Industry is promising, provided the profession gears itself to the challenges and new demands of the world of business and industry. Social work educators would need to upgrade their educational program for industrial social work and practice with sound business principles.

CHANGING SCENARIO OF INDUSTRIAL SOCIAL WORK IN INDIA: RECENT LABOUR REFORMS IN INDIA

The labour scenario is the milieu in which Industrial Social Work operates and therefore it is imminent to know the recent labour reforms that are launched in India. For ensuring workers' right to minimum wages, the Central Government of India has amalgamated *4 laws in the Wage Code, 9 laws in the Social Security Code, 13 laws in the Occupational Safety, Health and Working Conditions Code, 2020* and *3 laws in the Industrial Relations Code*. A social worker must be aware of similar labour reforms and laws in its working environment that changes from country to country and state to state. These four Labour Codes directly influence workers of both organized and unorganized sector in India. Now, Employees' Provident Fund (EPF), Employees' Pension Scheme (EPS) and coverage of all types of medical benefit under Employees' Insurance will be available to all workers.

These codes have been developed by amalgamating laws.

Table 3: Key Highlights of the New Labour Codes in India: A Big Paradigm Shift for Industrial Social Work Practice

Labor Code	*Key Highlights*	*Changes Occur Due to*
Wage Code (2019)	Review of minimum wages in every 5 years for the labour; Guarantee of timely payment of wages; Equal remuneration to male and female workers; workers of unorganized sector to get these rights; To remove regional disparity in minimum wages the provision of floor wage has been introduced; skill level and geographical area to determine the minimum wages; wage ceiling from Rs. 18000/- to Rs. 24000/- under payment of wages act from 2017 onwards;	Amalgamation of 04 laws

Labor Code	*Key Highlights*	*Changes Occur Due to*
Social Security Code (2020)	Through a small contribution, benefit of free treatment is now available under hospitals and dispensaries of ESIC; ESIC now to be opened for the workers of all sectors along with the workers of the unorganized sector; Expansion of ESIC hospitals, dispensaries and branches upto district level. This facility to be increased from 566 districts to all the 740 districts of the country; Even if a single worker is engaged in hazardous work, he would be given ESIC benefit; Opportunity to join ESIC for platform and gig workers engaged in new technology; Plantation workers to get benefit of ESIC; Institutions working in hazardous area to be compulsorily registered with ESIC; Benefit of pension scheme (EPFO) to all workers of organized, unorganized and self-employed sectors; Creation of social security fund for providing comprehensive social security to the unorganized sector; Requirement of minimum service has been removed for payment of gratuity in case of fixed term employees; Employees engaged on fixed term to get same social security benefit as permanent employees; Employees engaged on fixed term to get same social security benefit as permanent employees; Creating a national database of workers of unorganized sector through registration on Portal; Employers employing more than 20 workers to mandatorily report vacancies online; A Universal Account Number (UAN) for ESIC, EPFO and Unorganized Sector workers; Aadhaar based Universal Account Number (UAN) to ensure seamless portability	Amalgamation of 09 laws
OSHWC Code (2020)	Making life simpler for Inter-State Migrant Workers by (a) enabling to self-declare about their status on national portal, (b) making provision for providing travelling allowance annually to an Inter-State Migrant Worker for undertaking a to-and-fro journey to his native place, (c) making it mandatory for employers to conduct free annual health checkups for employees and providing them appointment letters; a worker engaged in building and other construction work in one State and moving to another State, benefit from the Building and other Construction Workers' Cess fund to be provided; Inter-State Migrant Worker would get ration facility in the State he is working in and the remaining members of his family would be able to avail of the ration facility in the State where they reside under one-nation one ration-	Amalgamation of 13 laws

* Under the Atal Bimit Vyakti Kalyan Yojna, a worker of organized sector who loses his job gets financial aid from the Government. This is a type of unemployment allowance, the benefit of which is admissible to the workers covered under the ESI Scheme

Labor Code	*Key Highlights*	*Changes Occur Due to*
	card initiative; mandatory helpline for interstate migrant workers; national database for inter-state migrant workers; better leave provisions; right to work in all types of establishments with safety and security with equal wages to women workers; enhanced maternity benefits for pregnant women workers and child care facilities for lactating mothers	
Industrial Relations Code (2020)	In case of job loss, a worker will get benefit under the Atal Bimit *Vyakti Kalyan Yojna**; At the time of retrenchment a worker would be provided 15 days' wages for re-skilling; Faster justice to the workers through the Tribunal; Workers disputes to be resolved within a year in the Tribunal; If there is no trade union with majority vote share then negotiation councils will be empowered to negotiate and make agreement with employer	Amalgamation of 03 laws

Review Questions

(a) Revisit the roles of Industrial Social Workers in India.

(b) Explain the opportunities for Industrial social workers in modern times.

(c) Describe how the turf for social work practice in Indian industries is changing as the changes in new labor code unfold.

MODELS OF INDUSTRIAL SOCIAL WORK

Straussner (1998) had developed a typology of FIVE models of occupational social work that may be useful in future for practice in the world of work.

1. **Employee Service Model:** This model gives importance to worker's micro level system in which employees and their families function. In this model social work functions include counselling employees their families, providing educational programmes to employees and their families providing educational programmes to employees, referring employees to other agencies, implementing recreational programmes, counselling with management regarding individual employee problems and training supervisors in recognizing and dealing appropriately with employee problem. The broad range of social, psychological, vocational and financial needs of workers and their families are meeting through direct service delivery in work place and labour sponsored settings.
2. **Consumer Service Model:** This model focuses in intervention at a broader level with in the same system, This model views employees as consumers and assist them in identifying needs and advocating to get these needs met. Social workers work with consumer's employees

in assessing their needs, developing strategies to best meet the needs identified, identifying and providing community resources to meet the needs, serving as a liaison between consumer-employee group and social services agencies and developing outreach programmes to meet employee needs.

3. **Corporate Social Responsibility Model:** Linkage of work organization resources to the wide range of community will play an increasing role in the activities carried out by occupational social worker in the future. Social workers broadened their activities within work organization to include the use of community organization skills in networking, needs assessment, and programme development within the community, in tandem with more traditional roles of advertisement and consultation in corporate giving endeavour. Social workers operating within the realm of this model work with the work place, community, and society in general in developing employees and their families.
4. **Employee/work Organization Service Model:** Changes in the workforce and structure of work organizations will require and expanded rate for social workers in the area of policy development and programme planning. social work consultation to organizations will increasingly be aimed at influencing work organization policy in the areas of health and safety practices, conflict meditation, benefit structures, training and development, and affirmative action.
5. **Work-related Public Policy Model:** Policy planning and analysis in the world of work has been identified as an area requiring further emphasis and development. The trends in the work place and among the work force identified the areas for social policy development in the world of work, including, training and educational needs within a given community or among the working age population as a whole, the effect of work place production processes an employee and community health, and the degree to which work organization human resources and health benefit policies meet the needs of a changing workforce and family structure.

In addition to these popular models of practice of Industrial Social Work propagated by Straussner (1998), we would also like to present three models of Industrial/Occupational Social Work, which are in line with the practice of social work in industrial settings. Based on experiences we propose the three models namely (1) WAD model, (2) VIVAD model and (3) VED model. Let us go little deeper in these models.

Some Emerging Models Observed: *WAD*, *VIVAD* and *VED*

These models are classified by the authors based on practice patterns of Industrial / Occupational Social Work in India in recent years. *WAD Model* of Industrial Social Work stands for *Welfare and Assistance for Development* during occupational social work. In modern times there are organizations which are offering the mix of employee welfare and employee assistance programmes towards facilitating the employees at the workplace. Many times it is observed that various Employee Welfare Programs (EWPs) and Employee Assistance Programs (EAPs) are part of the occupational social work. Thorough such programs organizations justify that they take care of employees. The limitation of this model is that it is confined to overall work environment only and it has no outreach to other stakeholders of the organizations like customers, co-creators, other beneficiaries and community members.

VIVAD Model of Industrial Social Work or Occupational Social Work stands for *Voluntary Initiatives and Vocational Assistance for Development.* Here, note that emphasis has been given to two points, (a) voluntary initiatives and (b) vocational assistance for Development. Voluntary initiatives count for all actions that are taken by an individual willingly without any pressure, external force or action. So, actions of pro-social behaviour like distribution of free food, clothes to needy etc., are performed by the people working at an organization, plant or factory/ facility of similar nature. As part of another strategy towards employee and other stakeholder welfare, an organization may encourage vocational assistance as well. Vocational assistance would be anything pertaining to helping employees grow and develop in them on skill or vocation. At times, encouraging vocational initiatives and providing voluntary assistance is also possible. Either way, it is going to be a combination of initiatives and assistance pertaining to voluntarism and vocational development. Such a model can be executed through Voluntary Initiative Program (VIPs) and/or Vocational Assistance Programs (VAPs).

VED Model stands for Volunteering and Engagement for Development. Many times it is observed that corporate houses and other organizations make employees volunteer for a pro-social / social welfare cause through some activity or event. Such activities are known as Employee Volunteering Programs (EVPs) and Employee Engagement Programs (EEPs). There is slight difference in VIPs and EVPs, as the previous one stands for self-motivated action on part of the employee and the later indicates the deployment of employees for voluntary activity or initiatives. Since ultimately every action and initiative in industrial social work is meant for overall development, all these models have development of all as their common objectives. These are models are imagined based on the pattern of practice of employee welfare, employee engagement, employee assistance, employee initiatives for development.

Challenges in Practicing Industrial Social Work

Practice of social work in business and industry is not without its share of hurdles and problems, some of which are enumerated below:

1. A social worker in industry has to accept the fact that her/his job would be limited by various factors. The limits could be professional by virtue of the job assignment, the organisational structure and by additional assignments.
2. Industry has not always defined its needs where a social worker can fit in as the logical resource person and the social workers have also not identified tangible areas of service that are significant to industry. Further, there is still not a proper understanding of the type of social work skills and knowledge, which are specifically transferable to Industry. A service becomes meaningful when there is a defined need and a defined service.
3. Many a time, the social workers may find themselves in a business that does not cherish the same values that social work stands for. The value orientation of social work is that the resources of the society must be used to bring about maximum opportunities for the individual, whereas that of business is profit.
4. Social workers today are appointed in large numbers as welfare/personnel functionaries in industry. As such, they are busier carrying out their legal and administrative tasks rather than pure social work tasks, hence they are not very much identified with social workers working in other fields. Many a times, they find themselves in a business, which does not value the same concerns that social work stands for. The varied duties specified for the welfare officers in Indian Industries, ranging from welfare and personnel to legal and conciliation responsibilities, indicate lack of uniformity and consistency. It also reflects the lack of clarity regarding social work in industry and the true role of a social worker in that environment.
5. The alignment of social work and personnel management, which was considered as a good combination once, as it gave a big boost to the growth of social work profession, is now considered a bane of the profession by many social work educators. The multiplicity of the tasks carried out by the personnel/welfare functionary does not allow him to carry out his social work role.
6. There are practical difficulties faced in the practice of the various social work methods and they may have to be adapted and defined to the peculiar needs of industry. Since the practice of these methods demands a lot of time and skill, the personnel functionaries, burdened

with numerous responsibilities, do not always give adequate time and emphasis to them. The management will ultimately judge the value of these methods to the extent they contribute to organisational objectives.

7. Social work in industry today will have to drastically change itself not only in term of the course content but in priority in use of its various well accepted methods which are generally practiced today in an integrated form. Because human resource is most important concern of every industrial organization at present and individualized attention is being given even to the personal problems of all the different kinds of human constituents of industrial establishments. Helping employees to maintain a quality life in the work place and at home is increasingly accepted as a goal of management and trade unions. In this context the social work profession is being solicited to deliver various services.

Review Questions

(a) Explain various contemporary models of practicing Industrial Social Work, e.g. WAD, VIVAD and VED.
(b) Explain the traditional models of Industrial Social Work
(c) Describe the modern-day challenges of practicing industrial work.

If we accept that business and industry are not merely profit oriented institutions but have social obligations as well, then social work does have plenty of scope in industry, as it can help it to achieve its social goals. Today, it is not only the production or sale of goods and services that is the managements' concern, but the social climate inside the organisation, the work structure and the mental health of the employees is of equal concern. Industrial social work can go a long way in improving the social climate and quality of human relations in an organisation. Human relations propose in general that productivity should be achieved by means of building and maintaining employee dignity and satisfaction rather than at the cost of these values.

Occupational social work can be involved in Macro practice (such as organizational interventions on behalf of employees group) as well as individual clinical activities. Occupational social work also will require collective action for job-related services that will improve and humanize the quality of work life, by establishing co-operative relationships with management and trade unions and simultaneously ensuring that the clinical social workers efforts are not perceived as co-opting union responsibilities (Zink, 1983). Occupational social workers have to translate knowledge about the occupational settings in to specific skills. Although social work practice includes various assessment, intervention and evaluation techniques, most of these techniques focus on the individual. These techniques need to be supplemented with new skills, advocacy on behalf of employees, negotiation with management, persuasion of bureaucratic decision makers, and interpretation of industrial legislation. Occupational social work needs to be designed, modified, strengthened further by using information regarding worker's personal problems (which add to the cost of company operation)job performance problems, extent of social services, major personal problems of service users, and programme outcome distribution (Yamatani, 1988).

SUMMARY

In social work, human dignity is always upheld and man is helped to integrate and adapt to his social environment. There is plenty of scope for social work practice in industry. This is because the larger the organisation, the more complex are the problems faced by human beings. In small organisations, employees have direct access to the managers and so many of their problems get sorted out early.

In larger organisations, there is no such opportunity for the employees, as everything has to go through proper channels and, thus, they have access only to the supervisors and junior managers, who are not decision makers. Relationships between employees and management are more formalized and availability of the management to the employees is reduced. Paternalistic attitudes towards employees and authoritarian kind of approach seem more prevalent in organisations.

This chapter summaries need, scope and changing concept of Industrial Social Work right from evolutionary perspective to modern times. While doing so, various roles of Industrial social workers have been discussed. Traditional and Contemporary models of industrial and occupational social work have been discussed. Challenges of Industrial Social Work practice and challenges before practicing industrial social work have also been highlighted. It has been shown as to how the scenario of labour welfare changes as new labour codes in India emerged.

GLOSSARY

- **CSR: Corporate Social Responsibility** – A business model where companies integrate social and environmental concerns into their operations and interactions with stakeholders.
- **DWSPBM: Dislocated Worker's Services, Plans, and Benefits Management** – A program that helps workers who have lost their jobs due to economic shifts or downsizing by providing services, benefits, and career planning.

- **EWP: Employee Welfare Program** – Initiatives aimed at improving the well-being, health, and morale of employees by providing various benefits and support services.
- **EVP: Employee Volunteering Program** – Corporate-supported opportunities for employees to volunteer in community service activities, fostering social responsibility.
- **IR: Industrial Relations** – The study and management of the employment relationship between employers, employees, and trade unions, focusing on conflict resolution and cooperation.
- **ISW: Industrial Social Work** – A branch of social work that addresses employee welfare and work-related social issues within industrial settings.
- **OSW: Occupational Social Work** – Social work services provided in the workplace to help employees deal with personal and job-related challenges, enhancing productivity and well-being.
- **OD: Organizational Development** – A planned, systemic approach aimed at improving the effectiveness, health, and performance of an organization through interventions and change management strategies.
- **VAP: Vocational Assistance Programs** – Programs designed to provide career counseling, training, and job placement services for individuals seeking new employment or career advancement.
- **VIPs: Voluntary Initiative Program** – A corporate program encouraging employees to voluntarily engage in community service or environmental sustainability initiatives.

TOP TEN TAKEAWAY POINTS

1. Industrial Social Work is that area of social work practice where the social worker is engaged in welfare, engagement, and development of the employees at the workplace using the specific knowledge and skills acquired for the said purpose.
2. There are social, psychological, economic and environmental (ecological) spaces for employee welfare in industrial social work.
3. A major breakthrough was achieved with the series of experiments conducted by the Hawthorne Works in Chicago from 1926 onwards. Later World War II created instigated need of social work at the work places.
4. In India the factories act of 1948 proved to be the game changer and it played a pivotal role in generating the requirement for industrial social workers.
5. Industrial Social Work evolved a great deal of being a space for labour welfare to modern human resources development. Most of the modern

human resource development practices are now part of Industrial Social Work alternatively known as Occupational Social Work.

6. Industrial Social Worker has to play a preventive, developmental and curative levels of roles.
7. Modern workplace has several challenges which amalgamate with each other and makes the practice of industrial social work more complex. These challenges are more women in workforce, aging workforce, increased Stress at workplace, sexual harassment at workplace, occupational health hazards, work-life balance, and issues of working parents.
8. CSR has enabled an environment full of opportunities for the Occupational Social Work in the form of EWP (Employee Welfare Programs), EVP (Employee Volunteering Programs), EAPs (Employee Assistance Programs), EVIP (Employee Voluntary Initiative Programs), VAP (Vocational Assistance Programmes), and VIPs (Voluntary Initiative Programs).
9. Straussner (1998) has given popular five models of Industrial Social Work Practice namely Employee Service model, Consumer Service Model, Corporate Social responsibility Model, Employee/work Organization Service model, and Work-related Public Policy Model. Extending the same logic this chapter three more models applicable on Occupational Social Work Practice namely WAD, VIVAD and VED.
10. Work place concept becoming more and more complex and flexible the practice of occupational social work is also getting complex and wide.

MULTIPLE CHOICE QUESTIONS

1. Industrial Social Work mainly deals with
   (a) Employees (b) Labours
   (c) Employees and Labours (d) None
2. Which of the act mentioned below was primarily responsible for growth of Industrial Social Work in India?
   (a) Factories Act 1948 (b) Indian Trust Act 1882
   (c) Societies Registration Act 1860
   (d) None
3. Who among the following has written about Occupational Social Work:
   (a) Ram Ahuja (b) Jesintha Paul
   (c) MM Desai (d) JC Bose
4. Industrial Social Work and Occupational Social Work are used interchangeably:
   (a) Sometimes (b) Always
   (c) Never (d) None of the above

5. Government of India has asked this institution to train manpower to meet the growing demand of Industrial Labour Welfare Officer which played key role later in the development of Industrial Social Work in India:
   (a) University of Bombay
   (b) Indian Institute of Management, Ahmedabad (IIM A)
   (c) Tata Institute of Social Sciences (TISS)
   (d) University of Delhi (DU)
6. Under the new labour reforms OSH code (2020) has been developed by amalgamating below mentioned number of laws:
   (a) 17 (b) 16 (c) 12 (d) 13
7. Under the new labour reforms Industrial Relations Code (2020) has been developed by amalgamating below mentioned number of laws:
   (a) 04 (b) 03 (c) 04 (d) 10
8. Creating a national database of unorganised sector workers at a national portal is a reform which is part of:
   (a) Wage Code (b) Social Security Code
   (c) OSH Code (d) IR Code
9. WAD model stands for:
   (a) Welfare and Assistance for Doers
   (b) Welfare and Assistance for Decoding
   (c) Welfare and Alternative Direction
   (d) Welfare and Assistance for Development
10. EVP stands for:
   (a) Employee Vigilance Program
   (b) Employee Volunteering Program
   (c) Employee Vacancy Program
   (d) Employee Victory Program

Answers

1. (c), 2. (a), 3. (c), 4. (b), 5. (c), 6. (d), 7. (b), 8. (b), 9. (d), 10. (b)

REFERENCES

1. Crawley, Brenda (1992),The Transformation of the American Labour Force: Americans and Occupational Social Work, *Social Work*, Vol. 37, No. 1, January.
2. Desai, M.M. (1979), Industrial Social work, Bombay, Tata Institute of Social Work.
3. Jacob, K.K. (1973), Personnel Management in India, Udayapur, SJC Publications.
4. Sehgal, Ranjana (2005), Social Work and Industry – Dilemma of Partnership, *Contemporary Social Work*, Vol. XXII, April.

5. Singh Surendra (2004), Social Work Industry – Issues and Challenging, *Contemporary Social Work*, Vol. XXI, April.
6. Sinha, Debotosh (2007), Aspects of Industry and Occupational Social Work, Delhi, Abhijeet Publications.
7. Sinha, D. (1998), Combating the Problems of Older Workers in Industries – Implication for Social Work, *Contemporary Social Work*, Vol. XV, April.
8. Smith, M.L. (1989).Social Work in the Work Place: An Overview, New York, Springer.
9. Straussner, Shulamith (1999), Occupational Social Work Today: An Overview. New York, The Haworth Press.
10. Yamatani, H. (1988), Client Assessment in an Industrial setting: A Cross Cultural Method, *Social Work*, 33(1), NASW.
11. Zink, V.M. (1983), Organizational Labour Role, In. E.Griffes (ed). Companies Act and amendments of 2013. Retrieved from Ministry of Corporate Affairs – Companies Act, 2013 (mca.gov.in), on June 2, 2023.

RECOMMENDED READINGS

1. Paul A. Kurzman, Ph.D., Sheila H. Akabas, Ph.D., Industrial social work as an arena for practice, *Social Work*, Volume 26, Issue 1, January 1981, Pages 52–60, https://doi.org/10.1093/sw/26.1.52
2. Bryan, Laura L. Koppes, and Andrew J. Vinchur, 'A History of Industrial and Organizational Psychology', in Steve W. J. Kozlowski (ed.), *The Oxford Handbook of Organizational Psychology*, Volume 1, Oxford Library of Psychology (2012; online edn, Oxford Academic, 18 Sept. 2012), https://doi.org/10.1093/oxfordhb/9780199928309.013.0002, accessed 26 Apr. 2023.
3. Forgey, M. A., He, K., & Cai, Y. (2023). Occupational Social Work: A Field of Practice in Need of Revival. *Families in Society*, 0(0). https://doi.org/10.1177/10443894231151315
4. Oxford Bibliographies of Occupational Social Work: Retrieved on June 02, 2023 from https://www.oxfordbibliographies.com/display/document/obo-9780195389678/obo-9780195389678-0094.xml"Occupational Social Work - Social Work - Oxford Bibliographies

CHAPTER–7

Social Work Intervention in Health Care System

Kasturi Sinha Ghosh

Asstistant Professor, Social Work, Netaji Subhas Open University
E-mail: kasturisghosh@gmail.com

Of all the forms of injustice, inequality in healthcare is the most shocking and inhumane.

– Martin Luther King

Abstract: *Health has always been a priority in our country. Since the beginning of civilization, people have been concerned about their health and medical care. According to evidence from numerous writings, India has made significant contributions to the fields of medicine and surgical training. Since the Vedic period Ayurveda, Siddha, and Unani were the traditional medical systems practiced in India. Indian medical system has always aimed to cure illnesses using a combination of science and compassion. We consider health as our basic human right and no one should be deprived of it. As social workers, it is our duty to ensure that all the community members have access to the health care system. This chapter will enable us to understand the role of social workers in promoting good health and making aware the community about their health rights and the role of government in augmenting health care system in our nation.*

Keywords: *Social Work Intervention, Health Care Service, Health Culture, Indigenous Medicine, Right-based Approaches*

Learning Objective

After reading this chapter, you will be able to:

- Understand the concept of health, health rights and health care system.
- Examine the role of social work in the promotion of health care service.
- Examine the initiatives and interventions of social workers and the government in augmenting health care facilities in our country.

INTRODUCTION

Health and health care has been a matter of concern since the ancient time, we have evidences from various scripts, that since the Vedic era, India has made remarkable contribution in the field of medicine and surgical training. Ayurveda, Siddha, and Unani are the traditional medicinal systems that existing in India since the ancient period. We get evidences about these medical systems in the Vedas and other scripts. Ayurveda, in particular refers to 'Science of life'. This medical system is believed to have a much user friendly approach and is supposed to be a highly interactive way of treating diseases. It educates people to become self–empowered and be responsible to keep themselves as well as their surroundings healthy, and thus promote positive health in the society. Along with this, the use of indigenous medicine has also been a very popular practice in ancient Indian culture. It has been an old heritage of using herbal plants for curing illness and promotes health particularly in Tribal and Rural parts of the communities. Since these plants could be easy accessible therefore the traditional and indigenous health care is still considered as the best alternative and an integral part of today's health care system. The indigenous people of some societies possess a broader knowledge about the existing ecological system and practice this knowledge quite successfully in treating diseases. We must therefore truly acknowledge the intense relationship between the tribal people with the forest. Healers or doctors were the elderly and experienced persons of the tribal community who were committed to work for the well-being of the people. It is a well-known concept that the Indian traditional system of medicine has gained a lot of importance in the global health care system and will continue to do so in near future also.

Thus the rich historical background of Indian Medical System suggests that, health has always been a priority in our country and Indian medical system has always intended to treat diseases with a scientific and humane approach.

HISTORY OF SOCIAL WORK IN HEALTH CARE SYSTEM

Social workers from the twentieth century got involved in health care system with the aim of providing services to the deprived people, or worked with the elderly as well as patients suffering with tuberculosis. The World Association of Social Work published standards for the provision of health care services in hospitals in 1977 and in 1980; the standards for social workers replaced the hospital standards. Between 1981 and 1982, the National Association of Social Work Board's further added some more agendas to the previous standard of care. The new set of agenda included the activities of social workers in the field of health care service for critically ill patient, disability. Social Workers by now concentrated much more on transferring the patient or refer him or her to home and in some cases even resolve the financial problems as well.

An ideal health care system must comprise:

1. Ethics and values

2. Health inequalities
3. Cultural competence
4. Privacy professionals
5. Knowledge
6. Assessment
7. Intervention and treatment
8. Leadership in social work
9. File management
10. Crisis intervention
11. Empowerment

CONCEPTS OF HEALTH AND HEALTH CARE SERVICE

The World Health Organization (WHO) defines health as 'a state of complete physical, mental, and social wellbeing and not merely the absence of disease or infirmity'. The World Health Organization has considered the primary health approach as the basis for an effective delivery of health care services.

According to WHO, Primary health care is:

- A philosophy for guiding health policy that is population focused
- A strategy for organizing health services that are integrated and needs based.
- A level of intervention which is delivered by a team
- A set of activities which include health promotion, prevention, early intervention, treatment and follow-up.

Let us look into the five key principles of primary health care:

- Public Participation
- Accessibility of services
- Appropriate Technology
- Interdisciplinary Collaboration
- Health Promotion

Today, increased attention is being focused on Human Resources Management (HRM) within the health care systems. Human resources is one of three principle health system inputs, while the other two major principles are physical capital and consumables.

Human resources, within the health care service, can be defined as the different kinds of clinical and non-clinical staff responsible for public and individual health intervention. As arguably the most important of the health system inputs, the performance and the benefits the system can deliver depend largely upon the knowledge, skills and motivation of those individuals responsible for delivering health services.

HEALTH: A BASIC HUMAN RIGHT

Right to health is recognized by many international human rights treatises. There is also a body of international standards and declarations relating directly or indirectly to the right to health. Right to life is a fundamental right guaranteed by Article 21 of the Indian Constitution. The Directive Principles mentioned in Part IV of the Constitution of India, imposes duty on the State to provide health care to its public. The Supreme Court and the various high courts through their judgements have recognized right to health as a fundamental right and have laid down the obligation on the state to provide medical health services. Everyone has the right to health. It relates to both the right of individuals to obtain a certain standard of health and health care, and the state obligation to ensure a certain standard of public health with the community generally.

It is the duty of the state to ensure both the health rights as well as entitlements. The right to control one's health and body, including sexual and reproductive freedom, and the freedom from interference such as torture, non-consensual medical treatment and experimentation are bracketed under the basic health rights. While entitlements include access to adequate health care facilities and services, as well as access to appropriate infrastructure to promote good health. State must also cater to the socio-economic determinants of health, such as food, water and sanitation, safe and health working conditions, housing, and address the problem of poverty.

The right to health is further closely related to with several different human rights issues, including the rights to food, water, housing, work, education, life, non-discrimination, privacy, access to information, the prohibition against violence.

The UN Committee on Economic, Social, and Cultural Rights provided detailed guidance to States regarding their obligations to respect, protect and fulfil the right to health. The Committee also noted that the right includes the following interrelated and essential features:

- **Availability:** States should ensure the provision of enough functioning of public health and individual health care facilities within their jurisdiction, arrange for safe water and sanitation facilities, and train medical professionals, and make sure to supply essential medicines.
- **Accessibility:** To enhance the accessibility to health, State must fulfil the four key elements, i.e. non-discrimination, physical accessibility, economic accessibility, and information accessibility. Health facilities and services should be accessible to everyone in the society without any discrimination, especially the most vulnerable. The facilities and services, as well as underlying determinants of health such as water

and sanitation amenities, must be within safe physical reach. Health care facilities, goods and services must be affordable for all, with any payment based on the principle of equity so that poorer households are not disproportionately burdened with health-related expenses. States must ensure that every person has the right to seek, receive and impart information on health, in balance with the confidentiality of medical information.

- **Acceptability:** Health facilities should be respectful of medical ethics and the culture of individuals and communities, as well as attentive to gender and life-cycle requirements.
- **Quality:** Health facilities should be scientifically and medically appropriate and of good quality. Among other things, this requires the provision of necessary medicines and equipment, skilled medical professionals, and adequate water and sanitation.

Review Questions

(a) Give a brief History of Social Work Intervention in the field of Health Care System.

(b) Develop an ideal Health Care system particularly for Rural Communities.

(c) Discuss the concept of Health as given by World Health Organization

UNDERSTANDING THE HEALTH CARE SYSTEM IN INDIA

India ranks 130 out of 189 countries as depicted in the Human Development Index Report 2018 issued by the UNDP. This shows that we still have to work hard to reach upto the mark in the health care sector .

Although India we know is one of the fastest developing economies of the world yet the essential aspects of primary health care like, promotion of food supply, proper nutrition, safe water and sanitation and provision for appropriate health information, is still largely ignored in this part of the world. People do not have access to healthcare services, and lack of provisions for essential medicines and paucity of doctors are other chalxlenging issue in the primary health care scenario.

Ensuring Health Rights through Social Work Intervention

Most of the Indian communities are deprived of adequate health conditions due to lack of preventative and treatment care. Majority of the families do not spend much of their earnings in addressing health emergencies. Unfortunately, families who are economically not sound, are at more risk of suffering from poor health conditions, as they do not have equal access to health services. Moreover, the Indian health care system is, under-resourced, and does not have the specialists and trained professionals

Did You Know?

- A report suggests that 469 million people in India do not have regular access to essential medicines. (Source: WHO)
- It has been recorded that 63 per cent of primary health centres did not have the facility of operation theatre and 29 per cent did not have any labour room, and the community health centres were short of specialists–surgeon, gynaecologists and paediatricians. (Source: India Spend, January 2018)
- In 2014, 58 per cent Indians in rural areas and 68 per cent in urban areas said they use private facilities for inpatient care, according to the 71st round of the National Sample Survey (Source: India Spend, January 2018)
- Different reports show that the rising out-of-pocket expenditures on healthcare is pushing around 32-39 million Indians below the poverty line annually.
- About 23 per cent of the sick can't afford healthcare because of poverty. (Source-Oxfam-India)
- Major cause of deaths in India is due to cardiac arrest and stroke. (Source: Oxfam-India)
- In Indians about 55 million are pushed into poverty in a single year due to unaffordable healthcare. (PHFI, 2018)
- A report states that. 33 out of 55 million fell under the poverty line due to expenditure on medicines alone. (PHFI, 2018)
- World Health Organisation (WHO), has reported that 1 7 million Indian deaths are caused by heart diseases.
- Approximately 5.8 million people in India die due to Diabetes, heart attack, cancer etc each year in our country. – Report by WHO

to meet these out of their reach, or it is too expensive. Further, relevant information about the welfare schemes and programs do not often reach such marginalized communities. Low literacy rates, limited access to resources, are also reasons for poor access to health care service in our community. But we know, Health is the basic Human Right and no one should be deprived of this Right. Every single person of our society is entitled to avail all the Health Care facilities that are available. However due to lack of proper information and awareness most of the people in our society remain deprived of this facility. Health care services are those services which are provided to individuals or communities by the health professions, for the purpose of promoting, maintaining, monitoring, or restoring good health in a right way.

Social workers who are engaged in Health Care Services, and work with individuals suffering from some health issues need to adopt some unique approaches and gain wide-range of knowledge to contribute in this field. The professionally qualified social workers involved in this sector must develop the required conceptual frameworks and skills needed to practice effectively as well as develop effective partnerships and collaboration with agencies to enhance the service delivery system

Social workers must apply the primary and secondary methods of Social Work as and when required and should follow the professional ethics while working in the community setting. The profession of social work working in this field are engaged in enhancing the social well-being of individuals, families, groups and communities. Social workers work to ensure the rights and dignity of all individuals and establish social justice in our society. Thus Social workers who are committed to work in the health care sector are responsible to assess, resolve, prevent or lessen the impact of socio-economic problems on the health of the people.

The social work profession has a history of interdisciplinary collaboration and a commitment to the importance of early intervention, prevention and health promotion. The Medical social work is a sub-discipline of Social Work. Which work in a hospital setting, outdoor clinic, community health centres, or in long-term rehabilitation centres. They work with patients and their families in need of psychosocial assistance. Social workers have to make assessments of the psychosocial functioning of clients and families and intervene as needed. The role of a social worker is to strike a balance in an individual's personal, family and social environment, in order to help people, maintain or recover their health and strengthen their ability to adapt and reintegrate in the communities. The various kinds of interventions may include connecting clients and their families to the required resources and extend support to the community such as preventive care; providing psychotherapy, supportive counselling, or dealing with trauma and helping the client to expand and strengthen their network of social supports. Professionals in this field have to simultaneously work with other disciplines like. medicine, nursing, physical, occupational, speech and recreational therapy. Social worker needs to collaborate with the medical professionals who usually treat patients. Social work in healthcare must be aware of the healthcare legislation and not solely by social laws

Social Workers Association Act & CASW Scope of Practice Statement has given the following key points to ensure Right Based Health Care Service:Ensure community development and community capacity building to understand the health rights.

- Promoting delivery of health care services in collaboration with other professions.
- Adoption of right legislation and social processes to enhance social and health services.
- Providing counselling and psycho-therapy.
- Assisting people to obtain their basic human needs.
- Conducting social research activities in this field.
- Generating awareness on the impact of social and environmental issues on health.

Role of Social Workers

The professionally qualified social workers are responsible for providing individuals, families, and groups with the required support needed to overcome their illnesses. These services involve dealing with the family caregivers, providing appropriate information to the patients and even carryout counselling sessions, along with other referrals services. They also provide care management or other crisis interventions in the communities to promote health, prevent disease, and remove barriers to access to healthcare. The health care professionals must maintain a strong 'person in environment' approach while working with individuals, families, groups and communities. Social workers working within the framework of health care service must make necessary links between the physical, social, emotional and economic impacts of health

A social worker must work with lots of empathy which is the core concept of social work discipline, as it leads to the development of a therapeutic relationship with the patients, and thus providing the basis for therapeutic change. Empathy is especially an important aspect for the social work profession. It may be noticed that empathy helps in better understanding of the patient's perspectives and feelings. It plays a crucial role in health care service as empathy is one of the most important skills which the health professionals must employ while working in this field. Social workers who work with empathy may bring about desired social change in the social environment as they may understand and feel compassionate towards the community people in need of health care service. Empathy enables the people to express their thoughts and problems without any hesitation. Thus empathy leads to the development of trust, augments therapeutic change and there is an improvement in the overall social functionality. All these efforts of Social Workers would be a big step towards ensuring the health rights of the people of our society.

The National Association of Social Workers (NASW) Standard for Social Work Practice in Health Care Setting (2016): We may go through the following eight Standards of Practice prescribed for Health Care Social Workers, which is in accordance with the guidelines of NASW, with the intention to strengthen the health care service, so that they may deliver their services efficiently:All medical social workers in the healthcare arena must practice in accordance with the social work code of ethics.

- Advocate for client's right to self-determination, confidentiality, access to supportive services and resources, and appropriate inclusion in decision making that affects their overall health and well-being.
- Encourage social work participation in the development, refinement, and integration of best practices in health care.

- Enhance the quality of social work services provided to clients and families in health care settings.
- Promote social work participation in system wide quality improvement and research efforts within health care settings.
- Provide a basis for the development of continuing education materials and programs related to social work in health care settings.
- Promote social work participation in the development and refinement of public policy at the local, state, federal, and tribal levels to support the well-being of clients, families, and communities served by the rapidly evolving U.S. health care system.
- Inform policymakers, employers, and the public about the essential role of social workers across the health care continuum.

We may further propose the following approaches to ensure quality health care within the society, as per the recommendation made by the 'Social Workers in Hospitals and Medical Centre's Occupation Profile' in (2017):

- To conduct health assessments and screenings on regular basis as well as making referrals for individual, family and or group within the community.
- Promoting education and general awareness in health care and hygiene among the community members. Aware the community about the various kinds of illness and available treatment options as well as possible outcomes of various treatments and also about the consequences of refusal of treatment.
- Extending support to the patient and their families to adjust with the hospital dynamics and understanding the emotional and social responses to the illness and treatment.
- Making the patient and family understand about the roles of the healthcare team. Helping the patients and their families to communicate comfortably with the members of the Health Care providers.
- Encourage the patients and families to make their own decision.
- Training the hospital staff to handle the patient's psychosocial matters.
- Coordinating patient discharge with a safety plan and planning by providing care to patient through navigation services;
- Arranging resources for finances, medications, medical equipment and other special needs services.

At last, we may say that one of the major roles of all social workers is advocacy for the interest of community people. Social workers can do this by making their representation, promoting change, speaking on behalf of the community people regarding their health rights and entitlements, assessing these rights and benefits, and finally securing social justice.

Review Questions

(a) How can we ensure Health Rights of the people belonging to weaker segment of our Society?

(b) Discuss the role of a Professional Social Worker in strengthening the health care service?

MODES OF HEALTH SERVICES PROVISION IN INDIA

In India, health care services are provided at three levels which may be categorized in the following way:

1. **House Hold and Community Level:** Services like empowering families to provide services like breast feeding, nutrition, home-based newborn care, diarrhea management (ORS Depot, Drug distribution centres, Fever treatment depots) Physical exercise etc. The service providers like ASHA & AWWs and Community Based Organizations and Non- Governmental Organization volunteers empower the mothers and family and community members through awareness creation and skill building support.
2. **Outreach Services:** These are services that are delivered at community level on periodical basis. These include monthly Routine immunization, Antenatal care, contraceptive distribution, prophylaxis against nutritional anaemia with daily/weekly supplementation of Iron and folic acid tablets to all pregnant mothers and all school going age children and half yearly supplementation of Vitamin-A and Anti-helminthic in endemic communities.
3. **Individual Care:** This is the most critical of the three modes of services, delivered at the above two levels by paramedical workers and at the facilities starting from PHC to the tertiary level care institutes. Though many studies suggest that the private sector meets two thirds (78 per cent) of OPD care and nearly half (60 per cent) of inpatient care but It is a fact that if one desegregates the proportions by socio-economic status and communicable diseases (TB, Leprosy, Malaria, Dengue, H1N1 and Chikungunya) majority of the population seek care in Public sector. The field observations during the implementation of Integrated Diseases Surveillance Project (IDSP-2004–10) supported by The World Bank has brought this fact out in 2005–06 for the first time. The outbreaks studied over last decade have confirmed this trend of reach and coverage by public health system services over the last decade.

Government Initiatives in Promoting Health Care Service in India

Indian Government has launched several National level programmes, to encourage people to adopt a healthy lifestyle and promote good hygiene practice. These programmes are designed to meet the health needs and health culture of the community people, making them much more Right-based in nature. As discussed earlier, Indians still have a lot of faith in the indigenous way of treatment.

Did You Know?

In the year 2014, the Indian Government established a separate Ministry of AYUSH, which deals with Ayurvedic, Yoga, Unani, Siddha and Homeopathy so that these systems of medicines may easily reach the masses.

Government of India launched another important programme in 2013, named 'National Health Mission'. Under the National Health Mission, the government has launched several schemes like:

1. **Reproductive, Maternal, Newborn, Child and Adolescent Health (RMNCH+A):** This programme primarily addresses the major causes of mortality among women and children as well as the delays in accessing and utilizing health care and services. It initiated the use of Score Card to track health performance, National Iron + , further address the issue of anemia across all age groups and the arrange for comprehensive screening and early detections and interventions for defects during the time of birth and deficiencies among children and adolescents.
2. **Rashtriya Bal Swasthya Karyakram (RBSK):** This is a crucial step to identify diseases and make early intervention for children from birth to 18 years to cover 4 'D's viz. Defects at birth, Deficiencies, Diseases, Development delays including disability.
3. **The Rashtriya Kishor Swasthya Karyakram:** The primary aim of this programme is adolescent participation and leadership, Equity and inclusion, Gender Equity and strategic partnerships with other stakeholders. Through this programme all adolescents in India would be enabled to realize their full capacity by making informed and responsible decisions about their health and well-being by accessing the health care services.
4. **Janani Shishu Suraksha Karyakaram (JSSK):** The Government of India has launched JSSK Programme to motivate pregnant women to go for institutional deliveries. It is an initiative with a goal that all the states would come forward to ensure that benefits under JSSK would reach every needy pregnant woman coming to government institutions.

5. **National AIDS Control Organisation (NACO):** This programme was taken up so that every person infected with HIV may have complete access to quality care and would be treated with due respect and dignity. This would be done in collaboration with NGOs, women's self-help groups, community-based organizations, and communities; NACO aims to improve access and accountability of the services. It is committed to building up an enabling environment so that those infected by HIV may play a key role to address the epidemic at state, district and grassroots level.
6. **Revised National TB Control Programme:** The programme is a state-run tuberculosis control initiative of Government of India with a vision of achieving a TB free India. The programme provides, various free of cost, quality tuberculosis diagnosis and treatment services across the country through the government health system.
7. **National Leprosy Eradication Programme:** This programme was taken up by the government for early detection through active surveillance by the trained health workers and to provide appropriate rehabilitation and leprosy care services.
8. **Mission Indradhanush:** Mission Indradhanush a Government-run programme , aims to cover maximum immunization in the country. It aimed to achieve at least 90 per cent immunization coverage by December 2018 and reach out to all unvaccinated and partially vaccinated children in rural and urban areas of India.
9. **National Mental Health Programme:** Government of India has implemented National Mental Health Programme to ensure the availability and accessibility of minimum mental healthcare for all in the foreseeable future.
10. **Pulse Polio:** The Pulse Polio programme is an immunization campaign established by the government of India to eliminate polio from India by protection all children under the age of five years against the polio virus by vaccination.
11. **The Pradhan Mantri Swasthya Suraksha Yojana (PMSSY):** The above mentioned programme is a very crucial programme which was announced with objectives of correcting regional imbalances in the availability of affordable/ reliable tertiary healthcare services and also to augment facilities for quality medical education in the country by setting up of various institutions like AIIMS and upgrading government medical college institutions.
12. **Rashtriya Arogya Nidhi:** The Government of India launched several programmes to address the huge income disparities, and support the financially backward class of the country. The most important

programme launched by the government is Rashtriya Arogya Nidhi which provides financial assistance to the people who are below poverty line and are suffering from life-threatening diseases, so that they may receive medical treatment at any government run hospital at a very low cost.

13. **National Tobacco Control Programme:** The National Tobacoo Control Programme was launched with the aim to bring about awareness and enhance consciousness about the harmful effects of the use of tobacco and promote effective implementation of the Tobacco Control Laws.
14. **Integrated Child Development Scheme Service (ICDS):** ICDS was launched on 2nd October 1975, with the intention to improve the nutrition and health status of children in the age group of 0–6 years. It laid the foundation for proper psychological, physical and social development of the child, effective coordination and implementation of policy among the various departments and to enhance the capability of the mothers to look after the normal health and nutrition needs through proper nutrition and health education.
15. **Rashtriya Swasthya Bima Yojana:** The above programme is an insurance programme run by the government for the Indian poor. It provides health insurance coverage to the unrecognized sector workers belonging to the below poverty line.

Review Questions

(a) Briefly write about the three levels of Health Care Services.
(b) What do you understand by 'Integrated approach of Social Work Intervention in the Health Care System'?
(c) In what ways can we make the Health Care system Right-based in nature?

SUMMARY

We may conclude by stating that the role of the health workers is really very important, in health promotion direction. Health services need to be expanded with a mandate which is sensitive and respects the cultural needs of our community people. This mandate should cater to the needs of individual, group and communities for a healthier life, and widely open the channels between the health sector and broader social, political, economic and physical environmental components. In recent years we have witnessed the beginnings of a paradigm shift, with the gradual introduction of new concepts, theories and frameworks into the health care system which would enrich the entire health care system and be more systematic and humane in nature.

Further an interdisciplinary approach in primary health care may improve the quality of service, and thus we may work more effectively with the people in need of health care All physicians, nurses, social workers, administrative staff, and patient care workers must abide by all policies to produce effective outcomes for the organization. The generalist social work interventions can be used to address issues such as early risk identification, issues related to rehospitalisation and disease management, particularly among vulnerable populations as it is much more scientific, humane and democratic in nature. It may be suggested that application of social work intervention which is much scientific and humane in nature can improve medical outcomes by addressing psychosocial and environmental aspects of chronic conditions such as cancer, hypertension, infectious diseases and depression. The noble profession of Social Work is thus responsible to enhance people's health, and empower the vulnerable individuals by enabling them to meet their primary health needs by filling up the gaps between the people with some disease and the health care facility available within the existing setting.

GLOSSARY

- **Health:** According to the World Health Organization, Health is 'a state of complete physical, mental and social well-being and not merely the absence of disease and infirmity'
- **Health Care Service:** Health Care Services consist of medical professionals, organizations, and ancillary health care workers who provide medical care to those in need. Health services serve patients, families, and the communities as a whole. They cover emergency, preventative, rehabilitative, long-term, hospital, diagnostic, primary, palliative, and home care. These services are centered around making health care accessible, high quality, and patient-centered.
- **Health Culture:** The Health Culture is broadly defined as one, in which good health and well-being flourish across geographic, demographic, and social sectors; fostering healthy equitable communities guides public and private decision making; and everyone has the opportunity to make choices that lead to healthy lifestyles.
- **Health Right:** Right to Health ensures that everyone should have access to the health care services whenever they need them, without suffering financial hardship. No one should get sick or lose their life due to poverty, or because they cannot access the health services they need.
- **Primary Health Care:** Primary Health Care is a whole-of-society approach to health that aims at ensuring the highest possible level

of health and well-being and their equitable distribution by focusing on people's needs and as early as possible along the continuum from health promotion and disease prevention to treatment, rehabilitation and palliative care, and as close as feasible to people's everyday environment.

- **Indigenous Medicine:** Knowledge about various materials and practices employed for treatment of disease in a specific region and popular in a localized area.
- **AYUSH:** AYUSH stands for Ayurveda, Yoga and Naturopathy, Unani, Siddha and Homeopathy and is the six Indian systems of medicine prevalent and practiced in India and in some of the neighbouring Asian countries.
- **National Health Mission:** The major components-Health System Strengthening, Reproductive-Maternal-Neonatal-Child and Adolescent Health and Communicable and Non-Communicable Diseases. The National Health Mission envisages achievement of universal access to equitable, affordable & quality health care services that are accountable and responsive to people's needs.
- **Social Work Intervention:** Social Work Intervention is a process when a social worker takes action or provides support to a client to help change behaviour or resolve an issue.
- **Rights-based Approach:** A rights-based approach develops the capacity of duty-bearers to meet their obligations and encourages rights holders to claim their rights.

TOP TEN TAKEAWAY POINTS

1. India has a made a remarkable contribution in the History of Medicine since the Vedic Period.
2. The World Association of Social Work published standards for the provision of health care services in hospitals in 1977.
3. India ranks 130 out of 189 countries as depicted in the Human Development Index Report 2018 issued by the UNDP.
4. Health is the basic Human Right and no one should be deprived of this Right.
5. In India the three level of Health Care services are- House hold & Community Level, Outreach Services and Individual Care.
6. Primary Health Care is a whole-of-society approach to health that aims at ensuring the highest possible level of health and well-being.
7. AYUSH comprises of Ayurveda, Yoga and Naturopathy, Unani, Siddha and Homeopathy.

8. Social Worker must work with lots of empathy which is the core concept of social work Profession.
9. The role of a social worker is to strike a balance in an individual's personal, family and social environment.
10. An inter disciplinary approach is required to the make the entire Health Care system Right-based and easily accessible.

MULTIPLE CHOICE QUESTIONS

1. Since when did social workers get involved in the health care system?
   (a) Twenty-first Century (b) Twentieth Century
   (c) Nineteenth Century (d) Eighteenth Century
2. Which System of Medicine is known as 'Science of life'
   (a) Unani (b) Yoga (c) Ayurveda (d) Siddha
3. Which of the following is not one of the five key principles of primary health care?
   (a) Women Empowerment (b) Accessibility of services
   (c) Appropriate Technology (d) Interdisciplinary Collaboration
4. According to WHO, approximately how many people in India die due to Diabetes, heart attack, cancer etc each year in our country?
   (a) 5.6 million (b) 6.8 million
   (c) 8.5 million (d) 5.8 million
5. Which Scheme under Government of India motivates pregnant women to go for institutional deliveries?
   (a) Rashtriya Arogya Nidhi
   (b) Rashtriya Swasthya Bima Yojana
   (c) Janani Shishu Suraksha Karyakaram
   (d) Mission Indradhanush
6. When did the World Association of Social Work published the standards for the provision of health care services in hospitals?
   (a) 1978 (b) 1977
   (c) 1975 (d) 1987
7. Choose the age group of children covered by ICDS:
   (a) 0–6 years (b) 6–12 years
   (c) 0–5 years (d) 6–10 years
8. When was the National Health Mission launched in India?
   (a) 2006 (b) 2009 (c) 2013 (d) 2010
9. Which level of Health Care services is committed to empowering families to provide services like breast feeding, nutrition, home-based newborn care?
   (a) Outreach Services (b) Household & Community Level
   (c) Individual Care (d) None of the above

10. In which year did the Indian Government established a separate Ministry of AYUSH?
    (a) 2015 (b) 2014 (c) 2013 (d) 2018

Answers

1. (b), 2. (c), 3. (a), 4. (d), 5. (c), 6. (b), 7. (a), 8. (c), 9. (b), 10. (b)

REFERENCES

1. Armstrong, L.J. (2019). Health, Rights, and Culture: Reflections on the meanings of the word 'rights" from a cross cultural health worker. *Christian Journal for Global Health*, 6(1), 64–69. https://doi.org/10.15566/cjgh.v6i1.269
2. Clarke, G.M., Conti S., Wolters, A.T., Steventon, A Evaluation of the impact of healthcare intervention using routine data BMJ 2019, 365:12239 doi 10.1136/bmj.12239
3. Lewis, M.E. (2020) The Effects of an Indigenous Health Curriculum for Medical Students. Med.sci.Educ.
4. Moudatsou, M., Stavropoulou, A., Philalithis, A., & Koukouli, S. (2020). The Role of Empathy in Health and Social Care Professionals. *Healthcare*, 8(1), 26. MDPI AG. Retrieved from http://dx.doi.org/10.3390/healthcare8010026
5. M.M. Pandey, Subha Rastogi, A.K.S. Rawat, 'Indian Traditional Ayurvedic System of Medicine and Nutrition Supplementation', *Evidence-Based Complementary and Alternative Medicine*, 2013. https://doi.org/10.1155/2013/37632
6. Okech, V., Neszméry, Štefan, & Mačkinová, M. (2020). 'Roles of Social Workers in Mental Health Care teams: A systematic review of the literature'. in *Proceedings of CBU in Social Sciences*, 1, 167–72.
7. Ruth, B. J., Sisco, S., Wyatt, J., Bethke, C., Bachman, S. S., & Piper, T. M. (2008). Public Health and Social Work: Training Dual Professionals for the Contemporary Workplace. *Public Health Reports* (1974-), 123, 71–77. http://www.jstor.org/stable/25682043
8. Trevillion, S. (2007). Health, Disability and Social Work: New Directions in Social Work Research. *The British Journal of Social Work*, 37(5), 937–46. http://www.jstor.org/stable/23722541
9. Venneri. E.(2016). Community Care and Professions: What is the Role of Social Work?', *International Journal of Applied Sociology*, Vol. 6 No. 3, 2016, pp. 33–37.
10. https://courses.lumenlearning.com/diseaseprevention/chapter/culture-beliefs-attitudes-and-stigmatized-illnesses/
11. https://www.casw-acts.ca/en/social-work-primary-health-care
12. https://www.escr-net.org/rights/health
13. https://www.oxfamindia.org/blog/15-healthcare-schemes-india-you-must-know-about?gclid=Cj0KCQiA3rKQBhCNARIsACUEW_YgHwLm8naj4dt_s1x_VqC92f3idoHTFKL13JsAZYa79-sRf_-4mWcaAtgUEALw_wcB

RECOMMENDED READING

1. Allen, K. & Spitzer,W. (2015). *Social Work Practice in Healthcare Advanced Approaches and Emerging Trends*. Sage Publication
2. Davidson, K. (1990). *Social Work in Health Car: A Handbook for Practice.* Routledge Publication
3. Lewis, M.E. *The Effects of an Indigenous Health Curriculum for Medical Students*. Med. Sci. Educ.
4. Shaista Sidiq Pandit, Nahidah Nazeer and Dar Nazir Ahmad (2018). *An Overview of Medical Social Work* 6 (Sep). 211-214] (ISSN 2320-5407).
5. www.journalijar.com

CHAPTER–8

Social Work Practice with Youth in India for Strong Nation-Building

Vishal Mishra and Rambabu Botcha

Assistant Professors, Department of Social Work, Rajiv Gandhi National Institute of Youth Development (RGNIYD), Ministry of Youth Affairs and Sports, Government of India, Sriperumbudur, Tamil Nadu, India

A brave, frank, clean-hearted, courageous and aspiring youth is the only foundation on which the future nation can be built

– Swami Vivekananda

Abstract: *Social work is a practice-based profession and academic discipline that deals with various sections of society. As youth play an important role in creating sustainable societies for strong nation-building, the social work profession significantly contributes to harnessing the potential of youth for nation-building. This chapter explores the vital role of social work practice in empowering youth in India, crucial for strong nation-building. It delves into global and national scenarios, highlighting the potential of young people and the emphasis of national youth policies on harnessing their capabilities. The chapter discusses various models and approaches, including strengths-based practice, and methods of social work, such as youth development index and professional social work interventions. It also emphasizes the significance of social work practice with youth, categorizing those who require support and illustrating the positive impact of effective social work practice. The chapter concludes with key takeaways, a glossary, and multiple-choice questions, making it a comprehensive resource for understanding the dynamic role of social work in youth empowerment and nation-building in India.*

Keywords: *Social Work, Youth, Nation Building, Models and Approaches*

Learning Objectives

After reading this chapter, you will be able to:

(a) Understand the Youth Development Index on Youth Engagement
(b) Importance of National Youth Policy
(c) Models of Youth Work
(d) Application of social work methods while working with youth
(e) Use of Strengths-based practice when working with youth

INTRODUCTION

The Commonwealth Secretariat defines youth as individuals aged 15–29. However, the delineation of the youth age bracket lacks universality, with varying definitions across contexts. Young people are frequently characterized more by what they are not rather than by their defining characteristics. They are often perceived as occupying the transitional space between childhood and adulthood, yet the precise age range remains a subject of debate (Furlong and Cartmel, 1997).

Youth, being the most enthusiastic, vibrant, innovative, and dynamic segment of the population, holds a pivotal role in the progress and success of a nation. Their strong passion, motivation, and willpower make them the most valuable human resource for fostering economic, cultural, and political development. The size of a country's youth population is a key determinant of its ability and potential for growth, emphasizing the importance of harnessing, motivating, and skillfully streamlining this demographic to bring about rapid progress.

India, with 66 per cent of its population (808 million) below the age of 35, boasts the world's largest youth population. Despite projected declines, the country is set to remain 'young' in 2030, with 24 per cent of its population (365 million) in the 15-29 age group. This demographic reality places a significant responsibility on the shoulders of young people to contribute to building the nation and competing on the global stage. As several countries grapple with the challenges of an aging population, India's approach to nurturing its youth will undeniably shape its future growth trajectory.

The youth's role extends beyond mere numbers; they are vital for the progress and success of a nation. The United Nations' Sustainable Development Goals (SDGs) underline the critical importance of investing in youth, recognizing them as a crucial national demographic. Young people are not just passive beneficiaries but active participants in sustainable development, serving as digital innovators within their communities. Their eagerness to contribute positively underscores the need to address multifaceted challenges, such as access to quality education, healthcare, employment, and gender equality.

Youth, as the most energetic and productive section of society, represent the driving force behind a nation's growth. The belief that developing countries with substantial youth populations can experience tremendous growth underscores the importance of investing in their education, health, and safeguarding their rights. Today's young generations are tomorrow's innovators, creators, builders, and leaders, demanding more just, equitable, and progressive opportunities and solutions. Addressing the pressing challenges faced by young people has become more imperative than ever, reflecting a collective responsibility to shape a more inclusive and sustainable future.

The youth demographic is a crucial and dynamic segment of the global population, representing around 85 per cent of the world's youth, constituting 18 per cent of the population, particularly prominent in developing nations. India stands out as one of the youngest nations, with a predicted 470 million young people by 2020 actively participating in economic activities. In 2000, nearly 20 per cent of India's population was under the age of 15, and a third of that group was young adults aged 15 to 24. From 1995 to 2000 and 2005, there were 210 million people in the 15 to 24 age range, up from about 175 million in 1995. The average age of a person in India in 2020 will only be 29, compared to 37 in China, the US, 45 in West Europe, and 48 in Japan.

The current global scenario of youth is a vibrant tapestry woven with threads of opportunity and challenge, with over 1.2 billion young people aged 15 to 24 representing 16 per cent of the world's population. While their potential to shape the future is undeniable, navigating this landscape comes with its own set of complexities, necessitating an understanding of the diverse realities young people face worldwide. Across the globe, a massive youth population phenomenon is unfolding, driven by a high birth rate and a low death rate. Recognizing and addressing the unique challenges and opportunities associated with this demographic, especially in developing nations like India, becomes imperative.

Worldwide, the population of young people is growing overall, but the age structure and relative size of the youth population vary widely. Economic development leads to demographic transitions, marked by industrialization, urbanization, and skills-dependent economic production, resulting in a decline in fertility and child-age dependents. As the relative number of children decreases, populations experience a growth in youth as a share of the total population, creating what is known as a youth bulge. Understanding these global trends is essential for comprehending the complexities of the youth demographic and devising effective strategies for their empowerment and development.

NATIONAL SCENARIO OF YOUTH

With nearly one out of every four persons between the ages of 15 and 29, India boasts an enviable youth population, currently estimated to constitute more than 34 per cent of the total population. While projections indicate a decline in these numbers in the coming years, youth will still comprise almost 24 per cent of India's population, amounting to 365 million people by 2030. This demographic advantage places India in a position of strength compared to countries like China, Japan, and the USA, which grapple with the challenge of an aging population, offering India the potential to drive economic growth.

Youth represents a vital social capital for economic growth globally, and the Government of India recognizes the current youth bulge as an abundant asset. This demographic offers immense leverage in terms of skilled labor, entrepreneurship, innovation, and knowledge to accelerate the country's developmental needs.

However, despite the opportunities presented by India's youthful population, action must be catalyzed to address the barriers to youth development and prepare them for a rapidly changing world. The onset of the COVID-19 pandemic has accelerated trends such as automation, e-commerce, remote work, and technology integration. While these changes offer new opportunities, they also underscore the need for stronger protections for all youth, particularly the millions who migrate from rural to urban areas in search of better opportunities. This migration adversely affects rural economies and imposes resource burdens on urban areas.

India is undergoing rapid urbanization, mirroring global trends. While urbanization can create more opportunities for youth, it also exposes them to various risks and vulnerabilities. Youth in peri-urban areas face challenges such as social insecurity, unemployment, exposure to higher rates of crime and violence, leading to detrimental behaviour patterns. Addressing these challenges is essential to harnessing the full potential of India's youth population and ensuring inclusive and sustainable development.

EMPHASIS OF NATIONAL YOUTH POLICIES ON YOUTH POTENTIAL

There was no national youth policy in India till 1987. However, youth has always been a concern of the Government of India. Various youth development programmes undertaken by the Union Government after Independence, like National Cadet Corps (NCC), National Service Scheme (NSS), Nehru Yuva Kendra Sangathan (NYKS) and the schemes for financial assistance to NGOs engaged in youth development bear ample testimony to this fact.

The National Youth Policy(NYP) of India, implemented in 2014, aims to empower the youth of the country to achieve their full potential and enable India to find its rightful place in the community of nations. It emphasizes creating a productive workforce, developing a strong and healthy generation, instilling social values, promoting community service, and facilitating participation in politics and governance. The policy outlines specific objectives and priority areas to address the needs and challenges faced by the youth population. The NYP-2014 proposes a holistic 'vision' for the youth of India, which is 'To empower youth of the country to achieve their full potential, and through them enable India to find its rightful place in the community of nations'. In order to realize this Vision, the NYP-2014 identifies 5 clearly defined 'Objectives' which need to be pursued and the 'Priority Areas' under each of the objectives.

The National Youth Policy 2014 provides a comprehensive overview of the state of youth in India, highlighting the critical role they play in the country's progress and development. With youth comprising 27.5 per cent of the population, the policy emphasizes the need for their representation and active participation in various spheres, including politics, governance, education, employment, entrepreneurship, health, sports, and social values. According to the National Youth Policy (NYP)-2014, the youth of this country are contributing 34 per cent of the Gross National Product (GNP) in our nation. It has gradually increased as the youth population is increasing. It acknowledges the challenges faced by the youth and aims to empower them to achieve their full potential, thereby enabling India to secure its rightful place in the global community. The policy underscores the importance of creating a conducive environment for youth development, addressing specific gaps, and investing in interventions that will have a maximum impact in each of the identified priority areas. Furthermore, it emphasizes the necessity of concerted efforts from all stakeholders to ensure the successful implementation of youth-focused initiatives and programs.

Recently the government has come out with the draft National Youth Policy 2021. The draft National Youth Policy 2021 (NYP 2021) has been recently introduced by the government, outlining a ten-year vision for youth development in India by 2030. Aligned with the Sustainable Development Goals (SDGs), the policy aims to unlock the potential of youth to advance the nation. It focuses on five priority areas: education, employment and entrepreneurship, youth leadership and development, health, fitness and sports, and social justice, with a core principle of social inclusion. In the education sector, the policy emphasizes imparting career opportunities and life skills to all young people, ensuring access to sustainable livelihoods, and encouraging rural economic development and entrepreneurship. To foster leadership among youth, the NYP 2021 advocates for strengthening the volunteering ecosystem, expanding leadership development opportunities, and leveraging technology for a vibrant youth enablement platform. Addressing health and well-being, especially for young women, is another key aspect. The policy proposes strengthening healthcare services, including mental health and reproductive health, while promoting a culture of sports and fitness. Furthermore, the policy outlines measures to empower youth and ensure safety, strengthen the legal system, and provide support for rehabilitation. Special emphasis is placed on social justice for marginalized and vulnerable youth. The NYP 2021 serves as a national-level framework, to be adopted by states for formulating their youth policies. Effective implementation will require collaboration among government entities, the social sector, civil society, and the private sector. The Ministry of Youth Affairs and Sports (MoYAS) will coordinate these efforts, ensuring strategic partnerships, strong coordination, and robust implementation. As the nodal ministry for youth, MoYAS will play a critical role in monitoring outcomes and ensuring effective delivery of the policy objectives, thus driving the vision for youth development in India.

OVERVIEW OF YOUTH DEVELOPMENT INDEX ON YOUTH ENGAGEMENT

The Youth Development Index (YDI) is a comprehensive tool that assesses youth development across 181 countries, measuring six key domains: Health and Wellbeing, Education, Employment and Opportunity, Political and Civic Participation, Equality and Inclusion, and Peace and Security. Ranging from 0 to 1, with 1 indicating the highest level of youth development, the YDI facilitates comparisons between countries and regions, offering valuable insights into areas requiring attention and action.

The YDI also monitors changes in the situation of young people, recognizing their contributions to the world and supporting them in pursuing the Sustainable Development Goals (SDGs). Providing valuable insights into global youth conditions, the index measures progress in youth development. It does not delve into specific inequalities within a country but serves as a benchmark for monitoring progress toward youth development and achieving the SDGs.

Closely related to most SDGs, the YDI indicates that countries excelling in youth development also tend to make greater progress toward the SDGs. As such, it becomes a valuable tool for monitoring progress and prompting action to scale up good practices or undertake reforms.

According to the 2020 Global Youth Development Index, young people's conditions improved by 3.1 per cent between 2010 and 2018, albeit at a slow pace. Serving as a resource for understanding the global state of youth engagement and development, the index offers key findings and insights to support youth empowerment and well-being. Through its comprehensive evaluation, the YDI emerges as a crucial tool not only for assessing youth development but also for aligning it with broader global sustainability objectives.

PROFESSIONAL SOCIAL WORK AND VARIOUS SECTORS/ AREAS OF INTERVENTION

The Social Work Profession not only works towards developing communities, uplifting disadvantaged sections, sensitizing different categories of people, capacitating them to cope up with the situations, generating awareness on the rights and providing sufficient information to avail the schemes and provisions from different service providers in the nation but also preparing them to manage crisis situations, giving psychosocial support and resolving conflicts within and among the individuals/ families/ groups and communities with the support of scientific knowledge and skills. Professional social work has certain methods, principles, tools and techniques to deal with the various categories of people and various types of problems. This professional programme was formally started in India in 1936 with the establishment of Sir Dorabji Tata Graduate School of Social Work, now popularly known as Tata Institute of Social Sciences (TISS), Mumbai.

Social work is a practice based profession just like medicine, engineering, law, agriculture; nursing, etc., the fraternity of social work is trained practically after understanding the theoretical background on various aspects in professional social work during their field work. Unfortunately, the professional outlook and recognition was not visualized for certain reasons in India. In all the western countries, it is a fully professional programme recognized by their Government, they practice it properly after the training is over, and the national and international professional bodies are taking care of the routine function of the profession in those countries which has become difficult in India.

International Definition of Social Work (IFSW, 2010), states that the social work profession promotes social change, problem solving in human relationships and the empowerment and liberation of people to enhance well-being. Utilizing theories of human behavior and social systems, social work intervenes at the points where people interact with their environments. Principles of human rights and social justice are fundamental to social work.

The Global Definition of Social Work (IFSW, 2014), states that *Social work is a practice-based profession and an academic discipline that promotes social change and development, social cohesion, and the empowerment and liberation of people. Principles of social justice, human rights, collective responsibility and respect for diversities are central to social work. Underpinned by theories of social work, social sciences, humanities and indigenous knowledge, social work engages people and structures to address life challenges and enhance wellbeing.*

It is emphasized that the focus of the social work profession is to promote social change, solve problems, promote empowerment, develop the communities, safeguard the justice and protect human rights etc. in the society. In those lines, the social work profession works across the globe towards development and wellbeing of the people in a professional manner on this earth. Youth development is not exceptional in the social work profession. In the Indian context, focus on youth development has been increased for the last four decades and currently, more focus has been given by the Government of India. Professional social work has been rendering its services in various sectors such as child development, adolescent development, youth development, women empowerment, elderly welfare etc. From the inception, social work has evolved from charity based profession to welfare based, from there to rights based and currently development based profession in India and other countries too. Various approaches such as strengths based approach, entrepreneurial approach and ecological approach etc. have become part of the social work practice in the current scenario. Youth development has become a crucial area of practice for social work in India as youth represent the majority of the population and India is the youngest nation in the world. However, there are many problems faced by the youth in India. Therefore, the presence of professional social work in the area of youth development is very essential. Professional social workers can address the problems and issues of youth by applying methods, following principles and using tools and techniques of social work.

EFFECTIVENESS OF SOCIAL WORK PRACTICE WITH VARIOUS CATEGORIES OF PEOPLE

Efforts of social workers in various sectors are very much essential in countries like India. The Social Work profession has been rendering its services in various sectors for the last nine decades with various categories of people.

Over the years, social work has been transformed from a simple helping profession into an empowering profession and in the process passed many milestones. With a well-defined and established value system, principles, skills and techniques, it occupies an important position in the society. Today, the social work profession is shouldering the unprecedented responsibility of maintaining a social order that promotes the good of everyone. It is playing an active role in bringing about planned change with an emphasis on humanization of social relationships and transactions for the overall betterment of society.

MODELS OF YOUTH WORK

In 1994, Youth Studies Australia published an article on Models of Youth Work Intervention by Cooper and White (1994). The stated purpose of the model(s) was to 'clarify the different orientations and practices associated with different kinds of youth work activity' (1994: 30). Six different models (or approaches) were presented and brought together through the organising principle of political ideology. The nomenclature used to describe each approach relates to the nature of the intervention. The main argument, implicit within this overall model, is that different political ideologies, worldviews and values spawn very different forms of youth work, and that these different forms continue to develop and co-exist. Structurally, this argument parallels the argument proposed by Hurley and Treacy about social analysis, and is consistent with Smith's analysis.

The six approaches discussed are Treatment, Reform, Non-radical Advocacy, Radical Advocacy, Non-radical Empowerment, and Radical Empowerment. Each approach is discussed in terms of its political ideological foundations, how it constructs young people's problems, its perspective on society, assumptions about human nature, core values of the approach, motivation for intervention, types of intervention, skills required of workers, and disciplines that inform practice. The model explicitly refers to the language used to describe young people and relates this to political ideological perspectives and assumptions about human nature. The focus on language highlights two aspects not discussed in other models. firstly, similar language is used to describe some quite different forms of intervention, see for example radical empowerment vs. Non-radical empowerment, and radical Advocacy vs. Non-radical Advocacy. Secondly, the focus on language provides a useful quick method to identify underlying values within new policy initiatives. Table 2 captures the main features of this model and the interested reader should refer back to the original journal article for a fuller account. The model is well-known in Australia, but not elsewhere.

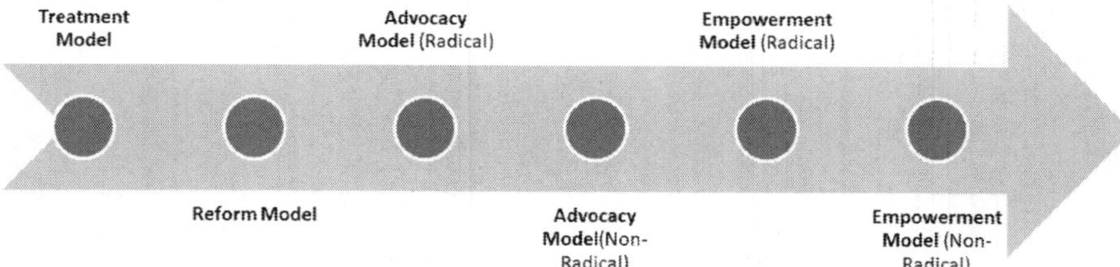

1. **The Treatment Model:** The Treatment model defines young people as deviant, mad or deficient. They present a social threat to the community. Young people must be treated or made to conform to societal 'norms'

to become productive members of society and if this is unsuccessful, action should be taken to protect society. The model assumes that all members of society agree on acceptable standards of behaviour. The values that underpin this model are social conformity, distinctions between class structures and self-improvement through competition. The model ignores social justice. The main motivation of this model is to promote good citizenship and conventional lifestyles. The interventions involved in the model require structured discipline and programs to limit anti-social behaviours and promote specific standards and values. If you think back to historical perspective of youth work, you will see how this model was popular in Britain, as well as the early days of Australian colonisation. In 2001 it could be argued that young offender (Juvenile Justice) programmes are delivered using this framework. Young people who become part of the Juvenile Justice programme, as a result of breaking the law and appearing before a Court, are often seen as misfits or deviants who must have their behaviour 're-shaped' in order to fit into society.

2. **The Reform Model:** The Reform Model defines young people as being socially disadvantaged by their environment and upbringing. This in turn may make them social outcasts and cause them to inflict violent behaviour on themselves or others. This model maintains that the values of society are acceptable and desirable but that some minor changes (reforms) may be necessary to improve conditions for disadvantaged groups. Supporters of this model believe that socio-environmental conditions affect people differently and individual coping skills will vary. Society will offer help to those who attempt to help themselves. The motivations for intervention are primarily to ensure social stability by supporting and encouraging the process of equal participation of young people in the community. Extreme suffering is considered morally unacceptable in modern society and all citizens have a duty of care to help the unfairly disadvantaged. Society should provide education and training to enable the young person to compete in the job market. Specific programs and services that target the needs of young people in education and training should be available. This should be coupled with personal development programs. Under this model, youth workers require skills in motivation, rapport building and the ability to help young people identify their own needs. The disciplines mentioned within the framework are social psychology, group work and personal development skills, which promote and encourage successful outcomes for young people.

3. **The Advocacy Model (Radical):** The Radical Advocacy Model defines young people as being marginalised by current society through inadequate basic rights or social protection. Young people are ill informed as to their rights and how to access them. Society is viewed under this model as fundamentally unjust in its laws and bureaucracy. The role of the youth worker is to expose inequality and get rid of bureaucratic and legal biases which disempower the young. The motivation for intervention is based on transforming society towards the adoption of values of equality and social justice. Interventions suggested are the development of group campaigns to promote and advocate the reform of institutional inequality. This is a human rights and social justice model of intervention. Youth workers need skills in campaigning, media and motivation and their role is to advocate on the behalf of individuals and groups for social change.
4. **The Advocacy (Non-Radical):** The young person is defined in this model as having problems because they are ignorant of their rights. Furthermore, bureaucratic barriers prevent their access to knowledge and information. Society is viewed in this model as complex and bureaucratic in nature – either it cannot be changed or it is the task of others (besides the youth worker) to change it. The underpinning values of this non-radical advocacy model are based on the belief that equality is present for those who have existing equality of opportunity and access to it. The youth worker's role under this model is to assist the young person in acquiring whatever they deserve or are legally entitled to. The youth worker should work to ensure that young people are aware of supports and entitlements and to work with bureaucracies so that young people achieve their rights. Examples of interventions under this model are welfare rights groups, Citizens Advice Bureaus and Legal Aid. The role of the youth worker is to maximise the young person's ability to benefit under legal and institutional frameworks through advocacy and participation. Skills needed by the youth worker under this model are an understanding of welfare and legal rights, networking and relationship building with bureaucracy.
5. **The Empowerment Model (Radical):** This model contends that institutions, which operate to protect the privileged or powerful, systematically disempower young people. Youth are seen as only one group disempowered under this framework. Society is viewed as unjust and controlled by the elite or upper classes. The basic values of the model are that youth workers should help young people to address power imbalances in society without disempowering other disadvantaged groups. Youth workers should not act as advocates for

young people but rather help them to obtain the skills to act on their own. The model also suggests that institutions, such as the media and education, are responsible for the belief that existing social hierarchical structures are natural. It focuses on oppression of marginalised groups and believes that the hierarchical structures create personal blame and apathy towards change. Examples of interventions under this model are welfare rights groups, Citizens Advice Bureaus and Legal Aid. The role of the youth worker is to maximise the young person's ability to benefit under legal and institutional frameworks through advocacy and participation. Skills needed by the youth worker under this model are an understanding of welfare and legal rights, networking and relationship building with bureaucracy. Young people should be encouraged to believe in themselves and identify oppressive factors so that they can overcome inequality. Workers should be aware of power imbalances and not assume a leadership role in the process.

6. **The Empowerment Model (Non-Radical):** This model holds that young people don't have enough control or power over their lives. Impacting on this is society's view that young people need to be protected from themselves and others. The core values framing the model are that young people need to be given more control over their lives and that they are capable of making independent decisions, providing adults allow them. It also states that empowerment can be achieved if the young person is assisted to become more powerful within whatever framework of values they individually choose. The sole motivation is to help young people gain control over their lives. The interventions adopted are to take on a 'laissez faire' approach and allow young people to take their own action. Youth workers need to be supportive and motivational without interfering in the process and should be seen in the role of a friend. While knowledge of these theoretical models is essential to the youth worker, there are other models of service delivery that are currently in practice. To find out more about these models, you may wish to explore Colleague's Advice in the Youth Work Agency.

METHODS OF SOCIAL WORK

There are six methods in professional social work that are practiced to work towards the development, solve the problems of different categories of people in the society: (1) Social Case Work, (2) Social Group Work, (3) Community Organization (4) Social Work Research (5) Social Action (6) Social Welfare Administration. These six methods were broadly divided in two categories such as primary methods and secondary methods, the first three methods come under primary methods and the next three methods come under secondary methods. Let us briefly know more about each method and its role in development of communities, particularly rural communities aiming at rural development. Apart from all these methods there is set of code of ethics, core values and principles to practice this profession.

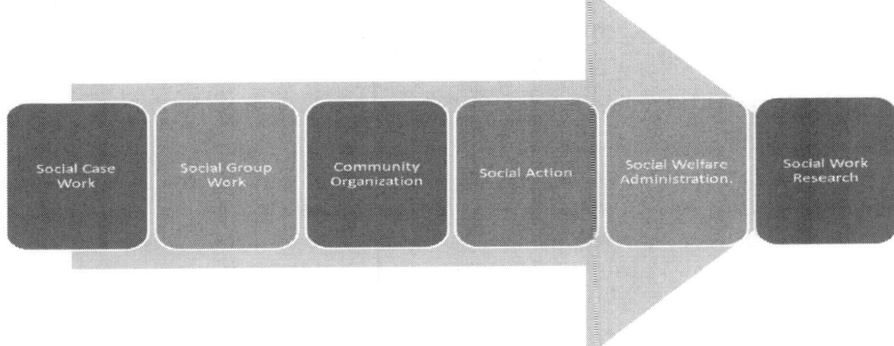

Social case work which is one of the primary methods deals with individuals towards solving individual problems, providing counseling, capacitating to address his/her issues, sensitizing towards better social functioning, improving quality of life and so on. Basically, the professional social worker applies this method while dealing with individuals. There are certain principles, tools and techniques in this method; all those are practiced while working with individuals scientifically and systematically. Through this method, the professionals applies the process of social work which includes Study, Diagnosis, Treatment (Intervention), Termination and Follow up and Evaluation.

Social group work deals with groups consisting of 10-15 members. It has its own process to enable, educate and empower the people in various settings and areas. This method helps all the group members in the group individually with a specific objective. Group work focuses on from planned group formation on wards to process of evaluation of the group at the end in achieving in stated objectives by following certain principles and steps. Through this method people can be capacitated, empowered, educated and enabled towards achieving their objectives and needs aiming better social functioning.

Community organization is one of the important primary methods of social work. This method is highly relevant to practice in India. Community organization focuses whole community as a unit. In that community it deals with individuals, groups, families and communities, ultimately it will work for the overall development of the whole community by taking support from various stakeholders with in the community. People's participation is important in this method in this method of practice. There are certain principles, models and approaches to practice this method to improve the quality of life of people in the community. The present chapter is the positive outcome of practice of this method.

Social work research focuses on finding facts and searching for truth of the problems and issues that are emerged in this society and design solutions to solve those problems in a scientific manner. This method also concentrates on problems and challenges that are emerged in social work practices as well. There are certain steps in the process of research including Identification of problem, need assessment, selection of social work research design, pre-intervention measurement, Intervention, Post-Intervention measurement and Inferences. The whole procedure will be followed to complete the research in social work profession. That research may be initiated with any category of clients

Social action has been used to signify a wide range of primarily voluntary initiatives to bring out change in social systems, processes and even structure. Social workers, more often than not, have divergent opinion about the scope and relevance of social action. This ambiguity has even accelerated the debate whether to recognize social action as a method of professional social work (Kaushik, 2010: 260). Social action focuses on mass problems; it mobilizes people to attack mass problems. There are certain techniques that are followed in this method such as rallies, awareness campaigns, strikes, boycotts, march and so on. It is basically a mass movement on mass problems for example Narmada Bachao Andolan (NBA), Anti-Corruption Movement, Movement on Delhi Gang Rape, Jallikattu Movement in Tamil Nadu, Kisan Andolan-1.0 and Kisan Andolan-2.0, etc.

As discussed earlier social work deals with individuals, families, groups, organizations and communities in the society. Social worker need to equip themselves with social welfare administration to work better in the field of social work (Beena, 2010: 317). As John C Kidneigh (1950) described social welfare administration as the 'process of transforming social policy into social services…a two way process: (i) transforming policy into concrete social service and (ii) the use of experience in recommending modification of policy. In this method of social work, several aspects are involved and practiced such as Planning, Organising, Staffing, Training Coordinating, Reporting and Budgeting as said by Luther Gallic. Administration of all the processes, available resources, fine tuning the exiting administration policies, execution of available programmes, etc.

As part of its education and training, both theory and practicum should be given equal importance. There are certain components in field work to train the learners of social work. Those important components are (1) Observation Visits (2) Concurrent Field Work (3) Internship (4) Block Field Work and (5) Rural Camp. The present chapter intended to explain the outcome of a Rural Camp conducted by the IGNOU School of Social Work with more than 100 master degree (Regular) students in the state of West Bengal. During that period, the group was involved in application of social work theories and skills in a group of rural villages by following a three dimensional approach which include (i) Identification of Problems (ii) Social Work Intervention and (iii) Evaluation. The community organization method was largely applied during the intervention, after the social work intervention during the rural camp; the author has drawn its positive outcome, and identified the possibilities and difficulties in developing rural communities in this country through professional social work interventions.

The significant opportunities for developing rural communities in this country were identified through that small social work intervention. Those opportunities were found listed out which include (1) Building Trust and Relationship (2) Verbalize the needs (3) Identification of Resources (4) Discover the Solutions (5) Promoting People's Participation (6) Planning, Execution, Monitoring and Evaluation (7) Empowering, Educating and Enabling (8) Applying social work theories and (9) Developing the whole communities.

Similarly, in any professional practice, the professionals experience and identify some challenges to execute their plans. The major challenges those were identified during the rural camp were (1) Bringing people together (2) Generating Awareness on Misconceptions (3) Dealing with sensitive issues such as values, customs etc. (4) Working with different stakeholder's perception (5) Ensuring equal and regular participation (6) Language barrier and (7) Challenges from Government Officers.

Based on the experiences and positive outcome drawn during the camp, the author has attempted to explain the role of the social work profession in rural development. One of the primary methods of social work is largely practiced and suitable to the Indian context. There may be changes among the people based on their culture, values and habits. As we all know, there is so much diversity in this country from state to state, region to region and district to district. Even though professional social work can deal with the people with different cultures by amalgamating their cultures and social work theories through various approaches aiming at developing their communities at individual, family and community level.

There are a lot of schemes, plannings and programmes for rural development but as we analyze the remote rural areas we find nothing for much improvement. For example: there is no electricity, health care centre, education system, road, etc., in most of the villages. In the field of education the poor people of rural areas are left far behind. There are government schools but teachers are not responsible They do not come in time. There is no proper education system in the rural area. Though some improvement is there but slow, one can definitely say that India will take another fifty years to get literature. We cannot say one is literate just by a little bit of writing and speaking languages (Bhattacharya, 2011).

Community development has the potential to effect changes that will combat poverty and social exclusion. Its role, above all, is to advocate for radical change in the structures that keep people poor. The analysis so far has pointed to the fact that the sector is not realizing its full potential. The question remains then whether alternative approaches and processes can be put in place to build the effectiveness of community development as a powerful force for social change (Lee, 2006).

CORE VALUES OF SOCIAL WORK

The following broad ethical principles are based on social work's core values of service, social justice, dignity and worth of the person, importance of human relationships, integrity, and competence. These principles set forth ideals to which all social workers should aspire.

Value: Service

Ethical Principle: Social workers' primary goal is to help people in need and to address social problems

Social workers elevate service to others above self-interest. Social workers draw on their knowledge, values, and skills to help people in need and to address social problems. Social workers are encouraged to volunteer some portion of their professional skills with no expectation of significant financial return (pro bono service).

Value: Social Justice

Ethical Principle: Social workers challenge social injustice.

Social workers pursue social change, particularly with and on behalf of vulnerable and oppressed individuals and groups of people. Social workers' social change efforts are focused primarily on issues of poverty, unemployment, discrimination, and other forms of social injustice. These activities seek to promote sensitivity to and knowledge about oppression and cultural and ethnic diversity. Social workers strive to ensure access to needed information, services, and resources; equality of opportunity; and meaningful participation in decision making for all people.

Value: Dignity and Worth of the Person

Ethical Principle: Social workers respect the inherent dignity and worth of the person.

Social workers treat each person in a caring and respectful fashion, mindful of individual differences and cultural and ethnic diversity. Social workers promote clients' socially responsible self-determination. Social workers seek to enhance clients' capacity and opportunity to change and to address their own needs. Social workers are cognizant of their dual responsibility to clients and to the broader society. They seek to resolve conflicts between clients' interests and the broader society's interests in a socially responsible manner consistent with the values, ethical principles, and ethical standards of the profession.

Value: Importance of Human Relationships

Ethical Principle: Social workers recognize the central importance of human relationships.

Social workers understand that relationships between and among people are an important vehicle for change. Social workers engage people as partners in the helping process. Social workers seek to strengthen relationships among people in a purposeful effort to promote, restore, maintain, and enhance the well-being of individuals, families, social groups, organizations, and communities.

Value: Integrity

Ethical Principle: Social workers behave in a trustworthy manner.

Social workers are continually aware of the profession's mission, values, ethical principles, and ethical standards and practice in a manner consistent with them. Social workers should take measures to care for themselves professionally and personally. Social workers act honestly and responsibly and promote ethical practices on the part of the organizations with which they are affiliated.

Value: Competence

Ethical Principle: Social workers practice within their areas of competence and develop and enhance their professional expertise.

Social workers continually strive to increase their professional knowledge and skills and to apply them in practice. Social workers should aspire to contribute to the knowledge base of the profession.

STRENGTHS-BASED PRACTICE IN SOCIAL WORK

A strengths-based approach focuses on identifying and utilizing an individual's strengths and resources rather than focusing solely on their problems. It is a person-centered, holistic, and outcomes-focused approach that promotes individual well-being. By looking beyond labels and asking the right questions, practitioners can uncover the potential and possibilities within each individual.

The focus of a strengths-based approach is on recognizing and building upon the strengths, talents, and resources of individuals. Rather than solely focusing on their problems, deficiencies, or needs, the approach shifts the attention to what is strong, capable, and resilient about the individual. The focus is on understanding the individual as a whole, including their skills, knowledge, abilities, character traits, relationships, and personal outcomes that are important to them. It seeks to identify and leverage these strengths to support the individual in achieving their goals and improving their overall well-being. By focusing on strengths, the approach acknowledges the unique qualities and assets that individuals possess, allowing for a more positive and empowering perspective. It helps individuals recognize their own capabilities and resources, and encourages them to take an active role in shaping their own lives. The strengths-based approach also extends beyond the individual, recognizing that their strengths and talents can integrate with their wider social network, including family, friends, community, and professionals. This collaborative approach maximizes the available resources and support systems to promote the individual's well-being. In summary, the focus of a strengths-based approach is on highlighting and utilizing the strengths of individuals, fostering a positive and empowering perspective, and leveraging the available resources to support their overall well-being and achievement of personal outcomes. Strengths-based practice in social work refers to an approach that focuses on a person's strengths, resources, and capacities rather than solely on their problems or deficits. It seeks to empower individuals, families, and communities by recognizing and building upon their existing strengths and capabilities.

In strength-based social work practice, the practitioner works collaboratively with the individual to identify their strengths, talents, skills, and support systems. This includes exploring their personal qualities, knowledge, relationships, cultural background, and community resources. By recognizing and valuing these strengths, the practitioner aims to promote self-determination, resilience, and positive change. Strengths-based practice in social work with youth involves focusing on the strengths, capacities, and potential of young people, rather than solely on their problems or deficiencies. It aims to empower and support youth in developing their skills, resiliency, and positive outcomes.

Here are some key elements of strengths-based practice when working with youth:

1. **Positive Youth Development:** Strengths-based practice recognizes and builds upon the inherent strengths and skills that young people possess. It emphasizes promoting positive youth development by fostering their talents, interests, and aspirations. One of the goals of positive youth development is to shift the paradigm for youth services from a programmatic focus on youth problems to a more comprehensive approach that views youth as having assets, resources, and capabilities that deserve full support and development.
2. **Empowering Youth Voice:** Social workers in strengths-based practice actively seek and value the perspectives, ideas, and contributions of young people. They involve youth in decision-making processes and encourage them to take ownership of their own lives.
3. **Identifying Strengths and Assets:** Social workers work collaboratively with youth to identify their strengths, interests, talents, and support networks. This process involves exploring their skills, passions, values, relationships, and community resources that can contribute to their well-being and success.
4. **Goal-Oriented and Solution-Focused:** Strengths-based practice encourages youth to set and achieve their own goals. Social workers help youth identify their desired outcomes and work together to develop strategies and solutions to overcome challenges and achieve those goals.
5. **Building Resilience:** Strengths-based practice emphasizes fostering resilience in young people. It focuses on nurturing their ability to cope with adversity, develop problem-solving skills, and maintain positive relationships and connections.
6. **Relationship-Building:** Social workers aim to establish positive and trusting relationships with young people based on mutual respect, empathy, and genuine care. This relationship serves as a foundation for supporting and empowering youth in their personal growth and development.
7. **Holistic Approach:** Strengths-based practice considers the whole person and their various contexts, including family, school, community, and cultural factors. It recognizes the impact of these contexts on youth and seeks to integrate and leverage the available resources to support their well-being.

By implementing strengths-based practice, social workers can promote youth empowerment, resilience, positive development, and improved outcomes for young people. It nurtures their strengths and capabilities, helping them to navigate challenges and thrive in their lives.

The positive youth development practice is explicitly strengths-based in the sense that it is grounded in a philosophy that places value on all youth, and emphasizes their strengths and potential for development and resilience rather than only overcoming their deficits. It is also more holistic in orientation than the risk reduction approach, which basically identifies problems and creates solutions to those problems.

SIGNIFICANCE OF SOCIAL WORK PRACTICE WITH YOUTH

Social Work practice with youth holds significant importance in addressing the unique challenges and opportunities faced by young people. Here are some key points highlighting the significance of Social Work practice with youth:

1. **Vulnerability and Risk Factors:** Social Work practice with youth focuses on addressing the vulnerabilities and risk factors that young people may face, such as poverty, homelessness, substance abuse, mental health issues, and involvement in the juvenile justice system.
2. **Empowerment and Support:** Social Workers play a crucial role in empowering and supporting young people to navigate complex systems, access resources, and develop skills to lead successful and fulfilling lives. By empowering youth, social workers help them build self-esteem, develop leadership qualities, and enhance their capabilities to contribute positively to society
3. **Advocacy and Social Justice:** Social Workers advocate for the rights and well-being of youth, working to address systemic inequalities and promote social justice for this population. Through advocacy efforts, social workers work towards creating a supportive environment that promotes the growth and development of youth. Social workers advocate for youth-friendly policies and programs that address the systemic barriers and inequalities affecting young individuals. By influencing policy decisions and promoting youth-centered approaches, social workers contribute to creating a more inclusive and supportive environment for youth development.
4. **Prevention and Intervention:** Social Work practice with youth involves both preventive measures to address risk factors before they escalate, as well as interventions to support young people in crisis situations. By providing early intervention and support services, social workers help prevent negative outcomes and promote positive youth development.
5. **Strengths-Based Approach:** Social Work practice with youth often adopts a strengths-based approach, focusing on the assets and

capabilities of young people rather than solely viewing them through a deficit lens.

6. **Youth Development:** Social Workers contribute to the positive development of youth by providing guidance, mentorship, and opportunities for growth and self-discovery.
7. **Collaboration and Community Engagement:** Social Workers collaborate with families, schools, communities, and other stakeholders to create a supportive environment for youth and promote their overall well-being. By involving youth in community activities, social workers promote a sense of belonging, responsibility, and civic engagement among young individuals.
8. **Skill Development:** Social workers focus on enhancing the skills, knowledge, and capacities of youth through various programs and activities. By providing opportunities for skill development, social workers equip youth with the tools they need to succeed academically, professionally, and personally.

Social Work practice with youth is essential for addressing the multifaceted needs of young people, promoting their empowerment, advocating for their rights, and fostering positive development and social inclusion. By addressing the unique needs of youth and advocating for their rights, social workers play a vital role in fostering positive youth development and creating a more equitable and inclusive society (Anaut-Bravo & Raya-Díez, 2020)

CATEGORIES OF YOUTH REQUIRE SOCIAL WORK PRACTICE

Youth may be viewed simultaneously as a human resource and a problem/risk group (Anaut-Bravo & Raya-Díez, 2020). As a result of changes in social institutions such as the family and factors such as industrialization, urbanization, and environmental factors, the youth are increasingly confronted with persistent and recurrent social problems, including those related to health, unemployment, and drug abuse. Since youth social exclusion is on the rise, social work focusing on youth development requires high levels of expertise (Merfeldaite & Dilyte, 2016). Social workers must address these new societal concerns while focusing their efforts on factors that degrade youth personalities, providing basic needs, enhancing relationships, coping with stress, and developing a positive attitude about oneself and others (Otieno et al., 2018).

1. **Adolescents and young adults with mental ill-health:** Individuals facing severe difficulties due to mental ill-health in combination with social vulnerabilities.

2. **Young people with complex needs:** Defined as adolescents or young adults receiving assistance from multiple welfare services due to mental ill-health and social vulnerabilities.
3. **Youth transitioning from one agency to another (eg. Foster Youth):** Young people who may need support during transitions between different service providers or care systems.
4. **Young people with addiction issues:** Some youth categorized as having complex needs may struggle with addiction, requiring specialized interventions and support.
5. **Youth with psychiatric diagnoses:** Individuals with psychiatric diagnoses may require tailored social work practices to address their specific needs.

'NASW Standards for the Practice of Social Work with Adolescents' outlines standards for social work practice with adolescents. The categories of youth that require social work practice can include, but are not limited to:

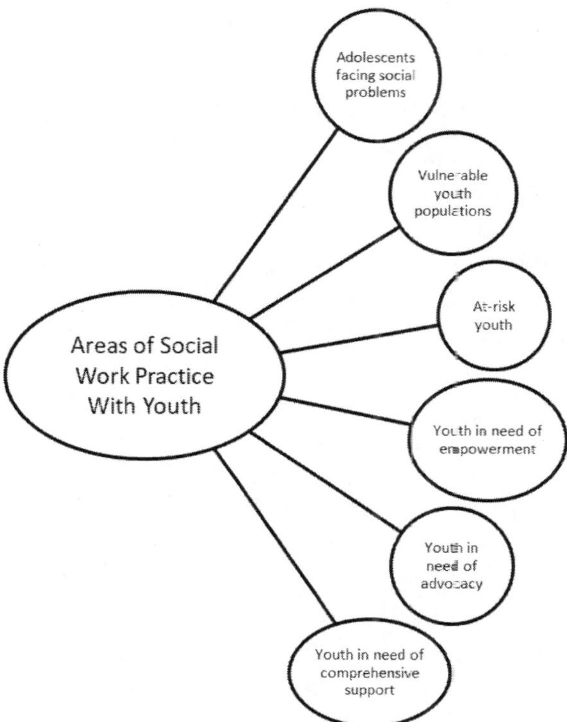

1. **Adolescents facing social problems:** Social workers may work with adolescents facing various social problems such as substance abuse, mental health issues, family conflicts, homelessness, or involvement in the juvenile justice system.

2. **Vulnerable youth populations:** Social workers may focus on vulnerable youth populations, including LGBTQ+ youth, youth in foster care, immigrant and refugee youth, or youth with disabilities, who may require specialized support and services.
3. **At-risk youth:** Social workers may engage with at-risk youth who are exposed to factors that increase their likelihood of experiencing negative outcomes, such as poverty, academic challenges, or involvement in risky behaviors.
4. **Youth in need of empowerment:** Social workers aim to empower adolescents by promoting their autonomy, decision-making skills, and self-advocacy to help them navigate challenges and achieve their goals.
5. **Youth in need of advocacy:** Social workers advocate for the rights and needs of adolescents, ensuring they have access to essential services, resources, and opportunities for growth and development.
6. **Youth in need of comprehensive support:** Social workers may provide comprehensive services to adolescents, addressing their physical, emotional, educational, and social needs to promote holistic well-being and positive outcomes.

SOCIAL WORK PRACTICE AND ITS IMPACT ON YOUTH

Social workers also should work to promote the social, emotional, spiritual and mental well-being of youth. Lacking these, youth cannot work and think properly. Social workers also should focus on generating opportunities for youth development as well as opportunities to express themselves. Youth are not getting too many opportunities to express themselves and in the context of developing countries youth should work under the elders and there they do not get a chance to use creativity, they cannot use their potential. So, social workers should provide opportunities to the youth to express and show their potentiality.

Youth are not getting opportunities to participate in politics, planning, policy making, etc. so social workers should conduct programs and activities to pressurize the authorized sector to provide opportunity for youth to participate in all parts of government and decision-making status.

Social workers should not work with youth but they should work with youth. As a social worker, workers should not feel that they are working for developing the youth capacity but they are working to enhance the potential capacity which all youth have but that may be hidden because they may not get a chance to express those hidden potentialities. To enhance the potential capacity of youth, social workers should focus on practical knowledge as well as skills where they can use those creativity, skills, and potentialities. Social workers should minimize the activities and knowledge which only gives theoretical aspects.

As everyone has their inherent worth and dignity the same way youth also has. As a social worker works with youth it does not mean that youth know nothing, social workers should respect the opinion and skills of the youth. Even though social workers do not know many things, youth can teach them so many things, so social workers should have the ability to accept the uniqueness of individuals.

Besides these, social workers should be able to connect youth with their communities and nation. Nowadays youth are dreaming about western countries and they always want to go abroad. But as a social worker we should convince them that they are the nation builder, without them the nation is nothing. Whatever they can do in western countries, the same can be done here. Social workers should be able to make them feel that they are needed and useful for their own communities and nation.

The social worker should conduct research and survey to find-out the needs of youth and the necessities of youth for development and then they should formulate programs which are really relevant with youth.

All youths are leaders. Some youth may not know how to lead. Social workers should build the self-esteem of youth and should provide training on leadership to develop and enhance their leadership. Social workers themselves might be the role model for youth to make them think about nation/community development. No sustainable development is possible if youth are not interested or if youth do not take leadership.

The social work profession also has a role in working with other stakeholders to support young people in job preparation and placement. Social workers are in a well-placed position to promote youth employment and reduce youth unemployment. To take a more proactive approach, social workers need to stay alongside young people, upgrade their knowledge and skills, and conduct practice research and program evaluation in helping young people to overcome the challenges of their transition to adulthood, within an ecological consideration.

Review Questions

(a) Explain how youth empowerment contributes to nation-building in India. Use examples from the chapter.

(b) Discuss the significance of strengths-based practice in social work with youth. How does it differ from deficit-focused approaches?

(c) What role do social workers play in addressing the barriers that prevent youth from realizing their full potential in India?

(d) Reflect on the models of youth work discussed in this chapter. How do they shape the interventions designed to engage and support Indian youth?

Did You Know?

- India has one of the world's largest youth populations, with over 66% of the population below the age of 35 (about 808 million people). By 2030, this percentage is expected to reduce slightly to 24%, yet will still include 365 million people aged 15–29.
- The National Youth Policy of 2014 highlighted that Indian youth contribute 34% of the Gross National Product (GNP), emphasizing their importance in the nation's economic progress.
- The Treatment Model views young people as deviant or deficient, aiming to make them conform to societal norms through structured programs to become productive members of society.
- The Empowerment Model (Radical) argues that institutions disempower youth, and social workers should assist them in overcoming societal power imbalances without assuming a leadership role.
- Among the six primary methods of social work, Social Case Work deals with individuals to solve personal problems and improve their quality of life through counselling and intervention.
- Community Organization focuses on mobilizing entire communities to address collective challenges by promoting people's participation and working with various stakeholders.
- Despite these opportunities, India's youth face challenges such as unemployment, urban migration, and a need for skills that align with technological advances and global competition.
- The Youth Development Index (YDI) assesses youth well-being globally, measuring domains like education, employment, and political participation. According to the 2020 YDI, youth development improved by 3.1% between 2010 and 2018 globally.

SUMMARY

The youth of India represent not only the future but also the present of the nation's development trajectory. With a staggering demographic advantage, India's young population holds immense potential for driving social, economic, and political progress. However, this potential can only be fully realized through concerted efforts in nurturing, guiding, and empowering the youth towards constructive engagement with society and its challenges. Throughout this chapter, we have examined the critical role of social work practice in facilitating the holistic development of young individuals and harnessing their capabilities for nation-building endeavors. By employing various models, approaches, and methods, social workers can effectively engage with diverse youth populations across different sectors and domains of intervention. Moreover, by upholding core values such as empathy, inclusivity, and social justice, social workers can create meaningful impact in the lives of young people, particularly those marginalized or at risk. Embracing a strengths-based approach, social work practitioners can empower youth to leverage their inherent assets and talents, thereby fostering resilience and self-efficacy. Furthermore, the significance of social work practice with youth cannot be overstated, especially in addressing the multifaceted challenges faced by this demographic, ranging from education and employment to mental health and social integration. By tailoring interventions to meet the unique needs and aspirations of each youth cohort, social workers can facilitate positive outcomes and contribute significantly to nation-building efforts. In essence, as India endeavors to emerge as a global leader in the 21st century, it must prioritize investments in its youth and leverage the expertise of social work professionals to ensure their holistic development and meaningful integration into society. By doing so, India can harness the demographic dividend offered by its youthful population and pave the way for a stronger, more inclusive, and prosperous nation.

GLOSSARY

- **Youth Bulge:** A demographic pattern where a large proportion of a country's population is comprised of young people, typically resulting from high birth rates and declining child mortality. This can lead to both opportunities and challenges in economic and social development.
- **Youth Development Index (YDI):** A tool used to assess youth development across various countries by measuring domains such as health, education, employment, political participation, equality, and peace. It helps in comparing the progress of youth development globally and identifies areas needing improvement.
- **Social Work Profession:** A practice-based profession and academic discipline that promotes social change, problem-solving in human relationships, and the empowerment and liberation of people to enhance well-being. It involves principles of social justice, human rights, collective responsibility, and respect for diversities.
- **Strengths-based Approach:** A practice framework that focuses on identifying and utilizing the strengths, talents, and resources of individuals, families, and communities to promote well-being and achieve goals. Instead of concentrating on problems and deficiencies, this approach emphasizes positive attributes and capacities.
- **Positive Youth Development (PYD):** A framework that promotes the strengths and potential of young people by fostering their skills, interests, and aspirations. PYD shifts the focus from addressing youth problems to supporting their overall development and resilience.
- **Holistic Approach:** A comprehensive perspective that considers the whole person, including their physical, emotional, social, and

environmental factors. This approach recognizes the interconnectedness of various aspects of a person's life and aims to integrate these elements to support overall well-being and growth.

TOP TEN TAKEAWAY POINTS

1. The varying definitions of youth globally emphasize their critical role in national progress despite age differences, focusing on economic, cultural, and political contributions.
2. India's youthful demographic presents a significant advantage for economic growth and global competitiveness, requiring attention to challenges such as urban migration and economic disparities.
3. National youth policies like NYP-2014 and the draft NYP 2021 signal India's commitment to empowering youth through education, employment, health, and social justice initiatives, preparing them for leadership and sustainable development.
4. Different models of youth work, rooted in diverse political ideologies, shape interventions ranging from treatment and reform to advocacy and empowerment, reflecting varying societal values and aspirations.
5. Language analysis within these models not only distinguishes between different intervention types but also reveals underlying values and biases, crucial for evaluating and adapting youth work policies and practices.
6. These models underscore the dynamic evolution and coexistence of youth work approaches, emphasizing the need for adaptive strategies to effectively address the diverse challenges and needs of today's youth.
7. Strengths-based practice in social work empowers youth by focusing on their inherent strengths and resources rather than their deficits, fostering resilience and self-confidence.
8. It takes a holistic approach, considering youth's personal qualities, relationships, and community resources to support comprehensive development.
9. Social workers collaborate with youth in setting and achieving goals, promoting a sense of ownership and empowerment in their journey.
10. The six Models of Youth Work Intervention are Treatment, Reform, Non-radical Advocacy, Radical Advocacy, Non-radical Empowerment, and Radical Empowerment.

MULTIPLE CHOICE QUESTIONS

1. What is the primary focus of a strengths-based approach in social work?
   (a) Identifying and labelling individuals based on their problems

(b) Recognizing and building upon individuals' strengths
(c) Assigning blame for societal issues
(d) Ignoring individual capabilities and resources

2. What does a strengths-based approach seek to achieve in individuals?
(a) Dependency on social workers for solutions
(b) Recognition of their own capabilities and resources
(c) Avoidance of personal responsibility
(d) Identification as a problem case

3. Which model defines young people as deviant or deficient, aiming to conform them to societal norms through structured programs?
(a) Reform Model
(b) Radical Advocacy Model
(c) Treatment Model
(d) Non-radical Empowerment Model

4. Which model focuses on exposing societal inequalities and advocating for systemic change through campaigns and media efforts?
(a) Non-radical Advocacy Model
(b) Radical Empowerment Model
(c) Reform Model
(d) Radical Advocacy Model

5. According to which model, young people are viewed as disempowered due to institutional structures that favour the elite?
(a) Non-radical Empowerment Model
(b) Radical Empowerment Model
(c) Reform Model (d) Treatment Model

6. Which model emphasizes providing young people with legal and bureaucratic knowledge to access their rights within existing frameworks?
(a) Reform Model (b) Radical Advocacy Model
(c) Non-radical Advocacy Model
(d) Non-radical Empowerment Model

7. According to the National Youth Policy (2014), youth is defined as individuals aged:
(a) 15–24 years (b) 15–29 years
(c) 18–35 years (d) 20–30 years

8. India's youth population is projected to be what percentage of its total population by 2030?
(a) 15% (b) 20% (c) 24% (d) 30%

9. The National Youth Policy of India 2014 emphasizes all of the following objectives EXCEPT:
(a) Youth participation in politics and governance

(b) Developing a strong and healthy youth generation
(c) Instilling cultural values among youth
(d) Expanding industrialization in rural areas

10. The Youth Development Index (YDI) measures youth development across countries in how many key domains?
(a) 4 (b) 5
(c) 6 (d) 7

Answers

1. (b), 2. (b), 3. (c), 4. (d), 5. (b), 6. (c), 7. (b), 8. (c), 9. (d), 10. (c)

REFERENCES

1. Furlong, A. and F. Cartmel (1997) Young People and Social Change: Individualization and Risk in Late Modernity (Repr). Milton Keynes: Open University Press.
2. Anaut-Bravo, S., & Raya-Díez, E. (2020). The social reality of youth and social work: Between visibility and invisibility. *Social Work Education*, 39(6), 737–49. https://doi.org/10.1080/02615479.2019.1682541
3. Social group work with young people in Tamil Nadu, India: A case study of civic engagement (2023, June 23). Youth & Policy. https://www.youthandpolicy.org/articles/social-group-work/

RECOMMENDED READINGS

1. Banks, S. (1999). Ethical Issues in Youth Work Practice. New Delhi: Routledge.
2. Batsleer, J. (2011). What is Youth Work? New Delhi: Sage Publications.
3. Bright, G. (2015). Youth Work: Histories, Policy and Contexts. New York: Palgrave.
4. Howard, S. (2010). Youth Work Ethics. New Delhi: Sage Publications.

CHAPTER – 9

Social Work with Families during COVID-19

Ragini Tyagi

Research Scholar, Department of Social Work, University of Delhi, Delhi

The strength of a family, like the strength of an army,
is in its loyalty to each other.

– Mario Puzo

Abstract: *COVID-19 has impacted the lives of each section of the society. Family as a fundamental unit of society got impacted too at multiple levels such as economic, political, social and various others. Family social workers can help understand the situation better by talking to the individuals of the family and practising an intervention for the sudden pandemic situation. This chapter helps to understand the family as an institution and its functions. It also elaborates the impact of COVID-19 pandemic on the family system. It enables the understanding regarding the role of family social workers during the COVID-19 and the challenges associated with it.*

Keywords: *COVID-19, Crisis, Families, Resilience Dyadic Relationships*

Learning Objectives

After reading this chapter, you will be able to:

- Understand the concepts and dynamics of family system vis a vis COVID-19 Pandemic.
- Develop the understanding regarding the problems and challenges faced by different stakeholders in family system (children, parents, husbands, wives, etc.) during the pandemic.
- Assess the adjustment and maladjustment of the family members during the lockdown situation.
- Discuss the role of social workers in family setting during the crisis situation like COVID-19 pandemic.
- Understand the emerging challenges for the social work professionals working in the field of family setting in the light of changes happened during the pandemic.

INTRODUCTION

The system of family is widely regarded as the most important social institution. It is a fundamental unit in the society performing various multifaceted functions making it a much-needed institution in the society.

It is one of the world's oldest and ancient social institutions. Families differ greatly across the globe, but they all share certain common concerns in their daily lives. The effect of the COVID-19 pandemic on the family system includes economic, social, psychological, impact on women, children, elderly, etc. Social Work practice with family is based on this system perspective. There are various methods and strategies in the profession, which can be applied to handle the multiplicity of family problems, especially during the pandemic.

IMPORTANCE OF FAMILY AS AN INSTITUTION

Definition: Family is a kinship group that includes two or more people who are related by either blood, marriage, or adoption. It is a group of individuals directly linked by kin connections, the adult members of whom assumes the responsibility for caring for children. The family system is kin based cooperative unit.

FUNCTIONS OF THE FAMILY INSTITUTIONS

- **Socialization:** Family is responsible for primary care and early learning. It is not just a producer of biological kind, but has a fundamental role of socializing the children (language, learning a set of values, beliefs, skills, etc). Parents and other relatives are responsible for teaching children the necessary knowledge and skills to survive.
- **Economic Support:** Families are the primary unit of economic support. Financial support is provided by the independent members to the dependent members of the family. Resource generation and allocation are important family function keeping in mind the needs of each family member.
- **Providing Care and Protection:** Every human being needs food and shelter. In addition, we all need to be among people who care for us emotionally, who help us with the problems that arise in daily life, and who back us up when we come into conflict with others. Undoubtedly, the family often is the one group in society that meets these needs.
- **Education:** Family provides formal as well as informal education to its members, so that they can better contribute to the family and the society.
- **Recreation:** Family provides recreational activities within the family and outside the family to its participating members.
- **Sexual Regulation:** Family system regulates the sexual activity of their members and hence control reproduction occurring within the specific boundaries. Marriage is a legally recognized relationship which is established by a civil or religious ceremony, between two

individuals who intend to live together as partners. There is no society which leaves people to express their sexual behaviours as they desire, but there are a whole set of written as well as unwritten rules/norms that prohibit certain ways of sexual behaviour of the people.

- **Reproduction:** It is the essential function of the society performed by the family. Each society needs new generations of young people to replace the old people and this can be merely in three ways: by reproduction, migration or conquest of other societies. In the absence of any biological reproduction, any society is sentenced to disappearance.
- **Providing Social Status/Social Placement:** Simply by being born into a particular family, each individual gets both material goods and the socially recognized position defined by ascribed status. These statuses include social class, caste membership and ethnic identity. Family background is the most important social factor affecting our lives in society.

Did You Know?

Social work is a broad and diverse field where the work extends across various settings. These professionals work with individuals, groups, families, schools, universities, institutions, non-profit agencies, corporations, hospitals and government agencies. They are actively participates in politics at all levels. Social workers also advocate for legislation and policies that help improve the quality of life for the children, adults and community as a whole.

COVID-19 PANDEMIC AND ITS IMPACT ON FAMILIES

COVID-19 has been declared as the global pandemic by the World Health Organisation on 11th March 2020. Indian government called for first complete lockdown on 24th March, 2020. The lockdown has induced an entirely different set of challenges of every section of society. In order to stop the risk of infection to spread, various countries implemented containment measures or lockdowns which includes the measures like closure of schools, educational institutes, universities, offices and other recreational activity areas. These situations are beyond normal experience which eventually leads to stress, anxiety and also helplessness. The COVID-19 pandemic created many stressful situations among the family system which impacted them at various levels including social, physical and psychological involving the aspects like job loss, financial hardships, social distancing, home confinement, etc.

Economic

Family as the basic institution is required to meet the fundamental and basic needs of the family members. Resource generation and allocation is one of the important functions of the family. During the COVID-19 outbreak, the economic situation of the family has suddenly worsened. It includes financial hardships in the families along with unprecedented rising levels of unemployment during the pandemic. The impact of the social disruption due to the COVID-19 pandemic (e.g., job loss, financial hardship, social distancing, confinement) needs to be considered in the context of the pre-existing vulnerabilities in the families too (e.g., marginalization, economic hardship, history of adversity, poverty). Although the current strain of the COVID-19 outbreak is unprecedented and it has affected all people globally, the impact of the virus can be rooted in historic as well as persistent social, economic, and educational disparities, resulting in greater vulnerabilities, inequality and difficulties in people of low-income families.

Social

Measures such as physical distancing and lockdown which were induced to curb the spreading of the corona virus have disrupted the social networks of the people. Individuals became socially isolated which created problems in reaching out to people. This home confinement has impacted the people psychologically also leading to problems like stress, anxiety, depression, anger, etc. In this situation, atmosphere at home and behaviour of other members of the family has a huge impact in dealing with the situation. However, external support by other family members might got disrupted and social support systems gets fade away due to social distancing measures.

Women

Women during the lockdown have faced multiple problems such as increased burden at home, job loss, domestic violence, etc. During the COVID-19 pandemic, most people's lifestyle and work have been negatively affected by the crisis. However, women's jobs and livelihoods are more vulnerable to the COVID-19 pandemic. Inequality is highly striking: Using the data and trends from unemployment surveys both in the United States and India, where the gender-disaggregated data are available, it has been seen that female job loss rates due to the COVID-19 pandemic are about 1.8 times higher than male job loss rates globally, at the 5.7 per cent versus 3.1 per cent respectively.

Gender disparities in the allocation of household duties during such confinement must also be addressed, as women are frequently expected to devote more time to household chores and home-schooling children, affecting their academic career (Mahapatra & Sharma, 2020).

United Nations Development Programme(UNDP) has shared frightening data in which 243 million women and girls suffered from the physical/sexual violence in 2020 globally. Many countries have even proclaimed the state of emergency over any kind of gender-based violence and feminicides.

Older People

Elderly in the family are particularly vulnerable to the risk of virus infection from COVID-19, especially those with chronic and age related health conditions such as hypertension, diabetes, cardiovascular diseases and others. They are not just facing greater health risks but are also not very well capable of supporting themselves in quarantine and isolation. Physical and Social distancing also lead to increased social isolation of elderly at a time when they may be at most need of the support. The norms around COVID-19 exacerbates the negative stereotypes about elderly population who may be viewed as very weak, unimportant and a burden on society. Adult family members at home became more cautious while living together with the elderly.

Children and Adolescents

Children and adolescents are a vulnerable group who are going through a difficult time. The COVID-19 outbreak and lockdown may have a variety of effects on the lives of the adolescents, including chronic and acute stress, concern for their families, unexpected bereavements, sudden school breaks and home confinement in many countries, increased time spent on the Internet and social media, and concern for their family's and country's economic future. People are staying at home. Their social relationships are being disrupted. Masks are becoming more common in some countries where people are not used to them, and people can no longer see each other's facial expressions (Guessoum, et al., 2020).

In comparison to adults, this pandemic may have increased long term adverse and harmful consequences on adolescents as well as children. The impact of the pandemic induced circumstances on children depends on many vulnerability factors like the transitional and developmental age, biological and behavioural changes, current educational status, having special needs particular to the adolescence, pre-existing mental health condition, being economically or socially under privileged and child/ parent being remained in isolation and quarantined due to the fear of infection (Singh et al., 2020).

Individuals are experiencing psychological impact as a result of COVID-19 pandemic (Asmundson and Taylor, 2020; Li et al., 2020). For adolescents with psychiatric disorders, lockdown might have resulted in a sudden break or shift in care for the teenagers who have psychological disorders. There is surge in several risks during the pandemic like disaster, such as Post-Traumatic Stress Disorder (PTSD), irritation, depression, anxiety, confusion, dilemma, anger, effecting teenager's mental health and brain development. The period of quarantine has negative and long-term impact on the psychological health of the individual. School closure is directly linked to the decrease in physical activities, increased screen time, change in sleeping patterns and poor diets among adolescents and children (Wang et al., 2020). The interaction of the brain with the social environment, as well as the emergence of adolescence coinciding with isolation, influences the psychotic disorders (Lamblin et al., 2017). Teenagers are going through a new period of insecurity, which includes worrying about their relatives' health and work, being separated from friends and peers unexpectedly, school disruption, deaths or thoughts of deaths.

There are many ways to deal with the stress and anxiety caused by adolescent psychosocial and physical transitions, such as problem-solving, rumination, support-seeking, escape, reaching out and distraction, all of which work on risk, resilience, and adversity (Zimmer-Gembeck & Skinner, 2010). Coping is also linked to the lifestyles and eating habits. To distract themselves, adolescents tend to eat more, it helps them cope with the situation at hand. Seeking help is one of the most important ways to cope with negative emotions. Adolescents are dependent on their significant adults such as parents, teachers, peers, and seek social support from them.

Many people are unfamiliar with digital learning. While most schools, colleges, and universities have moved to online class delivery and evaluation in order to avoid disruptions in education, the digital platform remains uncharted and unfamiliar territory for the majority of people in low-middle-income countries such as India. Although internet penetration in India is increasing in both urban and rural areas, with approximately 73.3 per cent of the population connected via mobile phones (Sood et al., 2019), the use of digital resources, particularly in mainstream education, has remained largely unexplored.

Disparity in access to digital education foreshadows academic stress in students who are unable to access online classes or submit assignments, falling behind their peers in their curriculum. This has resulted in reports of depression, anxiety, and, in severe cases, suicidal attempts in children and adolescents as a result of academic stress and concerns about the future.

According to Mahapatra and Sharma (2020), dissemination of learning and educating through a digital portal would necessitate students having access to a laptop/computer, which, given the socio-economic disparities, is out of reach for students from low-income families. According to the National Sample Survey, 2017–18, households having access to the internet amounts 24 per cent, while only 8 per cent of all households who have members from the age group 5 to 24 have both computer and an internet connection. It highlights the seriousness of the psychological consequences of being unable to access basic education due to socioeconomic and geographic barriers. In the absence of adequate social welfare and policy measures at the governmental and institutional levels, this could lead to a severe mental health crisis among the young, further undermining their academic prospects and triggering a vicious cycle of mental disorders, academic underachievement, and poor socio-occupational functioning. On the other hand, individuals having access to digital learning media, also show increase in gaming, problematic use of technology, and spending more time on internet and social media are all issues that may arise causing concern and necessitate intervention.

Migration

The migrants and their families are not very well familiar in the new atmosphere in which they live temporarily. They are already prone to various physical, social, psychological as well as emotional trauma in such circumstances, ensuing from the fear of neglect and rejection by the local community of that area and concerning about the wellbeing and safety of their families waiting in their native places.

The migrants have to leave their native places in search of the better opportunities and earnings, many times leaving behind their families. The families waiting in the native places depends partially or completely on the money sent by the migrant earning members of their family back home. During outbreak of communicable diseases, such a COVID-19, and the restrictions imposed on routine activities as part of social distancing norms to prevent the spread of the disease, scores of migrant workers tend to move back to their native places.

During the sudden outbreak of the COVID-19, and the restrictions imposed on the routine activities as part of the social distancing rules to prevent the spreading of the disease, migrant workers tend to move back to their native places. Many migrant workers used all the possible means to reach their particular destinations. However, many of them are stuck at the borders, including state, district or at national border areas.

They are the most marginalized sections of the society those are dependent on the daily wages for their living, and in the times of crisis and distress, they need sympathy as well as understanding of the society. Immediate needs and concerns of the migrant workers relate to food, shelter, safety, healthcare, fear of infection or spreading of the virus, loss of earnings, concerns about the family, stress, anxiety and fear. They also encounter harassment and negative reactions of the local community of the region which calls for strong social protection. As an immediate response to these problems, measures which has to be taken must include, community shelters and community kitchens, ensuring the availability of other relief materials, emphasising on the need for social distancing, identification of the suspected cases of infection and adherence to protocols for the management of such cases, putting up mechanisms to enable the migrants to reach out to their family members through telephone, or video calls etc. and ensuring their physical safety.

Dyadic Relationships

- **Husband-Wife:** It is a relationship based on understanding and companionship. But lockdown period had both positive and negative consequences on the relationship. Spending more time with each other can be seen as the positive side of the home confinement. However, increase in domestic violence, marital conflict are the negative consequences that emerged during the lockdown period.
- **Parent-Child:** Since the closure of schools, parents had assumed primary responsibility for their children's education. They were compelled to take on the task of home-schooling in order to maintain educational continuity. This added to their burden, as they are already dealing with issues such as work-from-home, and temporary unemployment leading to financial crisis, and household work management. Many parents do not have the time or educational qualifications so that they can help their children with assignments that were previously handled by their teachers. This is likely to lead to caregiver's frustration and burnout, as well as disruption in the children's academic activities, resulting in stress in both parents and children.
- **Grandparents-Grandchildren:** Elderly people and children both are more vulnerable to the effects of the pandemic. However, the bond of care, love and compassion can help them find solace in each other during the home-confinement.
- **Sibling:** It consists of brother-sister, sister-sister, or brother-brother dyads. During the lockdown, the increase in the time spent together might have benefitted the bonding between the siblings.

Did You Know?

In just first 20 months of the occurrence of the COVID-19 pandemic, 208 million cases had been reported worldwide. It has impacted children a lot and put 1.6 billion children out of school.

Review Questions

(a) What are the important functions of family as an institution?

(b) How are the dyadic relationships among the family has been impacted during the COVID-19 pandemic?

ROLE OF SOCIAL WORKERS

Social workers are concerned about the impact of COVID-19 on the society and the wellbeing of the people they provide services, their families and the community. Social work assessment and intervention can be done in accordance to the system's theory. As per system's theory, there are two parts of any system, i.e., system's environment (supra-system) and system's components (sub-systems). Dyadic relationships in the family are its sub-system and the social environment such as work, education, political system, media are the supra-system of the family.

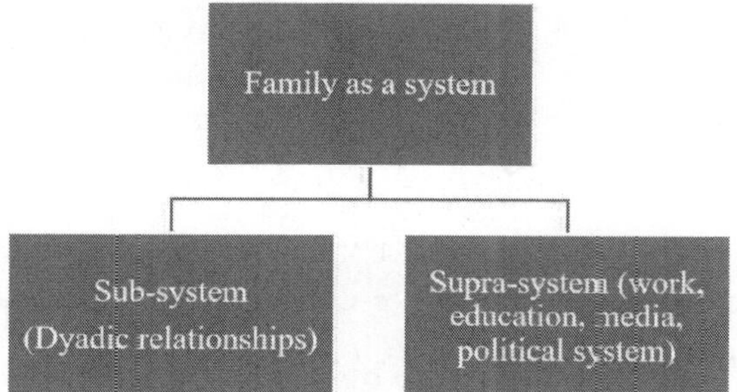

Figure 1: Family System and its Components

During the pandemic, there was a drastic change in both the sub-system as well as the supra-system of the family. For the holistic family assessment, social worker needs to study the impact of the pandemic on time spent together by the family members, parenting style, social as well as psychological behaviour of the members, sensitivity to the needs during the lockdown.

Figure 2: Social Work Intervention Methods with Family

Social Work with Individuals in Family Setting

While working with a family, the social worker may sometimes limit his/her interaction on a one-to-one basis with individual members of the family. Certain pandemic induced problems, such as increased screen time of children, poor academic performance, lethargy, emotional outbursts of children or some behavioural problems of parents, such as being strictness or authoritarian, too much demanding and over involvement may not require the need of other sub-systems of the family. In the cases of marital conflicts, the other spouse may be not be ready or hostile to the idea of working with the social worker. Such situations require the social worker to work with one member of the family to enable him to handle the particular problem.

Social Work with Groups in Family System

Instances where many parents will come across some common problems in dealing and bringing up their children especially during the home confinement. Similarly, the children or the spouses may also have certain problems that have a common pattern. Under such circumstances, it will be more beneficial to help and engage with them in groups rather than dealing with them individually. For example, if a group of parents feel that they need to understand better parenting methods, it will be better to bring them together in a group and enable them to share their problems, anxieties, ventilate their feelings and enable them to learn from each other's experiences. In the same way, children, who may have been indulged in delinquent behaviours or temper tantrums, may benefit a lot if they meet other children with similar problems or circumstances and work together to come out of the particular problem. In this context, working with groups assumes significance in social work practice with families. Groups provide its members with learning experiences, understanding and opportunity to share experiences and to engage in better dealing with the situation and mutual problem solving. Members also gets the opportunity to increase their confidence as well as understanding under the guidance of a professional social worker.

Crisis Intervention

Pandemic has induced a sudden crisis situation which has induced various challenges in the family. The challenges can be getting infected with COVID-19, death of family member, financial problems, behavioural problems, etc. The period can be very critical disrupting family's stability and harmony and puts at stake the security, safety and survival of the members of the family. It is in this context that some helpful external support is needed to these families through crisis intervention. It enables the members to ventilate their feelings, mobilise resources, and help them to gain a healthy equilibrium.

Family Therapy

It aims to establish more satisfying ways of living and co-existing for the entire family. The family is considered as a system where any maladjusted person is given treatment within the family system. It is assumed that the problem related to one person in the family is the product of his interaction with other family members and vice versa. Problem includes alcoholism, marital breakdown and family violence. Hence, it is necessary to work with the entire family or with at least those, who are concerned about the problem. During the lockdown, problems like marital conflict, domestic violence tremendously increased. Family Therapy is one such method, which can be used in Social Work Practice in crisis situations like pandemic.

At the Cognitive-Affective Level

- Coping must be emotion focussed which requires emotion expression and regulation to be more self-reliant during the uncontrollable crisis situations like pandemic. Accepting or developing the attribute of acceptance can be the most important factor to build positive coping strategies during such circumstances.
- Awareness generation among the family members.
- Laughter and humour can act as an important stress buster. It not just improves the mental health but enhance the immune system also.
- Making a good plan according to the goals and interest would not just help in active coping but also keeps the individual going in difficult situations.

Social Worker's Challenges during COVID-19 Pandemic

- Difficulty in reaching out to people and not able to have face to face interaction during the pandemic created the biggest challenge for the social workers.
- Maintaining the trust, empathy and confidentiality over the phone or internet is challenging.
- Prioritizing the services and needs according to the pandemic situation and its demand.
- Balancing between the need of the time and the safety of the social worker.
- Handling the emotions and fatigue while working in the stressful and unsafe circumstances induced by the pandemic.

- Learning the lessons to redevelop and rethink about social work practice according to the future's demand.

Review Questions

(a) Describe the major areas of social work intervention among the family system?

(b) What are the various challenges faced by the human service professionals practicing family social work during the COVID-19 pandemic?

(c) What can be the role of social workers during the pandemic?

(d) How can family therapy help in the crisis situation?

SUMMARY

Family is the fundamental institution in the society. During the pandemic, various challenges has been induced in the family system such as physical, social, psychological challenges. The problems included stress, anxiety, economic hardships, and various others. Hence, it is important that the family social workers are equipped with the skills as well as knowledge of working with families in the crisis situation like pandemic. We have also learnt that the problems faced by families during the COVID-19 pandemic are multifaceted in nature. We have also understood that family exists as a system, and so, handling the problem of any individual member in the family involves the cooperation of all other members of the family system as well as its external environment. This chapter has presented Social Work methods of working with individuals, groups of the family system and also other strategies, such as Crisis Intervention, family therapy, etc. Pandemic has also increased challenges for the human service professionals and it's very important to adapt the changes in social work practice according to the need of the future.

GLOSSARY

- **Family:** It is a group having certain obligations and the members of the group are related to each other by blood, marriage or adoption.
- **Family Dyads:** They are the family subsystems including dyads such as parent-child, siblings dyads, husband-wife dyad, grandparents-grant child dyads, in-laws dyads.
- **Family Social Work:** It is the practice and profession in which the family social worker helps families and the members of the family get through difficult times and get additional support. They assist and help by letting families know that there are special and proper services available to them which will help them get through the crisis situation.

- **Social Work Intervention:** It refers to actions which are taken by social workers to directly provide the service or support to at-need individuals, groups or community.
- **Pandemic:** A disease or infection that spreads all over the country or the world such as Corona Virus Disease (COVID-19).

TOP TEN TAKEAWAYS POINTS

1. Family is a kinship group that includes two or more people who are related by either blood, marriage, or adoption.
2. Functions of family as an institution are socialization, economic support, providing care and protection, sexual regulation, reproduction, recreation, education, social placement, etc.
3. The effect of the COVID-19 pandemic on the family system includes economic, social, psychological, impact on women, children, elderly, etc.
4. Pandemic has impacted the family system at various levels including social, physical and psychological involving the aspects like job loss, financial hardships, social distancing, home confinement, etc.
5. Family social work is the practice and profession in which the family social worker helps families and the members of the family get through difficult times.
6. Social work assessment and intervention can be done in accordance to the system's theory. There are two parts of any system, i.e., system's environment (supra-system) and system's components (sub-systems).
7. Dyadic relationships in the family are its sub-system and the social environment such as work, education, political system, media are the supra-system of the family.
8. Social work intervention with family can be done with the help of the methods like social work individual members of the family, or groups in the family like dyads, crisis intervention, marital counselling or family therapy.
9. Challenges for the social workers during the pandemic includes difficulty in face-to-face interaction and reaching out to people.
10. Human service professional should learn the lessons and apply them to rethink the social work practice according to the future's demand.

MULTIPLE CHOICE QUESTIONS

1. A group of people related by blood, marriage or adoption is called as __________.

   (a) Peer (b) Friends
   (c) Family (d) Community

2. Any disease which spreads over a large area is called as........
   (a) Epidemic (b) Pandemic
   (c) Endemic (d) Infection
3. A system consists of
   (a) Sub-system (b) Supra-system
   (c) Both of them (d) None of them
4. Which one of the following is not a family dyad?
   (a) Husband-wife (b) Parent-child
   (c) Grandparents-grandchildren (d) Teacher-student
5. A system theory is based on __________
   (a) Internal environment of the system
   (b) External environment of the system
   (c) Both of them (d) None of them
6. Functions of the family as an institution are:
   (a) Socialization (b) Reproduction
   (c) Education (d) All of the above
7. Social work intervention includes working with
   (a) Individual (b) Group
   (c) Community (d) All of the above
8. Individuals working with family helping them dealing with their problems and provide them help is called as....
   (a) Teacher (b) Police
   (c) Family social worker (d) Academician
9. Important ethical consideration for the social worker are....
   (a) Maintaining trust (b) Confidentiality
   (c) Empathy (d) All of the above
10. Pandemic has created problems such as...
   (a) Fear of infection (b) Financial hardships
   (c) Psychological impact (d) All of the above

Answers

1. (c), 2. (b), 3. (c), 4. (d), 5. (c), 6. (d), 7. (d), 8. (c), 9. (d), 10. (d)

REFERENCES

1. Asmundson, G.J.G., Taylor, S., (2020). Coronaphobia: Fear and the 2019-nCoV outbreak. *Journal of Anxiety Disorders* 70, 102196. Doi: https://doi.org/10.1016/j.janxdis.2020.102196
2. Chen, C.V., Byrne, E. & Velez, T. (2021). Impact of the Impact of the 2020 pandemic of COVID-19 on Families with School-aged Children in the United States: Roles of Income Level and Race. *Journal of Family Issues*. Doi: https://doi.org/10.1177/0192513X21994153

3. Guessoum, B.S., Lachal, J., Radjack, R., Carretier, E., Minassian, S., Benoit, L., & Moro, M.R. (2020). Adolescent psychiatric disorders during the COVID-19 pandemic and lockdown. *Psychiatry Research*, 291. doi:10.1016/j.psychres.2020.113264
4. Lamblin, M., Murawski, C., Whittle, S., Forrito, A., (2017). Social connectedness, mental health and the adolescent brain. *Neuroscience and Biobehavioral Reviews* 80, 57–68. Doi: https://doi.org/10.1016/j.neubiorev.2017.05.010
5. Li, S., Wang, Y., Xue, J., Zhao, N., Zhu, T., (2020). The Impact of COVID-19 Epidemic Declaration on Psychological Consequences: A Study on Active Weibo Users. *International Journal of Environmental Research and Public Health* 17 (6). Doi: https:// doi.org/10.3390/ijerph17062032.
6. Mahapatra, A. & Sharma, P. (2020). Education in times of COVID-19 pandemic: Academic stress and its psychosocial impact on children and adolescents in India. *International Journal of Social Psychiatry*. doi: https://doi.org/10.1177/0020764020961801
7. Okafor. A. & Walla, P. (Reviewing editor) (2021). Role of the social worker in the outbreak of pandemics (A case of COVID-19), *Cogent Psychology*, 8:1, DOI: 10.1080/23311908.2021.1939537
8. Singh, S., Roy, D., Sinha, K., Parveen, S., Sharma, G., & Joshi, G. (2020). Impact of COVID-19 and lockdown on mental health of children and adolescents: A narrative review with recommendations. *Psychiatry Research*, 293:113429. doi:10.1016/j.psychres.2020.113429
9. Sood, M., Mahapatra, A. & Chadda, R.K. (2019), Use of mobile phones by patients with serious mental illness attending a general hospital psychiatric outpatient service in India. *Asian Journal of Psychiatry*, 45:61-62. Doi: 10.1016/j.ajp.2019.08.015
10. Vanderhout, S.M., Birken, C.S., Wong, P., Kelleher, S., Weir, S. & Maguire, J. L. (2020). Family perspectives of COVID-19 research. *Research Involvment and Engagement*, 6, 69. Doi: https://doi.org/10.1186/s40900-020-00242-1
11. Wang, G., Zhang, Y., Zhao, J., Zhang, J., Jiang, F., (2020). Mitigate the effects of home confinement on children during the COVID-19 outbreak. *The Lancet 395* (10228), 945–947. https://doi.org/10.1016/S0140-6736(20)30547-X
12. Zimmer-Gembeck, M. J., & Skinner, E. A. (2010). Review: The development of coping across childhood and adolescence: An integrative review and critique of research. *International Journal of Behavioral Development*, 35(1), 1–17. doi:10.1177/0165025410384923

RECOMMENDED READINGS

1. Abrams, L. S., & Dettlaff, A. J. (2020). Voices from the Frontlines: Social Workers Confront the COVID-19 Pandemic. *Social Work*. doi:10.1093/sw/swaa030
2. Banks, S., Cai, T., de Jonge, E., Shears, J., Shum, M., Sobočan, A. M., Storm, K., Truell, R., Úriz, M. J., & Weinberg, M. (2020). Practising ethically during

COVID-19: Social work challenges and responses. *International Social Work*, 63(5), 569–583. doi:10.1177/0020872820949614

3. Broadhurst, K. (2003). Engaging parents and carers with family support services: What can be learned from research on help-seeking. *Child and Family Social Work*, 8(4), 341–350.
4. Copson, R., Murphy, A. M., Cook, L., Neil, E., & Sorensen, P. (2022). Relationship-based practice and digital technology in child and family social work: Learning from practice during the COVID-19 pandemic. *Developmental Child Welfare*, 4(1), 3-19. https://doi.org/10.1177/25161032221079325
5. Early, T. J., & GlenMaye, L. F. (2000). Valuing families: Social work practice with families from a strengths perspective. *Social work*, 45(2), 118–130.
6. Fisher, J., Languilaire, J. C., Lawthom, R., Nieuwenhuis, R., Petts, R. J., Runswick-Cole, K., & Yerkes, M. A. (2020). Community, work, and family in times of COVID-19. *Community, Work & Family*, 23(3), 247–252.
7. Holland, S. (2010). Child and family assessment in social work practice.

CHAPTER – 10

Social Work with Women: Practices, Policies and Scope

GAYATRI MENON

PhD Scholar – ICSSR Doctoral Fellow, Department of Social Work, University of Delhi, Delhi

A feminist is anyone who recognises the equality and full humanity of women and men.

– Gloria Steinen

ABSTRACT: *Violence against women has been a very common phenomenon globally. There are many underlying causes and consequences in this context that needs immediate and urgent attention. Of late, even in the context of Covid, gender based violence specifically against women are in a rise. Vulnerability of women is a major challenge in the contemporary world. Age old practices and societal taboos are still becoming a reason for the same. This chapter will define a few important concepts in the context of women. It will also try to examine and make the social work students understand the forms of vulnerabilities that women undergo. It will also cover the skills and strategies required among the budding social workers to empower women in the larger context.*

Keywords: *Gender, Gender Based Violence, Social Work with Women, Vulnerability of Women, Social Work Skills and Strategies*

Learning Objectives

After reading the chapter, you will be able to:

- Understand the various needs and challenges faced by women.
- Understand the causes and consequences of these challenges on women.
- Know the possible ways to ensure welfare of women through social work strategies.

INTRODUCTION

Gender has been a profound subject of debate cutting across areas of studies. Globally, a differentiation can be found in the way society treats a man and woman. This differentiation reflects from the way women are treated as the pride and honor of a family. They are also sometimes considered as people who can preserve the tradition and ritual of the families. In this context, there are several challenges that women face on a day to day basis. If we look into the data of sex ratio in the world, men outnumber women. For instance, in a data that was brought out in 2019, it was found that, globally, there are around 105 boys for every 100 girls. In India, there are 943 women for every 1000 men born as per the Census 2011. Though this is considered as the natural sex ratio at birth, it is vital to reflect on this stark difference.

BASIC CONCEPTS

- **Gender** is the socio-cultural attribute given by the social norms of society to men and women. They are characterized with masculine and feminine roles in society. This characterisation has the power to differentiate men and women into unequal groups which sometimes lead to unequal access to opportunities and resources. This leads to the next concept of Gender Equality.
- **Gender equality** is globally defined as the access to rights, opportunities, resources and protection for every individual irrespective of gender. But it is a challenge to acquire this state of context without a mass scale change in the behaviour and mindset of people in the society. To ensure this they should be provided with fair access and equal opportunities to all irrespective of their gender. This is commonly referred to as Gender Equity. But these states of equality among genders are sometimes interrupted by the assigned gender roles.
- **Gender roles** are those stereotyped attitudes, attributes and actions assigned to individuals by the society that brings the differences in their access and opportunities. For instance, women are considered as individuals who are caring, nurturing and as the one who should carry out the household chores. These typical roles may sometimes mar the accessibility and opportunities of women. This can also sometimes lead to Gender based violence. This is defined as any harm penetrated to a person or group due to their sex, gender, sexual orientation and gender identity. And unfortunately, most of the time women become prey to such violence. In this context, patriarchy is another aspect that affects women in a society. Patriarchy is the system in which the male breadwinner of the family is the authority and oppresses the women based on their gender roles. They provide for the women in the family rather than making them independent.
- **Womanhood** is considered to be the state of being a woman and is different from being a girl. It is considered as a universal term. But, feminists opine that, womanhood cannot be defined in a specific way, because in today's times, the roles and responsibilities of women are prescribed by the society. They do not emanate from their choices and thoughts. The abilities, attributes and capacities of women cannot be prescribed and should be considered a biological make.

Challenges faced by women due to gender inequality and stereotyping have been a global issue since ages. It is the time to understand and confront the same comprehensively. In the next few sections we will discuss the proportions of gender based violence against women and policies to curb this at the global and national level.

GENDER EQUALITY – A GLOBAL SCENARIO

The United Nations recognizes gender equality as a human right for all. This can contribute to the social, economic and sustainable development of any country. But, unfortunately gender inequality is a prevalent practice globally. From ancient Victorian times, gender inequality has been a common phenomenon especially against women in the world.

Globally, it is recognized that about 50 per cent of the women population in their productive age is not in the labour market. The unpaid domestic and care work in the households are held responsible for this scenario. There is a gender gap found in the labour market and also there is a significant difference in the pay given to men and women all over. It is estimated that, only 46 per cent of the total female population is in the labour market compared to the 74 per cent among men. Apart from this, women also due to the prevalent patriarchal system faces domestic violence, intimate partner violence, sexual abuse, harassment at workplace, lack of access to education, health and employment opportunities.

Did You Know?

Globally,

- 1 in 3 women are victims of domestic violence.
- 45% of women do not make their sexual and reproductive decisions for themselves.
- 24% of women have undergone violence before they turned 15 years.
- 38–50% of murders of women are committed by intimate partners.

It is important to note that gender equality is an important global agenda for most of the countries. It is a major goal in the Sustainable Development Goals of the United Nations and the allied countries. Sustainable Development Goals is a set of 17 goals put forth by the United Nations in the year 2015–30. Each goal has several targets that cover every agenda for the development and maintenance of the economies across the globe touching all kinds of communities. In these 17 goals, SDG 5 - Gender Equality is the most important goal that aims at protecting and empowering females.

GENDER EQUALITY - AN INDIAN SCENARIO

According to Census (2011), about 48.5 per cent of the population are females. The sex ratio of age group 0–6 years is 923 and 0–19 years is 908 per 1000 births. Also, sex ratio among the economically productive age group (15–59 years) is 944 per 1000 births. When we look into the literacy status of women in India, it is only 64.4 per cent which is lesser compared to the literacy rate among men. The gender gap in the rural and urban literacy rate is 16.5 per cent and 9.4 per cent respectively. Though there is a hike in enrolment rate, there is an increase in the dropout rate among women. There has even been a steady increase in this status during the Covid period. Even the National Crime Record Bureau marked an increase in gender based crimes against women in India.

Did You Know?

- 30% of women of the age group 18- 49 years have experienced sexual violence in their households (NFHS 5).
- 1 woman in India died per hour due to dowry (NCRB, 2020)
- 4 women were raped every hour in India.
- 14 cases are reported under 'Cruelty of Husband' every hour in India.

Is it not alarming and high time to take action against these practices in India or abroad? And it is important for social work as a profession to grow and disseminate its knowledge in this direction to ensure safety and security of the women of its country.

Minimal gaps between men and women in India on gender attitudes

% of Indian adults who say ...

	Women	Men
Men in a family should be primarily responsible for making decisions about expenses	19%	21%
Men generally make better political leaders than women	21	29
Sons should have greater rights to inheritance from parents	33	34
Sons should have the primary responsibility to care for parents as they age	37	40
Men in a family should be primarily responsible for earning money	42	45
Sons should have the primary responsibility for a parent's last rites or burial rituals	62	64
A wife must always obey her husband	86	89

Source: PEW Research Centre (2022)

The above figure above shows a very important and minute aspect of gender inequality in households of India. This research vividly shows the opinion on the gender attitudes on various indicators related to patriarchy. Men and women more or less share the same attitude when it comes to gender roles in India. It is observed that a strong attitudinal problem is observed among women themselves on gender roles and its influence. This may also stand as a major reason for the widening gender disparity in the country.

Review Questions

(a) What is gender-based violence?

(b) What are the forms of gender-based violence?

Vulnerabilities Faced by Women

This section will cover various challenges and vulnerabilities of women globally and in India. This will describe the magnitude of the issue at the global and national levels, the causes and consequences of the same on the women population in the world and in India specifically. The hunting down of women in the Indian context started even before the Mughals. The women were looked upon as individuals who serve the men and also considered a burden as their wedding should be with huge pomp and pageantry. This section will try to make the reader aware about the various issues faced by women right from their birth to during their life course.

Female Foeticide is a gender based violence that starts from the womb of the mother. It is an illegal abortion of a female fetus after recognising her sex through sex determination tests. This is identified as a gross violence of human rights and child rights on a larger perspective. It can also have its own repercussions on women who undergo the process. The pressure of having a girl child can mount pressure on the mother too. They may even drop to Post Traumatic Stress after the process. It is often referred to as 'missing women' from the global population by UNFPA. It is reported in a , in the year 2007, China reported 17.3 million births out of which 1 million girls were 'missing'.

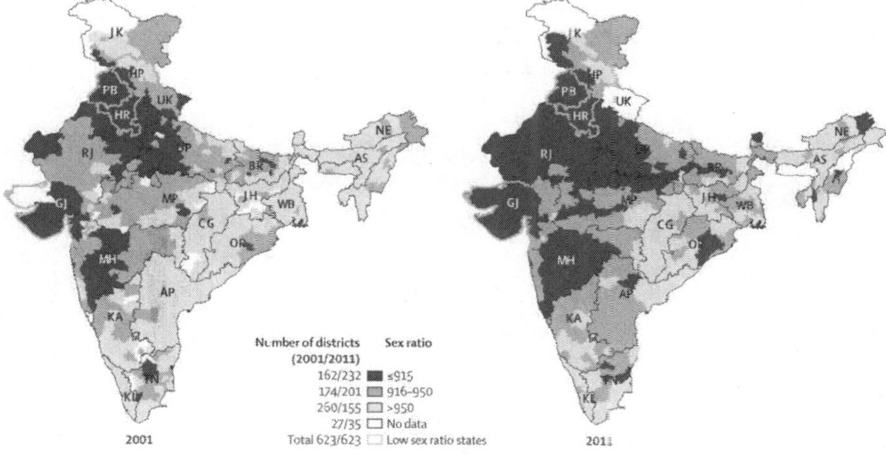

Source: Census (2011) represented by mtholyoke.edu

The challenge of missing women from the realm of birth ratio and sex ratio is a major social problem. From 1987–2016, it is found that 13.5

million women are missing based on the sex ratio 950 girls per 1000 births. Based on the 5 National Family Health Surveys, the trend is sex ratio is observed to be reducing. It is also further estimated based on the existing data, that about 10 million females are illegally aborted in India. The magnitude of this problem is further estimated to be a loss of 5 lakh women annually. The state with the highest sex ratio is Kerala 1058 for every 1000 births and lowest is Haryana 861 for every 1000 births.

In the Indian context, there are several causes of female foeticide. This problem is interlinked to the cultural and social factors in the Indian fabric. They are:

- Indian family systems are mostly patriarchal in nature. Its roots are strong in every sphere of Indian society. Sex selective abortion through pre-natal sex determination is an illegal practice, but still the rate of foeticide is high in the country.
- Dowry system in India is connected to female foeticide. Due to this system and fear of providing dowry for the prospective marriage of the unborn baby, the girls are aborted in the womb.
- Females are considered a financial burden or financial obligation by the family. Females are provided with gender roles of getting married and taking care of family for years together. Investing in their marriage or education is not greatly ideated by families.
- On the other side, inflation is considered as another major reason for female foeticide. The families take crucial decisions regarding giving birth to girl children, their education and marriage.
- The lack of robust implementation of Pre-conception and Pre-natal Diagnostics Techniques Act, 1994 is another reason for the increasing rate of sex selective abortion.
- Corruption and technological advancement are the reasons for the same.

Female foeticide denies a woman their basic constitutional right to life. This social problem is a major cause of the skewed sex ratio of India. This can also cause a decrease of the women population at large. Due to this disparity, it is recognised that this results in trafficking of women in India. This is an organized crime in which women are sold for marriage due to the scarcity. When there is a paucity of women in the country, the instances of rape and assault in India can increase. So, it is important to curb this major social issue posing women in India.

Child Marriage or Early Marriage is another major problem that is faced by females at a very young age. It is a marriage of a female or man before their legal adult age. This robs a female of their rights, childhood and brings in early adulthood responsibilities on them. Looking at the trends in

India, this marriage is prevalent mostly among women in India. This can pose a major challenge to the health and education of women.

Magnitude of Child Marriage in India	
Global Perspective	*Indian Perspective*
• 700 million women alive today are married before the age of 18 years. • More than 1 in 3 women entered into union before the age of 15 years. • Girls are disproportionately affected by the practice. • This is a common practice in South Asian and Sub-Saharan countries. • Niger has the largest number of child marriages in the world. • South Asia accounts for 42% of the total early marriages globally.	• The magnitude of the problem in India is in a reducing trend from 47.7% to 25.8%. • Highest prevalent states: Rajasthan, Uttar Pradesh, Madhya Pradesh, Jharkhand, Chhattisgarh and Bihar • Jammu and Kashmir has the lowest Child marriages in India. • Odisha's Ganjam is declared as child marriage free district in India in 2022.
Source: UNICEF, 2014	*Source:* NFHS 5

Child marriage is a very complex and intertwined problem. It is considered as a form of gender inequality. The following figure shows that 33 per cent of the marriages among children are reported from India in the South Asian region.

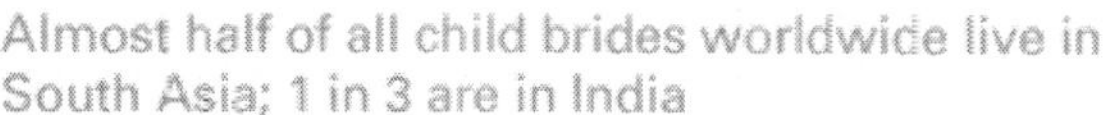

Percentage distribution of women aged 18 years and older who were married or in union before age 18, by region

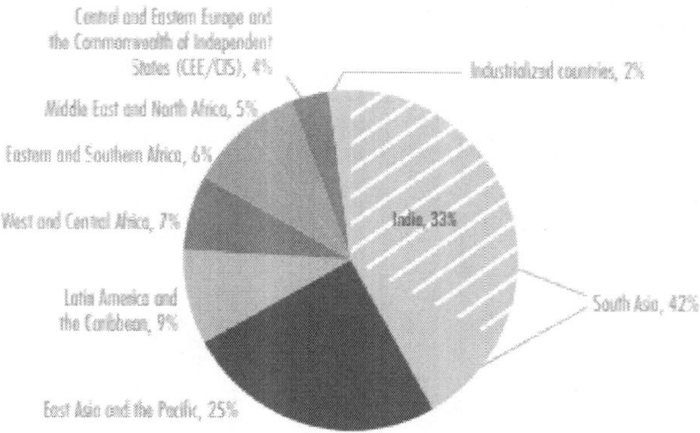

Source: UNICEF (2014)

- The primary causes of this practice is gender inequality and patriarchal norms. The gender norms and roles of women is a strong construct that leads to this practice.
- Poverty is another reason for child marriage in India. It is said that 40 per cent of the world's poor countries are married off at a very young

age. This relates to the family's cost burden and financial security. Economic or financial distress causes child marriages. Dowry and expenses of marriage is believed to be higher as the age of the girls are higher. The family prefers early marriage. Lack of access to education and welfare schemes for females in the lower income families can result in such marriages. Early adulthood responsibilities limit their access to emancipatory resources. Families with resources would invest it on the boy children in the family. Their access to job opportunities are limited due to gender norms at home.

- Bride price or dowry is another cause of child marriages in India.
- The relevance given to female reproductive and sexuality rights is a cause to child marriages of girls. This can lead to an overall control over her life through the institution of marriage.
- This criminalizes her sexuality and access to care.
- Family finds it a dishonour for the girls to have a relationship or pregnancy outside of the community and finds marriage as the option to protect their children.
- Social and cultural norms of the community on the age of marriage despite the existence of legal provisions causes rampant child marriages.
- Displacement from native lands is another reason for child marriages in India. This phenomenon also displaces their native social relations which make girls vulnerable to marriages.
- Human trafficking is hidden through child marriages. They are put into risk of exploitation and even slavery.

Child marriage has its own effects and influences on girls and women. The **basic rights of women are violated** at a very young age. It is divided into three major forms namely, (1) Violence of women rights, (2) health related challenges, and (3) gender based violence.

1. **Violation of rights:** The following rights of girl children gets violated with child marriage:
    - Right to survival
    - Right to health
    - Right to education
    - Right to protection
2. **Health related challenges:**
    - ***Adolescent pregnancy:*** is a major health risk. They are more vulnerable to physical problems among adolescent mothers. It can lead to low birth weight, preterm birth and severe neonatal condition. Adolescent pregnancy is sometimes caused by lack of usage of contraceptives. Child sexual abuse in such marriages are

also a major cause of it. The maternal health of the adolescent may not stay stable and can sometimes lead to mortality and morbidity.

- ***Sexually transmitted diseases:*** It can lead to sexually transmitted infections and violation of sexual-reproductive health rights. Early sexual debut can cause HIV and AIDS among girls. Unprotected sexual activity and usage of contraceptives are another reason for such diseases. Inaccessibility to SRHR is another cause for HIV-AIDS due to marriages among adolescents. Intimate partner violence in child marriages may sometimes make the girls vulnerable to STIs. Lower education levels and awareness about STIs can also cause the same.
- ***Mental health of children:*** can be depreciated with child marriage. Unintended pregnancies and domestic violence during childhood or adolescence can pose risk to the mental health of women. They may slip into depression and suicidal tendencies due to this challenge. On a larger landscape, this problem

3. **Gender-based violence:**
   - ***Physical, sexual and psychological violence:*** is another major result of child marriage. Sexually transmitted infections, unintended pregnancy, unsafe abortion, poor mental health, depression and femicide is associated with gender based physical and sexual violence.
   - ***Lower educational, economic and employment opportunities*** can result from child marriage.
   - ***Child marriage*** also results in intimate partner violence. As the age difference increases in the marriage the possibilities of violence are higher.

DOMESTIC VIOLENCE OR INTIMATE PARTNER/NON-PARTNER VIOLENCE

Violence against women perpetuates in each stage of their lives. It is sometimes carried into each generation. They also stated that violence against women, especially domestic violence is one of the most underrated and under-reported forms of violence around the globe. It is positioned that domestic violence or any forms of violence against women is a major human rights violation. One out of three women, i.e. 30 per cent of women globally have already gone through abuse and violence in their entire life time. One third of the women of age 15–49 years, i.e. 27 per cent are subjected to sexual or physical violence by their intimate partner. In the South Asian region including India it has a 35 per cent prevalence rate of Domestic Violence. Suicide due to domestic violence is a major reason for deaths of women between the age group of 15–39 years.

Did You Know?

- 81,000 women and girls were killed in 2020 out of which 58% were killed due to intimate partner violence.
- 1 woman dies every 11 minutes due to domestic violence globally.
- Gender related killings have been higher in Western Europe (11%), Southern Europe (5%), North America (8%) and South America (5%).
- 1.6 million women aged 16–74 years are victims of domestic violence in England and Wales.

There are different ways in which domestic violence can be inflicted – Physical abuse, Sexual abuse, verbal abuse, emotional abuse, social abuse and economic abuse. This practice causes physical, psychological and sexual harms in a relationship. It is a form of emotional abuse and controlling behaviour. Even though domestic violence is reported irrespective of gender, its prevalence is higher among women and girls. Causing violence on women in the family is due to the toxic masculinity, gender inequality and deep rooted patriarchal thoughts in the society. Domestic Violence is often only counted as a violent behaviour in a marital relationship. Violence is inflicted on women irrespective of them being a daughter, daughter-in-law or wife. It may be noted that women are found to be vulnerable and submissive in this society. They are prone to violence of different forms. As a result, domestic violence may have its own consequences on the physical and mental health of women. Even it can be assumed that women may be at times habitual of this form of violence.

Dowry system has a strong root in the Indian social structure. Every marriage carries a bride price and if it is way less than expected then the consequences are borne by the women. Dowry deaths are on the rise today. Even literate states like Kerala and Tamil Nadu reports very significant fatal cases of induced suicide and violence among women in India.

Gender based violence was termed as shadow pandemic during the COVID 19 pandemic. During the pandemic since 2020, there are 243 million women and girls of the age group 15–49 years who experience violence sexually and physically by an intimate partner. Most of the time, domestic violence is caused due to: (i) limited security, wealth and money; (ii) cramped living conditions; (iii) isolation with abusers at home; (iv) movement restrictions on women; and (v) deserted public spaces due to lockdown.

Domestic violence is a major challenge on the public health system of the country in the context of securing the physical, psychological, sexual and reproductive health of women. It can lead to social and economic consequences on women. The effects perpetuate to families and their children too. The consequences are divided into: (i) health impacts; (ii) social consequences; and (iii) economic effects.

Health Impacts

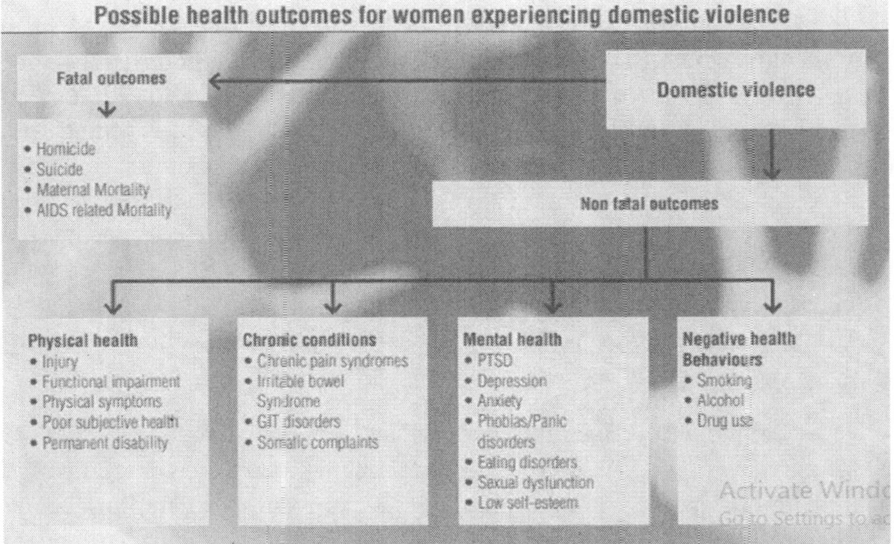

Source: 'A Question of Maternal Health.' Campbell D. (2010). *WIN*. Vol 11 Issue 9 https://inmo.ie/MagazineArticle/PrintArticle/8654

Fatal Outcomes

- **Femicide** is identified as a criminal act globally. It is reported that six women are killed every hour by their intimate partner or family members around the globe, identifying homes as the most dangerous place for women to live. They also identified that these women were killed because of gender norms, gender stereotyping and patriarchy. Further it was also explained that homicides are due to physical assault and dowry related issues. Homicides include poisoning, burns, hitting and planned road crashes.
- **Suicide** is another effect of domestic violence. It is found that in India, domestic violence in itself is a life stressor that can cause suicide tendencies among women. It was pointed out that women victims of suicide either consume pesticides, drugs, self-immolate or hang themselves. It is realized that, India reports 36 per cent of suicide among women around the globe. And more than half these cases are due to domestic violence.
- **Maternal Mortality** is a concern that can be a by-product of domestic violence. It is a key health indicator for women and which is identified

to be preventable. The National Sample Registration System (2018) reported a decline in maternal deaths over these years. Bihar has a high rate of maternal deaths. The women have undergone prolonged pre-delivery complications and also consequences of nutritional deprivation which causes death. It is also identified that the trauma and physical consequences of domestic violence contributes to the same.

- **Sexual Transmitted Diseases (STDs)** is another fatal consequence of domestic violence. STDs were found among women who are married and sexually violated by intimate partners. It is also identified that women get infected with HIV-AIDS, Chlamydia and Gonorrhea. These are major impacts of non-consensual and unprotected sexual practices among couples. It is considered to be a major violation of reproductive health rights of women across the globe. Violence, alcoholic partner, lack of economic independence and partners withholding physical intimacy as the reasons for HIV infection in married women in India.

Non-fatal Outcomes

- **Physical health consequences** of domestic violence include immediate injury, functional impairment, physical symptoms, poor subjective health and permanent disability. WHO enunciates that the immediate health related consequences of violence against women will include burns, bites, fractures and bruises. Physical violence can cause injuries on sensitive body parts like eyes, ears, chest, breast and abdomen. Chronic conditions may include body pain, irritable bowel syndrome, gastroenteritis, sleeplessness, back pain, headache and other somatic disorders.
- **Sexual and reproductive health rights** are also violated thereby affecting their health. Women may undergo gynecological disorders and trauma WHO (2012) also identified that women are not given the right to decide their pregnancy, access to safe sex and abortion rights. Men in the family take the decisions and females go by it. In such circumstances women suffer from pregnancy complications, painful sexual intercourse, vaginal bleeding and sexual dysfunction. Apart from these, they also undergo medical conditions like STDs, pelvic infection, cervical cancer, urinary tract infection and fistula. Another important aspect is female genital mutilation. In the familial system, genital mutilation is undertaken by women that is decided by men. In India, women who are battered are four times more at risk of STDs.
- **Mental health consequences** are also identified as a result of repeated violence from intimate partners. Marital violence and abuse can cause mental health issues in women. This may be manifested as Post

Traumatic Stress Disorder (PTSD), depression, anxiety, phobias/panic attacks, dietary disorders, sexual dysfunction and low self-esteem. The most prevalent forms of mental health disorder may also include insomnia, self-harms and attempts to suicide. Wife Battering Syndrome (WBS) is another important concept in the context of mental health. In this state, the woman shows diagnostic symptoms like psychologically re-experiencing the violence, staying aloof from people and activities, disrupted interpersonal skills, sexuality and somatic concerns.

- **Negative behaviour modifications** may combine smoking, alcoholism and usage of drugs. Violence in any form since childhood can cause an inclination to sexual activity at a very early stage of life, drug abuse, multiple partners, abusive partners and lower usage of contraceptive measures. These behavioral modifications take place as a result of continuous and unprecedented violence against them.

Social Consequences

As a consequence of domestic violence the victim stays away from their peer groups. They are not allowed to visit their natal home and peer groups in the community. The gender norms at home as part of the patriarchal practices may include serving the men and taking care of the household. So, their responsibilities are undervalued. Psychological and emotional trauma that women undergo due to violence affects their social life and reduces their presence in their peer circles. The lack of access to education is an effect of domestic violence. They are provided little access to education, crippling their ability to grow and contribute. She also elucidated that domestic violence victims have weaker family and peer ties. They are sometimes discriminated against with respect to the dowry.

Economic Consequences

Economic abuse may include economic exploitation, sabotage and control. It can be assumed that when a woman in the house undergoes violence, her productivity and ability to work reduces. Due to health and emotional consequences her opportunities to work also comes down. This may end up reducing the overall income of the family and the family perpetuates the violence intergenerationally. With this, the women may be economically dependent, threatened with their own security and self-sufficiency.

As part of a larger picture, domestic violence can cause reduced contribution of women to the global workforce. IMF recognizes that, with an increase in domestic violence cases, women would show absenteeism at workplace as their productivity goes less. Due to physical problems caused by violence women's participation at work, usage of their skill sets and education will be reduced. Due to reduced workforce, the overall income generated reduces and more budget is channelized to health and legal services.

It is very evident that as social workers there are many directions in which we can work for the welfare of women. Every challenge faced by them paves way to the next. Their welfare is dependent upon the family and also their own empowerment. Empowerment of girls and women in their lifetime can be done by elevating them to self-sufficiency and independence. Social work has a very strong means to ensure this. The next section will discuss about the legalities and provisions provided at the global and national level for protection and security of women.

Other Major Challenges

Human Trafficking of Women:

- Important problem among women that leads to immoral trafficking in the form of human smuggling, prostitution, intimate partner violence and child abuse.
- Violation of human rights
- Disrupts their social and economic life.
- Girls and women may encounter physical and psychological violations.
- Physical symptoms lead to neurological disorders, STIs and traumatic injuries.
- Mental health disorders like anxiety, depression, suicidal ideation, PTSD and disassociative disorders.

Review Questions

(a) What is Child Marriage in the Context of India?
(b) What are the causes and consequences of intimate partner violence?

POLICY FRAMEWORKS AND LEGISLATIONS

The Global and national provisions for women and their protection includes a structured set of legislation and frameworks. This section will be derived from:

- **Universal Declaration of Human Rights (1948):** provides for equal rights and dignity to every human without any type of discrimination. It also pronounces that, the right to live, be safe and secured. It also identified that every human in the world should be considered equally before the rule of law.
- **Convention on the Elimination of All Forms of Discrimination against Women (1979):** dissuades all forms of violence and inequality based on sex, gender, social, economic and cultural grounds. It also embodies the relevance legal provisions and rights perspective of women across the globe. It also calls upon every country to take up the agenda of economic independence of women and the significance of their contribution to the economy. It identifies the importance of

women in a family, to the economy and to the society at large. In 1993, India ratified this treaty.

- **World Conference on Human Rights (1993):** recognized violence against women a basic violation of their rights. This conference called off all the violence against women and also encouraged the world to make women a better part of all developmental decisions.
- **Declaration on Elimination of Violence against Women (1993):** propounded that violence against women is a comprehensive violation of their rights. It condemns and raises the requirement of legal frameworks against physical, sexual and psychological violence against women at the family and community levels.
- **International Conference on Population and Development (1994):** recognized the importance of women rights linked to reproductive health. It recognized that securing the rights of women and girls contributes to development. The conference primarily focused on agenda like gender equality, human rights, women's reproductive health rights, maternal deaths and unwanted pregnancies.
- **Beijing Platform for Action (1995):** called upon governments of various countries across the globe to contemplate and formulate legal frameworks on violence against women (UN Women, 2015). Taking this agenda forward, UN Women (2020) unfolded that 166 countries in the world compiled to and implemented the legal frameworks in the last 5 years.
- **Secretary-General's In-Depth Study on All Forms of violence against Women (2006):** concluded that without progress in reducing all forms of violence against women, there will not be any transformation in the issues related to equality, development and peace. This study recognized that it is very important for countries to punish the perpetrator and provide legal aid to the victims. It has called upon channelized work from government, NGOs, women's group and researchers to end such forms of violence.
- **Council of Europe Convention on preventing and combating violence against women and domestic violence (2011):** became a globally accepted instrument for securing the women from all forms of violence.
- **Commission for the Status of Women (1946):** As per the guidelines of ECOSOC Resolution 11, 1946, the Commission for the Status of Women was formed. This commission primarily focused on strengthening gender equality and women empowerment. The commission is formed to address global women protection issues and also to take measures that will be implemented at the field.

From the above frameworks, it may be identified that women are basically vulnerable due to gender based violence faced by them. All the global strategies reflected on the preventive and curative strategies that help in betterment of women. It calls for robust legal and policy level decisions that can help women at the grass-root level. This chapter will further take us through the legislations, policies, schemes and service delivery structures to combat violence against women in India.

Indian Context

The history of evolution of legislations on violence against women. In India, the colonial period saw a number of social reformers like Raja Ram Mohan Roy who spoke and worked eloquently for the rights of women. They were strongly against the social evils like sati and also harsh widowhood. They recognised that women also have rights to live and survive happily after her husband.

The Immoral Traffic (Prevention) Act, 1959: is a legislation that came into place after India signed the trafficking suppression treaty of the UN. It aims at reducing and abolishing various provisions of sex work in the country. According to Section 23 of the act, immoral trafficking of human beings is prohibited. By this, it means that forced transfer of people for economic abuse, labour and sexual abuse. A person who is involved in recruiting, transportation, transferring, harbouring and receiving people for prostitution is liable for punishment. If the person is involved with a child and found guilty for it would be punishable for seven or more years.

Dowry Prohibition Act, 1961: Indian culture always welcomed grand weddings associated with huge dowry. This system was supposed to strengthen the relationship between the partners. But, he further recognizes that the practice is a huge violation of rights. But even with the enactment of such legislations, such practices still continued. During the 1980s, India saw a steep hike in the dowry deaths. The provisions related to domestic violence were first implicated in the Indian Penal Code (1863) in 1983 under section 498(a) favouring women who undergo cruelty from her partner and non-partner relationships. In 1986, the IPC also introduced Sec 304 B, which states that any suspicious deaths within 7 years of marriage of a woman at her in-laws' home will be an offence.

Way back from the 1970s, combating violence against women became a very clear agenda of the government and legal system in India. Tukaram and other v/s State of Maharashtra – a case that was registered in session's court which shook the entire country. A 16-year-old girl was raped by a police official and the session's court passed a judgement that the victim was lying and she was consensual to the act. Later, the High Court revoked the decision of the session's court and found the accused to be guilty. In 1979, on appeal by the defendants to the Supreme Court of India, the judgement of the High Court was cancelled. The Supreme Court of India passed a judgement that defendants were not guilty as the victim was not vocal about any lack of consent or did not survive any bruises on her body. The Hon'ble Court also stated that the victim was habituated to sex according to the two finger test. It is notable that during this period, the victim has to prove her innocence. Every street of Delhi was flooded with women led movements against the judgement of the Supreme Court. This uprising has led to positive changes in the existing legislations related to women in the country.

Indecent Representation of Women (Prohibition) Act, 1986: prohibits the indecent depiction of women through advertisement, publication, writing, paintings, figures or photographs. In this context, for first conviction, the term of imprisonment can be up to 2 years with a fine of Rs. 2000. In the second conviction, the imprisonment may not be less than 6 months up to 5 years and a fine from Rs. 10,000 to 1 lakh.

Preconception and Prenatal Diagnostic Technique Act, 1994: was amended in 2003 and 2011 respectively. This legislation was an effort to prohibit the prenatal diagnostic technique for sex determination to avoid female foeticide in India. This act was a result of the increasing disparity in sex ratio in India. The provisions of this legislation basically keeps ultrasound scanning and amniocentesis in purview in the context of sex determination. Also, it allows detection of genetic abnormalities, chromosomal abnormalities, malformations and hameoglobinopathisis. Anyone who engages in sex determination techniques can be imprisoned for 3 years with a fine of Rs. 10,000.

The Protection of Women from Domestic Violence Act, 2005: The legal provisions under this act recognizes physical abuse, sexual abuse, verbal & emotional abuse and economic abuse as domestic violence against women. The act designates the Protection Officer for women and the police official of the respective jurisdiction to be responsible for the safety of the aggrieved. Examining the depth of the consequences of the violence on women, the court will pass the orders on compensation. With the strong legal provisions under the Act, the stronger implementation of the act is very important. Quoting the data from NCRB, 2014 they analysed that out of the 426 cases registered under the Act only 19.1 per cent was convicted. And the acceleration of the pace of implementing the act is important.

The **National Policy for Women, 2006** highlights the fight on violence against women. This policy comprehensively covers all forms of violence. Following the life cycle approach, the policy highlights the importance to reduce sex selective abortion, child marriages and combat violence at any stage of life with the robust utilisation of the existing legal provisions. It recommends the placement of strong enforcement agencies and members in the field to identify violence against women in the communities. It also brought out the importance of participation of men in advocacy and awareness programmes based on gender sensitisation.

Prevention of Sexual Harassment at Workplace Act, 2013: attempts to protect against sexual harrassment and abuse of women at workplace. It seeks to ensure a safe and protective environment for women. It also intends to create awareness on sexual harrassment and also provides necessary steps for legal remedies for victims. It brought out the necessity of Internal Complaints Committee (ICC) within the workplace to ensure a safe working environment for women. It not only ensures a harassment free environment in the office but also ensures that the rights of women are protected.

Mission Shakti converges two major subcategories of programme – *Sambal & Samarthya*. The schemes under the mission are completely for the safety and security of women as well as children. One Stop Centre, Mahila Police Volunteer, Women Helpline, *Swadhar*, *Ujjwala* and Widow Home are under *Sambal*. *Beti Bachao Beti Padhao*, Creche system, Pradhan Mantri Mathru Vandana Yojana, Gender Budgeting and Research comes under *Samarthya*.

Sambal Schemes

- **One Stop Centre** is a major mission for the rehabilitation of victims who face gender based violence. This centre has a team of 7 staff members who provide medical assistance (referral), police assistance, psychosocial counselling services, legal aid and shelter. Any aggrieved women will be provided with immediate aid and then provided with long term solutions. They handle domestic violence cases along with the protection officers appointed under the PWDV Act, 2005 and comprehensively provides services for their safety (Ministry of Women and Child Development.
- **Mahila Police Volunteers** is a pilot project that started in Haryana. It is formed to report violence against women taking place in villages in Haryana. It may include child marriage, domestic violence and dowry harassment. This was envisioned as a strong engagement between the police and society at large. This scheme also aimed at facilitating outreach programmes with the communities along with the police personnel.
- **Swadhar Scheme** is a project for women victim of domestic violence or any other difficult situations. It provides temporary shelter, basic

amenities, vocational training, counselling services and legal guidance to them. Widow Homes is a project piloted in UP, which provides for the overall well-being of widows. They are provided with safety, security, place of stay, health services, and nutritious meal, legal as well as counselling services.

- **Beti Bachao Beti Padao (BBBP)** is a flagship programme that aims at reducing sex selective abortion by enabling safety of girl children. It also encourages education and to fulfil the participation rights of girl children. This is mainly implemented through community and mass level programmes. This programme is designed based on advocacy and media campaign. As a whole, this programme aims at maintaining gender equality at all levels.

So, these are the basic legal, policy and service related frameworks in India that help in betterment of the women and their protection. It is very important for the women to know about these facilities and legal framework to move forward from toxic relationships. All the schemes and service delivery structures aim at addressing domestic violence, its forms and causes.

Social Work with Women

Social work with women is a branch of the discipline that works for the welfare and empowerment of women. Welfare denotes their safety, protection, access and opportunities, whereas empowerment is about action. Gender is a very important aspect of social work. The non - discriminatory nature of interventions in the field is a valid example for the same. It is important to empathetically understand that men and women are socialized differently. Men are generally considered assertive, competitive and forceful whereas women are considered tender and timid. This differentiation creates the domination of men and oppression of women to a large extent. Social work as a profession has specific principles and values that guides them to work in any field or specific area. The inherent nature of social work practice includes empathy and optimum use of resources should be considered at this point. Dealing with women in distress is complex and hence a skillful task. It is important for young social workers to possess a set of key professional skills that will help them to transition easily in the context of protection and empowerment of women.

Social work with women aims at:

- Provides students with the strengths of empowering women in distress.
- Exposing students to the programmes and services provided at the field level.
- To build skills to work with women.
- Engaging them with the emerging policy and its implementation

- Social work with women engages the students in the following areas:
- Human Rights
- Women empowerment
- Vulnerability of women
- Causes of violence against women
- Consequences of gender based violence
- Policy level interventions for women

It is critical for social workers to practice strategies in the context of women. It is critical for the professional to contribute towards their socio - economic stability, empowerment and also on gender based violence. It is vital for social workers to also work on the fields of sex selective abortions, woman's inability to bear children especially male child, female foeticide, discrimination against women on food and education, forced sex work, dowry deaths, domestic violence, access to health etc. are some of the examples of such discrimination (Gandhi, n.d.). Social work with women is to empower and educate family and community about the challenges and vulnerabilities faced by them at large. It is to sensitize the community about the deep rooted patriarchal processes and the ways in which it can be reduced. Social workers can be a catalyst in this context to ensure that women understand their problems and challenges.

Social work as a professional practice can have the following aspects covered:

- Synthesis between practice and theoretical framework based on feminist literatures as well as social realities.
- Unbiased approach to field level practice of social work among women.
- Use of philosophies and ethics of social work in the process of empowering women.
- Fieldwork with women implementing the methods of social work namely, case work, group work and community organisation.
- Clearing off bias from the minds of social workers themselves. This is self-centric approach in which their interventions are also unbiased.

In order to carry out them, it is important for social workers to possess skills like:

- Self-awareness
- Skill of positive evaluation of women
- Skill of self-disclosure to encourage women
- Skill of intensive interviewing
- Skills related to negotiation, reconciliation and networking
- Ability to work with self-help groups of men and women
- Ability to work with reluctant clients and stakeholders

- Ability to work in team with allied professionals
- Ability for narrative, analytical and reflective recordings

Measuring Gender Inequality

Gender Equality Index (GII) is the composite metric for gender inequality based on reproductive health, empowerment and labour market. Lower the GII value, lower is the inequality between men and women. This was put forth by the United Nations Development Programme (UNDP). The figure below shows the indicators that is primarily used to measure this for various countries:

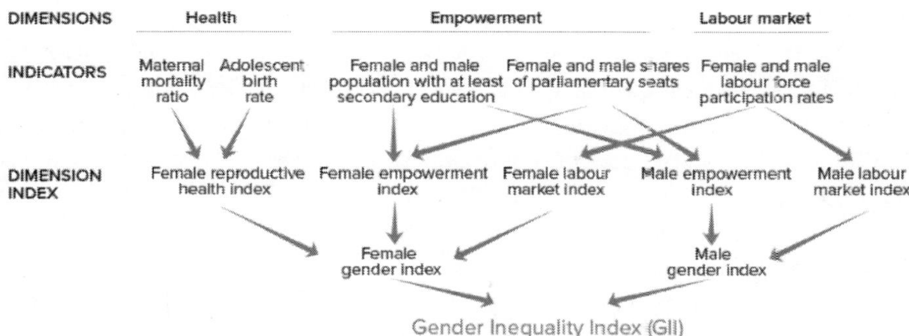

Gender Inequality Index (GII)

On the basis of these indices, India stands at the 122th position globally standing at the medium human development index. So, it is important to note that skills of Management Information System (MIS) and Monitoring & Evaluation need to be acquired to measure and understand the gender based modalities of women's vulnerabilities.

Challenges and vulnerabilities of women are a global phenomenon. It is caused due to patriarchy, gender norms, gender inequality and gender roles. Gender based violence against women are female foeticide, child marriage, domestic violence and dowry deaths. It is caused by gender based challenges, patriarchy and gender roles given by the social system. Social work with women can bring changes in the field that comprehensively converges the programmes and services in the country to make a change in the social set up of the country. The interventions will cover the physical, psychological, familial and social aspects with respective social work strategies.

Review Questions

(a) What are the major frameworks globally to combat violence against women?

(b) What are the major legislations in India for violence against women?

SUMMARY

In this chapter, we understood the concept of gender, gender equality, gender equity, gender roles, patriarchy and womanhood. It also looked into the causes and consequences of gender based violence among women. The chapter also explained about specific forms of violence like domestic violence, dowry, female foeticide and child marriage. The section also looked into the policies and legislations in the global and national levels. Also, the chapter covered the required skills and proficiencies for working with women.

GLOSSARY

- **Missing women** is defined as a deficit in the total number of women to be present in a geographical area. It is measured by measuring the sex ratios, sex-selective abortions, female foeticide, and inadequate healthcare and nutrition for female children (Sen, 1990).
- **Sexuality** is defined as a concept of understanding our bodies, desires, relationships, gender, thoughts and feelings (Sexuality Education Research Centre, 2023).
- **Sexual and reproductive health** is a state of physical, emotional, mental and social well-being in relation to all aspects of sexuality and reproduction, not merely the absence of disease, dysfunction or infirmity (Guttmacher Institute, 2023).

TOP TEN TAKEAWAY POINTS

1. Women face several challenges globally.
2. Gender based violence (GBV) is a major challenge posed against women.
3. GBV includes various forms of violence like female foeticide, child marriage, domestic violence, dowry system and sexual abuse.
4. Gender roles lead to gender based violence
5. There are several causes to gender based violence which includes patriarchy, gender roles and social standards.
6. Consequences of violence against women can be physical, social, economic, psychological and health related.
7. Violence against women can exploit their basic human rights.
8. Social work profession can ensure organised strategies to prevent such forms of violence.
9. Following the basic social work principles and values can bring strong interventions and changes in the field in the context of women.
10. Gender Equality Index (GII) is a composite metric introduced by UNDP to measure gender inequality in work place, health set up and empowerment.

MULTIPLE CHOICE QUESTIONS

1. The socio-cultural attribute given by the social norms of society to men and women:
   (a) Gender (b) Patriarchy
   (c) Social Norms (d) Gender Norms
2. The access to rights, opportunities, resources and protection for every individual irrespective of gender:
   (a) Equality (b) Norms (c) Gender Equality (d) Gender
3. Providing fair access and equal opportunities to all irrespective of their gender is called:
   (a) Gender Equality (b) Gender Equity
   (c) Gender based violence (d) Matriarchy
4. Stereotyped attitudes, attributes and actions assigned to individuals by the society that brings the differences in their access and opportunities is denoted as:
   (a) Gender Equality (b) Gender Roles
   (c) Patriarchal Norms (d) Social Norms
5. _________ is the system in which the male breadwinner of the family is the authority and oppresses the women based on their gender roles.
   (a) Matriarchy (b) Patriarchy
   (c) Social Structure (d) Social work norms
6. Domestic violence includes all except _____________.
   (a) Stalking (b) Date rape
   (c) Marital rape (d) Intimate Partner Violence
7. Which of the following Act is made to prohibit the practice of dowry?
   (a) Dowry Prevention Act, 1971 (b) Dowry Prohibition Act, 1961
   (c) Dowry Prohibition Act, 1951 (d) Dowry Prohibition Act, 1941
8. When was Prohibition of Child Marriage Act passed?
   (a) 2010 (b) 2006 (c) 2022 (d) 2001
9. In which case references does the Sexual Harassment of Women at Workplace Act come into place?
   (a) Nirbhaya (b) Vishaka (c) Mariam (d) Bhanwari
10. Child marriage is a cause for domestic violence.
    (a) True (b) False

Answers

1. (a), 2. (c), 3. (b), 4. (b), 5. (b), 6. (d), 7. (b), 8. (b), 9. (b), 10. (a)

REFERENCES

1. American Psychological Association (2017). Facts about Trafficking of women and girls. https://www.apa.org/topics/women-girls/trafficking-women-girls

2. Baxter J. and Hoffman H. (2019). Gender. Oxford Bibliographies. DOI: 10.1093/OBO/9780199756384-0022
3. Barik S. (2022). Ganjam district is now child marriage free. *The Hindu*. https://www.thehindu.com/news/national/other-states/ganjam-district-is-now-child-marriage-free/article38103390.ece
4. Chatterjee I. (2009). The Evil of Female Foeticide In India: Causes, Consequences and Prevention. *Legal Service India e-Journal*. https://www.legalserviceindia.com/legal/article-777-the-evil-of-female-foeticide-in-india-causes-consequences-and-prevention.html
5. Diamant J. (2022). In India and many other countries, there is little gap between men and women in attitudes on gender issues. PEW Research Centre. https://pewrsr.ch/3CIQDgf
6. Kehinde E.O. (2007). Womanhood: A Philosophical Appraisal. *African Journals Online*, Vol. 9, No.1. DOI: 10.4314/sophia.v9i1.38760
7. Kidman, 2017, Child marriage and intimate partner violence: a comparative study of 34 countries, *International Journal of Epidemiology*, Volume 46, Issue 2, 1 April 2017, pp. 662–75.
8. Ritchie H. and Roser M. (2019). Gender Ratio. https://ourworldindata.org/gender-ratio
9. Sexuality Education Resource Centre (n.d.). What is Sexuality. https://serc.mb.ca/sexual-health-info/the-basics/what-is-sexuality/
10. Starrs, Ezeh, Barker, Basu, Bertrand, Blum, Coll-Seck, Grover, Laski, Roa, Sathar, Say, Serour, Singh, Stenberg and Temmerman (2018). Accelerate Progress – Sexual and Reproductive Health and Rights for all. Guttmacher Institute. Germany.
11. Vikaspedia (2019). Status of Women in India. https://vikaspedia.in/social-welfare/women-and-child-development/women-development-1/status-of-women-in-india
12. UNICEF (2022). Gender Inequality Overview. https://data.unicef.org/topic/gender/overview/#:~:text=Gender%20equality%20means%20that%20women,%2C%20resources%2C%20opportunities%20and%20protections.
13. UN Women (n.d.). The Shadow Pandemic: Violence against women during COVID 19. https://www.unwomen.org/en/news/in-focus/in-focus-gender-equality-in-covid-19-response/violence-against-women-during-covid-19
14. World Health Organisation (2022). Adolescent Pregnancy. https://www.who.int/news-room/fact-sheets/detail/adolescent-pregnancy#:~:text=Adolescent%20mothers%20(aged%2010%E2%80%9319,birth%20and%20severe%20neonatal%20condition.

RECOMMENDED READINGS

1. Alston M. (2015). Working with Women: Gender Sensitive Social Work Practice. Working with Particular Groups and Communities of Interest. Oxford University Press.

2. Dominelli L. (2010). Social Work in a Globalising World. Cambridge: Polity, pp. 3–18.
3. Moulding, Nicole & Wendt, Sarah (eds) (2016). Contemporary Feminisms in Social Work Practice. London: Routledge.
4. National Family Health Survey (2015–16). India Factsheet – National Family Health Survey. Indian Institute of Population Studies.
5. National Family Health Survey (2019–21). National Family Health Survey 5 India Report. International Institute of Population Studies.
6. Neuman S. (2013). The Issues of Sexual Violence against Women in Contemporary India. School of Social Sciences, Linnaeus University, pp. 1–63.
7. Singh A., Chokandre P., Singh A.K., Baker K.M., Kumar K., McDougal L., James K.S. & Raj A. (2021). *Developing of the India Patriarchy Index*. Social Indicators Research. doi: https://doi.org/10.1007/s11205-021-02752-1
8. Slabbert I. (2006). *Domestic Violence and Poverty: Some Women's Experience*. Research on Social Work Practice. https://doi.org/10 1177/1049731516662321
9. Walker, L.E. (1979). *The Battered woman*. New York: Harper & Row.

CHAPTER – 11

Social Work Practice with LGBTQIA+

SAYANTIKA SEN[1] AND VANI NARULA[2]

[1]*PhD Scholar, Department of Social Work, Jamia Millia Islamia*
[2]*Professor, Department of Social Work, Jamia Millia Islamia*

LGBT people are some of the bravest and most potent change agents and leaders I have encountered, and the most forceful defenders of the vulnerable and voiceless, because they know what it's like to be there.

– Ronan Farrow (2018)

ABSTRACT: *The concept of LGBTQIA+ (Lesbian, Gay, Bisexual, Transgender, Queer, Intersex, Asexual) came into existence after breaking the stereotypical norm of binary gender identity. A transgender is a person whose gender (which is a social construct) does not match with the sex (which is formed biologically at birth). A person of different sexual orientations (lesbian, gay, bisexual) than heterosexual have sexual preferences for the same gender as oneself or towards different genders. This chapter aims to explore the differences between gender and sexual orientation and how each of the identity is different from the other. It also discusses how Social Work as a profession plays an integral role in supporting the needs of the gender minority population as advocates and allies of the LGBTQIA+ community. Finally, the chapter examines the social challenges faced by the community and builds up the solution of developing inclusivity and cultural competency models of Social Work to address the situation.*

Keywords: *LGBTQIA+, Sex, Gender, Legislation, Discrimination*

Learning Objectives

After reading this chapter, you would be able to:

- Develop an understanding of the differential terminologies of LGBTQIA+ population.
- This chapter explain the differences of the concepts of sex, gender and sexual orientation.
- Describe the history and transition of social status of the LGBTQIA+ community in India and world
- A preview to the national and international legislations for the LGBTQIA+ community
- How social work professionals' change current and potential roles in the care, support, and well-being of the LGBTQIA+ community.

INTRODUCTION

The initials of LGBTQIA+ stands for lesbian, gay, bisexual, transgender, queer, intersex, asexual and other additional genders. LGBT is commonly used as an inclusive umbrella term for all the sexual and gender identity who is non-cisgender (whose gender does not identify with assigned sex at birth) and non-heterosexual (who is sexually attracted to the same sex). The letter Q often identifies as queer or who are questioning their sexual or gender identity. It is to be believed that there may be as many genders in this world as many population is there. To include this idea, the symbol + is used to signify the existence of other genders as well. These group of individuals are called non binary, who are, individuals who do not identify as exclusively male or female. This population includes people who identify as a combination of male and female, neither male nor female, or something else entirely. Non-binary individuals (who have different gender orientations) may also identify as gender fluid, meaning their gender identity changes over time or in different contexts. Over the years, the stigmatization and marginalization of the LGBTQIA+ population has increased because of the fact that the society has unjustly blamed them and associated them largely with HIV/AIDS risk behaviours. This kind of structural and social barriers which prevents the LGBTQIA+ community is to be identified so that these community members are not prevented from accessing life support resources.

CONCEPTS OF SEX, GENDER AND SEXUAL ORIENTATION

Sex refers to the physical and physiological features including chromosomes, gene expression, hormone levels and function, and reproductive/sexual anatomy. Sex can be classified as male, female or intersex. Sex is determined the moment the sperm fertilizes the egg and is biological in nature. It is defined by XX chromosome in female, XY chromosome male and XXY or XYY chromosome among intersex.

Whereas, gender refers to the socially constructed roles, behaviours, expressions and identities. Gender is influenced by how people perceive themselves and express themselves in the society. Gender is expressed through how they act, interact and dress up. Gender can be both binary and non-binary. Binary gender means where the gender expression is limited to male and female while non-binary gender can consist of any gender expression. Again, gender can be dynamic, meaning that gender expression may change from time to time (e.g., gender fluid) or it may exist along a continuum. Thus gender is perceived by how individuals understand the roles they take on, experiences they live and relationships built up with others based on the gender identity formed by them.

If observed intriguingly, it will be noticed that through long time duration since civilization established gender has been shaped by political, religious, philosophical, linguistic, traditional, and other cultural forces while many subtle trails continue to influence gender constantly.

DEFINITION OF LGBTQIA+ TERMINOLOGIES

To go by the definitions, a lesbian is 'a woman whose enduring physical, romantic, and/or emotional attraction is to other women. Some lesbians may prefer to identify as gay or as gay women'.

Gay is the adjective that describes people who are romantically or physically attracted to the people of same sex.

Bisexual is someone 'who can form enduring physical, romantic, and/or emotional attractions to those of the same gender or more than one gender. People may experience this attraction in differing ways and degrees over their lifetime. Bisexual people need not have had specific sexual experiences to be bisexual; they need not have had any sexual experience at all to identify as bisexual'.

A transgender is an umbrella term for people whose gender identity or expression differs from their sex assigned at birth. A transgender person can be both binary and non-binary. Some transgender individuals take medical assistance like surgery, hormone therapy to bring their bodies into alignment with their gender identity. Not all transgender people go through it and transgender identity is not dependent upon physical appearance or medical procedures. It focuses more on how the individual wants to express one's gender in the society.

A queer is an inclusive adjective for non-binary, gender-fluid, or gender nonconforming identities. Questioning gender identity describes someone who is questioning or not yet confirmed about their sexual orientation or gender identity. Intersex people are individuals with one or more innate sex characteristics, including genitals, internal reproductive organs, and chromosomes which does not confirm with the traditional male or female biological constructs. Intersex are different from transgender since intersex people are assigned at birth. It is more of biological than a social construct and often they are identified as male or female which is decided by medical providers and parents after birth.

Asexual person does not experience sexual attraction. It has several divisions like demisexual (who experience some sexual attraction), graysexual (who may not fit the strictest definition of the word asexual) and aromantic (who does not experience or desire to form romantic attractions).

The symbol + is used to signify the existence of other genders as well. These groups of individuals are called non binary, who are, individuals who do not identify as exclusively male or female. This population includes people who identify as a combination of male and female, neither male nor female, or something else entirely.

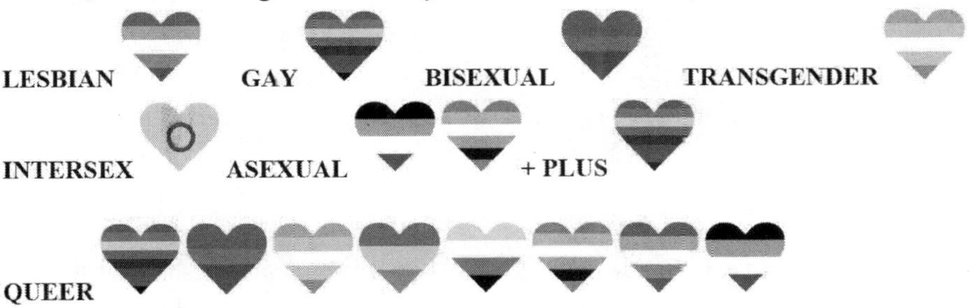

Figure 1: Different Pride Flags of the LGBTQIA+ Community
Source: https://gaycenter.org/about/lgbtq/

Review Questions

(a) What do you understand by binary and non-binary gender?
(b) What is the difference between sex and gender?
(c) What are the different terminologies of LGBTQIA+? Give a brief definition of each of them.

HISTORY OF LGBTQIA+ COMMUNITY

The history of the LGBTQIA+ community in India is complex and multifaceted. Same-sex relationships and gender diversity have been documented in India's ancient religious texts, such as the Kama Sutra and the Arthashastra, which suggest that attitudes towards same-sex relationships have varied across different regions and time periods.

During the British colonial period, India adopted laws from Britain that criminalized homosexuality, with Section 377 of the Indian Penal Code making same-sex sexual activity illegal. This law was challenged by LGBTQIA+ activists and allies for many years, culminating in a historic judgment in 2018 by the Indian Supreme Court, which declared Section 377 unconstitutional and decriminalized consensual same-sex sexual activity.

Despite this progress, the LGBTQIA+ community in India still faces significant legal, social, and cultural challenges. Many LGBTQIA+ individuals face discrimination, harassment, and violence, and are often ostracized by their families and communities. While there is no explicit legal recognition of same-sex relationships in India, some state governments have taken steps to provide recognition and support for LGBTQIA+ individuals, such as through the provision of healthcare and welfare services.

TRANSITION OF MINDSET TOWARDS THE LGBTQIA+ COMMUNITY

Transgender individuals have been documented in various ancient religious texts, including those from Hindu mythology. Here are a few examples:

- **Lord Shiva:** In Hindu mythology, Lord Shiva is often depicted as Ardhanarishvara, a deity who is half-male and half-female. This representation of Shiva is meant to symbolize the unity and balance of male and female energies and the possibility of transcending binary gender categories.
- **Lord Vishnu:** In some versions of the Hindu epic Mahabharata, the god Vishnu is said to have taken on a female form, Mohini, in order to trick demons and obtain the elixir of immortality. This story has been interpreted as an example of gender fluidity and the potential for divine beings to transcend gender boundaries.
- **Kinnars/Hijras:** Hijras, Kinnars or transgender individuals who are assigned male at birth, have been documented in Hindu mythology and in historical texts dating back to the Mughal era. Hijras are often associated with the goddess Bahuchara Mata, who is said to have granted them special powers and blessings. In some Hindu traditions, hijras are considered to be auspicious and are invited to perform at weddings and other ceremonies.

These examples suggest that gender diversity has been present in Hindu mythology for thousands of years and has been acknowledged and celebrated in various ways. While contemporary attitudes towards transgender individuals in India can be complex and varied, the history of transgender individuals in Hindu mythology provides a rich and diverse cultural legacy that continues to be relevant today.

The history of transgender individuals in Muslim texts and cultures is complex and diverse. Throughout history, there have been examples of transgender individuals and gender-nonconforming people in Muslim cultures, including Sufi mystics, poets, and artists. For example, the Persian poet Rumi is said to have had a close relationship with a male disciple, Shams Tabrizi, that has been interpreted as a same-sex relationship or as an example of spiritual love beyond gender boundaries.

Hijras, also known as eunuchs or transgender individuals, played a significant role in the Mughal era of India (1526-1858). In the Mughal court, hijras held important positions as trusted advisors, guards, and servants. They were often seen as powerful and mystical figures, capable of granting blessings and curses. The Mughal emperors, including Akbar and Shah Jahan, were known to have eunuchs in their courts. These eunuchs were highly respected and given important roles, such as serving as personal attendants and advisers to the emperor. They were also used as guards and were trusted to protect the emperor's harem and the royal family. Hijras were also present in Mughal society at large, and were often marginalized and stigmatized. They were viewed as a separate and distinct group, and were often subject to discrimination and persecution. However, they also had their own communities and networks, and were sometimes able to establish their own power and influence.

The influence of British colonialism on attitudes towards transgender and homosexual individuals in India and other colonized countries has been significant. British colonial authorities introduced laws and policies that criminalized same-sex relations and gender non-conforming behaviour, and these laws continued to have a lasting impact even after colonial rule ended.

One of the most notorious examples of this influence was the introduction of Section 377 of the Indian Penal Code in 1860, which made "carnal intercourse against the order of nature" a criminal offense. This law was widely interpreted to include same-sex relations, and it was used to justify discrimination and violence against LGBTQIA+ individuals for many decades.

The British also introduced a system of gender binary that was more rigid than many traditional cultural practices in India and other colonized countries. This system prioritized a binary understanding of gender, with men and women expected to conform to certain norms and behaviours based on their biological sex. This often meant that individuals who did not conform to these norms, such as hijras or other gender non-conforming people, were stigmatized and marginalized.

The status of LGBTQ+ individuals in India has been a complex and evolving issue since the country gained independence in 1947. Prior to independence, homosexuality was criminalized under British colonial rule through the introduction of Section 377 of the Indian Penal Code, which criminalized "unnatural offenses" including same-sex sexual activity. This law remained in place even after independence and was often used to discriminate against and persecute LGBTQ+ individuals in India. In recent years, there have been significant developments towards LGBTQ+ rights in India. In 2009, the Delhi High Court declared Section 377 unconstitutional in a landmark ruling, which was a major victory for the LGBTQ+ community. However, this ruling was later overturned by the Supreme Court in 2013, reinstating the criminalization of homosexuality. In 2018, the Supreme Court once again struck down Section 377, decriminalizing consensual same-sex sexual activity and paving the way for greater legal protection and recognition of LGBTQ+ rights in India. Since then, several significant advancements have been made towards recognizing and protecting the rights of LGBTQ+ individuals, including: The Transgender Persons (Protection of Rights) Act, 2019, which recognizes transgender people as a third gender and provides for their protection against discrimination and violence. The Indian Air Force became the first branch of the Indian military to allow transgender individuals to serve in 2021. Several Indian cities have hosted Pride parades and events to celebrate and advocate for LGBTQ+ rights. However, discrimination and violence against LGBTQ+ individuals still persist in India, and there is still a long way to go towards achieving full equality and protection under the law. LGBTQ+ individuals continue to face social stigma and discrimination in many aspects of their lives, including employment, healthcare, and education. Nonetheless, the progress made in recent years is a testament to the efforts of activists and allies in India's LGBTQ+ community, and offers hope for a more just and equal future.

Review Questions

(a) What role did the British have to play with changing the mindset of Indians towards transgender community?

(b) State few examples of mention of transgender in religious texts and mythologies.

DEMOGRAPHIC FACTS – INDIA AND WORLD

Table 1: State-wise Distribution of Transgender in India

#	*State*	*Transgenders*	*Child (0–6)*	*SC*	*ST*	*Literacy*
–	India	487,803	54,854	78,811	33,293	56.07%
1	Uttar Pradesh	137,465	18,734	26,404	639	55.80%
2	Andhra Pradesh	43,769	4,082	6,226	3,225	53.33%
3	Maharashtra	40,891	4,101	4,691	3,529	67.57%
4	Bihar	40,827	5,971	6,295	506	44.35%
5	West Bengal	30,349	2,376	6,474	1,474	58.83%
6	Madhya Pradesh	29,597	3,409	4,361	5,260	53.01%
7	Tamil Nadu	22,364	1,289	4,203	180	57.78%
8	Orissa	20,332	2,125	3,236	4,553	54.35%
9	Karnataka	20,266	1,771	3,275	1,324	58.82%
10	Rajasthan	16,517	2,012	2,961	1,805	48.34%
11	Jharkhand	13,463	1,593	1,499	3.735	47.58%
12	Gujarat	11,544	1,028	664	1,238	62.82%
13	Assam	11,374	1,348	774	1,223	53.69%

#	*State*	*Transgenders*	*Child (0–6)*	*SC*	*ST*	*Literacy*
14	Punjab	10,243	813	3,055	0	59.75%
15	Haryana	8,422	1,107	1,456	0	62.11%
16	Chhattisgarh	6,591	706	742	1,963	51.35%
17	Uttarakhand	4,555	512	731	95	62.65%
18	Delhi	4,213	311	490	0	62.99%
19	Jammu and Kashmir	4,137	487	207	385	49.29%
20	Kerala	3,902	295	337	51	84.61%
21	Himachal Pradesh	2,051	154	433	118	62.10%
22	Manipur	1,343	177	40	378	67.50%
23	Tripura	833	66	172	181	71.19%
24	Meghalaya	627	134	3	540	57.40%
25	Arunachal Pradesh	495	64	0	311	52.20%
26	Goa	398	34	9	33	73.90%
27	Nagaland	398	63	0	335	70.75%
28	Puducherry	252	16	40	0	60.59%
29	Mizoram	166	26	1	146	87.14%
30	Chandigarh	142	16	22	0	72.22%
31	Sikkim	126	14	9	37	65.18%
32	Daman and Diu	59	10	1	2	75.51%
33	Andaman and Nicobar Islands	47	5	0	3	73.81%
34	Dadra and Nagar Haveli	43	5	0	22	73.68%
35	Lakshadweep	2	0	0	2	50.00%

Source: Census of India, 2011

The 2011 census of India was the first census to include a category for transgender individuals. This was a significant step towards recognizing and acknowledging the existence of transgender individuals in India.

According to the 2011 census, there were approximately 487,000 transgender individuals in India. However, it is important to note that this number is likely an underestimate, as many transgender individuals may not have disclosed their gender identity on the census due to fear of discrimination and stigma.

Additionally, the census data only allowed individuals to identify as "male" or "female" or "other," which may not accurately reflect the diversity of gender identities and expressions within the transgender community. The 2011 census data on transgender individuals was a step in the right direction towards recognizing the rights and needs of this community, but more comprehensive data collection methods are needed to better understand and support the diverse experiences of transgender individuals in India.

Review Questions

(a) From the Census data of India, Identify the states with largest and smallest transgender population in India.

(b) From the global data of LGBTQIA+ what do you understand regarding the distribution of LGBTQIA+ across the globe?

GLOBAL DATA

Data on the size and characteristics of the LGBTQIA+ community varies by country and region, and is often difficult to obtain due to stigma, discrimination, and social and legal barriers. However, here are some examples of data on the LGBTQIA+ population.

- In the United States, an estimated 4.5% of adults identify as LGBTQIA+, according to a 2021 Gallup poll. Among millennials, the percentage is higher at 15.9%.
- In Europe, a 2020 survey conducted by the European Union Agency for Fundamental Rights (FRA) found that 6% of the European Union population identifies as LGBTQ, with higher percentages among younger age groups.
- In the United Kingdom, a 2020 survey conducted by the Office for National Statistics found that 3.5% of the population identified as LGB, while a separate survey found that 2% of the population identified as transgender or non-binary.
- In Canada, a 2019 survey conducted by the federal government found that 2.4% of the population identified as gay or lesbian, while 1.4% identified as bisexual. The survey did not include data on transgender or non-binary individuals.
- In Australia, a 2021 survey conducted by the Australian Bureau of Statistics found that 1.9% of the population identified as gay or lesbian, while 1.2% identified as bisexual. The survey did not include data on transgender or non-binary individuals.

It is important to note that these data sources have limitations and may not accurately reflect the diversity of experiences and identities within the LGBTQIA community. Additionally, data may be impacted by factors such as social stigma and discrimination, which can make it difficult for individuals to disclose their sexual orientation or gender identity.

INTERNATIONAL AND NATIONAL LEGISLATION FOR THE LGBTQIA+ COMMUNITY

The United Nations (UN) has taken several steps to promote and protect the rights of LGBTQ+ individuals worldwide. Here are a few examples of key legislative initiatives:

1. **Yogyakarta Principles:** In 2006, a group of international human rights experts drafted the Yogyakarta Principles, a set of principles related to sexual orientation and gender identity that apply international human rights law to address the specific challenges faced by LGBTQ+ individuals. The principles have been endorsed by many UN member states and have served as a basis for policy and legal reform in many countries.
2. **Joint Statement on Ending Violence and Discrimination Against LGBTQ+ Individuals:** In 2019, a group of 27 UN member states, including Argentina, Brazil, Canada, and the United States, issued a joint statement calling for an end to violence and discrimination against LGBTQ+ individuals. The statement called on UN member states to take concrete steps to protect LGBTQ+ individuals from violence and discrimination, including by decriminalizing same-sex relations and enacting anti-discrimination laws.
3. **Free and Equal Campaign:** In 2013, the UN launched the Free & Equal campaign, which aims to raise awareness of the human rights challenges faced by LGBTQ+ individuals worldwide and to promote greater acceptance and equality. The campaign has included public events, social media initiatives, and other outreach efforts aimed at changing attitudes and promoting inclusivity.
4. **International Day Against Homophobia, Transphobia and Biphobia (IDAHOTB):** In 2004, a group of activists in Canada launched the first International Day Against Homophobia, which was later expanded to include transphobia and biphobia. The day is now recognized by the UN and celebrated annually on May 17th to raise awareness of the ongoing challenges faced by LGBTQ+ individuals and to promote greater acceptance and inclusion.

These initiatives and others demonstrate the UN's commitment to promoting and protecting the rights of LGBTQ+ individuals worldwide, and to creating a more inclusive and equitable society for all.

In recent years, there has been significant legislative and social progress for transgender individuals in India, including the following:

- **NALSA Judgment:** In 2014, the Indian Supreme Court issued a landmark judgment in the case of National Legal Services Authority

(NALSA) v. Union of India, recognizing the legal rights of transgender individuals and directing the government to provide them with equal opportunities in education, employment, and other areas.

- **The Transgender Persons (Protection of Rights) Act, 2019:** In 2019, the Indian Parliament passed this legislation, which aims to protect the rights and welfare of transgender individuals and prohibit discrimination against them. The law recognizes transgender persons as a third gender, and provides for legal recognition of their gender identities.
- **Social Movements:** There have also been significant social movements and initiatives in India aimed at promoting the rights and well-being of transgender individuals. For example, the Hijra Habba festival in Bangalore, Karnataka celebrates transgender culture and identity, while the Kinnar Akhara is a group of transgender individuals who participate in the Kumbh Mela, a major Hindu religious festivals.
- **Reservation:** In some states of India, transgender individuals have been granted reservations in education and employment.

While there has been progress in recent years, transgender individuals in India still face significant challenges, including discrimination, harassment, and violence. The implementation of the Transgender Persons (Protection of Rights) Act has also faced criticism from some advocates who feel that the law falls short of providing adequate protections and recognition for transgender individuals. However, there is hope that continued advocacy and activism will lead to further progress and a more inclusive and equitable society for all.

Review Questions

(a) What idea do you get about the transgender community from the Census of India, 2011?

(b) What are the steps taken by the UN to protect the rights of the LGBTQIA+ community?

CHALLENGES FOR THE LGBTQIA+ COMMUNITY

Despite legislative progress and increasing social acceptance in many parts of the world, LGBTQIA individuals still face significant challenges. Here are some of the main challenges:

1. **Discrimination:** LGBTQIA individuals often face discrimination in employment, housing, education, healthcare, and other areas. This can include verbal harassment, physical violence, and exclusion from social or community events.

2. **Legal challenges:** In many countries, same-sex sexual activity is illegal and punishable by law. Even in countries where homosexuality is legal, LGBTQIA individuals may not have the same legal rights and protections as heterosexual individuals. For example, they may not be able to marry, adopt children, or inherit properties.
3. **Family rejection:** LGBTQIA individuals are more likely to experience rejection from their families, which can lead to social isolation and mental health problems,
4. **Mental health:** LGBTQIA individuals are more likely to experience depression, anxiety, and other mental health issues due to the discrimination and stigma they face.
5. **Health care:** LGBTQIA individuals may face challenges in accessing quality health care. For example, they may be denied health insurance or have difficulty finding providers who are knowledgeable about their specific health needs.
6. **Hate crimes:** LGBTQIA individuals are at a higher risk of being the victims of hate crimes, including physical assaults and murders.
7. **Intersectionality:** LGBTQIA individuals who belong to other marginalized groups, such as people of color or those with disabilities, may face additional challenges and discrimination due to their intersectional identities.

Overall, it is important to recognize the ongoing challenges faced by LGBTQIA individuals and work to promote greater acceptance, inclusion, and equity for all people, regardless of sexual orientation or gender identity.

ROLE OF SOCIAL WORKERS IN SAFEGUARDING RIGHTS OF LGBTQIA+ COMMUNITY

Social work with LGBTQIA+ individuals is an important and specialized field within social work. Social workers who work with LGBTQIA+ individuals are trained to understand the unique challenges that this population faces, such as discrimination, stigma, and prejudice.

Here are some key points to keep in mind when working with LGBTQIA+ individuals:

1. **Be respectful and non-judgmental:** Social workers should always treat LGBTQIA+ individuals with respect and dignity. It's important to create a safe and non-judgmental space where clients feel comfortable sharing their experiences and feelings.
2. **Understand the diversity within the LGBTQIA+ community:** The LGBTQIA+ community is diverse, and it's important to recognize that

individuals within this community may have different experiences, values, and beliefs.

3. **Use inclusive language:** Social workers should use language that is inclusive and affirming of LGBTQIA+ identities. For example, instead of assuming a client's gender identity or sexual orientation, social workers should ask for and use the client's preferred pronouns.
4. **Be knowledgeable about resources:** Social workers should be knowledgeable about resources that are available for LGBTQIA+ individuals, such as support groups, advocacy organizations, and legal services.
5. **Advocate for LGBTQIA+ rights:** Social workers should be advocates for LGBTQ+ rights and work to create policies and practices that promote equality and social justice for all individuals.

Overall, social workers who work with LGBTQIA+ individuals should be knowledgeable, culturally sensitive, and committed to creating a safe and affirming environment for their clients.

Review Questions

(a) State the challenges faced by the LGBTQIA+ community.
(b) How can a social worker safeguard the rights of the LGBTQIA+ community?

Did You Know?

- Research suggests transgender people's brain structure aligns with their identified gender, not assigned sex.
- Many transgender people experience gender dysphoria (discomfort) from a young age, with 75% reporting feelings by age 7.
- India's Supreme Court recognized transgender people as a third gender in 2014, granting them legal rights and protections.
- Hindu mythology and ancient texts like the Mahabharata and Ramayana contain references to third-gender characters, indicating a long history of transgender presence in Indian culture.
- India's hijra community, estimated to be over 1 million, has a distinct culture and history, with many hijras living in close-knit communities.
- Transgender people in India face significant barriers in education and employment; only 2% complete higher education, and 60% are unemployed.
- India introduced the "Third Gender" option on passports in 2011, allowing transgender people to identify themselves accurately.
- Some Indian states offer reservations and quotas for transgender people in education, employment, and politics.
- India celebrates various transgender cultural festivals, such as the Koothandavar Festival in Tamil Nadu, promoting visibility and acceptance.
- American Psychological Association recognizes that being transgender is not a mental disorder; the focus is on supporting individuals with gender dysphoria.

SUMMARY

In Social Work the Cultural competency models are important tools for social workers working with diverse populations, including the LGBTQIA community. Here are some cultural competency models that can be used to effectively engage and support LGBTQIA individuals.

- **Intersectionality Model:** The intersectionality model emphasizes the importance of understanding and acknowledging the multiple identities and experiences of LGBTQIA individuals. This model recognizes that LGBTQIA individuals often face discrimination and oppression based on multiple factors, such as race, gender, and socioeconomic status. Intersectionality is a framework that recognizes that individuals are not defined by a single aspect of their identity, but rather by the intersection of multiple identities and social categories, such as race, gender, sexuality, class, and ability. Applying this framework to LGBTQ+ issues highlights the unique experiences and challenges faced by individuals who hold multiple marginalized identities. For example, LGBTQ+ people of color may face discrimination based on both their race and sexual orientation, and may therefore experience compounded forms of oppression. Similarly, LGBTQ+ individuals with disabilities may face additional barriers to accessing healthcare and support services, and may experience discrimination based on their disability as well as their sexual orientation or gender identity. Applying an intersectional framework to LGBTQ+ advocacy and activism involves recognizing and addressing the ways in which different forms of oppression intersect and reinforce each other. It involves centering the experiences of marginalized LGBTQ+ individuals and advocating for policies and practices that address their specific needs and concerns. For example, intersectional LGBTQ+ activism may involve advocating for policies that support the needs of LGBTQ+ people of color, such as anti-discrimination laws that specifically address discrimination based on race and sexual orientation or gender identity. It may also involve advocating for accessible healthcare and support services for LGBTQ+ individuals with disabilities, and addressing the ways in which ableism and homophobia/transphobia intersect.
- **Socio-Ecological Model:** The Socio-Ecological Model is a framework that recognizes the interrelated factors that influence individuals' health and well-being, including individual, interpersonal, community, and societal factors. Applying this framework to LGBTQ+ issues involves examining how different levels of influence impact the experiences and outcomes of LGBTQ+ individuals. At the individual

level, factors such as sexual orientation, gender identity, and gender expression can impact the experiences of LGBTQ+ individuals. Discrimination, stigma, and violence directed towards LGBTQ+ individuals can negatively impact their mental and physical health outcomes. This can include experiencing depression, anxiety, and other mental health issues as well as facing higher rates of substance abuse and suicide. Interpersonal factors such as familial, peer, and romantic relationships can also impact the experiences of LGBTQ+ individuals. Acceptance or rejection from family members, friends, and partners can significantly affect the mental health and well-being of LGBTQ+ individuals. Community factors such as social norms, cultural values, and political policies also play a significant role in the experiences of LGBTQ+ individuals. Discriminatory laws and policies can negatively impact the daily lives and opportunities of LGBTQ+ individuals. In contrast, inclusive policies and programs that promote equality can have positive impacts on the health and well-being of LGBTQ+ individuals. Societal factors such as media representations and cultural attitudes towards LGBTQ+ individuals can also impact the experiences of LGBTQ+ individuals. Positive representation and increased visibility of LGBTQ+ individuals in media and society can help reduce stigma and promote acceptance. Overall, the Socio-Ecological Model helps us understand the complex and interrelated factors that impact the lives of LGBTQ+ individuals. Applying this model to LGBTQ+ issues highlights the need for systemic changes at all levels of influence to promote equality, reduce discrimination, and improve the health and well-being of LGBTQ+ individuals.

- **Person-in-Environment Model:** The Person-in-Environment (PIE) Model is a framework that recognizes the interactions between individuals and their environment. It emphasizes the importance of understanding the individual's social and cultural context in order to fully understand their experiences and behaviors. Applying this framework to LGBTQ+ issues involves examining the ways in which the environment and social context impact the experiences of LGBTQ+ individuals. The PIE Model recognizes that LGBTQ+ individuals face unique challenges due to societal stigma and discrimination. Discrimination based on sexual orientation and gender identity can negatively impact the mental and physical health of LGBTQ+ individuals. For example, LGBTQ+ individuals may experience higher rates of depression, anxiety, and suicide, and may also face barriers to accessing healthcare and other support services. The PIE Model also recognizes the importance of social support and networks for LGBTQ+

individuals. Supportive families, friends, and communities can have positive impacts on the well-being of LGBTQ+ individuals. However, many LGBTQ+ individuals face rejection and discrimination from their families and communities, which can lead to social isolation and other negative outcomes. Applying the PIE Model to LGBTQ+ issues also involves recognizing the intersectionality of different social identities. For example, LGBTQ+ individuals who also belong to marginalized racial or ethnic groups may face compounded forms of discrimination and oppression. Overall, the PIE Model helps us understand the complex interactions between LGBTQ+ individuals and their social and cultural context. It highlights the need for supportive environments and policies that promote equality and reduce discrimination, as well as the importance of social support and networks for LGBTQ+ individuals. Top of Form

- **Empowerment Model:** The Empowerment Model is a framework that focuses on empowering individuals and communities to take control of their own lives and advocate for their own needs and rights. Applying this model to LGBTQ+ issues involves promoting the empowerment of LGBTQ+ individuals and communities to address discrimination, promote equality, and improve the well-being of LGBTQ+ individuals. The Empowerment Model recognizes that LGBTQ+ individuals often face discrimination and marginalization, which can lead to a sense of powerlessness and a lack of agency. Empowerment involves recognizing and challenging these power imbalances and supporting LGBTQ+ individuals to take control of their own lives and advocate for their own needs and rights. At the individual level, empowerment can involve providing LGBTQ+ individuals with the knowledge, skills, and resources they need to navigate systems of discrimination and advocate for their own needs. This can include education about legal rights, access to healthcare and other support services, and training in advocacy and leadership. At the community level, empowerment involves supporting LGBTQ+ communities to come together, build social networks, and advocate for their own needs and rights. This can involve providing funding and resources for LGBTQ+ organizations and initiatives, creating safe spaces and support groups for LGBTQ+ individuals, and promoting LGBTQ+ visibility and representation in media and society. Applying the Empowerment Model to LGBTQ+ issues also involves recognizing the intersectionality of different social identities and promoting the empowerment of LGBTQ+ individuals from all backgrounds. This means addressing the specific needs and concerns of LGBTQ+ individuals who hold multiple marginalized identities, such as LGBTQ+ people of color, transgender and gender non-conforming individuals, and LGBTQ+ individuals with disabilities.

Overall, cultural competency models are important tools for social workers working with the LGBTQIA community. By understanding the social and cultural context of LGBTQIA individuals and the challenges they face, social workers can better support and empower them to live healthy, fulfilling lives.

GLOSSARY

- **Cisgender:** A person whose gender identity and expression matches the sex they were assigned at birth.
- **Gender Identity:** A person's internal sense of being male, female, and neither or other gender.
- **Gender Expression:** How a person externally expresses their gender through clothing, behaviour, interests, appearance, etc.
- **Heteronormativity:** The assumption that heterosexuality is the default, normal or preferred sexual orientation.
- **Homophobia:** Fear, hatred, discomfort with, or mistrust of people who are attracted to the same gender.
- **Intersex:** A person born with sex characteristics that do not fit typical binary notions of male or female bodies.
- **LGBTQIA+:** An acronym that stands for lesbian, gay, bisexual, transgender, queer, intersex, asexual and other sexual and gender identities.
- **Non-binary:** A spectrum of gender identities that are not exclusively masculine or exclusively feminine,Äźidentities that are outside the gender binary.
- **Pronouns:** The words used to refer to someone's gender identity, such as he/him, she/her, they/them, etc.
- **Sexual Orientation**: A person's emotional, romantic and/or sexual attraction to other people.
- **Transgender:** A person whose gender identity or expression differs from the sex they were assigned at birth.
- **Transphobia:** Fear, hatred, discomfort with, or mistrust of people whose gender identity or expression differs from traditional gender norms.

TOP TEN TAKEAWAY POINTS

1. The chapter explores the differences between gender and sexual orientation, and how they are distinct concepts.

2. LGBTQIA+ is an umbrella term that includes Lesbian, Gay, Bisexual, Transgender, Queer, Intersex, Asexual, and other gender and sexual identities.
3. Sex refers to the biological and physiological features, while gender is a social construct around roles, behaviours, expressions, and identities.
4. Transgender individuals are those whose gender identity or expression differs from their sex assigned at birth. They may or may not undergo medical transition.
5. Bisexual individuals are attracted to people of the same gender as well as other genders. Lesbian and gay refer to same-sex attraction.
6. Queer is an inclusive umbrella term for non-binary, gender-fluid, or gender non-conforming identities. Intersex individuals have biological sex characteristics that do not fit typical male or female categories.
7. Asexual individuals do not experience sexual attraction, with further divisions like demisexual, graysexual, and aromantic.
8. The chapter discusses the history and transition of social status of the LGBTQIA+ community, and the social challenges they face.
9. It highlights the important role of social work professionals as advocates and allies in supporting the needs and well-being of the LGBTQIA+ community.
10. The chapter emphasizes the need to develop inclusivity and cultural competency models in social work practice to address the issues faced by the LGBTQIA+ population.

MULTIPLE CHOICE QUESTIONS

1. According to the passage, what does the term "LGBTQIA+" stand for?
   (a) Lesbian, Gay, Bisexual, Transgender, Queer, Intersex, Asexual
   (b) Lesbian, Genderfluid, Bisexual, Transgender, Queer, Intersex, Asexual
   (c) Lesbian, Gay, Bisexual, Transgender, Questioning, Intersex, Agender
   (d) Lesbian, Gender, Bisexual, Transgender, Queer, Intersex
2. What is the primary difference between sex and gender as described in the chapter?
   (a) Sex is a social construct, while gender is biological.
   (b) Sex is determined at birth, while gender is a spectrum.
   (c) Sex refers to physical and physiological features, while gender refers to socially constructed roles and identities.
   (d) Sex is binary (male/female), while gender can be binary or non-binary.

3. What is the key characteristic that distinguishes transgender individuals from cisgender individuals?
   (a) Transgender individuals undergo medical procedures to align their bodies with their gender identity.
   (b) Transgender individuals' gender identity differs from their assigned sex at birth.
   (c) Transgender individuals often identify as non-binary or gender fluid.
   (d) Transgender individuals face greater social stigma and marginalization.
4. Which of the following is not considered a part of the LGBTQIA+ spectrum?
   (a) Lesbian (b) Gay
   (c) Pansexual (d) Heterosexual
5. What is the primary difference between intersex and transgender individuals?
   (a) Intersex individuals are assigned a gender at birth, while transgender individuals self-identify their gender.
   (b) Intersex individuals have biological variations in their sex characteristics, while transgender individuals have a mismatch between their gender identity and assigned sex.
   (c) Intersex individuals face more social stigma and discrimination than transgender individuals.
   (d) Intersex individuals require medical intervention, while transgender individuals do not.
6. What is the primary purpose of the "+" symbol in the LGBTQIA+ acronym?
   (a) To include individuals who identify as non-binary or gender fluid.
   (b) To represent the diversity and fluidity of sexual and gender identities.
   (c) To signify the existence of other genders and sexual orientations not explicitly mentioned.
   (d) All of the above.
7. Which of the following is not considered a part of the asexual spectrum?
   (a) Demisexual (b) Graysexual
   (c) Pansexual (d) Aromantic
8. Which of the following is not a key difference between sex and gender as described in the passage?\
   (a) Sex is determined at birth, while gender is a social construct.
   (b) Sex is binary (male/female), while gender can be binary or non-binary.

(c) Sex refers to physical and physiological features, while gender refers to socially constructed roles and identities.
(d) Sex is influenced by political, religious, and cultural forces, while gender is biologically determined.

9. Which of the following statements about the history and social status of the LGBTQIA+ community in India and globally is accurate?
(a) The LGBTQIA+ community has always been accepted and celebrated in India and globally.
(b) The LGBTQIA+ community has faced increasing stigmatization and marginalization over time, often being associated with HIV/AIDS.
(c) The LGBTQIA+ community has been recognized and protected by national and international legislation in most countries.
(d) The LGBTQIA+ community has had a consistent social status and level of acceptance over time.

10. What is the primary role of social work professionals in supporting the LGBTQIA+ community according to the passage?
(a) To provide counselling and mental health services.
(b) To advocate for the rights and well-being of the LGBTQIA+ community.
(c) To develop inclusive and culturally competent models of social work practice.
(d) All of the above.

Answers

1. (a), 2. (c), 3. (b), 4. (d), 5. (b), 6. (d), 7. (c), 8. (d), 9. (b), 10. (d)

REFERENCES

1. American Psychological Association (2009a). *Report of the Task Force on Gender Identity and Gender Variance*. Available at: http://www.apa.org/pi/lgbt/resources/policy/gender-identity-report.pdf
2. Bartlett, A., Smith, G., and King, M. (2009). The response of mental health professionals to clients seeking help to change or redirect same-sex sexual orientation. *BMC Psychiatry* 9:11. doi: 10.1186/1471-244X-9-11
3. Coleman, E., Bockting, W., Botzer, M., Cohen - Kettenis, P., DeCuypere, G., Feldman, J., et al. (2012). Standards of care for the health of transsexual, transgender, and gender nonconforming people, 7th version. *Int. J. Transgend.* 13, 165–232.
4. D'Augelli, A. R., Pilkington, N. W., and Hershberger, S. L. (2002). Incidence and mental health impact of sexual orientation victimization of lesbian, gay, and bisexual youths in high school. *School Psychol. Q.* 17, 148–167. doi: 10.1521/scpq.17.2.148.20854

5. European Union Agency for Fundamental Rights (2014). *European LGBT Survey: Main Results.* Luxembourg: Publications Office of the European Union.
6. Lawrence, A. A. (2008). "Gender identity disorders in adults: diagnosis and treatment," in *Handbook of Sexual and Gender Identity Disorders*, eds D. L. Rowland and L. Incrocci (New York, NY: Wiley), 423–456.
7. *LGBT.* (2023, February 10). Retrieved from Wikipedia: https://en.wikipedia.org/wiki/LGBT
8. Molerio, Pinto. (2015). Sexual orientation and gender identity: review of concepts, controversies and their relation to psychopathology classification systems. *Frontiers in Psychology*.
9. Mustanski, B. S., Garofalo, R., and Emerson, E. M. (2010). Mental health disorders, psychological distress, and suicidality in a diverse sample of lesbian, gay, bisexual, and transgender youths. *Res. Pract.* 100, 2426–2432. doi: 10.2105/AJPH.2009.178319
10. Shelton, K., and Delgado-Romero, E. A. (2011). Sexual orientation microaggressions: the experience of lesbian, gay, bisexual, and queer clients in psychotherapy. *J. Couns. Psychol.* 58, 210–221. doi: 10.1037/a0022251
11. *What is gender? What is sex?* (2023, February 2). Retrieved from Canadian Institute of Health Researches: https://cihr-irsc.gc.ca/e/48642.html
12. *What is LGBTQIA+?* (2023, February 23). Retrieved from The Center: https://gaycenter.org/about/lgbtq/#lesbian

RECOMMENDED READINGS

1. Capuzza, Jamie C, and Leland G Spencer. *Transgender Communication Studies: Histories, Trends, and Trajectories*. Lanham, Lexington Books, 2015.
2. Elliot, Patricia. *Debates in Transgender, Queer, and Feminist Theory: Contested Sites*. New York, Ny; London, Routledge, 2016.
3. Enke, Anne. *Transfeminist Perspectives in and beyond Transgender and Gender Studies*. Philadelphia, Temple University Press, 2012.
4. Stryker, Susan, and Stephen Whittle. *The Transgender Studies Reader*. New York, Routledge, 2006.
5. Taylor, Jami K, and Donald P Haider-Markel. *Transgender Rights and Politics: Groups, Issue Framing, and Policy Adoption*. Ann Arbor, University of Michigan Press, 2015.
6. Valentine, David. *Imagining Transgender*. Duke University Press, 30 Aug. 2007.
7. Zabus, Chantal J., and David Coad. *Transgender Experience: Place, Ethnicity, and Visibility*. New York, Routledge, Taylor & Francis Group, 2014.

CHAPTER – 12

Social Work in Urban Setting

Chandrakala Diyali

Assistant Professor (Senior Scale), Department of Social Work, Amity University, Noida

'Comforts comes with a price and Sustainable living is an answer.'

– Anonymous

Abstract: *The chapter provides the conceptual understanding of the terms urbanisation, Industrialisation and modernisation. It also highlights various factors that lead to urbanisation and has also discussed the various problems and challenges faced due to urbanisation. It also briefly discusses the evolution of urban cities as well as the charactreistices of urban cities. The chapter also discusses the role of professional social workers work in different areas in the Urban setting in order to help resolve their problems across all aspects of life.The chapter also specifically discusses various strategies for alleviating urban poverty.*

Keywords: *Rural and Urban Settings, Urbanisation, Industrialisation, Modernisation, Poverty, Slums, Homelessness, Social Work Practice, Indianisation, Sustainability*

Learning Objectives

- The students would be able to understand the different broad settings of social work practice, i.e. rural, and urban settings.
- The students can understand the distinction among urbanisation, industrialisation, and modernisation and the characteristics of urban communities.
- The students would be able to understand the factors that lead to urbanisation.
- The students would be able to understand the historical context on the rise of urbanisation.
- The students would be able to understand the different problems and challenges of Urbanisation and will be able to analyse the sustainable solutions towards the same.
- The students would be able to understand the Constitutional provisions, programmes for urban community development, and roles of professional social work practice in different areas /settings in the urban milieu.

INTRODUCTION: URBANIZATION AND URBAN SOCIAL WORK

Social work, philanthropy, social welfare and charity are taken as similar terms that are interchangeably used by a layman. The social workers are the trained professionals who follow scientific and systematic strategy and intervention approaches by using their knowledge and skills to strive for the welfare and development of the impoverished and disadvantaged at individual, groups and community level to deal with their socio-economic, psycho-emotional issues at multi-dimentional levels to help them to help themselves, to improve their quality of life for the sustainable development.

From the perspective of Social Work, it is crucial to understand the geographical location or area or locality of our practice (Green, 2003; Turbett, 2009; Mason, 2011). The area has a broad demarcation as urban or rural setting in which they are based, that has a huge impact on how social work is practised.

The different setting has distinctive features in all aspects of their life and layouts. Hence, it become important for the social workers to focus on their upbringing, interests, familiarity, comfort, capabilities and competence in deciding to work in any specific setting.But in the neo-liberal and urbanisation era with the hyper development of Information and communication technology (ICT) across all verticle and horizontal spectrums, the spectular distinctiveness of rural and urban divide has been withering with time. That is a serious cause of concern for the sustainability of human civilization that is deeply rooted in the rural belt.

The global advocacy for sustainability as the philosophy and goals has been keeping the balance to sustain the essence of this broad distinctiveness of both rural and urban areas focussing on the rurality.

DIFFERENCE BETWEEN URBANIZATION, INDUSTRALIZATION, MODERNIZATION

Urbanisation is often taken as a synonym to modernization and Industralization. The industrialization and urbanization in simple term is the sub-processes of the process of Modernization that helps in the process of social change and development resulting chiefly from technological or ICT advancement.

James O' Connell (1976) defines 'modernization as a process through which a pre-technological society altered into machine technology where rational and secular attitudes and highly differentiated social structures prevails'.

Industrialization is the process of socio-economic revolution by which the economy source moves from primarily agriculture to manufacture of goods in the factory-based system of production which revolutionised to mass production and innovation for the catastrophic changes in society.

Urbanisation is a structural process of change that shifts from rural to Urban. As per the 2011 Census, India's 69 per cent of the population resides in Rural areas and rest of 31 per cent in Urban areas.Out of these 31 per cent , 25 per cent dwells in slums out of which 50 per cent are in Maharashtra.The country's majority of urban population resides in five states of Maharashtra, Uttar Pradesh, Tamil Nadu, West Bengal, and Andhra Pradesh. Maharashtra accounts for 14.4 per cent of the nation's total urban population, while Tamil Nadu and Uttar Pradesh each make for 12.1 per cent and 9.5 per cent..

FACTORS THAT LEAD TO URBANISATION

1. Economic Opportunities - It affects in two ways:
   (a) Income higher
   (b) As jobs opportunities grow
2. Companies agglomeration
3. Development of Infrastructure/Utility-Water, Electricity, Communication
4. Better Public Facility-Health Edcation
5. Globalisation

CLASSIFICATION OF URBANISATION

(i) Demography: This deals with the Nature of Work the population are engaged for eg.MSME,Carpenter,PSU,Financial Capital etc

(ii) Sociological: It focuses on the Heterogenity (Caste, creed, language, religion) quality of life, Interdependence, Pattern of culture

The concept of Urbanization is systematically analysed as a process of population concentration that encompasses two elements: 'the multiplications of points of concentration' and 'the increase in size of individual concentrations' that increases the percentage of the population living in urban places.

The phenomenon of Urbanization refers to the increasing concentration of people in urban areas. There has been rapid rate of increase of proportion of Urban population for the past few decades due to increasing number of people moving from rural areas to the Urban sophistication due to the interplay of many pull and push factors.

The fast increasing urbanisation is a positive sign of progress and development for any country as the cities are hubs of economic activity that leads to growth of businesses and industries for creating job opportunities for people for accelerating economic growth, reducing poverty and improving living standards.The influx of people in urban areas prompts economies of scale that makes the essential services such as healthcare, education, and transportation more accessible and effective.

Urbanization has its darker side too that is manifested with the negative effects on society, the environment, the economy, demography and others, leading to multi-dimensional and Inter-generational problems. Hence, the increasing problems of socio-economic,psychological and cultural problems in the urban areas have validated the emergence of a social work professionals in the urban settings.

Urbanisation has given way to problems that has gone vicious cycle. Due to increasing migration there is huge congestion that is built in the cities.That has led to the palpable problem like slums. Slums have given rise to a big social problem as there is fast increasing crime rate.The cause of concern is that, there is increase rate of participation of women in the prevailing crime.The networking of the NGOs and GOs have to stretch here for the community to be well integrated with the mainstream for their holistic growth and development.There is a big jolt and pressure built on the transportation and communivcation means due to population rise.We experience congestion every corner of the city irrespective of anytime in the day and mid night.

The housing also face the same problem. The slums have over congested houses that has make- shifts and sub-standard housing with no civic amenties like water and other basic needs of life like proper food, water, etc. Urban unemployment has risen from 15 per cent to 25 per cent, the unskilled labour force is fast increasing, manifesting and transforming into multiple problems in the city area. Environmental sanitation also suffers equally as the industries, factories and domestic sewerage and the problem of solid wastes management of non-biodegradable and E-waste has become impossible due to lack of land fill for disposal or treatment plant, that are randomly dumped into the river causing it to pollute beyond repair and ultimately it dries up forever. Concretisation and pollution has made the land loose all wet land in every city in the country. Public utilities and all elements of nature on and under the ground are under a huge strain due to hazardious chemicals and thus leads to the formation of 'Heat Island'. Due to fast deteroriating condition of environment and ecological balance, there is fast emergence of chronic communicable and non-communicable diseases accompanied by the life style diseases. The education system is not inclusive of disadvantaged, discriminated and have-nots population. Who are often excluded in the process of skillful human resource formation in their formative years of life and are in the clutches of child labour in the unorganised sector.

There have been structural and functional change in the cities that have caused multiple and complex problems due to degrading human values system with growing influence of social media and free access to all informations that place no age appropriate restriction. Moreover, the wild rush of competition,stress has already given rise to Mental Health Problems in the urban areas.

Hence, the Professional social workers work in different areas in the Urban setting in order to help resolve their problems across all aspects of life.

RISE OF URBANIZATION: A HISTORICAL CONTEXT

Evolution of Towns, Cities and Urban Areas

In India the evolution of urban areas (towns and cities) have occurred in different stages with different objective of the given time.It is broadly classified into ancient,medieval and modern towns.

The ancient towns had developed to serve the need of administrative, religious and cultural centers. The most popular are Harappa, Mohenjodara, Varanasi, Allahabad and Madurai.

Medieval towns were developed as headquarters of territories and kingdoms. The most famous ones are Delhi, Hyderabad, Jaipur, Lucknow, Agra and Nagpur.

As far as the modern India is concerned, the Europeans first developed some coastal towns such as Surat, Daman, Goa and Pondicherry. Then the British developed Madras, Bombay and Calcutta as the administrative headquarter and the trading centers. The newly developed towns are hills towns, industrial towns, court towns, railways station towns, cantonments and administrative towns.

Characteristics of Urban Communities

Urban communities have certain distinct features and characteristics that set them apart from rural communities. These characteristics are shaped by a range of social, economic, and environmental factors, and can have significant implications for the way that people live, work, and interact with each other. Here are some of the key characteristics of urban communities:

- **Population density:** One of the essential characteristics of urban communities is their high population density. The Cities and towns are bound to have a dense population, with large numbers of people living and working in a relatively small area.
- **Diverse population:** Urban communities tend to be more diverse than rural communities, with people from a wide range of ethnic, cultural,

and socio-economic backgrounds living in close proximity to each other.

- **Infrastructure and amenities:** Urban communities tend to have a more developed infrastructure and a wider range of amenities and services, including transportation, communication, healthcare, education, and entertainment options.
- **Higher levels of economic activity:** Urban communities are previledge to be centers of economic activity, with a range of industries, businesses, and services operating within them. This can create more job opportunities and higher levels of economic growth.
- **Higher cost of living:** The cost of living in urban communities is naturally higher than in rural areas, due to higher property values, greater demand for goods and services, transport cost and other factors.
- **Higher levels of social and cultural diversity:** Urban communities tend to be more socio-culturally diverse with people from different backgrounds, religions, and lifestyles living in close proximity to each other. This can create opportunities for cultural exchange and interaction, but can also lead to tensions and conflicts.
- **Greater exposure to environmental hazards:** Urban communities can be more vulnerable to environmental hazards such as pollution, congestion, and natural disasters due to their high population density and infrastructure.

Overall, urban communities are complex, dynamic environments that are shaped by a wide range of social, economic, and environmental factors. While they offer many opportunities and advantages, they also present significant challenges and risks that must be addressed through careful development planning and management.

Problems/Challenges Faced by Urban Areas

Excessive size in terms of population that gets multiplied in geometrical order vis-à-vis with area that is static in nature.The economic foundation of the cities is not strong enough to handle the problems brought in by the population size.

The government has a difficult time providing all of the human services that people want or expect because there are too many people living in cities. Everywhere in the world, there is a housing scarcity. Overcrowding and poor living conditions makes the slum dwellers more vulnerable to certain diseases in poor environmental and socio-economic conditions and are different from squatter settlements where people build houses without any legal title to land (UN-Habitat 2003).

Air and water pollution, high noise levels, and ugly landscapes as a result of bad planning are additional important worldwide issues.

Inadequate sewage disposal damaged the city's drinking water, causing epidemics.

Urban areas, by their nature, are often characterized by a range of problems and challenges that can impact the well-being of residents and the sustainability of the community. These challenges are embedded in a range of factors, including social, economic, and environmental factors.

Here are some of the most common challenges faced by urban areas:

- **Housing affordability:** One of the most pressing challenges facing urban areas is the affordability of housing. As urban areas become more desirable places to live and work, demand for housing increases, which can drive up prices and make it difficult for low-income residents to find affordable housing.
- **Traffic congestion:** With high population densities and large numbers of people commuting to work and other destinations, urban areas often suffer from traffic congestion, which can lead to longer commute times, air pollution, and other negative impacts.
- **Crime and safety:** Urban areas often experience higher levels of crime and safety concerns than rural areas, due to factors such as higher population densities, greater economic inequality, and greater social diversity.
- **Environmental issues:** Urban areas can be more vulnerable to environmental issues such as pollution, heat islands and natural disasters, which can impact the health and well-being of residents and the sustainability of the community.
- **Access to basic services:** Despite the greater availability of services in urban areas, some residents may face challenges accessing basic services such as healthcare, education, and social services due to economic or social barriers.
- **Economic inequality:** Urban areas can be marked by significant economic inequality, with some residents enjoying high levels of income and access to opportunities, while others face significant economic hardship and limited opportunities.
- **Urban sprawl:** As cities expand, they can face issues related to urban sprawl, including loss of green space, increased traffic congestion, and greater dependence on automobiles.

Overall, addressing these challenges requires a multi-faceted approach that involves government, civil society, and the private sector working together to create sustainable, equitable, and resilient urban communities.

MAJOR PROBLEMS IN THE URBAN LANDSCAPE

Poverty

The concept of poverty in a layman word is when people or communities are deprived of fundamental human needs or means of subsistence or material resources, but also includes a lack of access to basic necessities such as adequate housing, clean water, wholesome food, education, healthcare, and clean water etc.

Poverty is a complex and multi-faceted issue that affects millions of people around the world.

India's recent reports suggest that below the poverty line population in rural areas accounts for more than a quarter (25.7 per cent) of the total population living in the rural areas,. In the urban areas,the situation is comparatively better with 13.7 per cent of the population living below the poverty line. The common poverty estimation method in India is based on the income or consumption levels.The household falls in the category of Below Poverty Line (BPL) if the income or consumption falls below a given minimum level.In India as per the methodology approved by the Union Cabinet, income limit was Rs 27,000 per annum for households. Each country may have its own standards for establishing the poverty line and calculating the proportion of its population that lives in poverty.

Causes of Poverty

There are many determinant to poverty that could include economic inequality which can be perpetuated by factors such as unequal distribution of wealth, low wages, and limited job opportunities, political instability can also play a role, as it can lead to economic instability,social unrest also reduces investment in infrastructure and basic services.Environmental degradation can aggravate poverty that lead to reduced agricultural productivity, increased health risks, and limited access to natural resources. The socio-cultural exclusion like caste and other various variables that include race, sexual orientation, sexual identity, can also be a factor, to limit access to education, healthcare, and other basic services.

Urban poverty is multifaceted in nature that has multiple causes. Some important reasons for urban poverty are:

- **Economic inequality:** One of the main causes of urban poverty is economic inequality, which can be perpetuated by a range of factors, including limited job opportunities, low wages,uneven distribution of wealth and limited job opportunities.

  This can result in large segments of the urban population being unable to access the basic necessities of life, such as housing, food, and healthcare. social unrest also reduces investment in infrastructure and basic services.

- **Lack of affordable housing:** The cost of housing in urban areas is often very high, and many low-income households are unable to afford decent housing. This can lead to overcrowding, sub-standard living conditions, and other health and safety hazards
- **Inadequate education and skills training:** A lack of education and skills training can make it difficult for individuals to access better-paying jobs, leading to a cycle of poverty and economic insecurity.
- **Discrimination and social exclusion:** Individuals who belong to marginalized groups, such as low caste, ethnic minorities, immigrants, and third gender, may face discrimination and social exclusion, which can limit their access to education, healthcare, and job opportunities.
- **Limited access to basic services:** Urban poverty is often characterized by limited access to basic services such as healthcare, sanitation, and safe drinking water. This can result in poor health outcomes, reduced life expectancy, and other negative consequences.
- **Environmental degradation:** Urban poverty can be exacerbated by environmental degradation, such as air pollution, water pollution, and inadequate waste management. This can lead to health problems, reduced economic opportunities, and other negative outcomes.
- **Political instability:** Political instability can lead to economic instability and social unrest, which can exacerbate poverty and limit opportunities for economic development.

In conclusion, urban poverty is a complex issue that is influenced by a range of factors.Addressing these factors requires a comprehensive approach that involves government, civil society, and the private sector working together in a coordinated manner.

Consequences of Poverty

Poverty is a complex and multifaceted issue that affects millions of people around the world. It is caused by a range of factors.The consequences of poverty are wide-ranging and can have significant impacts on individuals, families, and communities. However, there are a range of strategies that can be used to address poverty, including economic development, social safety nets, education, and healthcare. By working together to address poverty, we can create a more just and equitable world for all.

Strategies to Address Poverty

The range of strategies for combating the poverty on a war-footing are:

- **Economic development:** The growth and development of Economic activities that is more sustainable in nature and that involves the community and its indigenous skills and resources can be an effective way to reduce poverty as it can create new job opportunities,local enterprenural skills and hence increase income.

- **Social safety nets:** Social safety nets, such as cash transfers and food subsidies, can provide a safety net for the most vulnerable populations.
- **Education:** Education is also critical, as it help a child to develop specialised skills through training and can increase opportunities for personal and social development, as well as improve access to better-paying jobs
- **Healthcare:** Health is a wealth hence, healthcare is also critical, as it can improve health outcomes and reduce the financial burden of illness.

Growth of Slums

The concept of 'culture of poverty' was propagated by the anthropologist Oscar Lewis in his best-selling ethnographic realist books on family life among the urban poor.He reinstated the theory that the poverty become inter-generational due to the poor mentatlity of people born in poverty.The scenrio of slums and poverty and its vicious circle fits well to the theory in the class-strategized and fiercely individualist capitalist society.

The characteristics found in the poverty striken slums are:

- Patterns of expenditure,
- Human value systems,
- Knowledge and importance of time and its time management, and
- The social milieu of people's relationships with family and friends.

Political and Social Aspects

Slums are contentious issue which has an intricate connect with many political, economic, and social elements. The political ground has a great influence on the continued existance in the urban landscape.

- The government may use the slums dwellers as a cheap vote bank.
- Somehow their prevalence is beneficial to serve their own political agenda, hence eviction of slum inhabitants is not seen as priority
- Political representatives are corrupt and would ignore the slums rehabilitation in the urban planning agenda.

Homelessness in India: Causes and Consequences

As per the article 25 Universal Declaration of Human Rights (1948) and article 11.1 (1966) International Covenant on Economic, Social and Cultural Rights, the right to adequate standard of living recognises adequate housing too along with all basic requirement of life and others.

As per UN Habitat for the better Urban future, Homelessness is 'One of the most acute forms of material deprivation'. Homelessness refers to the inability of people to enjoy a permanent accommodation. Homelessness can include many conditions, ranging from:

- 'rough sleepers' (i.e. people sleeping rough on the street)
- living in inadequate or insufficient housing (e.g. in tents)

Different definitions of homelessness creates different perceptions and policy priorities

- Street Homelessness / Rough Sleepers
- Housing with inadequate conditions
- Temporary / Emergency Accommodation
- 'Hidden' Homelessness

According to the International Declaration of Human Rights, 'Homelessness' refers to a condition in which a person lacks a stable, regular, and appropriate place of habitation. Globally about 150 million People are projected to be homeless.

The 2011 Census informs 17,73,040 (1.8 million) people includes the homeless people in India. The urban areas accounts for 9,38,348 (52 per cent) population and 8,34,692 resides in rural areas (Ministry of Housing and Urban Affairs).

Despite government's policy of 'Housing for All-2022', officials demolished 53,700 homes in 2017, displacing 260,000 (2.6 lakh) people as a result of projects like slum-free city beautification (HLRN – Housing and Land Rights Network India 2018).

Issues of Inclusion and Exclusion

The people who are excluded from the mainstream society and participation in the process of development have a strong link to historical caste-based discriminatory treatment towards them and others, that includes Schedule Castes,Women, divyang, socio-economically weakers class, third genders, etc. They totally feel excluded and alienated from the mainstream society. Moreover, its an added challenge to build and sustain social connections for those who are struggling with mental health disorders and/or drug use issues that are quite common. Social inclusion offers chances to re-engage with the neighborhood and form healthy connections with their family and the mainstream society.

It is hence critical to help them avail services and social security measures that are made available for marginalised group who are under the perview of government's provision under different policies/ acts/ laws to help them get included in our march towards sustainable development of the country.

URBAN COMMUNITY DEVELOPMENT: CONCEPT AND STRATEGIES OF URBAN DEVELOPMENT PROGRAMMES

Constitutional Provisions for Urban Areas

The 74th Constitutional amendment act was passed in 1992 to constitutionalize the system of Urban Local self Government, the Municipalities.It was for the decentralization of powers to Urban local bodies (ULBs) or city governments as the lowest unit of governance in cities and towns.

After the 74th Amendment was enacted the framework for the decentralisation of obligations and duties to the Municipal bodies with its three categories of urban local bodies:

- Mahanagar Nigam (Municipal Corporation)
- Nagar Palika (Municipality)
- Nagar Panchayat (Notified Area Council or Town Panchayat)

Jawaharlal Nehru National Urban Renewal Mission

JNNURM was a massive city-modernization scheme launched by GoI on December 3rd, 2005 under the aegis of Ministry of Urban Development. With its implementation,it was anticipated that urban regions would contribute 65 per cent of the nation's GDP.The productivity of the urban areas was dependent on the availability of adequate infrastructure such as roadways, telephones, solid waste management, and service delivery mechanisms, community participation, and accountability of ULBs agencies towards citizens that directly affects urban reforms and development.

Objectives of JNNURM

JNNURM's main goal is to transform cities into economically successful, productive, equitable, and responsible places. For the same, it emphasizes:

- Infrastructure development with integrated services
- Ensuring a strong link between the assets developed and their upkeep so the project may operate for longer periods of time sustainably.
- Ensuring that there is a flow of capital for urban infrastructure services to complete the development.
- Ensuring that urban expansion, including urban outgrowths and corridors, occurs in a planned manner.
- Cities' interior spaces should be updated or rebuilt as necessary.
- To make sure that urban services are accessible to all residents, not only those who are wealthy or middle-class, in these places.

The Smart Cities Mission

The area-based development for transformation and development of current regions through redevelopment is the primary emphasis of this project.

1. **Atal Mission for Rejuvenation and Urban Transformation (AMRUT) Project:** This initiative was started in conjunction with the Smart Cities Mission to improve living conditions through infrastructural improvements.
2. **Pradhan Mantri Awas Yojana (PMAY) or Housing for All:** It gives central aid to States and UTs for the building of dwellings for all qualified groups, with a concentration on urban slums and economically disadvantaged populations. As a result, the project's key components are slum restoration and affordable housing for economically underprivileged neighborhoods.
3. **Heritage City Development and Augmentation Yojana (HRIDAY):** HRIDAY Programme launched to build heritage cities holistically. Its goal is to maintain and enhance the particular character of India's historic cities.The central government, which has allotted Rs 500 crore, is responsible for providing all of the financing for the program's initial phase.
4. **Swachh Bharat Mission (SBM):** A significant element of the related programme for urban development is cleaning up India's urban areas. All 4041 statutory towns and cities will have scientifically managed municipal solid waste by 2019 according to the SBM.

SOCIAL WORK PRACTICE IN DIFFERENT SETTINGS: ROLES AND RESPONSIBILITIES

Few enlisted elements that an Urban social workers requires to understand before he/she begins her work in the urban areas are:

- Social workers has to be familiar with the geographic layout of the particular city they are working
- Its imperative for the social workers to be well aware about the social layout of the area
- Its highly recommended in the contemporary time to follow safety precautions to work in any particular urban setting.
- Even have to be aware about multiculturalism and diverse communities and understand the way towards its inclusive strategies.

The professional social work practice is best understood and experienced with effective intervention when taken into account the local context.The urban context of social work practice brings with it unique problems and opportunities that is far different than suburban and rural contexts.

The goal of social work professionals is to help people resolve problems(socio-psychological and associated problems) to improve their well-being by developing their positive personality Social workers, work in a variety of sub-settings/sectors including hospitals, schools, community organizations, government agencies, and private organisation by providing them with support, guidance, and access to resources.The range of services they avail are multi-dimensional in nature like counseling, case management, advocacy, and community outreach. They work with individual, families, groups and community at large, who are struggling with issues such as poverty, abuse, addiction, mental health problems,chronic illness,unresolved crisis among others.The social workers plays pivotal roles in providing direct services at different levels from a micro to macro, to promote social justice for social change by advocating for change in policies and laws that perpetuate social inequalities.They work to build and strengthen communities through grassroots organizing and community development initiatives through intervention at individual,group,families enveloping all at different levels in different broad settings like rural and urban.

World Health Organization (WHO) as per recent report has come out with a fact that by 2050, more than 70 per cent of the word population will be living in the urban areas.At the present time it is more than 50 per cent of the world's population who thrives in the urban area. With this exponential growth and rise in density of population in urban areas.There is going to be man resource conflict that would lead to vast population disparities in socio-economic,culturalpositionandahugeriseinthecasesofcrimes,psychological stressors and an increased incidence of have -nots/excluded populations.

These set of population settle in the unauthorised areas or becomes the slum dwellers. They lack citizen's right of any government provisions under any schemes like health insurance,PDS and other quality social services for the marginalised groups as they are undocumented citizens.The vicious cycle of poverty becomes inter-generational due to low socio-economic, cultural status that prevent them from basic access to quality education, healthcare, housing, sanitation, employment opportunity in the organised sectors where specialised skills is required. Whereas there is limitless opportunities available in cities that give rise to stark population divide as per their socio- economic and cultural background. Therefore, it become important for social work professionals to work for the equity,justice and re-distribution.

The practice of social work in the urban areas may be divided into a number of distinct categories and disciplines of work in various contexts. Social Work Practice encompasses a wide range of contexts, particularly in the public, private, and civil society sectors. The social work practice in the government sector is most prevalent in metropolitan areas. It has a role in influencing social policies for the wellbeing and welfare of general public and larger society as well as in the delivery of social services through appropriate government departments and organizations.With the fast pacing urbanisation and and its implications, the difficulties are escalating in different aspects and sectors, seriously disrupting society's ability to operate. The issues vary from poverty, homelessness, slums development, morbidity and to issues with children and adolescent mental health, epidemics,pandemics, patients in the hospital, third gender, students, etc. The social workers with their unique skills, and intervention strategies aid the weak, disadvantaged, and marginalized people of society for different issues and areas of social work practice.

In the broader term the social work practice is important in the urban areas as much as in the rural setting that includes hospitals, schools, community organizations, government agencies, and private practice so on and so forth.

Here are some examples of social work practice in different settings,areas and sectors of urban settings:

- Healthcare Settings in urban areas:
  - Health care settings in Urban areas is comparatively advance and they come both in a public and private set-ups.
  - They work both with the patients and theirs families /carers to help them cope with medical conditions,illnesses,injuries and their mental and emotional health.
  - They may provide counseling, case management, and assistance with accessing community resources.
  - Social workers in urban areas healthcare settings may work in hospitals, clinics, hospices, and other healthcare facilities.
- School Settings in Urban areas:
  - Social workers in school settings work with students, families, and teachers to address issues that affect academic performance and overall well-being as they face various challenges and problems in the urban areas.
  - They may provide counseling, advocacy, and support for students with special needs, those experiencing bullying or discrimination, and those facing family or personal problems.
  - Social workers in school settings in urban area may work in elementary, middle, high schools and even higher education institutes.
- Community Organizations:
  - Social workers in community organizations work to improve the lives of individuals and families in the communities.
  - They may work with low-income families, immigrants, refugees, and other marginalized groups to provide support and assistance with accessing community resources.

  - Social workers in community organizations may work in nonprofits, advocacy groups, or government agencies.
- Government Agencies:
  - Social workers in government agencies work to provide assistance to individuals and families who are eligible for government benefits, such as food stamps, Medicaid, or housing assistance. They may also work in child welfare, adult protective services, or other programs that provide services to vulnerable populations.
  - Social workers in government agencies may work at the local, zonal, block and state, or federal level.
- Private Practice:
  - Social workers in private practice provide counseling and therapy services to individuals, couples, and families.
  - They may specialize in areas such as mental health, substance abuse, or family therapy.
  - Social workers in private practice may work in solo or group practices, or they may work as independent contractors.

Review Questions

(a) What is difference between Urbanization and Industrialization?
(b) What are the factors leading to Urbanization?
(c) What are the problem and challenges of Urban areas in the new liberalized India?

Did You Know?

- The United Nations projects that by 2050, 68% of people on Earth will live in cities, underscoring the ongoing trend of urbanization.
- Suburban city growth creates serious environmental problems because it increases carbon emissions and destroys natural habitats.
- Urban landscapes frequently depict issues like socio-economic inequality, cultural diversity, and seclusion in the middle of a crowded place, reflecting the complexity of contemporary life.
- Cities' physical attributes, such as how people move through congested areas and engage with strangers, can have a big impact on relationships and character behavior.
- Urban settings are frequently used in stories to set the stage for conflict, whether that conflict is rooted in personal problems amidst a busy environment or in social issues like poverty and crime.

SUMMARY

Social work pratice in Urban setting is carried out in urban environments, that poses diverse challenges to the profession.The urban life and living with its unique surroundings in complexities of different aspects of life raises new questions in relation to increasing conflicts or disintegration, mounting inequality, discrimination or apartheid, homelessness, social exclusion, and environmental problems.

Due to dearth of much research conducted on the roles , functioning and performance of social workers in urban settings.The Urban social work remains conceptually indistinct and not well rooted.Now with expanding Urbanisation, Industralisation and modernization along with its infrastructural development and vast opportunities there is growing migration towards urban locations that has prompted more interest in these areas.

At the same time,urban cities are faced with challenges in different fronts that envelops questions on social, economic, and environmental justice combined by race, gender, and class..There are various issues concerning to isolation and exclusion due to socio- economic and cultural status.

Now due to population explosion, the resources and opportunities that were for the well-being of people are limited and the environmental hazards has become a common phenomena that further suppresses vulnerable populations creating a huge gap due to structural disparities.

The urban areas undergoing rapid gentrification is a new crisis for the poor and marginalised that has caused a new type of social problem of displacement of vulnerable population. The social work professionals in general and urban social workers have to wear the gear of socio-economic, political, environmental change-agent to bridge the gap with justice, equity, re-distribution and inclusion keeping all diversity in different aspects and forms well protected and promoted so that our development process in Urban area is more sustainable through people-centric approach through awareness generation, advocacy, collaboration, negotation for the holistic and inclusive development of urban areas.

GLOSSARY

- **Developed countries:** Developed countries are those with stronger, more diversified economies that are generally more industrialized, as well as higher living standards than emerging nations.
- **Developing countries:** Developing countries are defined as those that are categorized according to a variety of economic and social factors, including life expectancy and per capita income, but are still in the early stages of economic growth.
- **Homelessness:** The condition of lacking stable, permanent housing, often resulting in living on the streets or in temporary shelters.
- **Poverty:** A state of insufficient financial resources to meet basic living needs, such as food, shelter, and healthcare.

- **Slum:** A densely populated urban informal community that may be defined by substandard housing and a dearth of dependable utilities including electricity, potable water, sanitary facilities, and law enforcement.
- **Suburb:** A region of a city that is surrounded by rural areas and has low density housing there.
- **Urban agglomerations:** Urban agglomerations are composed of a central metropolis and the surrounding contiguous suburbs.
- **Urban area:** A densely populated region characterized by developed infrastructure, including buildings, roads, and facilities, typically a city or town.
- **Urbanization:** The process through which a growing percentage of a population lives in cities and their suburbs is known as urbanization.

TOP TEN TAKEAWAYS POINTS

1. The readers would be able to understand the different broad settings of social work practice i.e., rural and urban settings.
2. The readers can understand the distinction among urbanisation, industrialisation and modernisation.
3. The readers would be able to know the characteristics of urban communities.
4. The readers would be able to understand the factors that lead to urbanisation.
5. The readers would be able to understand the historical context on the rise of urbanisation.
6. The readers would be able to understand the different problems and challenges of urbanisation and will be able to analyse the sustainable solutions towards the same.
7. The readers would be able to understand the constitutional provisions and programmes for urban community development and roles of professional social work practice in different areas/ settings in the urban milieu.
8. The readers should be able to understand meaning of sustainability and adapt to and advocate for the cause, for the true Bharatiyakaran.
9. The readers should be able to understand and appreciate the rural areas as a gift of nature to help us realize to take the Urban areas development towards more organic, natural and sustainable in all aspects of life and living and to avoid any further intrusion into our serene Rural areas.
10. The chapter should be able to influence the legislative framework to tune towards upgrading the life and living conditions of people by following the paths of swacchata, Sarvodaya, Antyodaya and Sustainability.

MULTIPLE CHOICE QUESTIONS

1. What are the key differences in the settings of social work practice in rural and urban areas?
   (a) Urban social work primarily focuses on community development, while rural social work focuses on individual case management.
   (b) In rural areas, social work often involves addressing complex family dynamics, while urban social work tends to prioritize advocacy for policy change.
   (c) Rural social work is more likely to involve long travel distances, whereas urban social work is concentrated in centralized offices.
   (d) Urban social work typically deals with fewer cultural diversity challenges compared to rural social work.
2. Which state is highly urbanised in India?
   (a) Kerala (b) Maharashtra
   (c) Tamil Nadu (d) Delhi
3. In the historical context, what were some key factors contributing to the rise of urbanisation?
   (a) Increased availability of agricultural land and improved farming techniques.
   (b) The decline of trade routes and limited access to resources.
   (c) Industrialization was due to the growth of factories and job opportunities in cities.
   (d) Preservation of traditional rural lifestyles and strong agrarian communities.
4. What is the primary distinction between urbanization, industrialization, and modernization?
   (a) Urbanisation refers to the growth of cities and towns, industrialization involves the development of industries, and modernization relates to technological advancement. Urban communities typically have high population density and access to advanced infrastructure.
   (b) Urbanisation relates to the advancement of technology, industrialization involves the growth of urban areas, and modernization encompasses changes in cultural practices.
   (c) Urbanisation represents the shift from rural to urban living, industrialization involves the spread of education, and modernization refers to the adoption of traditional values. Urban communities are typically sparsely populated with limited access to amenities.
   (d) Urbanisation signifies the decline of cities, industrialization involves the decline of traditional industries, and modernization relates to the preservation of historical heritage. Urban communities often prioritize agriculture over industrial development.

5. What are some common challenges and problems associated with urbanisation?
   (a) Improved access to education and healthcare services.
   (b) Decreased environmental pollution due to modern urban planning.
   (c) Increased demand for affordable housing and infrastructure.
   (d) Reduced traffic congestion and ample parking spaces in cities.
6. What is the primary goal of sustainable development?
   (a) Maximizing economic growth
   (b) Protecting natural resources
   (c) Achieving social equity
   (d) Promoting technological advancement
7. When analyzing sustainable solutions for urbanization, which factor is most crucial for achieving long-term success in urban development?
   (a) Relying solely on fossil fuels for energy needs.
   (b) Ignoring public transportation and promoting private car usage.
   (c) Implementing eco-friendly infrastructure and promoting renewable energy sources.
   (d) Disregarding green spaces and natural ecosystems within cities.
8. What are some of the key roles of professional social work practices in urban community development?
   (a) Providing legal counseling to individuals in urban areas.
   (b) Offering medical services exclusively to children in need.
   (c) Advocating for social justice and equality in urban communities.
   (d) Focusing solely on economic development without considering social factors.
9. The Constitution (73rd Amendment) Act was passed in 1992 with the purpose of
   (a) To democratically centralise authority
   (b) To give effect to fundamental rights
   (c) Form self-governance units.
   (d) None of the above
10. What is the role of social worker in solving urban problems?
   (a) Building Sustainability in all aspects of life and Environment-friendly Cities.
   (b) Education
   (c) Uphold human right
   (d) Motivate.

Answers

1. (c), 2. (c), 3. (c), 4. (b), 5. (c), 6. (b), 7. (c), 8. (c), 9. (c), 10. (a)

REFERENCES

1. Sutton, S. E., and S. P. Kemp. 2011. The Paradox of Urban Space: Inequality and Transformation in Marginalized Communities. New York: Palgrave MacMillan. [Crossref], [Google Scholar]
2. Vertovec, S. 2007. 'Super-Diversity and Its Implications.' *Ethnic and Racial Studies* 30(6): 1024–1054. doi:10.1080/01419870701599465. [Taylor & Francis Online], [Web of Science ®], [Google Scholar]
3. Matthies, A.-L., P. Turunen, S. Albers, T. Boeck, and N. Kati. 2004. 'An Eco-Social Approach to Tackling Social Exclusion in European Cities: A New Comparative Research Project in Progress.' *European Journal of Social Work* 3(1): 43–52. doi:10.1080/714052811. [Taylor & Francis Online], [Google Scholar]
4. Dominelli, L. 2012. Green Social Work: From Environmental Crises to Environmental Justice. Cambridge, UK: Polity Press. [Google Scholar]
5. D. Węziak-Białowolska, Quality of life in cities – Empirical evidence in comparative European perspective Cities, 58 (2016), pp. 87-96, 10.1016/j.cities.2016.05.016
6. Addams, J. 1990 [1926]. Twenty Years at Hull House with Biographical Notes. New York: Macmillan.
7. Arksey, H., and L. O'Malley. 2005. 'Scoping Studies: Towards a Methodological Framework.' *International Journal of Social Research Methodology* 8(1): 19–32. doi:10.1080/1364557032000119616.
8. Aveyard, H. 2014. Doing A Literature Review in the Health and Social Care: A Practical Guide. 3rd ed. Berkshire: Open University Press
9. Congress, E. 2017. 'Immigrants and Refugees in Cities: Issues, Challenges, and Interventions for Social Workers.' *Urban Social Work* 1(1): 20–34. doi:10.1891/2474-8684.1.1.20.

RECOMMENDED READINGS

1. Addams, J. 1990 [1926]. Twenty Years at Hull House with Biographical Notes. New York: Macmillan.
2. Arksey, H., and L. O'Malley. 2005. "Scoping Studies: Towards a Methodological Framework." *International Journal of Social Resecrch Methodology* 8 (1): 19–32. doi: 10.1080/1364557032000119616.
3. Aveyard, H. 2014. Doing A Literature Review in the Health and Social Care: A Practical Guide. 3rd ed. Berkshire: Open University Press.
4. Fischer, C. 1995. "Subcultural Theory of Urbanism: A Twentieth-Year Assessment." *American Journal of Sociology* 101 (3): 543–577. doi: 10.1086/230753.
5. Geldof, D. 2011. "New Challenges for Urban Social Work and Urban Social Work Research." *European Journal of Social Work* 14 (1): 27–39. doi:10.1080/13691457.2010.516621.
6. Shlay, A.B., and J. Balzarini. 2015. "Urban Sociology." In *International Encyclopedia of the Social & Behavioral Sciences*, edited by J.D. Wright, 926–933. 2nd ed. Oxford: Elsevier.

CHAPTER – 13

Social Work with Families in Conflict Zones

SEILIENMANG HAOKIP

Assistant Professor, School of Social Work,
Martin Luther Christian University, Shillong, Meghalaya

If we desire a society of peace, then we cannot achieve such a society through violence.

– Bayard Rustin

ABSTRACT: *Violence generates a chain of problems that extend across time. Survivors and victims of violence are forced to endure a disrupted society in which displacement and poverty became rampant. Such an event deeply affect the younger generations as they found themselves entrapped in a cycle of violence and poverty. However, there is an innate hardiness in the structure of the society and the family that could provide resilience to individuals struggling with the aftermath of violence and disruption. This chapter is an attempt to provide an understanding of the concept of violence and the challenges imposed by it. It also focuses on the importance of family as a site of resilience in the aftermath of violence.*

Keywords: *Violence, Conflict Zones, Cultural Sensitivity, Resilience, Family, Social Work with Families*

Learning Objectives

- To understand the concept and nature of violence
- To understand the challenges of families in conflict zones
- To examine how the cycle of violence become endemic in a conflict zone
- To explore the significance of social work intervention in the mitigation of violence

INTRODUCTION

The devastation caused by wars and armed conflicts are manifested in different aspects of the everyday lives of the community. It affects individual children as well as their families through traumatic experiences and the complexities unleashed in the forms of displacement and poverty too. According to the United Nations High Commissioner for Refugees (UNHCR, 2017), conflict and human rights violation resulted in the forced displacement of more than 60 million people of which 51 per cent are children. Therefore violence continues to reproduce a specter in the post-conflict period and this set a stage for the perpetuation of further violence. The lasting impacts of war and armed conflict affect the physical, psychological and social functioning of the children. It can cause a rupture in the social fabric and services that render support to families and children. However, amid these complexities in conflict and post-conflict settings, family plays an important role in affecting the mental health and coping mechanism of the children. Social workers in conflict zones can play an important role in fostering a family approaches that can provide a conducive environment for the growth and development of children.

CONFLICT ZONES AND THE LASTING IMPACTS OF VIOLENCE

Violence is a global challenge that has been shaping behaviours of the individuals and groups throughout centuries. It is a global menace that doesn't spare any country during the course of history. According to the World Health Organization (2002), 1.6 million people annually lose their lives due to violence. The toll on violence-induced injuries is even higher with impairments ranging from physical to mental and social health. However, due to the lack of proper record keeping systems in many countries it is impossible to define the magnitude of the mortality and morbidity due to violence. The twentieth century remains a blot in history as the violence of nations have left a heavy burden that shattered communities and caused social suffering. According to Rummel (1994), violent conflicts took the lives of around 191 million people. Half of this population were civilians. The World Health Organization (2002) also reports that in the year 2000, violence resulted in the death of nearly two lakh youth in the USA. According to Kloos (1994), armed conflict in Ethiopia resulted in the death of a million people while physically disabling at least 40, 000 people. In Cambodia too, survivors of armed conflict continue to bear the brunt of the violence and landmines (Stover, 1994).

The impact of violence on the socio-economic aspects of the society is also extremely high. It resulted in poverty and victims are continually haunted in their everyday lives as they struggle to find adjustment in the post-conflict environment. The administration of a country is also left in shambles due to the devastating effects of violence. The destruction of infrastructures including the health-care system and social services of a country also hampered the processes of rebuilding and resilience. The case of Bosnia and Herzegovina reflects how violence can have a devastating toll on different institutions of the country. Before the violence in 1994, it was reported that about 95 per cent of the children were immunized. However, following the violence, the number of immunized children went down drastically to 35 per cent. Therefore, a huge part of the impact and cost of violence is borne by different institutions including the health-care system (Miller, Cohen and Rossman, 1993). As a result the United States of America began to give proper attention to the impact of violence based on the Surgeon General's report of 1979. Such a move is strongly coherent with the advocacy against violence because of its impacts on the health of the nation. Immediately in 1996 the World Health Assembly made the important and relevant declaration that violence is a leading public health challenges.

The devastation of violence is also strongly felt by the trade and commerce sector of a region or a country. Warfare, combat as well as rehabilitation of the population demand huge amount of government budget. The flow of production and the promises of profits of industrial countries are also impacted by violence. The World Health Organization's report (2002) also shows how the death of more than 40 million people are caused by conflict-induced famines. Refugees and children are among the groups of people being hit hard by the consequences of violence as poverty and the aftermath of chaos destroy different government mechanisms including health-care system. Malnutrition and unavailability of proper medicines are inevitable to such consequences. The Table 1 highlights a report of the Institute for Economic and Peace (2020) that lists the five countries with the highest expenditure on containment of violence on their respective GDP.

Table 1: Expenditure on Violence Containment (percent of GDP)

Country	*Expenditure*
North Korea	27.5 %
Syria	23.8 %
Liberia	22.7 %
Afghanistan	21.2 %
Libya	19.6 %

Several researches reveal the deleterious effects of violence on health and well-being of the children and youth groups (Arafat & Boothby, 2003; De Jong et al., 2005). There are also many studies that depict the impact of violence on the mental health of an individual. Anxiety, depression and Post Traumatic-Stress Disorders (PTSD) are common to the war-affected communities around the world (Barber, 2008; de Jong, et al., 2003). Scheeringa and Zeanah (1995) show that a child witnessing violence, in the homes or community, exhibit constant fear, sleep disturbances and excessive irritability. Exposure to wars and the experiences of growing up in conflict zones also influences unwanted and risky behavior among children that can include smoking, alcohol and unsafe sexual practices

(Anda et al., 1999; Dube et al., 2001). These challenges of the conflict zones demand proper social work intervention at the level of the family because the family is an important unit of social fabric that can reproduce creativity and resiliency in the aftermath of the conflict.

Did You Know?

Global displacement is at a record high with conflicts becoming more violent and protracted, and root causes more complex. At the end of 2018, 70.8 million were forcibly displaced as a result of persecution, conflict, violence, and human rights violations. Double the amount compared to 20 years ago.

Source: UNHCR

UNDERSTANDING VIOLENCE: CONCEPT AND DEFINITION

The definition of violence entails a complex process. While violence is basically understood as a behavior that can harm a person or an object, this meaning fails to encompass the multidimensional nature obscured by the themes of war, terrorism, and securitization. Bufacchi (2005) notes the lack of a scholarly consensus in defining violence. He categorizes violence, firstly, as the use of excessive force, and secondly as a violation. He also argues that the definition of violence as the abuse of physical force limits our understanding because it obscures other manifestation of violence that includes the psychological, structural and the institutional dimensions.

There is also a strong degree of subjectivity involved in the definition of violence. The conceptualization of violence is a process shaped by how one understands culture. Galtung (1969) classifies violence into direct and indirect violence. The latter form of violence is inherent in a culture. Galtung's classification shows that the pervasiveness of a norm or culture of violence in the society channels a process of internalization of

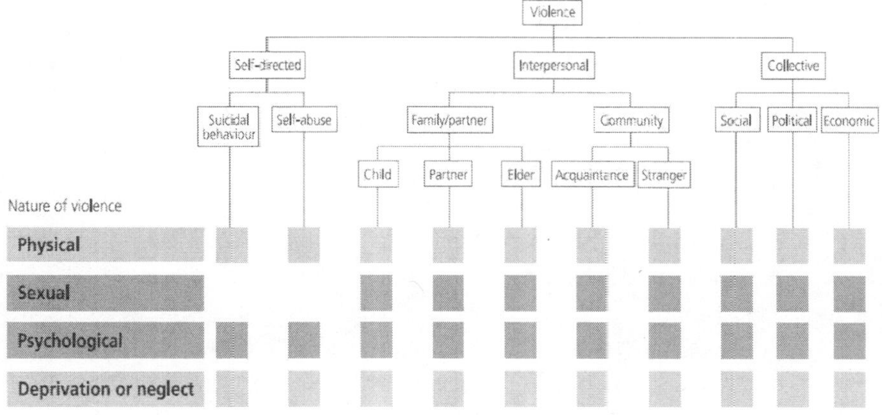

Figure 1: Typology of Violence (WHO, 2002)

violence as a normal and acceptable behaviour. The conceptualization of violence is also complicated by the multidisciplinary and interdisciplinary approaches.

The World Health Organization (2002) classifies violence into self-directed violence, interpersonal violence and collective violence. Self-directed violence includes suicidal behaviours and self-abuses, while interpersonal violence is commonly found in families between parents and children, and the abuse of elders. Interpersonal violence also includes community violence whereas collective violence is the type of violence associated with groups induced by ideologies, race, or ethnicities.

Review Questions

(a) Discuss the various types of Violence as given by WHO, 2002.

(b) Discuss briefly the impact of violence on the socio-economic aspects of the society.

SOCIAL WORK WITH FAMILIES IN CONFLICT ZONES

Violence and the consequences such as migration can produce a socio-ecological shock to the victims particularly the children. Boothby (2008) echoes the need for a protective shield to reduce the impact of such shocks. The impact of wars and conflicts are aggravated by the experiences of stressors during the processes of conflict-induced displacement and rehabilitation that are impaired by poverty (Denov and Shevell, 2019). This place refugee families and children at a high risk due to the experiences of torture and trauma (Kirmayer et al., 2011). Denov and Shevell argues the need for studying the entire family system as family support is significant to a sound mental health for young refugees (Kovacev and Shute, 2004). The emotional stress associated with wars and displacement can hamper the care-giving and nurturing capacity of the adults (Betancourt et al., 2015). According to Annan, Blattman and Horton (2006), high levels of family connectedness can decrease the degree of distress threatening the youth. Given these potentials of the family system, it is vital to focus on a social work approach with families in conflict zones that can offer support to war-affected children. This approach of social work can help locate protective shields or factors in different levels of the child's environment.

According to Bronfenbrenner's (1986) socio-ecological model, the development of a child is shaped by different reciprocal processes at different levels of the social ecology. These levels include the family, community and the society. This model of development has been commonly applied by scholars and researchers studying the realities and experiences of migrations and refugees. The model gives a holistic understanding of the well-being of refugees. Miller and Rasco (2004) also asserts the inextricability of environmental demands and adaptive resources available to a person. This interaction stemming out of the demands of the environment with the adaptive resources of a refugee shapes the processes of healing and adaptation. The family remains a vital supportive factor for both the social and emotional needs during the process of the resettlement of refugees. A social worker in a conflict zones can observe the importance of family members in the transformation of adversities into source of strength that provides chances of survival of the psycho-social, cultural and economy of the family. Such observation and intervention can be made possible by facilitating the process of rebuilding a meaningful universe.

Several scholars opine that the traditional approaches to the psycho-social support have been dominated by the focus on individualism (Denov and Shevell, 2019; Bilotta and Denov, 2017). These approaches focusing on trauma and the individual often obscure indigenous conceptualization. Through the use of a cultural lens, Rabiau (2019) analyses culture and the formation of identity among adolescents in a post-migratory context. Rabiau's work reveal the significance of cultural idioms of distress and the processes of acculturation inherent in the family. Cultural idiom aids in the interpretation of symptoms of distress. Bond (2019) focuses on the roles of fathers who have generally been excluded in clinical social work practices. Bond stresses on the critical roles of fathers in child development and observes that proper engagement of father can bring about a protective factor in the process of resilience and well-being of families and youth. These works focusing on families are based on a socio-ecological orientation that takes into consideration the cultural aspects of the society.

Review Questions

(a) What is the role of social workers with children living in conflict zones?

(b) Discuss scope of social work practice with families in conflict zones..

Did You Know?

Half of the refugee population worldwide are children and youth below the age of 18, more than 110,000 are separated from their families. In 2018, 27,600 unaccompanied and separated children sought asylum in countries around the world. Forced displacement has severe consequences for children's education opportunities, and currently 3.7 million refugee children are out of school.

Source: UNHCR

SUMMARY

Cultural sensitivity is an important starting point in the process of social work in conflict zones. The North-East region is an example that reinforces this idea. Governmental interventions have failed to bring about a halt in the insurgency movement because of the dominant theme of securitization that often obscure the histories of the locals. The Armed Forces (Special Power) Act, 1958, is an example of government intervention that fails to contain the violence and unrest in the region. A holistic understanding of this region shows how colonial legacies of administration continue to have an influence in regenerating disputes between states and different ethnic groups of the region. A contextualized knowledge can improve the practice of social work by initiating a process of adaptations that are relevant to the culture and sensitive to the realities of families undergoing the challenges of everyday in a conflict zone. A social worker can facilitate the intergenerational transmission of memories, promote cultural understanding of conflict mitigations inherent to the cultures of different groups in the conflict zones. The pedagogy of schools and religious institutions can also be oriented toward stories of resilience and narratives that promote peaceful coexistence.

GLOSSARY

- **Collective Violence:** Acts of violence committed by larger groups or communities, often during conflicts, wars, or social upheaval.
- **Conflict Zones:** Geographic areas where active fighting or armed conflict occurs between opposing groups, often affecting civilians.
- **Cultural Sensitivity:** Awareness and respect for cultural differences, ensuring that actions and behaviors are appropriate within diverse cultural contexts.
- **Ethnic Conflict:** Disputes or violent clashes between different ethnic groups, often based on identity, culture, or historical grievances.
- **PTSD (Post-Traumatic Stress Disorder):** A mental health condition triggered by experiencing or witnessing traumatic events, leading to symptoms like flashbacks, anxiety, and emotional distress.
- **Refugee:** A person who flees their country due to war, persecution, or natural disaster, seeking safety and asylum in another nation.
- **Resilience:** The ability to recover from adversity, stress, or trauma and adapt positively to challenging circumstances.
- **Violence:** The use of physical force or power to harm others, causing injury, damage, or death.

TOP TEN TAKEAWAYS POINTS

1. The Armed Forces Special Powers Act (AFSPA), 1958, was implemented and put into force in the context of increasing violence in the North-eastern states

2. Cultural sensitivity requires an understanding of another person's set of beliefs and values that is attributed to the latter's ethnic or cultural background. A Social Worker must be ready to adopt an accommodative approach in dealing with people of diverse cultural background and experiences.
3. Pedagogy refers to the method of teaching. It is imperative for Social Work educators to emphasize Critical Pedagogy grounded on a vision of justice and equality through transformative knowledge.
4. Pedagogy in the context of conflict zones requires a content of education inclusive of the specific needs. Trauma-informed teaching and management of behaviour are necessary to address the psychological harm and traumatic memories embedded in a culture of conflict zones.
5. According to the United Nations High Commissioner for Refugees (UNHCR, 2017), conflict and human rights violation resulted in the forced displacement of more than 60 million people of which 51 per cent are children.
6. Social workers in conflict zones can play an important role in fostering a family approach that can provide a conducive environment for the growth and development of children.
7. The impact of violence on the socio-economic aspects of the society is also extremely high. It resulted in poverty and victims are continually haunted in their everyday lives as they struggle to find adjustment in the post-conflict environment.
8. Global displacement is at a record high with conflicts becoming more violent and protracted, and root causes more complex. At the end of 2018, 70.8 million were forcibly displaced as a result of persecution, conflict, violence, and human rights violations. Double the amount compared to 20 years ago.
9. According to Bronfenbrenner's (1986) socio-ecological model, the development of a child is shaped by different reciprocal processes at different levels of the social ecology. These levels include the family, community and the society. This model of development has been commonly applied by scholars and researchers studying the realities and experiences of migrations and refugees. The model gives a holistic understanding of the well-being of refugees.
10. A social worker can facilitate the inter-generational transmission of memories, promote cultural understanding of conflict mitigations inherent to the cultures of different groups in the conflict zones.

MULTIPLE CHOICE QUESTIONS

1. The World Health Organization classification of violence consists of
   (a) Self-directed violence (b) Interpersonal violence
   (c) Collective violence (d) All of the above
2. What hampers the care-giving and nurturing capacity of adult during wars and displacement?
   (a) Emotional Stress (b) Unemployment
   (c) Financial burden (d) All of the above
3. The Socio-Ecological Model (SEM) was first introduced by
   (a) Carl Jung (b) Sigmund Freud
   (c) Urie Bronfenbrenner (d) Erik Erikson
4. ________________ can act as a prevention strategy from distress and risk factors for children and youth.
   (a) Increasing connectedness to people
   (b) Strict policing of conflict zones
   (c) Education (d) Proper isolation
5. How many people lose their live due to violence in every year?
   (a) 1.6 billion (b) 1.6 million
   (c) 2 million (d) 1 million
6. Which of the following is NOT a reason for global displacement?
   (a) Human rights violations (b) Violence
   (c) Job opportunities (d) Conflict
7. What is one of the significant impacts of violence on society as mentioned in the provided content?
   (a) Increase in educational opportunities
   (b) Improvement in healthcare services
   (c) Rise in poverty levels
   (d) Strengthening of community bonds
8. Community violence is primarily a form of:
   (a) Systemic violence (b) Interpersonal violence
   (c) Self-directed violence (d) Collective violence
9. Which aids in the interpretation of symptoms of distress?
   (a) Cultural idiom (b) Stress
   (c) Violence (d) Poverty
10. Which is an important starting point in the process of social work in conflict zones?
    (a) Systemic approach (b) Interpersonal Relationship
    (c) Violence (d) Cultural sensitivity

Answers

1. (d), 2. (a), 3. (c), 4. (a), 5. (b), 6. (c), 7. (c), 8. (b), 9. (a), 10. (d)

REFERENCES

1. Annan, J., Blattman, C., & Horton, R. (2006). The state of youth and youth protection in Northern Uganda (pp. 23). Uganda: UNICEF.
2. Anda, RF., Croft, JB., Felitti, V.J., Nordenberg, D., Giles, WH., Williamson, DF. & Giovino, GA. (1999). Adverse childhood experiences and smoking during adolescence and adulthood. *Journal of American Medical Association*, 282(17), 1652–658.
3. Arafat, C., & Boothby, N. (2003). *A psychosocial assessment of Palestinian children*. United States Agency for International Development.
4. Barber, Christopher. (2008). Domestic violence against men. *Nursing Standard: Official Newspaper of The Royal College of Nursing*, 22(51), 35–39.
5. Betancourt, T. S., Abdi, S., Ito, B. S., Lilienthal, G. M., Agalab, N., & Ellis, H. (2015). We left one war and came to another: Resource loss, acculturative stress, and caregiver–Child relationships in Somali refugee families. *Cultural Diversity and Ethnic Minority Psychology*, 21(1), 114.
6. Bilotta, N., & Denov, M. (2017). Theoretical understandings of unaccompanied young people affected by war: Bridging divides and embracing local ways of knowing. *The British Journal of Social Work*, 48(6).
7. Bond, S. (2019). The Essential Role of the Father: Fostering a Father-Inclusive Approach with Immigrant and Refugee Families. *Journal of Family Social Work*, 22(1).
8. Boothby, N. (2008). Political violence and development: An ecologic approach to children in war zones. *Child and Adolescent Psychiatric Clinics*, 17(3), 497–514.
9. Bufacchi, V. (2005). Two concepts of violence. *Political Studies Review*, 3(2), 193–204.
10. De Jong, J.T.V.M., Komproe, I. H., & van Ommeren, M. (2003). Common mental disorders in postconflict settings. *The lancet, 361(9375),* 2128–130.
11. De Jong, J.T., Punamäki R.L., Komproe, I., Qouta, S. & El-Masri, M. (2005). The deterioration and mobilization effects of trauma on social support: childhood maltreatment and adulthood military violence in a Palestinian community sample. *Journal of Child Abuse Neglect*, 29(4), 351–73.
12. Dube, S.R., Anda, R.F., Felitti, V.J., Chapman, D.P., Williamson, D.F., & Giles, W.H. (2001). Childhood abuse, household dysfunction, and the risk of attempted suicide throughout the life span: Findings from the adverse childhood experiences study. *Journal of American Medical Association*, 286(24), 3089–096.
13. Galtung, J. (1969). Violence, Peace, and Peace Research. *Journal of Peace Research*, 6(3), 167–91.
14. Kirmayer, L. J., Narasiah, L., Munoz, M., Rashid, M., Ryder, A. G., Guzder, J., … Pottie, K. (2011). Common mental health problems in immigrants and refugees: General approach in primary care. *Canadian Medical Association Journal*, 183(12), E959–E967.

15. Kloos, H. (1992). Health impacts of war in Ethiopia. *Disasters*, 16(4), 347–54.
16. Kovacev, L., & Shute, R. (2004). Acculturation and social support in relation to psychosocial adjustment of adolescent refugees resettled in Australia. *International Journal of Behavioral Development*, 28(3), 259–67.
17. Miller, T.R., Cohen, M.A., & Rossman, S.B. (1993). Victim costs of violent crime and resulting injuries. *Health Affairs*, 12, 186–97.
18. Rabiau, M. (2019). Culture, Migration, and Identity Formation in Adolescence: A Family Perspective. *Journal of Family Social Work*, 22(1).
19. Rummel, R.J. (1994). Death by government: Genocide and mass murder since 1990. London: Transaction Publication.
20. Scheeringa, M.S. & Zeanah, CH. (1995). Symptom expression and trauma variable in children under 48 months of age. *Infant Mental Health Journal*, 16(4), 259–70.
21. Stover, E., Keller, A., Cobey, J., & Sopheap, S. (1994). The medical and social consequences of landmines in Cambodia. *Journal of the American Medical Association*, 272(5), 331–36.
22. World Health Assembly, (1996). World Health Organization. Geneva: WHO.
23. World Health Organization. (2002). *Word Report on Violence and Health.* Geneva: WHO.

RECOMMENDED READINGS

1. Bronfenbrenner, U. (1986). Ecology of the family as a context for human development: Research perspectives. *Developmental Psychology*, 22(6), 723.
2. Denov, Myriam & Shevell, Meaghan C. (2019). Social work practice with war affected children and families: The importance of family, culture, arts, and participatory approaches, *Journal of Family Social Work*, 22:1, 1–16.
3. Denov, M. & Shevell, M.C. (2019). (Eds.). Social Work Practice with War Affected Children. Routledge.
4. Figley, C.R., Yarvis, J.S. & Thyer, B.A. (2020). (Eds.) Combat Social Work: Applying the Lessons of War to the Realities of Human Services, Oxford University Press
5. Miller, K. E., & Rasco, L. M. (Eds.). (2004). The mental health of refugees: Ecological approaches to healing and adaptation. Mahwah, New Jersey: Taylor & Francis.

CHAPTER – 14

Social Group Work Practice in Tribal Communities

VEENA SURESH AND VIVEK S.

Assistant Professors, Department of Social Work, Amrita Vishwa Vidyapeetham, Amritapuri Campus, Kerala, India

Coming together is a beginning. Keeping together is progress. Working together is success.

– Henry Ford

ABSTRACT: *Social group work method is a best way to break the silence of individuals who live in groups. During several instances of fieldwork, social workers have experienced that tribal communities are more relaxed in discussing in groups and they express more in group than individually. They take group consensus in most of the critical decisions in their life and follows group conformity in every action they do. Consequently, a group work method works wells with such a population since they already have social cohesiveness which strengthens team effort. However, the effectiveness of group work can be enhanced by the application of principles of social group work which serve as guidelines for conducting group work method. It sets standards to the code of conduct for the group worker during the interactive process. These principles follow all ethical considerations starting from informed consent of the participants, their volunteerism in engaging in the group activities, democratic participation of group members, their likes, and dislikes. Therefore this chapter elaborates how each principle in social group work method is applied to engage with tribal communities. The findings can be used by academicians, BSW, and MSW students to understand the scope and relevance of principles in social group work method.*

Keywords: *Social Group Work, Principles of Social Group Work, Tribal Community*

Learning Objectives

- To orient social group work principles in a tribal community setting.
- To get familiar with the actual case scenarios that a social work trainee may encounter during the field visit.

INTRODUCTION

Social Group Work is one of the core methods of social work. Its objective is to enhance social functioning, solve social problems through group effort, helps individuals to cope with difficulties via social support, and promote social change through teamwork. These methods have a broader scope in various settings like hospitals, psychiatric units, counselling centres, schools, shelter homes, etc. Social workers and group members' code of behaviour and attitude in different group work settings are governed by principles formulated from empirical evidence. Therefore, understanding the social group work principle is essential for a successful group work practice. Therefore, this chapter aims to discuss the application of social group work principles in a tribal community setting.

When we think about tribal communities, we can say that they are a group of people living in a closed community with specific community boundaries, social norms, customs, and practices. They live in tune with nature, efficient at managing natural resources. They are a group that has a strong group culture and identity. Because of these characteristics, it is easy for a group worker to ensure social cohesion in group work practice and the group work method works well with this group. However, these strengths of the tribal community may not produce the actual outcome if we conduct a group work session with certain false assumptions from a laymen perspective.

Let us discuss the false assumptions with an example. Imagine that you want to eradicate social problems like school dropout and unemployment in tribal hamlets. Our first step is to motivate them to join the school because we assume that a typical school education system will empower them. But the community may have alternative thoughts like whether this school will satisfy my need for livelihood, whether it provides an education in my local language, and exposure to experiential learning of life skills to deal with my daily life activities like fishing, hunting, collecting forest resources, etc. Probably the answer is NO for most of the questions. The problem is we are trying to enforce them to follow the system set by us, and in a way, we are making them vulnerable to stigma and discrimination from the external world.

Moving to the second assumption, if they are not interested in education, you decide to form different groups in the community and offer some random vocational training program. You may skip the need assessment tasks like checking the group's interest, feasibility, scope, and capacity to admit to such a program. The third assumption is that we think we are the so-called developed, cultured, educated fellows who know how to live, and we are supposed to change the lifestyle of the tribal population. So, we prepare a group work session to explain the development plan for the tribal community without collecting any feedback from them nor giving much attention to the socio-cultural contexts of the tribal community. So, is there a way to eliminate these false assumptions andand ensure an inclusive group work practice with this population? The answer is YES if we adhere to social group work practice principles.

CONCEPT AND DEFINITION

Principles in Social Group Work Practice

Principles are the foundational facts that guide action and are tested via empirical evidence. It provides practitioners with a theoretical framework when working with individuals and groups. Our understanding of principles evolves as we gain more experience and new insights. Principles of social group work is a set of guidelines that need to be followed by the group worker during the group work process. The classic book of 'Social Group Work: Principles and Practice' by Harleigh B. Trecker (1948) theorized Ten Social Group Work Principles, briefly covered below. The following sections discuss each principle and how it can be applied in real-time scenarios.

Review Questions

(a) Give an example of a false assumption related to tribal community development in India?

(b) What is the significance of applying principles in social group work practice?

(c) What do you mean by principles of social group work?

Did You Know?

The Ministry of Tribal Affairs (2022) provides the following relevant data on tribal communities in India:

- The tribal population in India was 104.3 million according to the 2011 Census, constituting 8.6% of the total population.
- Literacy rates among tribal communities have improved from 47.1% in 2001 to 59% in 2011, but remain significantly lower than the national average of 73%.
- The sex ratio in tribal communities is 990 females per 1000 males, which is higher than the national average of 940.
- Approximately 40.6% of tribal people live below the poverty line, compared to the national average of 20.8%.
- The infant mortality rate among tribal communities is 44.4 per 1000 live births, notably higher than the national average of 33.6.
- About 44.7% of tribal children under five years of age are stunted, while 45.3% are underweight.
- Only 46.1% of tribal households have access to clean drinking water, compared to the national average of 85.5%.
- Forest rights titles have been distributed to over 4.9 million tribal and other traditional forest dwellers under the Forest Rights Act, 2006, covering about 4.1 million hectares of forest land.

The Principle of Planned Group Formation

This principle proposes that the group work should be aware of the client demographic. It includes the gender, age, level of education, family details, the socio-cultural environment in which the client lives. The group is formed by considering all these factors to ensure the smooth functioning of the group work. So, suppose you are a social worker who works for tribal development. In that case, you need to make sure that the group consists of people from similar backgrounds, likes, dislikes, interests, and common problems.

Example: Group formation in a tribal community.

A group worker got an opportunity to work with tribes in a specific region. In the group formation phase, the groupworker interacted with all the tribes and invited them for the first group meeting. But a group of people from a specific tribe did not show up for the meeting even if they had agreed to attend the same the previous day. Further investigation proved that everyone who was called for the meeting represents tribal community, but each tribe has differences in their culture, values, and customs. According to the norms of this tribe (who did not show up for the meeting), they are not supposed to mingle with the other tribe. If they do so, they are outcasted from their community. Here the group worker ignored the importance of considering the cultural difference and community norms of the community during the group formation.

The Principle of Specific Group Objectives

The social worker formulates group objectives following the group's wishes and capabilities and the agency's mission. The group work should be clear about the precise aims they intend to achieve and the advantages they expect the members to get from the group work process. When designing the purposes and actions to be carried out in group work, the members' interests and desires should be considered.

Example: Open defecation free tribal hamlets.

You are working as a social worker in an NGO that works to achieve open defecation free tribal hamlets. The objective set by the NGO is to build toilets for each house. As per the objective, you make a toilet for each house, educate them on the consequences of open defecation and coordinate behaviour modification related to the usage of toilets. However, you found that the community members are still not using the toilets. Through in-depth discussion with the members, you related that none of the householders would prefer a bathroom attached to their house. They believe they should not defecate near their living space; it should be done outside their community to ensure water purity. This issue can be avoided if the social worker has taken the initiative to discuss the community preference before building the toilets. The objective of the NGO is GOOD, but if it is not set in line with the community preference, we cannot achieve the desired outcome.

The Principle of Purposeful Worker Group Relationship

The social worker's relationship with the group is informal with a clear purpose. Connection with the group must achieve some goals and satisfy members' needs. The extent to which the group can be assisted in achieving its full potential is determined by the quality and strength of this relationship.

Example: Monetary benefits for group participation v/s skill-building.

When a social worker forms a group, we ensure that the worker and the members know the group's purpose, goals, and outcome. For example, there are cases where people join a group expecting monetary support. However, our purpose as a social workers is to upskill the group members rather than distribute financial aid. The mismatch in group purpose can happen when a third person (mediator) between the group worker and members can provide false assurance that they will get money if they participate in a group meeting. So, it is always preferable to explain the group's purpose at the beginning of the group work process.

The Principle of Continuous Individualization

Each group must be distinct from others, just as the group members. Rather than a uniform response, the worker should be prepared for different responses. The social worker should realize that everyone's talent and growth differ. Strive to help people understand themselves and change their attitudes about people with exceptional needs.

Example: One Development plan for all tribal in India.

Development Programs are planned in a standardized format. However, these programs can be effective if it is offered in a way to address the uniqueness of the group. For example, a social worker followed a standardized format for vocational training in all tribal hamlets. But the worker realized that vocational training on pickle making is profitable in one hamlet and jewellery making for another depends on contextual factors like availability of resources, the scope of markets of the product, travel cost, skill, capacity, and motivation of group members. Therefore, if the social worker says they will only offer pickle making training in all hamlets, it may fail.

The Principle of Guided Group Interaction

Guided group interaction is when two or more persons are in meaningful contact and modify their behaviour. The exchange is happening between-group workers and the group members. Both are expecting a significant outcome from the conversation. It can be a conversion that instils hope among the members, encourages them to react to a social problem they face, enhances social functioning, changes irrational thoughts into rational through open group discussion, and promotes favourable behaviour modification.

Example: Group therapy session to build coping skills.

The group worker conducted group therapy with the tribal children who faced stigma and discrimination at school. The purpose of group work is to help them ventilate the painful experiences of discrimination and build positive coping mechanisms to react to such events in life. The group work interaction may go long and boring if everyone starts sharing their painful stories. There is a chance to deviate from the actual purpose of building coping skills if the group work is not prepared to moderate the interaction.

The Principle of Democratic Group Self-Determination

A group has the right to make its own decisions and the ability to succeed. The social worker's role is to make the group responsibly self-determining by assisting them in developing a conscious group-self. They may require the help of a social worker during the group formation phase, and transition of responsibility happens gradually if the social worker provides an environment of democratic group participation and engagement in group activities.

Example: Democratic participation of women in Self-Help Groups.

Group workers have helped the tribal women to form a Self-Help Group (SHG) for economic empowerment. A social worker can promote the SHG's activities. At the same time, the group members have the right to decide how much money could be collected from members, distribution of loans, and repayment procedures with the group consensus. This ensures the democratic participation of all members. Gradually the group became responsible; they could identify their needs and plan accordingly for their development.

The Principle of Flexible Functional Organization

A formal organization should be in place to assist the group in achieving its goals. This formal organization should fulfil a perceived need, be flexible and adaptable, and change as the group does. Depending on their context, every group can set a hierarchical organizational structure, including the board of directors, managers, president, secretary, treasurer, and members. They must decide the roles and responsibilities of each member in the group meetings. A standardized set of group norms, rules and guidelines are necessary to prevent failure or group conflicts. A group worker needs to be flexible in the functioning and decision-making process during the group work practice.

Example: Flexible functioning of group activities.

A group worker has planned a group evaluation meeting at the end of a month since they need to report to the agency. But the group members shared their inconvenience in attending the same due to some cultural festival in their community. In this context, the social worker must be flexible in organizing the group meeting according to the convenience of the group.

The Principle of Progressive Program Experiences

The group's programme experiences should start at the level of member desire, demand, ability, and expertise. The program is designed in line with the group's capacity to achieve the goals set by the group. It is unrealistic to expect the group to perform the same thing all the time. After completing simple tasks, the group can be encouraged to more complicated experiences.

Example: From group farming to environment protection.

A group of unemployed tribal youth decided to start group farming by mobilizing all youths in their community. When they became successful in farming, they formed an association of young farmers and started availing farming subsidies. So, they become a powerful group, and once they need to face an issue of land rights, they start raising their voice for their rights and become a group of people who protect their land. Here the group was initiated from a small group farming. Gradually they transformed into a group that fought for their rights.

The Principle of Resource Utilization

Group members are making the most use of the agency's and community's internal and external resources. Groups are encouraged to take charge of economic and human resources mobilization and utilization. Social workers or group leaders need to oversee the members' use of available resources for the good of the community.

Example: Identifying community resources to tackle iron deficiency.

Group workers have conducted a focused group discussion among the community members to address anaemia among women and children. When asked about the daily diet, the women stated they used to have a meal once a day, mainly rice. But they are a community involved in exporting drumsticks, and they were clueless about the nutritional benefits of moringa leaves in tackling anaemia. Such insights about the community resources can be provided with the help of group work.

The Principle of Evaluation

Evaluation provides an insight into the effectiveness of the group effort to the social worker and the group members. The evaluation questions can be discussed in the middle or final stage of the group process to analyze the group's progress. The evaluation can also be done with the help of online/offline feedback forms. The social worker and members must be prepared to take necessary actions if they find that the group work process has not achieved the expected outcome. Sometimes they must reconstitute the group, reframe the group objectives, modify intervention plans and re-evaluate the progress.

Example: Women's Group Evaluation Meeting.

A group meeting was conducted to assess the progress made by the group of tribal women in jewellery making, and group workers realized that they hadn't made progress. The group worker started blaming the group members inefficiency for achieving the goal and behaved in a bossy attitude without asking for failure in achieving the target. The women groups were not cooperative from then onwards, and the group started failing. If it is an open discussion regarding the factors contributing to failure, the group could realize their mistakes and come back. Therefore, it is necessary to evaluate group progress, but we need to acknowledge the group members' feelings during the evaluation.

The principles of the social group work method are an essential guide for practising group work with grassroots level people. Application of principles ensures a bottom-up approach and democratic engagement of group members. Moreover, it enhances social consciousness and social responsibility. Ultimately sustainable way of managing the group is feasible with the help of group work practice principles.

SUMMARY

Social group work is a primary method of social work practice. Group work methods become a systematic process when the social worker incorporates different theories, models, therapies, and techniques in their action. However, the foundation for executing the above concepts lies in social group work practice principles. The principles help the social worker build the guidelines that decide the ground rules of a group work process. Many social scientists have discovered a variety of principles for group work practice. In this chapter, we have attempted to elaborate Ten principles of social group work practice formulated by Harleigh B. Trecker. According to him, the social worker needs to give attention to different factors during group formation, set objectives by group consensus, consider each group as unique, the interaction between worker and members needs to be guided, democratic and flexible participation of members is mandatory, Programs need to plan according to the capacity of group members from simple to complex tasks. Internal and external resources are utilized for the group work process, and evaluation of the group's progress should be done to improve the effectiveness of the group work process.

GLOSSARY

- **Social group work practice:** A primary method of social work that intends to enhance the social functioning of individuals and solve social problems with the help of groups.
- **Tribal hamlet:** A geographical location in which the tribal lives.
- **Tribal community/tribes:** A homogenous indigenous group of people who reside in a broad, familiar territory, speak a common language, and practice.
- **SHG:** Self-help group is a homogenous group of people working together to achieve a common goal.

TOP TEN TAKEAWAYS POINTS

1. The group work aims to help people process unpleasant discriminating experiences and develop positive coping mechanisms to deal with similar situations in the future.
2. The social group work method's principles are an essential guide toward doing group work with people at the local level.
3. The principles of social group work are a set of standards that the group worker must follow throughout the group work process.
4. Application of principles ensures a bottom-up approach and democratic engagement of group members.
5. The group members' interests and objectives must be considered whenever designing the goals and plans to be carried out in group work.
6. To ensure the group's smooth functioning, characteristics such as gender, age, level of education, family details, and the socio-cultural context in which the client lives are taken into account for group processing.
7. The social worker must recognize that everyone's talent and development is unique.
8. The social worker's role is to help the group create a conscious group-self to be responsible for themselves.
9. The social worker and members must be prepared to take necessary actions if they find that the group work process has not achieved the expected outcome.

10. When we gain more experience and new insights, our understanding of principles advances.

Analytical Questions

(a) Differentiate social group work methods from group activity considering the principles you learned in social group work practice.
(b) Social group work principles developed from evidence-based practice. It provides a framework for social workers to work with the group. Interpret in your own words the ten principles of social group work practice.
(c) Examine the scope of social group work practice in other social work settings.

MULTIPLE CHOICE QUESTIONS

1. Which of the following is NOT a principle of social group work?
   (a) Exploring individual problems
   (b) Guided group interactions
   (c) Progressive programme development
   (d) Evaluation of the progress made by the group
2. All the following are TRUE about social group work EXCEPT:
   (a) It is a method of social work
   (b) It helps individuals to enhance their social functioning
   (c) It allows group members to cope more effectively with their personal, group or community problems.
   (d) It helps to change the personality flaws of group members.
3. If a client has an outburst, my first step as social group work is to remain calm. However, if I get emotionally irritated, it could worsen a difficult situation, so I focus on staying clear and professional. Then, I'll reiterate that my goal is to help and commit to working through this together as a team.
   Which social group work practice principle is followed by the social worker in this context?
   (a) The Principle of Specific Group Objectives
   (b) The Principle of Purposeful Worker Group Relationship
   (c) The Principle of Continuous Individualization
   (d) The Principle of Evaluation
4. A school social worker wants to do group intervention to handle bullying among students. They might engage in a needs assessment with different groups to determine the nature and extent of the problem, what is needed to eradicate it, and how the issue is being addressed

in the school. The social worker might also check the progress of his group intervention and make the necessary changes to improve group efficacy. Which social group work practice principle is followed by the social worker in this context?
   (a) The Principle of Specific Group Objectives
   (b) The Principle of Purposeful Worker Group Relationship
   (c) The Principle of Continuous Individualization
   (d) The Principle of Evaluation
5. As in other social work methods, this principle is significant in the Social Group Work method. The idea is to teach the members an ideology of democracy. Which principle emphasis this ideology?
   (a) The Principle of Specific Group Objectives
   (b) The Principle of Purposeful Worker Group Relationship
   (c) The Principle of Continuous Individualization
   (d) The Principle of Democratic Group Self-Determination
6. A Group worker designed a group process for a specific purpose of—
   (a) Encouraging social action,
   (b) Making community organization easier
   (c) Improve behaviour
   (d) Using collective procedures to tackle individual and group problems.
7. The process of social group work entails on
   (a) Instilling hope (b) Recreation plan
   (c) Personal engagement (d) Reassurance
8. Which of the following is NOT a principle of group work?
   (a) Experience with progressive and programme
   (b) Setting specific objectives for group work
   (c) Plan a group experiment
   (d) Keep track of the results.
9. The word 'group worker' appropriately describes the role of the group worker as __________.
   (a) Indirect leader (b) Enabler
   (c) Resource person (d) Programme planner
10. What distinguishes social group work from other types of work?
   (a) Being the primary group is natural
   (b) Client-worker relationship
   (c) Use of programme media in a unique way
   (d) None of the preceding

Answers

1. (a), 2. (d), 3. (c), 4. (d), 5. (d), 6. (d), 7. (a), 8. (c), 9. (d), 10. (c)

REFERENCE

1. Siddiqui H.Y (2011) Group Work: Theories and Practices, Rawat Publications. https://egyankosh.ac.in/bitstream/123456789/17164/1/Unit-3.pdf

RECOMMENDED READINGS

1. Friedlander W.A (ed.) (1958) Concepts and Methods of Social Work, Prentice Hall MC, Englewood Cliffs, N.J.
2. Garvin, Charles D. et al. (eds.) (2008) Handbook of Social Work With Groups, Rawat Publications, New Delhi.
3. Konopka Gisela (1963) Social Group Work: A Helping Process, Prentice Hall Englewood Cliffs, N.J.
4. Hepworth, Dean.H. and Larsen, Jo Ann (1992) Direct Social Work Practice: Theory and Skills, Brooks/Cole Publishing Company, California. 4th ed.
5. Trecker, H.B. (1955). Social Group Work: Principles and Practices. New York: Association Press.
6. Misra, P.D. (1994). Social Work: Philosophy and Methods. New Delhi: Inter-India Publications.
7. Bhattacharya, S. (2012). Social Work: An Integrated Approach. New Delhi: Deep and Deep Publications Pvt. Ltd.

CHAPTER–15

Social Work Practice in Child Welfare Setting

Kumar Satyam

Assistant Professor, Department of Social Work, Dr Bhim Rao Ambedkar College, University of Delhi, Delhi

'Every child comes with the message that God is not yet discouraged of man.'

– Rabindranath Tagore

Abstract: *The chapter highlights social work practice in child welfare settings in India. Child welfare is a broad field where a social worker offers great services to abused and neglected children. Children need special care and protection. But in the changing socio-economic and political environment children are suffering badly everywhere. The chapter describes the various issues and problems related to children within families and in the community. It is also stated in this chapter how these difficult and challenging situations impacted their life. A detailed analysis of existing programmes and schemes especially for children is included in this chapter.*

Considering the sensitivities and special needs, a social worker engages in the child welfare setting's needs and requires a unique ability to deal with the situation with an unbiased perspective and to take a variety of important factors into account. Additionally, they have to choose the best course of action through careful evaluation and planning. The chapter also discussed the different roles of social workers in this field.

Keywords: *Child, Child Labour, Child Abuse, Vulnerability, Social and Emotional Support*

Learning Objectives

After reading this chapter, you would be able to:

- Develop an understanding of the differential needs and vulnerabilities of the children;
- Know the reasons and factors of child abuse in family and society;
- Understand the role of social work professional in child welfare setting.

INTRODUCTION

Human being crosses various stages of life. Childhood is one of them. It is the best part of our life. It is first stage of the human life cycle where a child achieves many milestones. Child needs utmost care and protection for holistic development. But due to factors like poverty, illiteracy, migration, industrialization and urbanization etc., they face faulty and inappropriate socialization and because of these they have to face several challenges in present and later life. And in this way, they become a vulnerable social group. India has been developing in many fields like science, technology, medical and infrastructure. The result of these advancements comes as significant demographic change where we find a huge chunk of young population. The young population could change India's destiny. But still many challenges are there to counter like changing patterns of family system, absence of values and paucity of resources. Social work profession has the potential to deal with these problems and issues. This chapter sketches the outline of these barriers and prescribes professional supports to change the depressing picture.

CHILD: CONCEPTS AND FEATURES

Children are young human beings who are in the process of physical, mental, emotional, and social development. A child is a young human being who is typically under the age of 18 and has not yet reached adulthood. Children are characterized by their physical, cognitive, and social development. Some of the key features of children include:

- **Rapid physical growth:** Children undergo significant physical changes during their early years, including rapid growth and development of their organs, muscles, and bones.
- **Cognitive development:** Children's brains develop rapidly during their early years, and they begin to acquire language, problem-solving skills, and other cognitive abilities.
- **Emotional development:** Children also experience a range of emotional changes as they grow, including the development of self-awareness, emotional regulation, and empathy for others.
- **Social development:** Children learn how to interact with others and develop social skills through play, observation, and interaction with adults and peers.
- **Vulnerability:** Children are vulnerable to a range of physical and emotional risks, including abuse, neglect, and exploitation, and require protection and support from caregivers and society as a whole.
- **Playfulness:** Children have a natural inclination towards play, which helps them to learn, explore, and develop important skills.

Overall, children are dynamic and complex beings who require care, guidance and support as they navigate the process of growth and development.

Here are some key concepts and features related to children:

- **Development:** Children go through various stages of development, including physical, cognitive, emotional, and social development. Each stage is characterized by specific milestones that children typically reach at certain ages.
- **Play:** Play is an essential activity for children as it allows them to explore their environment, learn new skills, and develop social relationships with others.
- **Education:** Education is critical for a child's development, as it provides them with knowledge and skills needed for future success. Education can take place in various settings, including schools, homes, and communities.
- **Parenting:** Parenting is the process of raising and nurturing a child. Effective parenting involves providing a safe and nurturing environment, setting clear boundaries and expectations, and being involved in the child's life.
- **Health and well-being:** Children's health and well-being are critical for their development. This includes physical health, mental health, and emotional well-being. Children need access to healthcare, nutritious food, and a safe and supportive environment to thrive.
- **Rights:** Children have rights that protect them from harm, exploitation, and abuse. These rights include the right to education, healthcare, protection from violence, and participation in decisions that affect their lives.
- **Diversity:** Children come from diverse backgrounds, cultures, and experiences. It's important to recognize and celebrate this diversity and ensure that all children have equal opportunities to succeed.

Child welfare refers to the well-being and safety of children, typically those who are at risk of harm or in need of support. It encompasses a wide range of services and activities designed to promote children's safety, health, and development, while also addressing the needs of families and communities. Child welfare services may include:

- **Child protective services:** Investigating reports of child abuse and neglect, and intervening to protect children from harm.
- **Foster care and adoption:** Providing temporary or permanent homes for children who cannot live with their birth families.

- **Family support services:** Offering support and resources to families to help prevent child abuse and neglect.
- **Early childhood education and care:** Providing high-quality education and care for young children to support their healthy development.
- **Youth services:** Providing support and resources to older children and youth to help them succeed in school and prepare for adulthood.

Overall, child welfare is a critical area of focus for ensuring the safety, well-being, and future success of our youngest and most vulnerable members of society.

VARIOUS APPROACHES OF CHILD WELFARE

Organizations that provide services to promote the well-being and safety of children at risk of abuse, harass, neglect, or other harm is known as child welfare settings. There are different approaches to child welfare settings that focus on different aspects of child protection and support. Some of these approaches are as follows:

- **Prevention-oriented approach:** This approach focuses on identifying and addressing risk factors that may lead to abuse or neglect of children. It may include parenting classes, child development, education, and support services for families in need.
- **Child-centered approach:** This approach prioritizes child needs and interests. Therapeutic interventions, counseling, and advocacy for children in foster care or other out-of-home placements are few examples of this approach.
- **Family-centered approach:** This approach recognizes that families are the primary source of support and care for children. It involves working with families to identify and address issues that may affect their ability to provide a safe and nurturing home for their children.
- **Collaborative approach:** This approach involves working collaboratively with other service providers and community organizations to address children and families' complex needs. It involves partnerships with schools, healthcare providers, and social service agencies.
- **Strengths-based approach:** This approach focuses on building on children and families' strengths and resources to promote positive outcomes. Strengths-based programs may involve skills-building, goal-setting, and support services that empower children and families to overcome challenges and achieve their full potential.

Overall, the different approaches to child welfare settings reflect a range of perspectives and strategies for promoting children's well-being and safety. Effective child welfare programs often integrate multiple approaches to address the complex needs of the children and families they serve.

CHALLENGES IN SOCIAL WORK PRACTICE IN CHILD WELFARE

There are many challenges of Social work practice in child welfare settings. The complexity and sensitivity of the issues involved can discouraged and demotivate to social workers. They should have the understanding of a range of legal, ethical, social and cultural aspects. Some of the major and significant challenges in this area are like:

- **Reconciliation of child safety and family preservation:** Social workers must balance the need to protect children from harm with the objective of preserving and enhancing family relationships to the greatest extent possible. That requires thorough evaluation, cooperation and negotiation.
- **Trauma management:** Many children and families in child welfare settings suffer trauma, abuse, neglect or other forms of difficulties. Social workers must be prepared to address the complex emotional and psychological needs of these individuals and to assist them in healing and recovery.
- **Family involvement:** Social workers are expected to interact with families in a respectful, collaborative and culturally appropriate manner. It takes strong communication skills, a thorough understanding of family dynamics, and a willingness to overcome conflict and resiliency.
- **Working within finite resources:** Child welfare systems often have limited resources and face substantial budgetary constraints. Social workers should be creative and strategic in their approach to service delivery and advocate for additional resources where they can.

Did You Know?

Ministry of Women and Child Development formulated the following acts and legislations:

- The Juvenile Justice (Care and Protection of Children) Model Amendment Rules, 2022
- Adoption Regulations, 2022
- The Protection of Children from Sexual Offences (Amendment) Act, 2019
- The Immoral Traffic Prevention Amendment Bill, 2006
- The Infant Milk Substitutes, Feeding Bottles and Infant Foods Regulation of Production, Supply and Distribution Amendment Act, 2003
- The Commissions for Protection of Child Rights Act, 2005
- The Child Marriage Restraint Act, 1929

Review Questions

(a) What do you understand by social and emotional development of child?
(b) Explain the family-centered approach of Child Welfare.
(c) What are the challenges of practicing social work in Indian child welfare settings?

CHILD ABUSE

All forms of child abuse constitute violence against children. World Health Organisation defines child abuse or maltreatment as 'all forms of physical and/or emotional ill-treatment, sexual abuse, neglect or negligent treatment or commercial or other exploitation, resulting in actual or potential harm to the child's health, survival, development or dignity in the context of a relationship of responsibility, trust or power' (WHO, 1999).

RESPONSIBILITIES OF CHILDCARE PROFESSIONALS

The prevention, protection and treatment of child abuse require an interdisciplinary team of child care professionals. In West, the concept of a child advocacy centre linked to schools, hospitals and mandatory reporting of mistreatment has been effective in investigating numerous cases of abuse. They are also working to standardise the treatment protocol, legal procedures and support system for child victims of violence. These measures are gradually taking shape in India. We need comprehensive approach comprising health counselling, legal aid, and rehabilitation. Community-based prevention models can effect visible change supported by child advocacy centres to address the large number of incidents of child abuse in India. The current facilities are significantly inadequate. In doing so, no legislation and government can really help until adults see children differently. Adult education on children's vulnerability, the promotion of children's rights, improved health and education infrastructure, and poverty reduction programs will make a huge difference.

> Sexual abuse of children remains a hidden problem as there is a culture of silence and therefore the state must encourage families to report abuse even where the perpetrator is a family member – D.Y. Chandrachud, Chief Justice of India
>
> – *Indian Express*, 11 December 2022

Review Questions

(a) Describe child abuse and child rights.
(b) How will a child care professional deal with child-related abuse in India?
(c) Explain the causes of violence against children in your own words?

SKILLS REQUIRED TO WORK WITH CHILDREN

Working in a child welfare setting requires a combination of skills and attributes to effectively support and assist children and families in need. Some essential skills necessary for working in child welfare are Empathy and Compassion, Active Listening, Assessment and Observation, Crisis Intervention, Case Management, Communication and Advocacy, Cultural Competence, Knowledge of Child Development, Legal and Ethical Understanding, Teamwork and Collaboration. It's worth noting that working in a child welfare setting often requires on-going training and professional development to stay updated on best practices, policy changes, and emerging issues affecting children and families.

Throughout the discussion, it became apparent that working with vulnerable children and families requires a multi-dimensional approach based on compassion, empathy and a commitment to social justice. By integrating diverse theories, social workers can develop a comprehensive understanding of the complex dynamics involved in the lives of children and families. Social workers must take an anti-oppressive and anti-discriminatory stand to ensure equitable and just outcomes for all the children and families they serve. Social workers must work closely with other professionals, such as psychologists, educators, healthcare providers, and legal experts, to create a holistic support system that addresses the unique needs of each child and family. This collaborative approach enables a more comprehensive and coordinated response, resulting in improved child welfare in the child welfare system. To conclude, the practice of social work in child welfare institutions requires a comprehensive and multi-dimensional approach. It requires a comprehensive understanding of theories, cultural competency, interdisciplinary collaboration, evidence-based interventions, and self-care. By integrating these elements into their practice, social workers can make a significant and lasting impact on the lives of vulnerable children and families, promoting their safety, well-being, and overall positive development.

SUMMARY

In this chapter, we learnt about the definition of child, issues and problems of child and understood about the different approaches of child welfare. This helps in understand the multi-dimensional aspects of child and child welfare. Children are the future of a nation. Their issues and problems should properly addressed and resolve timely. A nation will not develop in all aspect without having a healthy and active child population. We tried to understand the factors by which the get impacted. We also learnt the role of professionals in child care system. There are lots of challenges in this field but a positive and holistic approach will give significant result. Social Work profession has the ability and expertise to rejuvenate and calibrate the standard of working culture in this area.

GLOSSARY

- **Chronological age** refers to the period that has elapsed beginning with an individual's birth and extending to any given point in time.
- **Child welfare services** are aimed at the physical, social and psychological well-being of children, especially those who suffer from the effects of poverty or who do not receive normal parental care and supervision.
- **Child Protection Officer** designates an officer attached to a children's home to perform the instructions given by the Committee.
- **Child Care Institution** means Children Home, open shelter, observation home, special home, place of safety, Specialised Adoption Agency and a fit facility recognised under this Act for providing care and protection to children, who are in need of such services.
- **Family** is a social group characterized by common residence, economic co-operation and reproduction. I includes adults of both sexes, at least two of whom maintain a socially approved sexual relationship, and one or more children, own or adopted, of the sexually co-habiting adults.
- **Health** is a condition of complete physical, mental and social wellbeing and not simply the absence of disease or infirmity.
- **Institutional care** is provided within a congregate living environment designed to meet the functional, medical, personal, social, and housing needs of individuals who have physical, mental, and/or developmental disabilities.
- **Well-being** is a positive state experienced by individuals and societies. Similar to health, it is a resource for daily life and is determined by social, economic and environmental conditions.

TOP TEN TAKEAWAY POINTS

1. It has been discussed that social work practice in child welfare settings requires a deep understanding of the complex challenges faced by children and families involved in the child welfare system
2. How the collaboration and effectiveness of child welfare social work practices have been determined to ensure the well-being of children.
3. Child protection interventions should be family-centred and emphasize the needs, strengths and objectives of the entire family unit.
4. Social workers should be qualified in crisis response techniques to deal with emergencies and provide immediate support to children and families in need.

5. Child welfare is an area of specialized social work education that requires more training to meet a child's needs.
6. The chapter presents the challenges associated with the practice of social work in child welfare.
7. Children are at risk and can suffer trauma and distress. How social workers address challenges is a significant issue.
8. Important concepts and characteristics for children are briefly mentioned.
9. The strength-based approach allows social workers to determine the strengths and resources inherent in children and families and to take advantage of them.
10. Early response, education and support services can help prevent child maltreatment and neglect.

MULTIPLE CHOICE QUESTIONS

1. Which of the following is NOT a primary goal of social work practice in child welfare setting?
   (a) Ensuring the safety and well-being of children
   (b) Supporting families in maintaining or achieving stability
   (c) Providing therapy to children who have experienced trauma
   (d) Separating children from their families as a first response
2. When working with children in the child welfare system, what is the ethical principle that social workers must uphold?
   (a) Confidentiality (b) Trustworthy
   (c) Challenge social injustice (d) All of the above
3. Which of the following is an example of a strength-based approach in child welfare practice?
   (a) Focusing on a family's deficits and problems
   (b) Working collaboratively with families to build on their strengths
   (c) Removing children from their homes as the first course of action
   (d) None of the above
4. What is the role of a social worker in a child welfare setting?
   (a) To advocate for the child's best interests
   (b) To provide support and resources to the child's family
   (c) To collaborate with other professionals involved in the case
   (d) All of the above
5. Which of the following is an important skill for social workers in child welfare?
   (a) Active listening (b) Conflict resolution
   (c) Cultural competency (d) All of the above
6. According to the 2011 Census, which state has the highest number of children in India?

(a) Maharashtra (b) Madhya Pradesh
(c) Rajasthan (d) Uttar Pradesh

7. Which state has the highest child sex ratio (0-6 years) in India?
(a) Mizoram (b) Bihar
(c) Haryana (d) Jharkhand
8. What is Mental Age?
(a) Actual age of an individual
(b) Social Age
(c) A numerical scale unit derives in an IQ Test
(d) All of the above
9. Which of the following developmental principles is not correct?
(a) This is a continual process. (b) It is quite predictable
(c) There are individual differences when it comes to development.
(d) Development is the result of coincidental events.
10. Which of the following techniques may be used with younger children who are less capable of communicating and expressing their feelings orally?
(a) Psychodynamic therapy (b) Systemic family therapy
(c) Play therapy (d) Cognitive behavioural theory

Answers

1. (d), 2. (d), 3. (b), 4. (d), 5. (d), 6. (d), 7. (d), 8. (c), 9. (d), 10. (d)

REFERENCES

1. Maluccio, A. N., Pine, B. A., & Tracy, E. M. (2002). *Social Work Practice with Families and Children*. Columbia University Press. https://doi.org/10.7312/malu10766
2. Neela Dabir, & Mohua Nigudkar. (2007). Child Abuse: Confronting Reality. *Economic and Political Weekly*, *42*(27/28), 2863–866. http://www.jstor.org/stable/4419782
4. World Health Organisation. (2021). Health Promotion Glossary of Terms 2021. Retrieved from https://www.who.int/publications/i/item/9789240038349
5. World Health Organisation. (1946). Constitution. Retrieved from https://www.who.int/about/governance/constitution
6. Galik, E. (2013). Institutional Care. In: Gellman, M.D., Turner, J.R. (eds) Encyclopedia of Behavioral Medicine. Springer, New York, NY. https://doi.org/10.1007/978-1-4419-1005-9_1424

RECOMMENDED READINGS

1. Mohan Dash, B., Kumar, M., Singh, D.P., & Shukla, S. (Eds.). (2020). *Indian Social Work* (1st ed.). Routledge India. https://doi.org/10.4324/9780429321818
2. Mohan Dash, B. (Eds.). (2022). Introduction to Social Work. Sage India.

CHAPTER – 16

Development-Induced Displacement and Resettlement (DIDR): Social Work Perspectives

Aneesh T.V.

Assistant Professor, Department of Social Work, Aditi Mahavidyalaya, University of Delhi, Delhi

Development should not be at the cost of the people; it should be for the people. When progress uproots, it ceases to be progress.

– Anonymous

Abstract: *In this Anthropocene age, the extraction of natural resources, especially land, has adversely impacted the environment along with changes in the socio-cultural and economic lives of people. Land grabbing and development-induced displacement are some of the social as well as political problems of the Anthropocene. This chapter will attempt to analyse the impact of development-induced displacement on the socioeconomic and cultural lives of displaced persons in Kerala, India, with special reference to Cochin International Airport Limited (CIAL). The chapter emphasises that social work needs to address the violence and exploitative nature of the dominant Eurocentric development model. Within this paradigm, the chapter would try to argue that decolonial models of development and the Indigenous development paradigm need to be inserted into social work education and practice to address development issues in the context of the Anthropocene. Finally, the chapter will analyse the role and scope of social work to resist displacement and facilitate an effective, people-centred, inclusive resettlement and rehabilitation process.*

Keywords: *Anthropocene, Internal Displacement, Development Induced Displacement, Impoverishment Risks, Resettlement And Rehabilitation (R&R)*

Learning Objectives

After reading this chapter, you would be able to:

- Develop an understanding of internal displacement and types of internal displacement.
- Comprehend the nature and significance of development-induced displacement in the Anthropocene era.

- Understand the causes and ramifications of displacement on the lives of Displaced Persons (DPs) Learn various approaches and models of DIDR.
- Understand how social work education and profession will address the issue of DIDR.

INTRODUCTION

The term 'development' encompasses a wide range of concepts and meanings. There are ongoing debates and discussions about how to broaden the conceptualizations of terminology in terms of its definition, nature, and the development processes that should be used. -Throughout history, 'development' as a concept has had distinct meanings and methods that were intended to promote colonial growth and modernization among the native inhabitants. During colonial times, the concept of development was entirely based on colonial modernity, which the Europeans employed as a primary tool to manage resources in colonies of Asia, Africa, and Latin America. Colonial rulers believed it was the 'white man's burden' to bring about 'progress' among the colonial natives. After the Second World War, the term 'development' was used to divide the world into developed and underdeveloped countries. During the years after colonialism ended and colonies became independent, the world was bifurcated into binaries of core and periphery, with the core being the developed Global North and the periphery being the Global South. This bifurcation resulted in the emergence of the Global North as the exporter of development models and policies majorly funded through development projects, while the Global South became a market to execute and sell products manufactured in the core. The term 'development' functions as a synonym for social change through the implementation of new knowledge and technology, especially in underdeveloped areas. Consequently, many people tend to associate development with modernity in the sense that it brings a new or structured stage of change. However, modernity as a concept is susceptible to change over a period of time; as a result, what is considered modern in a particular space and time may not be necessarily understood as modern in another space and time.

From an economic perspective, modernity as a concept is portrayed mainly through social processes such as industrialization and urbanization, as well as the wide use of technologies (Willis, 2005). As a harbinger of change and progress, the modern state acts as an agent of development that works to promote the welfare of its citizens through economic development. Ashish Nandy writes 'Development comes to all, sometimes as part of a package that includes idea of the nation-state at the price of all social change, a full-blown theory of progress through historical stages, and large-scale massification through urbanization and industrialization,' (Nandy, 2003, 173). Anthropocentrism places humans at the centre of the planet and gives them the power to determine the fate of other species. This ideology encourages humans to exploit nature and other living things for material gain. Anthropocentrism results in the intensification of human activities in the Anthropocene, a proposed geological epoch that acknowledges the profound influence of human activities on Earth's systems, including climate, geology, and ecosystems. In 2000, Paul Crutzen, a Dutch Nobel Prize-winning chemist, coined the term 'Anthropocene' to describe the epoch in which humans have become a major force in shaping the Earth's systems. The Anthropocene epoch is marked by unprecedented levels of human impact on the planet, such as climate change, habitat destruction, higher levels of pollution, and species extinctions. This reflects on the centrality of mankind upon ecology as well as how human society's interventions are central to geological and ecological changes (Crutzen & Stoermer, 2000). The Anthropocene not only causes environmental problems but also has other effects, such as unequal wealth and income, the exclusion of marginalised communities, the destruction of the domestic and traditional market, and the destruction of indigenous and traditional lifestyles and their sectors of the economy. Evidently, development induces displacement, which is also an inevitable consequence of this aggravated human relationship with nature, the market, and human beings' predatory nature to exploit fellow beings for progress. Social work is the study of how people interact with each other in the family, within the community, and with the environment. This chapter, therefore, looks at the role of social work within the context of displacement and development in the Anthropocene.

INTERNAL DISPLACEMENT

Around the world, millions of people have been compelled to leave their homes and countries due to a variety of factors, including war, conflict, natural and man-made disasters, as well as financial and political instability. Since many communities are uprooted within their own nation, this type of forced eviction does not always result in border crossing. Internally Displaced People (IDPs) are different from refugees, who have crossed an international border and are seeking protection in another country. The United Nations Guiding Principles on Internal Displacement refer to internally displaced persons as 'persons or groups of persons who have been forced or obliged to flee or to leave their homes or places of habitual residence, in particular as a result of or in order to avoid the effects of armed conflict, situations of generalised violence, violations of human rights, or natural or human-made disasters, and who have not crossed an internationally recognised state border. 'Internal displacement was formerly not thought to be a serious issue, which is why it received less attention than international migration of refugees. Besides, internally displaced people were sometimes mistakenly referred to as 'internal refugees.' According to the Global Report on Internal Displacement prepared by the Internal Displacement Monitoring Committee, a total of 59.1 million people were displaced in 2021; out of these displaced persons (IDPs), 14.4 million were displaced by conflict and violence and 23.7 million by disasters. Disasters led to approximately 4.9 million displacements in 2021, and political and other forms of violence caused 13,000 displacements. Floods and cyclones, which are influenced by the southwest and northeast monsoon seasons, are the main triggers of displacement due to natural disasters (Internal Displacement Monitoring Center, 2022).

Types of Internal Displacement

- Conservation-Induced Displacement refers to the removal of people from their houses or land and property by using force for the cause of conservation. It occurs when national parks, wildlife reserves, and protected areas are established on territories populated by indigenous or native communities.
- Climate- or Disaster-Induced Displacement happens due to natural calamities and disasters such as earthquakes, floods, and tsunamis, to name a few.
- Development-Induced Displacement is understood as eviction caused by industrial expansion and infrastructure growth. Therefore, the mining industry, construction of dams and infrastructure, and macro-development projects such as airports, roads, railways, port developments, special economic zones, and industrial corridors lead to the acquisition of land and the subsequent displacement of the population inhabiting those acquired lands.
- Conflict-induced Displacement occurs when people flee to escape from armed conflict, widespread violence, or other forms of insecure vulnerable situations such as communal riots and ethnic genocide. Conflict-induced displacement can be seen in the case of a vast exodus of Muslims from Myanmar and Kashmiri pandits from Kashmir.

Review Questions

(a) What is internal displacement?
(b) What are the types of internal displacement?

DEVELOPMENT INDUCED DISPLACEMENT

The term 'displacement' has many implications that differ depending on the context. The definition of 'displacement' used in this study, however, is oriented towards a primary understanding of the term as found in the Oxford Learner's Dictionary, which states that it is the 'act of driving anyone or something away from their home or position' (Oxford Learner's Dictionary, n.d.). Although we associate development with progress and growth but the forced removal of individuals from their property or natural habitats for infrastructure projects is consensually understood as inevitable collateral damage. In a normative sense, development as a process represents the enhancement of human welfare while on the other hand, forced displacement and the ensuing poverty actually negate the benefits of development and force us to rethink the idea of progress.

People who have been uprooted from their natural habitats often struggle to establish balance in new environments, which has a detrimental effect on their interests. According to Michael M. Cernea, scholarly discussions about displacement have centred around broad conceptualizations while a more specific definition is still lacking. Cernea broadly defines forced population displacement as caused by development or environment projects as those situations occurring when people lose, through expropriation, either their house or their land, or both simultaneously (Cernea, 2011, 94). He also observes that such a broad conceptualization of displacement triggered many further debates, especially in R&R policy practices. A major problem with this widely accepted definition is that it excludes people and communities who have suffered due to the loss of production activity as a result of loss of agricultural land or access to it without losing their house or land entirely through physical displacement. Such a situation arises when people get displaced from parks in environmental and conservation projects, as this loss has a direct impact on their identities and livelihood.

In general, macro-development projects and optimal infrastructure development are regarded as means for a country's economic development. Since independence, our first Prime Minister Jawaharlal Nehru's model of development has adopted a trickle-down approach to development. The construction of big dams was an essential part of macro-developmental projects that were considered iconic means of growth. These development projects were built in marginalised areas dominated by tribes, pastoralists, or subsistence agriculturalists (Mathur & Marsen, 2000). The magnitude of displacement in India cannot be determined by analysing the total number of Displaced Persons (DPs) or Project Affected Persons (PAPs). Fernandes indicates that the institutionalised attitude of neglect makes it hard to define and analyse various aspects of displacement due to the lack of reliable statistics of DPs in most projects (as cited in Padel & Das, 2011, 153).

The magnitude of displaced people in India is an ongoing debate. Various literature has quoted different numbers when it comes to the aggregate of DPs in our country. India does not have an official database on the number of DPs or PAPs and their types who have ousted for development projects after independence (Fernandes, 2011). Roy (1999) in her essay states that 56 million people were displaced by dam projects alone. But this argument has been questioned by Surjit Bhalla and based on a survey conducted by the Indian Institute of Public Administration (IIPA), he claims that 5 million people in India have been displaced by dam construction (cited in Fernandes, 2011, 302). Fernandes (2011) states that Roy's overestimated number and Bhalla's estimation of the average of 1360 per dam are too low even in the case of medium dams.

Table 1: Mining and Displacement

State	*Years*	*Numbers Displaced persons (DPs)*
Andhra Pradesh	1980–1995	1,00,541
Assam	1980–2000	41,200
Goa	1980s	4,740
Jharkhand	1980–1995	4,02,882
Odhisa	1960–1995	3,00,000
West Bengal	1960–2000	418,061

Source: Chakravorty, 2014

According to a rough estimate, the aggregate number of displaced people in India is between two to twenty million. The total number of displaced population by planned development from 1951–1990 could be from a conservative estimate of 110 Lakhs to an overall figure of 185 lakh (Pandey, 2008, 3). After independence, upward of 50 million acres of agricultural and non-agricultural land may have been converted and nearly 60 million people may have been affected (Chakravorty, 2014). One estimate about the number of DPs and Project Affected Persons (PAPs) is 60 million between 1947–2000 in India as a whole, and around 40 per cent of them are tribes (Fernandes, 2013).

Table 2: Selected Dams and Related Displacement

Name of Dam/Project	*State*	*Population Displaced*
Almatti	Karnataka	200,000
Narmada Sagar	Madhya Pradesh	200,000
Sardar Sarovar	Gujarat	200,000

Name of Dam/Project	*State*	*Population Displaced*
Narayanpur	Karnataka	160,000
Polavaram	Madhya Pradesh and Andhra Pradesh	150,000
Pong	Himachal	150,000
Sriramsagar	Andhra Pradesh	150,000
Bansagar	Madhya Pradesh	127,000
Kangsabati Kumari	West Bengal	125,000
Bargi	Madhya Pradesh	113,600
Hirakud	Odisha	110,000
Tehri	Uttar Pradesh	105,000
Gandhisagar	Madhya Pradesh	100,000
Somasila	Andhra Pradesh	100,000
Srisailam	Andhra Pradesh	100,000
Ukali	Gujarat	88,000
Rengali	Odisha	80,000
Upper Mullamari	Karnataka	80,000
Lower Manair	Andhra Pradesh	78,000
Nizamsagar	Andhra Pradesh	67,445
KoelKaro	Bihar	66,000
Majalgaon	Maharashtra	65,296
Gosikhurd	Maharashtra	65,198
Hippargi	Karnataka	62,480
Balimela	Odisha	60,000
Rihand	Uttar Pradesh	60,000
Bhima	Maharashtra	57,000
Tungabhadra	Karnataka	54,452

Source: Chakravorty, 2014

Impact of Development-Induced Displacement

The acquisition of land results in the expulsion of individuals from their property . The uprooting of a community, dependent on land, from its living space makes them vulnerable to homelessness and cultural isolation. Based on variables such as gender, class, caste, region, and the nature of the development project, the severity of the consequences of displacement tends to vary. Cernea in his Impoverishment Risk Reconstruction Model (IRRM), indicates the following eight risks after displacement: 'landlessness, homelessness, joblessness, marginalization, increased morbidity and mortality, food insecurity, loss of access to common property and services, and social disarticulation' (Cernea, 1999, 17, 18). This model is based on the managerial approach that considers development as inevitable for the progress of a nation and displacement as the natural outcome of development.

Those who depend on land, forest, and natural resources for subsistence are displaced from their homes (Mohanty, 2005). Farmers, agricultural labourers, and the entire agrarian society are marginalised when agricultural land is seized and transformed into business or industrial assets in the name of the public interest. The land not only serves as capital for producing crops and woods; it is also the centre of economic, social, and cultural life for humans. The land is not only an economic asset; it is also connected to the memories and deeds of generations of inhabitants who have lived and are buried there, and it is an integral part of the identities of generations who continue to live there (Faure, 2009). The loss of grazing land also directly impacts on the livestock breeding and livestock capital of DPs. The loss of livestock alters the consumption patterns and eating habits of the displaced persons. The loss of livestock and agricultural land has a negative impact on the income level of DPs, leading to their economic marginalisation. Loss of natural food habits and reliance on market products could result in food crises and famine among the displaced persons. The transformation of an agrarian society into a community reliant on markets and industries will marginalise it socially, economically, and culturally. The uprooting and fragmentation of socio-economic and cultural spheres of life that have been developed over many generations is a result of displacement. The long-delayed displacement project has changed the lives of the DPs and caused socio-cultural alienation and psychological traumas, as seen and according to lessons learned from earlier developmental projects (Pandey, 1998).

Long-standing relationships break apart as a result of the displacement of the kinship system. Tribal egalitarianism is replaced by hierarchical structures based on power and authority as a result of displacement, which also changes the lives of the displaced tribes from a natural to a material existence (Padel & Das, 2008). Larger social units, like extended families, frequently fall apart as a result of moving. After being displaced, resettlers become less and less concerned with their interactions with their former neighbours and members of the existing communities new surroundings (Terminski, 2015). Displacement and forced development have different effects on DPs. Removing people from their natural geographical spaces and cultural spaces causes socioeconomic poverty and cultural annihilation. The socio-economic and cultural context of DPs determines the degree of the impact. In other words, the effects of displacement vary across different age groups and communities. Children who are economically marginalised drop out of school and start working full-time to support their families. Among the project-affected persons and DPs, the impact of displacement is more severe for the poorest of the poor than for the privileged groups. The Asian Development Bank's (ADB) experience with displacement demonstrates that these groups are frequently more susceptible to poverty than other privileged groups when it comes to rebuilding their lives after relocation (Cernea, 1999).

Review Questions

(a) What do you understand by development- induced displacement (DID)?

(b) Discuss the major impact of DID?

Did You Know?

- In 2000, Paul Crutzen, a Dutch Nobel Prize-winning chemist, coined the term 'Anthropocene' to describe the epoch in which humans have become a major force in shaping the Earth's systems.
- According to the Global Report on Internal Displacement prepared by the Internal Displacement Monitoring Committee, a total of 59.1 million people were displaced in 2021; out of these internally displaced persons (IDPs), 14 4 million were displaced by conflict and violence, while 23.7 million were displaced by disasters.
- In India as a whole, the estimated number of DPs and Project Affected Persons (PAPs) is 60 million between the years 1947-2000, and around 40 percent of them are tribes.
- Dutch jurist Hugo Grotius invented the term 'eminent domain' in 1625. Land acquisition law in India is based on the 'eminent domain' concept, which empowers the state to acquire private property without approaching market transactions.
- The Right to Fair Compensation and Transparency in Land Acquisition, Rehabilitation, and Resettlement Act, 2013 (LARR Act) replaced the colonial Land Acquisition Act of 1894. Currently, the LARR Act regulates land acquisition and provides compensation, rehabilitation, and resettlement to the PAPs in India.
- Civil Society Organisations (CSOs) have a significant role in ensuring proper, effective, and timely R&R among the PAPs, especially among the DPs.

Case study of Cochin International Airport Limited (CIAL)

The CIAL was the first airport established along the lines of the Public-Private Participation (PPP) model for airport construction in India, inspiring many other development projects based on the PPP model in Kerala. mostly non-resident Indians, people of Kerala, and airport service providers collaborated together to construct an airport that meets international standards (Varkkey & Raghuram 2002). Land acquisition was carried out under the Land Acquisition Act (LAA) of 1894. An interview with a CIAL officer reveals that the project had acquired 1254 acres of land, and 872 families were displaced, primarily belonging to

Scheduled Castes (SCs) communities. The people who accepted the R&R package were allowed to resettle with 80 per cent of compensation (Murickan et al. 2003). The project covered 2,600 landowners, which included more than 800 households (Hooper & Walder, 2001). Even though displacement has affected all the Persons DPs irrespective of class, caste and gender, the impact it had on the lives of DPs is not of the same degree.

Impact of Displacement

- **Homelessness:** Majority (89.05%) of the displaced people had started their life in resettlement colonies before the completion of construction of houses in resettlement colonies. The CIAL has implemented the relocation of DPs immediately and did not provide enough time for the process of resettlement in the newly allotted areas.
- **Loss of land and livelihood:** Eviction and displacement from home and land have resulted in the loss of entire lands or a reduction in land size and the loss of livelihoods, which may lead to other forms of marginalisation among the displaced. Dispossession from land resulted in temporary joblessness and drastic change in job patterns.
- **Impact on cultural and social life:** In a survey among out 201 households, 135 respondents shared that they have lost old neighbourhood in resettlement colony. Loss of worshipping place and community place are the other major reasons for changes in socio-cultural life of displaced population in the study area. Creation of nuclear family is the main change taken place after displacement. After displacement, Lack of participation in festivals and family celebrations, individualism and lack of respect to elders is visible in family relationships. Common cremation ground, loss of worshipping place and community place are the other factors that contributed changes in the socio- cultural life of some of the DPs.
- **Loss of Common Community Places (CCP):** has not led to the loss of among the majority of DPs. SCs are the majority in the DPs who have suffered loss of CCP in comparison with general community.

Source: Aneesh, 2017

RESETTLEMENT AND REHABILITATION (R&R) EXPERIENCES IN IDIA

Most of the studies conducted on Development-Induced Displacement Resettlement (DIDR) experiences in India are evaluative in nature and try to evaluate the R&R process for a better and more effective R&R mechanism. Past DIDR experiences in India reveal that there is a gap between the R&R

programmes on paper and actual implementation in the field. In Orissa, the first wave of industrial projects such as the Rourkela Steel Plant, Hirkaud Upper Kolab, and Indravati Dam Project did not make any positive changes in the lives of resettlers (Padel & Das, 2011). In Gujarat, drinking water projects improved the life of resettlers in areas of drinking water facilities, toilets, and electricity connections. But the allocation of poor-quality land, lack of soil moisture, and inadequate irrigation facilities have failed crop cultivation. (Lobo, 2008). Tribal displacement for Polavaram dam and resettlement for various projects in Gujarat has faced the problem of loss of substance due to the non-accessibility of forest common property in forest land. In the Polavaram project, land for the land policy was adopted and land attend far away from the forest. the Polavaram Resettlement and Rehabilitation Package (PRRP) which was unable to offer employment opportunities outside of agriculture. So many settlers is not able to receive compensation due to the non-availability of land documents (Mariotti, 2015; Lobo, 2008).

In the case of the Tehari dam, displacement, and resettlement have taken place in the Resettlement town of New Tehri City a. resettlers has faced transportation issue in inside travel and with the outside world due to non-accessibility. The division of residential areas and administrative and educational places also created the problem of accessibility and travel issues, In addition, the dam cut off the eastern side of tehri from the distant capital which also deepened the isolation in the post-resettlement life of resettlers (Newton, 2008). Displacement has resulted in social disarticulation among the resettlers in the case of Kerala's Cochin International Airport Limited. Resettlement colonies were allocated within the premises of five kilometres of previous residing areas which helped to minimize cultural changes, and the non-accessibility of educational and other administrative facilities among the resettlers. But displacement has altered health-related practices and harmed value-related practices that were a part of their daily lives. Resettlement colonies are multicultural and multi-religious spaces, it has resulted in cross-cultural interaction and reduced the influence of religion and society on personal and educational advancement. Changes also happened in family ties and kinships; even disputes among family members regarding compensation money received under R&R and the division of families were evident after displacement (Vithayathil & Sunny, 2009).

Karba (2003) examine the R&R experiences of the Sahariya tribal in the Kuno Wildlife Sanctuary in northern Madhya Pradesh. R&R (relief and rehabilitation) efforts and practices carried out by the forest department are known as best R&R practices. The efforts of properly equipped and trained personnel, their autonomy and backup support to implement R&R for the officers helped in the successful execution of the task of rehabilitation. Relocation near to Mathura police station has resettlers to escape from isolation and the threat posed by dacoits in the sanctuary. The resettlement process was slow but it made a positive impact on health care system, road connectivity, and electrification in the rural area. The new resettlement village is near educational institutions which helped them to access education. The adverse impact of this project was the quality of allocated land under R&R is low quality compared with land available inside the sanctuary (Shahabuddin et al., 2005).

The Gujjar community in Rajasthan has been displaced from Sariska Wildlife Sanctuary. After resettlement, they were compelled to switch from grazing livestock to cultivation for livelihood. But the amount of land available is less than required for cultivation and R&R did not include the facilities for drinking water, or community properties such as schools, community halls etc. Similar issues of the non-availability of land for grazing cattle and agriculture are also visible in the R&R of Tadoba-Andhari Tiger Reserve in Maharashtra. The bureaucracy did not recognise first as resources used by the DPs so they did not consider as a loss for resettlers due to the displacement. the relocation package did not include provisions for a means of subsistence and the officers rejected this demand for employment for one member of each displaced family (Ghate, 2005). When analysing resettlement experiences, we can find that R&R affects people on both positive and adverse levels. Evaluation and analysis of past resettlement experiences may help policymakers, professionals, and social workers in developing and implementing better R&R.

LEGAL DIMENSIONS OF DEVELOPMENT-INDUCED DISPLACEMENT AND RESETTLEMENT (DIDR)

At the international level, UN Guiding Principles on Internal Displacement are the major legal provision on displacement and is an ambitious document that seeks to protect all internally displaced persons. In India, the LARR Act of 2013 addresses development-induced displacement and R&R. UN Guiding Principles on Internal Displacement states that any human being shall have the right to be protected from any form of arbitral displacement and it emphasises that states should seek alternatives to avoid displacement, it also states that state competent authorities have the primary duty to provide rehabilitation for the displaced persons. The term 'eminent domain' was invented by Dutch jurist Hugo Grotius In 1625. Land acquisition law in India is based on the 'eminent domain' concept, which empowers the state to acquire private property without approaching market transactions. Eminent domain proves state power over private property within the boundary (Lenhoff, 1942). In 1824, the British government enacted the first land acquisition law to acquire lad in Bengal provinces for public purposes. Later similar laws have enacted in the Bombay and Madras presidency. Later these acts in various presidencies have repealed and replaced by the Act VI of 1857, which aimed to unify various laws for a common land acquisition scheme. After independence, India required land for rapid industrialisation and infrastructure development which forced India to follow. Land acquisition act of 1894 (Chowdhury& Chowdhury, 2016). In Independent India, upward of 50 million acres of agricultural and non-agricultural land may have been converted and nearly 60 million people might have been affected (Chakravorty, 2014). Many issues and concerns have been raised in forceful land acquisition and failure to provide an effective R&R. It leads to conflicts in many parts of India and in some states, it resulted in state-tribal conflict and insurgency. These situations have forced the government to enact the new act LARR of 2013. Different from the old act, the new act incorporated the following provisions such as mandatory R&R provisions in land acquisition, provisions for mandatory Social Impact Assessment (SIA) and food security. It also states that the appropriate government shall ensure that the Social Impact Assessment Report is evaluated by an independent multidisciplinary Expert Group. For assuring food security, the act limits the acquisition of non-irrigated multi crops land. Whenever multi-crop irrigated land is acquired, an equivalent area of culturable wasteland shall be developed for agricultural purposes. Another important feature was the role of Gram Sabhas and local administrative bodies to decide on land acquisition. Ironically, in 2014, amendments 2014 scrapped and diluted major provisions including the exemption of five categories of projects from mandatory SIA and food security requirements, allowing private entities to acquire land under this act that expanded the scope of public purpose to acquire more land (Kohli, 2015).

IMPLICATION OF SOCIAL WORK EDUCATION AND SOCIAL WORK PROFESSION

'Anthropocentrism' refers to human beings' superiority over other living species because of exceptional value attributed to human lives while considering non-human species as mere resources. Kidner (2014) observes that anthropocentrism is not criticised for its focus as a human-centric concept, but it is condemned for its functions in the modern industrial capital world by the commodification of nature and human beings for wealth creation with the help of modern technology. He observed that homes are redefined as 'property,' human beings as 'human resources', and members of indigenous communities as 'raw materials.' The commodification of common resources such as water bodies, forests, land, etc., as well as accumulation of resources for creating assets for few privileged sections of the society creates irrevocable changes in ecology such as land expropriation, dispossession, and displacement. To understand the relevance of Social Work as a discipline in theorising Anthropocene and Anthropocentrism, it is important to reconsider the origin of Social Work as a consequence of industrialization and urbanization in Europe as a part of industrial revolution. Post-industrialization in Europe, social workers engaged in problems of industrial workers in urban areas who were either displaced from village farms or voluntarily migrated to seek employment. According to Gore (1997), modern social work was an attempt to help these DPs along with other issues of industrialization like poverty, unemployment, etc. In the context of industrialization, modern social work addressed the problems raised by the development and helped the victims to cope with issues. In contemporary times Social Work as discipline is actively engaging with the political side of social problems as well. For instance, globalization and market-led economic and political atmosphere, nature of social work intervention has changed according to growing inequality, privatization of social welfare schemes, migration, new forms of oppression, to name a few. Similarly new social movements such as feminist social work, anti-racial social work, and anti-oppressive social work have redefined social work as well as its theoretical orientations (Powell, 2001).

In the present scenario of climate change and environmental concerns, it is imperative that social work as a discipline should engage with critical ongoing debates about Anthropocene, especially in the areas of development and displacement. There have been some serious criticisms against social work in the past due to its failure to participate in popular social movements in the West. While traditional social work has limitations in addressing the political concerns of social problems, especially in cases of development and displacement, radical social work emerged as an alternative to mainstream social work theories. For its fight against social inequality and oppression, radical social work presented itself as an alternate idea to address the political cause. Radical social work has a significant role in pre-displacement resistance against eviction. Movementist Approach, sees displacement as the central issue rather than development. It does not accept displacement as an expected outcome of development but rather sees it as evidence of an irregular and unequal distribution of cost and benefit in development. The viewpoint of this displacement-based approach considers it an ugly face of development, and this viewpoint is most effectively articulated through people's movements and resistance to displacement (Dwivedi, 2002). For instance in the popular movement Narmada Bacchao Andolan is a fine example to understand the role of social intervention against displacement cause due to construction of dams. The success of the movement in the nature of its campaign that was never confined to only the locality where dams were being built or within the affected community, but the campaign tried to invoke mass consciousness about existing development paradigms and emphasized on the significance of alternative paradigms. In a similar vein, Civil Society Organisations (CSO) also have important role to play in initiating resistance and post-displacement R&R. Resistance plays a vital role in ensuring the effective implementation of R&R. Similarly, when social work is contextualized within Indian social and political movements, it is important to develop a framework that caters to the needs of Indian society. Within this contextual paradigm, Indigenous Social Work can be seen as an alternate concept for approaching contemporary social causes in India.

Indigenization of Social Work

The origin of social work traces back to the colonial history of India; the first school of social work was established by Dr Clifford Manshardt with the help of the House of Tata, a business-complex-industrial group in India. The foundation of the first school was connected with industrialists (Kulkarni, 1993). After Independence, professional social workers got connected and engaged with government rural welfare programmes in a broader manner; family planning and special rural development programmes, etc. were brought about under development planning (Gore, 1997; Kulkarni, 1993). The growth and specialisation of social work education depend on the nature of government welfare programmes and private industrial and capital growth. Just after independence, in the 1950s, community workers trained with social workers worked to strengthen the Community Development Programme as a co-producer in the project of the welfare state; the 1960s saw a surge in interest in working in rural areas. The 1970s and 1980s witnessed the active involvement of voluntary and nongovernment agencies in social development and transformation in nation-building. (Jaswal & Pandya, 2015; Bodhi, 2016). Nandy (2003) observes that development and violence are strong in the Southern world. In the beginning, development was not an oppressive idea. But now development exhibits the traits of primitive religious conflicts, colonial wars, and racism. He also observes that sometimes the success of development leads to the emergence of authoritarian politics in the Third World. Both the leaders, Hitler and Stalin, who considered authoritarian rule a means of development, instigated violence. In the First World War, fascist regimes preferred development over individual freedom. Displacement from the Nehruvian regime and constantly forced displacements in India, especially for establishing mining industries and larger dams, highlight the role of an authoritarian democratic state in violence and cultural genocide in the name of development (Nandy, 2003). Replicating the anthropocentric worldview in development has created environmental degradation, displacement, and the accumulation of wealth in the hands of a few. Most of these development projects in the global south have been funded by foreign funders from the North based on Euro-centric development models.

Indianisation of Social Work: Sarvodaya and Non-Violence (Ahimsa)

The current Indian social work profession, especially in social work academia, emphasises the decolonization process, but the funding and replication of development models from the global north are one of the crises or dilemmas of social work in the global south. Indian social work education does not give much importance to radical social work, which analyses the system politically. It may be because of the nature of the profession, which is largely connected with the market and private capital like CSR, foreign funds, and human resource training for corporations. The current political and economic system demands the involvement of private entities not only in industries and businesses but also in public health and education. Social work grew with the various development projects of the government, and many social work institutions and educators are part of many development projects as consultants and in the monitoring and evaluation processes of various health and development projects. This 'bureaucratic social work' or 'state-promoted social work' helps the government achieve political and economic goals through welfare measures. The decolonization of social work through the Indianization of social work education and profession is one of the alternate development paradigms against violent, anthropocentric, and Eurocentric development models in India.

Sarvodaya is a contribution of M.K. Gandhi that was greatly influenced by the ideology of 'Unto the Last.' 'Sarvodaya' is a complete form of socialism based on the principles of truth, Ahimsa (non-violence), love, cooperation, and good faith, supporting the construction of an ideal social system. It envisioned a society without any inequality or exploitation. The Bhoodan movement was started by Vinoba Bhave and greatly influenced by the concept of Sarvodaya. Vinoba's basic premise was that all citizens should accept that all land belongs to 'Gopal' (God). The Bhoodan movement symbolises this urge and ideal of a non-violent, decentralised democracy for India and other nations of the world. Instead of bringing about a social and economic revolution through the coercion of the state. (Bhattacharyya, 1958; Rawat, 2004; Leela, 1958) Redistribution of land resources and controlling coercive state action to acquire land for the few industrial elites need to be opposed on the basis of the Gandhian concept of Sarvodaya, which emphasises the development of all and reflects the same expression of 'right to development' without discrimination.

Review Questions

(a) What do you understand by the term 'Anthropocene'?
(b) What is the difference between 'Anthropocene' and 'Anthropocentrism'?
(c) How does 'Anthropocentrism' lead to environmental and developmental problems in this world?
(d) What is the meaning and purpose of the term indigenisation of social work?

According to the Gandhian philosophy of Sarvodaya, man is a member of the world's society, and through his wisdom, he can find a basis on which all of them can live in a family (Leela). Indian philosophy is different from the concept of the anthropocentric position of human beings, which fixes man as central in the universe and makes him powerful and a decider of the future of other species and the living planet. In planetary life, Indian philosophy emphasises the co-existence of human beings with nature and their fellow beings. The Anthropocene started due to a worldview based on Western predatory and exploitative ideologies. The post-independence development experiences focused on dams, mines, and large industries based on trickle-down theory, proving that replication of economic development models, whether based on capitalism or communism, is based on the world view of 'exploitation of nature for the material benefit of few. Social work promotes human rights and democratic values. Indian social work needs to redefine dominant development models and indicate the concepts and practices of development. Managerial approaches to R&R cannot find an ultimate solution to assure equal distribution of resources and democratic development. Alternative indigenous development models can only address and effectively solve the issue of maldevelopment created by the dominant Eurocentric development models.

SUMMARY

In this chapter, we learnt about the concept of internal displacement and types of internal displacement. Development-induced displacement comes under the broader definition of internal displacement. An approach based on Anthropocentrism increased the activities of human beings in nature and significant changes happened in nature. It also created various social issues such as displacement. We studied the meaning and definition of development induced and its impact on DPs. In this chapter, we discussed legal issues related to DIDR. We also learnt about social work implications in the field of DIDIR an alternate world view and indigenisation social work to address the issue of displacement in India.

GLOSSARY

- **Internal displacement:** People are forced out of their homes and lands for the development projects such as dance mines airport road constructions special economic sounds industrial codes by state and norms state actives. Development and displacement may happen with or without resettlement and habitation programs.
- **Development-induced displacement:** people are forcing offer their homes than reliance due to conflict disasters climate change war and development projects. It is different from refugees in that in India displacement people are not crossing the boundary.
- **Resettlement and rehabilitation:** Resettlement and rehabilitation packages assure the relocation of DPs will be relocated in the resettlement area. Resettlement includes livelihood, employment training, sharing of benefits and shares of the project. Rehabilitation emphasises on the reconstruction of socio-economic and cultural infrastructures for the easy resilience of displaced communities.
- **Anthropocene:** Dutch Nobel-prize-winning chemist Paul Crutzen coined the term 'Anthropocene' which denotes the proposed geological epoch and is considered an extension of the Holocene, the present geological epoch that began around 11,700 years ago. Holocene is characterised by relative stability in climate and ecosystem. But Anthropocene is characterised by human's ability to make significant changes in physical and natural environment.
- **Anthropocentric:** The term refers to describe a worldview or approach that places human beings as the centre of importance. It gives him the power to exploit other species and the environment for his material benefit.
- **Indigenisation of social work:** It refers to the process of adapting social work according to the socio-economic, political and cultural history of the native place on the basis of indigenous knowledge to address native problems and needs.
- **Decolonization of social work:** It refers to an approach to creating awareness of the effects of colonization in social work education and practice. It reduces the overdependence on the dominant global north

for theories and methods of delivering social services. Decolonisation may help social workers to work effectively with the local community and can apply indigenous approaches and methods based on native experience.

TOP TEN TAKEAWAY POINTS

1. Development-induced displacement is considered one of the negative adverse or limitations of the dominant development model based on Eurocentric and technocracy
2. Development-induced displacement has occurred in various regimes in India for various development projects which began from colonial rule till the present time.
3. Land acquisition and R&R in India is taking place under the
4. Rapid industrialisation and urbanisation have increased the magnitude of land acquisition and related displacement of people, especially in the global south
5. Displacement has inflicted socio-political and cultural changes in the lives of DPs.
6. Loss of commons, social as common community properties and common community services inflicted a change in the socio-cultural life and irreparable loss of social life of the people, especially the tribal population that depends on forest land and allied resources.
7. The Movementist approach does not consider development as a natural outcome of development. But conder as an unequal distribution of cost and benefit of development.
8. Social workers and civil society organisations have a significant role in the R&R process.
9. Effective and proper implementation of R&R among the PAPs may help to reduce the problems of displacement
10. Alternative development paradigms based on indigenous knowledge will help to avoid the adverse impacts of development such as environmental problems and displacement.

MULTIPLE CHOICE QUESTIONS

1. Name the sociologist who proposed the Impoverishment Risk Reconstruction model (IRRM)
   (a) Geroge Milton (b) Ferndandes
   (c) Michael M. Cernea (d) Michael Jackson
2. What is the name of the proposed geological epoch that considers human interaction has inflicted significant changes on the natural and the physical environment?

(a) Palaeontology (b) Holocene
(c) Anthropocene (d) Anthropocentrism

3. Choose among the following that does not fall under the imposition risks under IRM model?
(a) Landlessness (b) Homelessness
(c) Joblessness (d) Needlessness
4. Choose the major international legal document related to development-induced displacement.
(a) Guiding Principles on Internal Displacement
(b) Land Acquisition Act (c) Eminent Domani
(d) Universal Declaration of Human Rights
5. The power of the state to acquire private land within its territory is known as:
(a) Terrrus nellus (b) Resjudicata
(c) Eminent domain (d) Territorial jurisdiction
6. __________ is the process in which the social worker creates awareness of colonial influences and reduces the dependency on Eurocentric knowledge and theories.
(a) Decolonisation (b) neo-colonialism
(c) Postcolonialism (d) Colonial modernity
7. Name the process in the post-displacement phase that helps displaced persons to cultivate resilience at their relocation sites.
(a) Relocation (b) Resettlement and Rehabilitation
(c) Displacement (d) Renovation
8. First Land Acquisition Act was enacted in _______ province of British India.
(a) Bengal (b) Bombay (c) Delhi (d) Madras
9. Right to Fair Compensation and Transparency in Land Acquisition Rehabilitation and Resettlement Act (Land Acquisition Act) was introduced in:
(a) 2013 (b) 2014 (c) 2015 (d) 2020
10. The exodus of Kashmiri Pandits from Kashmir is an example of what type of Internal displacement?
(a) Conflict-induced displacement
(b) Conservation- Induced displacement
(c) Disaster-induced displacement
(d) Development–induced displacement

Answers

1. (c), 2. (c), 3. (d), 4. (a), 5. (c), 6. (a), 7. (b), 8. (a), 9. (a), 10. (a)

REFERENCES

1. Aneesh, T. V. (2017). Status of resettlement and rehabilitation in development induced displacement a study of Cochin International Airport Limited CIAL of Kerela [Doctoral dissertation, Jamia Millia Islamia]. Shodhganga: a reservoir for Indian thesis http://hdl.handle.net/10603/312300
2. Bhattacharyya, B. (1958). Sarvodaya. *The Indian Journal of Political Science*, 19(4), 375–87.
3. Bodhi, S.R. (2016). Professional social work education in India a critical view from the Periphery In Bodhi, S.R. (Ed.). *Social Work in India (tribal and Adivasi Studies: Perspective from Within)*. (pp. 229–247). Adivaani.
4. Cernea, M.M. (1999). Why economic analysis is essential to resettlement: A sociologist's view. In M. M. Cerna (Ed.), *The economics of involuntary resettlement questions and challenges* (pp. 5–38). World Bank.
5. Cernea, M.M. (2011). Broadening the definition of 'population displacement': Geography and economics in conservative policy. In Mathur, H. M. (Ed.), *Resettling displaced people policy and practice in India* (pp. 85–119). Routledge.
6. Chakravorty, S. (2014). *The price of land: Acquisition, conflict, consequences*. Oxford University Press.
7. Chowdhury, I.R., & Chowdhury, P.R. (2016). Holdout and Eminent Domain in Land Acquisition. *Indian Economic Review*, 51(1/2), 1–19. http://www.jstor.org/stable/44376233
8. Crutzen, P.J., & Stoermer, E.F. (2000). The Anthropocene. *Global change newsletter*, 41, 17–18.
9. Dwivedi, R. (2002). Models and methods in development–induced displacement. *Development and change*, 33(4), 709–732. https://doi.org/10.1111/1467-7660.00276
10. Faure, A. (2009). Displacements along the rivers of France: Affected people looking back. In R. Modi (Ed.), *Beyond relocation: The imperative of sustainable resettlement* (1st ed.). Sage.
11. Fernandes, W. (2011). Development-induced displacement in the era of privatisation. In Mathur, H. M. (Ed.), *Resettling displaced people policy and practice in India*. (pp. 301–16). Routledge.
12. Fernandes, W. (2013). Impact of displacement on the tribes. In S. Somayaji & S. Dasgupta (Eds.), *Sociology of displacement: Policies and practice*. Rawat.
13. Ghate, R. (2005). Relocation versus wildlife preservation. *Economic and Political Weekly*, 40(46), 4807–4809.
14. Gore, M.S. (1997). A historical perspective of the social work profession. *Indian Journal of Social Work*, 58(3), 442–455.
15. Hooper, P., & Jay H. Walder (2001). Cochin International Airport: The Gateway to God's Own Country http://cial.aero/userfiles/CIAL-Harward.pdf
16. Internal Displacement Monitoring Center. (2022). Global Report on Internal Displacement 2022. https://www.internal-displacement.org/global-report/grid2022/#part1

17. Jaswal, S., & Pandya, S. (2015). Social work education in India: Discussions on indigenisation. *The Indian Journal of Social Work,* 76(1), 139-158.
18. Kabra, A. (2003). Displacement and rehabilitation of an adivasi settlement case of Kuno wildlife sanctuary, Madhya Pradesh. *Economic and Political Weekly*, July 19, 3073–3078.
19. Kälin W. (2008). The Guiding Principles on Internal Displacement. The American Society of International Law, Washington. https://www.unhcr.org/43ce1cff2.pdf
20. Kidner, D.W. (2014). Why 'anthropocentrism'is not anthropocentric. *Dialectical anthropology*, 38, 465-480.
21. Kohli, K. (2015). Land Acquisition Ordinance 2014: Dismissing democracy, displacing safeguards? . Oxfam India. http://hdl.handle.net/10546/346708
22. Kulkarni, P.D. (1993). The indigenous base of social work profession in India. *Indian Journal of Social Work*, 54(4), 555–565.
23. Leela, R.H. (1958). Significance of sarvodaya. *The Indian Journal of Political Science,* 19(4), 365-367. http://www.jstor.org/stable/42753638
24. Lenhoff, A. (1942). Development of the Concept of Eminent Domain. *Columbia Law Review*, 42(4), 596–638. https://doi.org/10.2307/1117730
25. Lobo L. (2008). Development-induced displacement in Gujarat 1947 - 2004. In U. Mehta & R. Puniyani (Eds.), Sectarianism, politics and development. Jaipur. Rawat.
26. Mariotti, C. (2015). Development in practice resettlement and risk of adverse incorporation: The case of the Polavaram dam. *Development in Practice*, 25 (2). http://doi.org/10.1080/09614524.2015.1052373
27. Mathur, H. M., & Marsen, D. (2000). *Development projects and impoverishment risks: Resettling project – Affected people in India.* New Delhi: Oxford University Press.
28. Mohanty. B. (2005). Displacement and Rehabilitation of Tribals. *Economic and Political Weekly*, 40(13), 1318–1320. http://www.jstor.org/stable/4416394
29. Murickan, J., George, M.K., Emmnauel, K.A., Boban, J., & R., P.P. (2003). *Development -induced displacement:Case of Kerala.* Rawat.
30. Nandy, A. (2003). *The romance of the state: And the fate of dissent in the tropics.* (6th ed.). Oxford University Press.
31. Newton, J. (2008). Displacement and development: The paradoxes of India's Tehri Dam. *The Geographical Bulletin*, (49), 19–32.
32. Oxford Learner's Dictionaries (n.d) Displacement https://www.oxfordlearners dictionaries.com/definition/english/displacement
33. Padel, F., & Das, S. (2008). Cultural genocide: The real impact of development-induced displacement. In H.M. Mathur (Ed.), *India – Social development report 2008: Development and displacement* (pp. 103–126). Oxford University Press.
34. Padel, F., & Das, S. (2011). Resettlement realities :The gulf between policy and practice. In Hari Mohan Mathur (Ed.), *Resettling displaced people: Policy and practice in India.* (pp. 143–180). Routledge.

35. Pandey, B. (2008). The Kalinganagar tragedy: Development goal or development malaise. *Social Change*, 38(4), 609–626
36. Powell, F. (2001). *The politics of social work* (first). Sage.
37. Rawat, R.K. (2004). Vinoba Bhave's Conception of ' Sarvodaya'. *Peace Research*, 36(1), 25-32.
38. Roy, A. (1999). The greater common good. *Outlook*. Retrieved from http://www.outlookindia.com/magazine/story/thegreatercommongood/207509
39. Scudder, T. (1973). The human ecology of big projects: River basin development and resettlement. *Annual Review of Anthropology*, 2(1973), 45–55.
40. Shahabuddin, G., Kumar, R., & Shrivastava, M. (2005). Pushed over the edge village relocation from Sariska. *Economic and Political Weekly*, 40(32), 3563–3565.
41. Sharma, R. N. (2003). Involuntary displacement: A few encounters. *Economic and Political Weekly*, 38(9), 907–912.
42. Terminski, B. (2015). *Development-induced displacement and resettlement: Causes, consequences, and socio-legal context*. Ibidem-Verlag.
43. Varkkey, B., & Raghuram, G. (2002). Governance Issues in Airport Development: Learnings from Cochin International Airport Ltd. In S. Morris & S.R. (Eds.), *India Infrastructure Report Governance issues for commercialization.* Oxford University Press.
44. Vithayathil, P.N., & Sunny, C. (2009). Development projects and human right protection: The CIAL in Kerala. *Rajagiri Journal of Social Development*, 5(1).
45. Willis, K. (2005). *Theories and practices of development*. Routledge.

RECOMMENDED READINGS

1. Baviskar, A. (1995). *In the belly of the river: Tribal conflicts over development in the Narmada Valley*. Oxford
2. Levien, M. (2018). *Dispossession without development: Land grabs in neoliberal India*. Oxford University Press.
3. Mathur, H. M. (Ed.). (2012). *Resettling displaced people: Policy and practice in India*. Routledge
4. Terminski, B. (2015). *Development-induced displacement and resettlement: Causes, consequences, and socio-legal context*. Ibidem-Verlag.

CHAPTER – 17

Rural Development and Social Work

ARUL ACTOVIN C[1] AND SUNIL PRASAD[2]

[1]*Assistant Professor, Department of Social Work, Sri Ramakrishna Mission Vidyalaya College of Arts and Science (Autonomous) Coimbatore, India*
[2]*Assistant Professor, Department of Social Work, North Eastern Regional Institute of Management (NERIM), Guwahati, Assam*

India's place in the sun would come from the partnership between the wisdom of its rural people and skill of its professionals.

– Varghese Kurien

ABSTRACT: *Rural development aims to enhance the living standards of people in non-urban areas through community-led initiatives targeting social and economic progress. It stresses the fair distribution of benefits and the importance of ensuring development reaches everyone. In India, rural development is key to economic growth. Social workers play a vital role by addressing crises, advocating for change, and empowering communities through education and active involvement in social services. They also work to incorporate local knowledge and perspectives into development plans. Community development workers (CDWs) collaborate with various agencies, advocating for disadvantaged communities and ensuring their concerns are considered in policymaking at local and national levels. This chapter examines the connection between rural development and the social work profession.*

Keywords: *Social Work, Rural Development, Rural Community Development, Hermeneutic Phenomenological Approach*

Learning Objectives

- To understand the concept of rural development.
- To know the issues and elements of rural development.
- To get an idea about the importance of rural development in the field of social work.
- To understand the relevance of rural development in the social work profession.

INTRODUCTION

The rural community comprises the structural dimensions of occupations, ecology, and socio-cultural elements (Bealer, Willitis & Kuvesky, 1965). Development, as a practice, is meant to reduce exploitation and abuse, empower the economically weaker sections of society, and reduce the domination by social, economic, and political power. Development also means equal distribution of resources, better health care facilities and education for everyone. Rural development means an overall development of rural regions in economic, cultural, political and social contexts so that people can lead pleasant lives. The goal of rural development is social and economic growth, which emphasises equal distribution and the creation of benefits. Any development which does not benefit the masses and does not reach the masses cannot be justified.

Rural development is one of the most critical aspects of the prosperity of the Indian economy. Rural social work is social work with rural populations. Further, differs from similar types of work with urban groups in significant ways (Ginsberg, 2005; Johnson, 1980).

CONCEPT AND DEFINITION

Rural

A community can be classified as rural based on lower population density, less social differentiation, less social and spatial mobility, slow rate of social change, etc. Agriculture is the primary occupation of rural areas. Further, Rural is defined by Srivastava (1961) as an area where the people are engaged in the primary industry because they produce things directly for the first time in cooperation with nature.

Development

Development refers to growth, evolution, stage of inducement or progress. This progress or change is gradual and has sequential phases. Always there is increasing differentiation. It also refers to the overall movement towards greater efficiency and complex situations.

Rural Development

Rural Development is a process that aims to improve the well-being and self-realisation of people living outside the urbanised areas through a collective approach and designates utilising approaches and techniques under one programme, which rally upon local communities as units of action. It provides a large umbrella under which all the people are engaged in the work of community organisations, community progress and community relation. The term rural development connotes the overall development of rural areas to improve the quality of life of rural people. In this sense, it is a comprehensive and multi-dimensional concept. It encompasses the development of agriculture and allied activities, village and cottage industries and crafts, socio-economic infrastructure, community services and facilities, and human resources in rural areas. Rural development results from interactions between various physical, technological, economic, socio-cultural, and institutional factors.

According to the United Nations, rural development is a process of change by which the efforts of the people themselves are united, those of government authorities to improve the economic, social and cultural conditions of communities in the life of the nation and to enable them to contribute fully to a national programme.

According to **G. Shah,** rural development as 'the development of rural areas, often rural development has meant the extension of irrigation facilities, expansion of electricity, improvement in the techniques of cultivation, construction of school building and provision of educational facilities, health care, etc.'

Rural Development is a process of bringing change among rural communities from the traditional way of living to a progressive way of living. It is also expressed as a movement for progress. Rural Development is a subset of the broader term 'Development'. Howsoever we define it, development is universally cherished and it individuals, families, communities, and nations worldwide. The equipment is also natural because all life forms on Planet Earth have an inherent urge to survive and develop. Given these two attributes, i.e., its universal supremacy as a goal and its natural occurrence, development deserves a scientific study and analysis. Hence, it is surprising that scholars of all faiths, ideologies, and disciplines have studied the subject of development.

Rural development is a broad term. It essentially focuses on an action for the development of areas outside the mainstream urban economic system. We should consider what type of rural development is needed because the modernisation of the village leads to urbanisation, and the village environment disappears.

Did You Know?

In rural India, agriculture is the main occupation of the people, which provides them livelihood. Still, several other occupations keep people busy and engaged. India's economy can be thought of as comprising two main sectors: the rural sector and the non-rural sector. The rural sector is, in turn, composed of two main sub-sectors. i.e., the agricultural and allied sub-sector and non-agricultural sub-sector. The non-agricultural subsectors consist of economic activities relating to industry, business and services. The size of the rural sector could be measured in terms of the rural population, the population of livestock, the extent of land, forest and other natural resources. The Indian agricultural system, the backbone of the Indian economy, has its own features.

The following principles are suggested for implementing rural development programs:

- **Accessibility:** Try to ensure that the program and its benefits can reach those in need, and beware of the consequences if some farmers have access to the program while others do not.
- **Independence:** Devise a program that helps and supports the farmer but does not make him or his livelihood depend upon the program.
- **Sustainability:** Ensure that the programme's plans and solutions are relevant to the local economic, social, and administrative situation. Short-term solutions may yield quick results, but long-term programmes suitable to the local environment have more tremendous success.
- **Going forward:** Technological aspects of rural development programmes should help the farmer take the next step in his development and not demand that he take a giant technological leap. It is better to secure a modest advance that can be sustained than to suggest a substantial advance beyond most's ability.
- **Participation:** Always try to consult the local people, seek out their ideas, and involve them as much as possible in the programme.
- **Effectiveness:** A program should be based on adequate local resources and not necessarily on their most efficient use. While efficiency is essential, its requirements are often unrealistic. For example, the maximum use of fertiliser is beyond the means of most farmers. But effective use of resources, which is within the capabilities of most farmers, will have a better chance of a broader impact.

Rural development actions are intended to further rural communities' social and economic development. Rural development programmes were historically top-down approaches from local or regional authorities, agencies, NGOs, national governments or international development organisations.

Rural development aims to find ways to improve rural lives with the participation of rural people themselves to meet the critical needs of rural communities. The outsider may not understand the setting, culture, language and other things prevalent in the local area. Rural people themselves have to participate in their sustainable rural development. In developing countries like Nepal, Pakistan, India, Bangladesh, and China, integrated development approaches are followed.

Components of Rural Development

'Country improvement tries to change every one of the parts of the provincial economy – the essential area, the optional segment and the tertiary division.

'It is worried about improving the way of life of the ruralites through the arrangement of well-being and medicinal offices, business openings including professional preparation, instructive offices and so on.

'It realises critical improvement in the financial states of the planned positions, booked clans, the landless rural workers and the peripheral and little fanners' (Ashok, 2006, p.40)

The essential aspects of rural development (Rajvanshi, 2014) are as follows:

- Agricultural development constitutes a crucial aspect of rural development. Agricultural development is possible by using better seeds, adequate fertiliser, manures, and pesticides, adequate supply of water and effective implementation of land reform measures.
- By effecting changes in the socio-economic institutions, rural development seeks to change the socio-economic structure of the rural community.
- The effectiveness of the rural development programs necessitates non-political interference. The persons associated with these programs should be given adequate freedom to carry out their plans and programs with undivided attention.
- The success of the rural development programs depends on the cooperative orientation and attitude among the ruralites. The functioning of cooperative societies goes a long way in improving the conditions of the vulnerable sections of the rural setup.
- Rural development programs demand the active participation of the ruralites. While formulating these programs, the rural people's opinions, attitudes, drives, and interests should be considered. Further, dedicated and committed village leaders should come forward to guide the masses in bringing about rural development.

Review Questions

(a) Define Rural Community.

(b) What is Rural Development, and explain its essential aspects?

Did You Know?

According to UNESCO's definition, developmental activities are: conscious and scientific processes that involve five elements: population, social setup, environment, resources and technology; which when used proportionately and qualitatively ensure the quality of life at the macro and micro levels. As a community development worker (CDW), it is essential for you to have a thorough understanding of all the developmental needs and activities of a community.

RURAL COMMUNITY DEVELOPMENT

Objective

- Ensuring the development of both material and human resources.

- To develop local leadership and self-governing institutions.
- To develop the socio-economic and educational standards of the people.
- To make people self-reliant and increase productivity.
- To improve health and sanitation.
- Giving opportunity to all.

Approaches

There aren't any approaches for rural development that are generally acknowledged. It is a decision impacted by culture, time, and place. The following are five approaches identified to rural development:

1. **Process Approach:** More importance is given to the steps rather than the problem. An orienting community for mass participation and self-reliance.
2. **Area Applied Approach:** The main aim of this approach is the total development of area and quality of living for people. Development not only in agriculture but also gives importance to infrastructure (school, sanitation, health and nutrition family planning).
3. **Need-Based Approach:** The main aim is to fulfil the basic needs of the community.
4. **Spatial Approach:** It promotes the market-town connection between rural and urban, creating a rural marketing and industrial growth centre.
5. **Sectional Approach:** It takes a particular section (segment) of people and tackles them together.

   For example,

   (a) Green Revolution contributed to the wealth of the rich and not the poor.

   (b) Women empowerment.

Social Work

As a profession and scientific discipline, social work is of recent origin. Ordinary men are not aware of the significance of social work. A Social Worker is a trained person who receives remuneration for his services like any other profession. Social work is a helping activity that enables individuals, families, groups and communities to become self-reliant. Social work is based on principles and philosophies that help practice it with scientific knowledge and skills. It requires education and training for any person to practise it.

Social work is a problem-solving profession committed to improving the quality of human life by imparting various intervention techniques and strategies that are scientifically proved and artistically applied. Social work is a profession primarily concerned with the remedy to psycho-social problems and deficiencies in the relationship between the individual and his social environment. This phenomenon always existed in society in one form but achieved its scientific basis in the last decades of the 19th century.

According to the Indian Conference of Social work (1957), 'social work is a welfare activity based on humanitarian philosophy, scientific knowledge and technical skills for helping the individual, group or community to live a rich and full life.'

Defining the Practice

The approach is much less common and is often not explicitly stated in terms of a definitional issue. Still, it centres on the question: 'In what ways is rural social work different from urban practice?' Locke and Winship (2005) suggest five recurrent and significant themes in the literature on rural practice: Generalist's practise 'skilled working with individuals, families, small groups, organisations and communities' (p.6).

Community development - they note that as early as 1933, Josephine Brown called for rural workers to embrace casework and community work.

External relations are with significant people outside the immediate issue, such as local politicians and other influential actors.

Cultural influences: sensitivity to the particularities of local rural cultures and the needs of minority groups.

Desirable workers' characteristics include a visible commitment to the local community and the capacity to work without much professional support.

Rural Social Work

The idea that rural social work is social work with rural populations is compatible with rural social work's perspective as work in rural communities. Perhaps the most basic dialogue in rural social work is the one that contrasts rural social work in a rural community with one that defines rural social work as social work with rural populations. One school of thought is that rural social work is generally confined to rural or small communities.

The rural population approach to rural social work suggests a broader array of interventions and areas of interest because social workers work with individuals, families, groups, organisations, and communities.

Rural social workers deal with challenging issues of poverty, at-risk populations, and service delivery at the community, family, and individual intervention levels that are unique and different from urban practice. These and other factors raise crucial issues for social work practice and educational preparation for social work practice in rural areas.

NASW (2006), in its policy statement on rural work, recognises that social workers are well suited to helping rural people with their lives, sustain their families, and use their strengths to make a positive change in their lives.

Several sources are pretty clear in their support for rural social work as a field of practice distinctive from other practice fields (Ginsberg, 2005; Lohmann & Lohmann, 2005).

Did You Know?

The Community Development Programme 1952 has been the biggest rural reconstruction scheme undertaken by the Government of India. It has been described as the Magna Carta of hope and happiness for two-thirds of India's population, the testament of emancipation, the declaration of war on poverty, ignorance, squalor and disease under which millions have been groaning etc. The Planning Commission has defined the Community Development Programme as 'Community development is an attempt to bring about a social and economic transformation of village life through the efforts of the people themselves.' The Government of India launched 55 Community Development Projects, each covering about 300 villages or a population of 30,000. This programme was multi-dimensional, but the emphasis was on agricultural production. The areas selected for launching the project were located in irrigation schemes or where there was plenty of rainfall.

ROLE AND RESPONSIBILITIES OF SOCIAL WORKERS

The roles of the community social worker are enabler, advocate, broker, educator and counsellor. With their expertise in human relationships, the community social worker/organiser can hold the community members together under challenging conditions with the help of the local leadership. Through applying the knowledge and social work skills, the community social worker helps the community specify their need (problem), formulate effective and realisable goals, develop strategies for execution, identify financial resources, and *initiate direct action campaigns to achieve the required outcome*.

In 1969, Alex Sim wrote a seminal article on how social workers should enter communities. The first step Sim suggested is to become fully prepared. The social worker must make every effort to learn about the community, including culture and community structure. Gaining information from others who have known the community is of great help as well. This step is significant because first impressions are sometimes lasting, and a social worker who does the wrong things when first arriving can create problems for the future.

A hermeneutic phenomenological approach allows the social worker to sensitise him or herself to the community because this approach seeks to understand the lived experience of people within the context in which they live (Van Manen, 1990). Doing so validates the social worker's personal experience of the community while enabling the social worker to also understand that experience within the shared consciousness of the community. This, in turn, helps an outsider appreciate the language, values and perceptions used by insiders to explain behaviour or discuss phenomena.

The hermeneutic phenomenological approach supports using narratives or stories because it is respectful of the individual within the social context. By allowing an individual to relate how an event was experienced, one can gain insight into the individual based on such factors as what the person viewed as being noteworthy about the event, the aspects of the event which received the most attention, the language used to describe the event and the words used to describe any people involved in the event, and the value orientation driving the person's narrative. Moreover, as other people describe the event or hear this person's 'storying' of the event, insight can be gained into the congruence or lack of congruence among the various descriptions of the event, leading to a better understanding of the community's 'storying' of the event. Van Manen (1990) suggests that narratives have the following powers:

- 'To compel: a story recruits our willing attention;
- To lead us to reflect: a story tends to invite us to reflective search for significance;
- To involve us personally: one tends to search actively for the storyteller's meaning via one's own;
- To transform: we may be touched, shaken, or moved by the story; it touches us; and,
- To measure interpretive sense: one's response to a story is a measure of one's deepened ability to make interpretive sense' (p.121).

Social workers' roles have grown to include crisis management and roles of empowerment, and advocacy. Social workers can empower communities by encouraging individuals to take an active role in shaping social services, providing education programs and enabling economic independence long-term. Perhaps part of the social worker's role is to listen to these alternative voices and make room for the local ways of knowing, which may not have been storied.

Community development workers (CDW) usually work in teams and liaise closely with the police, social workers, teachers, probation officers and other agencies. They represent the voices and needs of target groups and disadvantaged communities to policymakers at the local and national levels. Four essential functions define the role of community development workers:

- Change agent: identifying gaps, developing innovative practice;

- Service developer: promoting joint working, education and training;
- Capacity builder in rural communities; and
- Access facilitator to services, community resources, overcoming language and cultural barriers.

These roles of community development workers may vary according to and be shaped by local community needs. The underlying principle for CDWs is; to analyse the reasons behind what is happening; and, with others, to work out what needs to be done, by whom, when and what support or resources they require at a strategic, developmental level. It is not (necessarily) about directly helping to effect a change in individual personal circumstances, although the strategic changes will help this occur. Community development workers can be

- seeking out strengths and abilities within local rural communities to help them to manage and address mental distress;
- supporting community development: helping groups and individuals to identify needs and concerns and work out local solutions;
- supporting local groups and networks so they can be partners in developing and improving mental health and social care services;
- helping to develop leadership locally;
- developing the skills, knowledge and confidence of individuals and communities to enable them to create local solutions; and
- Signposting people to information, resources and sources of funding.

Hopefully, this chapter has contributed to a better understanding between rural development and social work. We can continue to develop a better understanding of new approaches and ideas and advance this practice field.

Did You Know?

In 1957, a three-tier system of rural local government, called 'Panchayati Raj' (Rule by Local Councils), was established. These were Gram Panchayats (village level), Panchayat Samitis (block level) and Zilla Parishads (district level). The aim was to decentralise the decision-making process and encourage people's participation.

Review Questions

(a) Define Social Work Profession.
(b) What are the roles of a community development worker in a rural community?

SUMMARY

The goal of rural development is to enhance the quality of life for people who live in rural areas by working together on a variety of issues, including infrastructure, community services, and agriculture. The chapter emphasizes how crucial it is to comprehend regional customs and involve rural communities in development projects. It also looks at various strategies for rural development and the changing responsibilities social workers play in promoting long-term transformation and community empowerment. Ultimately, the paragraph emphasizes how intricately social work, rural development, and community involvement interact to promote positive change and raise rural residents' standards of living.

GLOSSARY

- **The National Association of Social Workers (NASW)**, founded in 1955, is the world's largest membership organization for professional social workers. Its mission is to promote the professional growth and development of its members, establish and uphold professional standards, and advocate for sound social policies that support both social workers and the communities they serve.
- **The Indian Conference of Social Work (ICSW)**, founded in 1947, is one of the most well-known professional organizations in India. However, it differs from the typical concept of a professional organization. It is largely dominated by volunteer social workers who lack formal professional training in social work and often come from non-social work backgrounds.
- **The United Nations Educational, Scientific and Cultural Organization (UNESCO)** is an organization dedicated to fostering international cooperation in the fields of education, the arts, sciences, and culture. Its mission is to promote peace, security, and sustainable development by encouraging collaboration among nations and supporting initiatives that improve education, preserve cultural heritage, and advance scientific progress.
- **Community development is a central aspect of social work**, where social workers adopt a professional and skilled approach to their roles. They focus on empowering both individuals and communities, ensuring that people have the tools and resources to shape their own futures. Social workers advocate for a bottom-up, participatory model of community development, which prioritizes inclusive decision-making and encourages communities to take an active role in addressing their own needs and challenges. This approach fosters sustainable, community-driven progress.
- **A non-governmental organization (NGO)** is a voluntary group of individuals or organizations that operates independently of

any government. NGOs are typically formed to provide services, address social issues, or advocate for specific public policies. These organizations play a crucial role in promoting social change, supporting humanitarian efforts, and giving voice to various community or global concerns.

TOP TEN TAKEAWAYS POINTS

1. The goal of rural development is to improve the quality of life for rural by working together on projects related to infrastructure, community services, and agriculture.
2. A variety of factors are involved in rural development, such as advancements in agriculture, changes to socioeconomic institutions, a cooperative mentality, and proactive community involvement.
3. With an emphasis on fair resource allocation and benefit distribution, rural development seeks to promote social and economic improvement in rural areas.
4. Social work plays a crucial role in rural development by promoting sustainable advancement, resolving socioeconomic inequities, and empowering communities.
5. In rural areas, social workers serve as educators, counselors, advocates, and catalysts, helping people in the community recognize needs, make goals, and put reform plans into action.
6. Strategies for rural development cover a wide range of techniques.
7. Effective rural development fosters community trust and collaboration by being sensitive to local cultures, traditions, and leadership structures.
8. In order to create a lasting impact, successful rural development efforts depend on the active participation of local inhabitants, taking into account their opinions, values, and interests.
9. Despite obstacles like poverty and resource shortages, rural development initiatives present chances for creativity, collaboration, and community capacity building.
10. Continuous learning, collaboration, and adaptation of innovative approaches are imperative for advancing rural development and enhancing social work practices to meet evolving community needs

Analytical Questions

(a) Describe the importance of rural social work practice among rural communities.

(b) What do you understand by rural community development? Discuss the roles of community development workers in the upliftment of rural communities.

MULTIPLE CHOICE QUESTIONS

1. Whose themselves have to participate in their sustainable rural development?
   (a) Politicians alone (b) Rural people
   (c) Urban People (d) Panchayat Members only
2. When has the community development programme been launched in India?
   (a) 1952 (b) 1957
   (c) 1987 (d) 1972
3. When Alex Sim wrote a seminal article on how social workers should enter communities?
   (a) 1969 (b) 1979 (c) 1962 (d) 1958
4. What does the rural community include
   (a) Ecological aspects only
   (b) Socio-cultural elements only
   (c) Occupations and ecology
   (d) Occupations, ecology, and socio-cultural elements
5. Which of the following is the primary aim of the Need-based Approach?
   (a) Providing resources to the community
   (b) Fulfilling advanced needs of individuals
   (c) Promoting equality among individuals
   (d) Enhancing economic growth of individuals
6. What is one reason why social work may be considered significant?
   (a) It is a highly specialized field
   (b) It helps people make money
   (c) It promotes equality and social justice
   (d) It is a prestigious profession
7. What is necessary for the effectiveness of rural development programmes?
   (a) Political interference (b) Non-political interference
   (c) Limited freedom (d) Undivided attention
8. What is the main reason for the hermeneutic phenomenological approach to support using narratives or stories?
   (a) To simplify the research process
   (b) To entertain the readers
   (c) To respect the individual within the social context
   (d) To follow a trend
9. When was Panchayati Raj established in India?
   (a) 1950 (b) 1957
   (c) 1978 (d) 1987

10. Which is not an approach to rural development?
    (a) Process (b) Area
    (c) Spatial (d) Local Development

Answers

1. (b), 2. (a), 3. (a), 4. (d), 5. (a), 6. (c), 7. (b), 8. (c), 9. (b), 10. (d)

REFERENCES

1. Bealer, R. C., Willitis, F. K., & Kuvlesky, W. P. (1965). The meaning of rurality in American society. *Rural Sociology*, *30*(3), 255–65.
2. Moseley, M. (2003). *Rural Development: Principles and Practice* (First ed.). SAGE Publications Ltd. https://doi.org/10.4135/9781446216439
3. Ginsberg, L. H. (2005). The overall context of rural practice. In L. H. Ginsberg (Ed.), *Social Work in Rural Communities* (4th ed., pp. 4–7). CSWE Press.
4. Johnson, W. H. (1980). Human service delivery patterns in nonmetropolitan communities. In W. H. Johnson (Ed.), *Rural human services: A book of readings* (pp. 67–69). F. E. Peacock Publishers.
5. Locke, B. L., & Winship, J. (2008). Rural Social Work Practice. In N. Lohmann & R. Lohmann (Eds.), *Social work in rural America: Lessons from the past and trends for the future* (Illustrated ed., pp. 3–24). Columbia University Press.
6. Manen, V. M. (1990). *Researching Lived Experience: Human Science for an Action Sensitive Pedagogy (SUNY series, The Philosophy of Education)* (2nd ed.). SUNY Press.
7. Narang, A. (2006). *Indian Rural Problems (pp. 40)*. Murari Lal & Sons.
8. Rajvanshi, A. (2014). *Romance of Innovation: Human interest story of R&D in a rural setting* (Revised ed.) [E-book]. Nimbkar Agricultural Research Institute (NARI). https://nariphaltan.org/roi.pdf

RECOMMENDED READINGS

1. Komol Singha, Rural Development in India: Retrospect and Prospects, Concept Publication, New Delhi, 2010.
2. K. R. Gupta, Rural Development in India, Atlantic Publishers, New Delhi, 2004.
3. Christine Polzin, "Institutional Change in Informal Credit: Through the Urban-Rural Lens" in Barbara HarrissWhite (Ed.), *Middle India and Urban-Rural Development: Four Decades of Change*, Springer Publication, New Delhi, 2016.
4. Sanjeev Prashar, Manish Didwania and Nitin Kishore Saxena, "Rural Development and Management in India: Opportunities and Challenges", Nova Science Publishers, New Delhi, 2017.
5. Katar Singh, "Rural Development: Principles, Policies and Management", Sage Publication, New Delhi, 1999.

Author Index

Actovin C, Arul 316
Aneesh, T.V. 293

Botcha, Rambabu 148

Dash, Bishnu Mohan 84
Diyali, Chandrakala 239

Gandhe, Rutwik 103
Ghosh, Kasturi Sinha 130

Haokip, Seilienmang 260

Jafri, Mehak 23
Joseph, Sheeba 84

Kaushik, Archana 1

Menon, Gayatri 193

Mishra, Vishal 148

Narula, Vani 218

Patil, Ravindra Ramesh 23
Prasad, Sunil 316

Satyam, Kumar 283
Sen, Sayantika 218
Sharma, Gauri 50
Simon, Richi 103
Suresh, Veena 271

Tyagi, Ragini 177

Varghese, Anna Taney 65
Vivek, S. 271

Zehra, Saniya 23

Editors' Profiles

Dr. Archana Kaushik is a Professor at the Department of Social Work, University of Delhi, India. Her areas of specialization and research interests include families and children, gerontological social work, thanatology, spiritual social work, empowerment of the marginalized communities, development administration and HIV/AIDS. She has nearly two decades of teaching experience at the postgraduate and doctoral levels. Under her supervision, more than 10 doctoral works and almost 25 M.Phil. dissertations have been accomplished successfully. She has many books and research articles on varied issues in the journals of national and international repute to her credit. She has conducted several research studies on varied topics and has undertaken evaluation studies with the Planning Commission, various ministries and other institutions in different capacities. She has occupied several administrative positions including Placement Director and Fieldwork Director. She has presented papers and chaired sessions at several national and international conferences on various social issues and participated as an expert in many television shows and other platforms.

Prof. Archana Kaushik has a wide teaching experience at the Department of Social Work, University of Delhi, Delhi. She is a *noted social work educator, a gerontologist and a social science researcher* with acclaimed writings in the form of books and research articles. She has developed a sizable amount of teaching-learning material from undergraduate to doctoral levels on varied themes of social work discipline.

Dr. Ravindra Ramesh Patil is presently a Professor in the Department of Social Work, Jamia Millia Islamia, New Delhi. He has been teaching graduate, postgraduate and doctoral students since October 2000 and has completed 22 years in the university. Apart from teaching, he has been continuously involved in research and publications. So far, he has 3 major research projects and more than 25 publications (national and international) including research articles, policy papers and books to his credit. He has authored/ edited 3 books, namely *Dalit Christians in India: Empowering Dalits, Non-Governmental Organizations*

in Western India, and *Tribal Development in India,* published by Manak and Sage publications. He has been regularly presenting papers and delivering lectures in national and international seminars and conferences.

Apart from academic contributions, Professor Patil has been serving universities in different administrative capacities. He has served as the head of the Department of Social Work and dean of the School of Social Sciences, Central University of Rajasthan, in the year 2012–14. Presently, he is the Director, Field Work and Placement at Department of Social Work, Jamia Millia Islamia, New Delhi. His research interest areas include development studies, environment, education and social work, marginalization, and civil society, and all his research and publications contribute towards enriching literature and documentation of the above research areas. Apart from this, he has been organizing seminars, conferences and workshops on different themes in the above areas.

Dr. Bishnu Mohan Dash, MSW (Visva-Bharati), MPhil (University of Delhi), PhD. (University of Delhi), ICSSR Post-Doctoral fellow, presently working as Professor, Department of Social Work at Dr Bhim Rao Ambedkar College (University of Delhi) has more than 15 years of teaching experience.

He is the recipient of '*Best Teacher Award*' from Government of Delhi 2019–20, and the '*Prestigious Delhi University Excellence Award*' for teachers 2021. He is also an editorial board member/ Advisory member in several national and international journals including *Practice: Social Work in Action* by Routledge, Taylor and Francis, London (Published by British Association of Social Workers), Associate Editor of *South Asian Journal of Participative Development*, and Member Editorial Board of *Bhopal Journal of Social Work.*

He has also authored, co-authored and edited 16 books. He has published more than 60 papers in various reputed national and international journals including Sage, Routledge Emerlad, Springer etc. and contributed chapters for Post Graduate Course in Social Work (MSW)/Social work and Counselling of Indira Gandhi National Open University, New Delhi and frequently contributes in leading national newspapers. He has presented papers and chaired sessions in various national/international conferences including Canada, Japan, and Srilanka and delivered invited lectures in various academic forums.

He was also member of the Expert Committee in the Course Revision/ Member, School Board, Indira Gandhi National Open University, New Delhi; Orissa State Open University, Mahatma Gandhi Antarrashtriya Hindi

Vishwa Vidyalaya, Maharashtra, BPS University, Sonepat and Member, Board of Studies in Social Work, Indore School of Social Work, Indore and Academic Advisory Board, School of Social Sciences, Doon University. He has completed a number of research projects sponsored by ICSSR and UGC and organized various workshops and seminars. His areas of interest are Rural Development, Child Welfare, and Social Work Education.

Dr. Sunil Prasad, BA (Hons) & MSW (University of Delhi), UGC NET, Ph.D. (Visva-Bharati University) is currently working as an Assistant Professor, Department of Social Work, North Eastern Regional Institute of Management, (NERIM), Guwahati, Assam. His areas of specialization and research interests include Rural Community Development, Sustainable Livelihood, and Social Work Education.

Dr Sunil has received recognition from his excellency the Governor of Sikkim, Shri Ganga Prasad, and from the Chief Minister of Sikkim, Shri P.S Golay, for community service and social work, in the year 2022. He has also been awarded the *Best Social Work Practitioner Award 2023*. He has several publications including articles in reputed Scopus Listed Journals, UGC listed Journals, study material chapters for Masters in Social Work Curriculum for Open Universities and book chapters in books by International and National Publishers. He has worked as a consultant with many other organizations in different capacities and delivered lectures in various academic forums. In addition to his contributions to academia, Dr Sunil has held many administrative positions. He is also the Training and Placement Officer for North Eastern Regional Institute of Management, (NERIM) Guwahati, Assam.